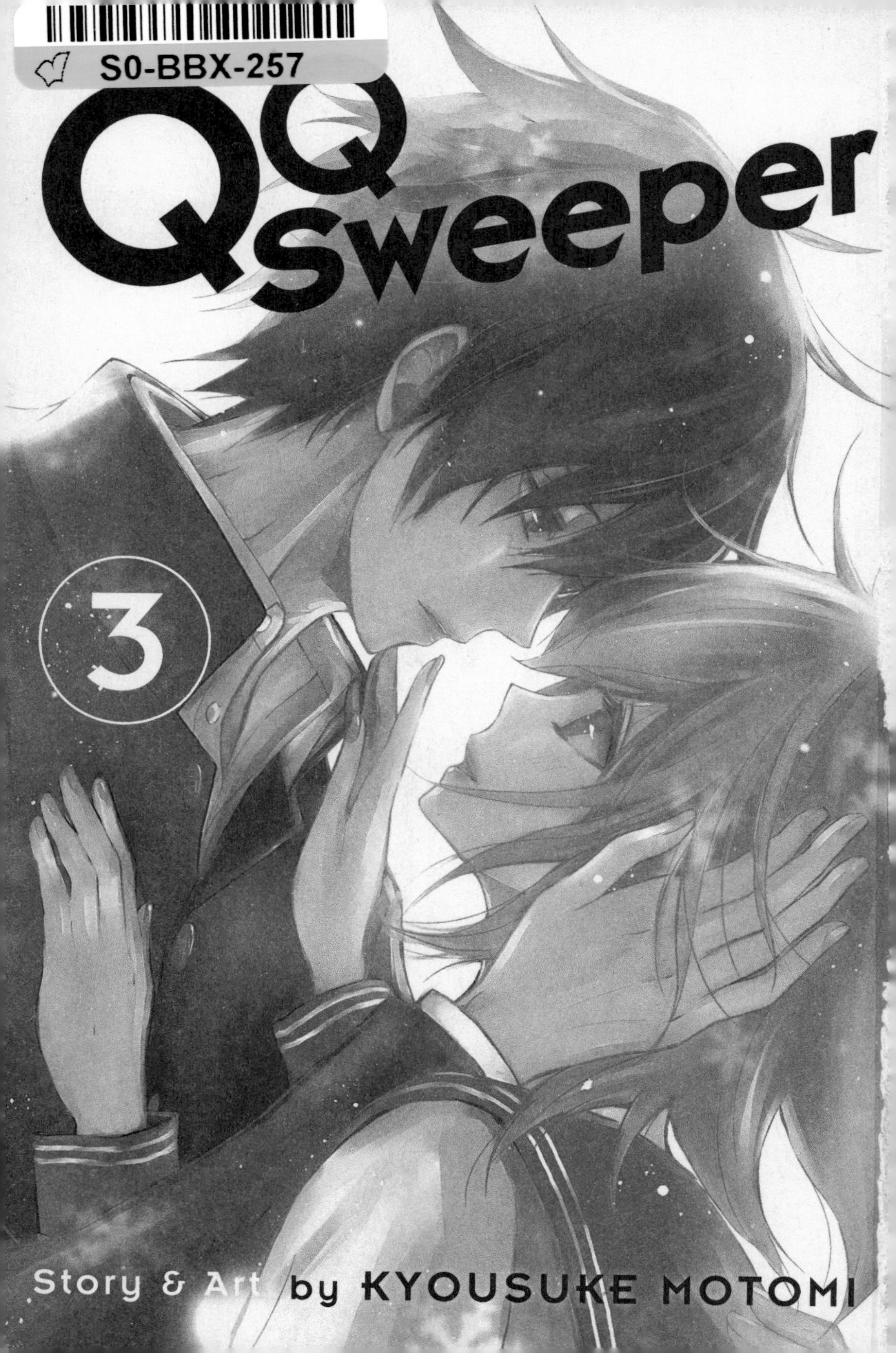

QQ Sweeper

3

Story & Art by KYOUSUKE MOTOMI

QQ Sweeper

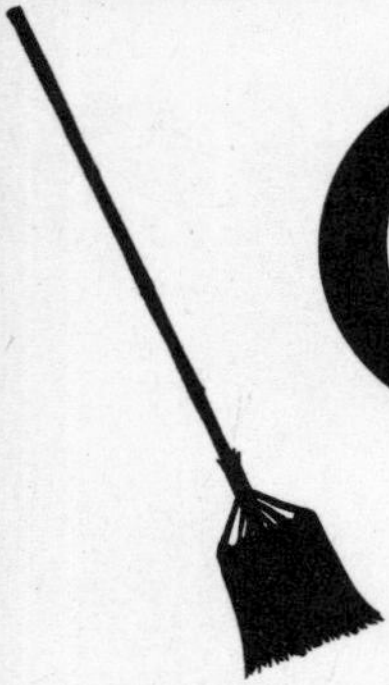

3

Sweep 11 — 3

Sweep 12 — 39

Sweep 13 — 75

Sweep 14 — 113

Sweep 15 — 149

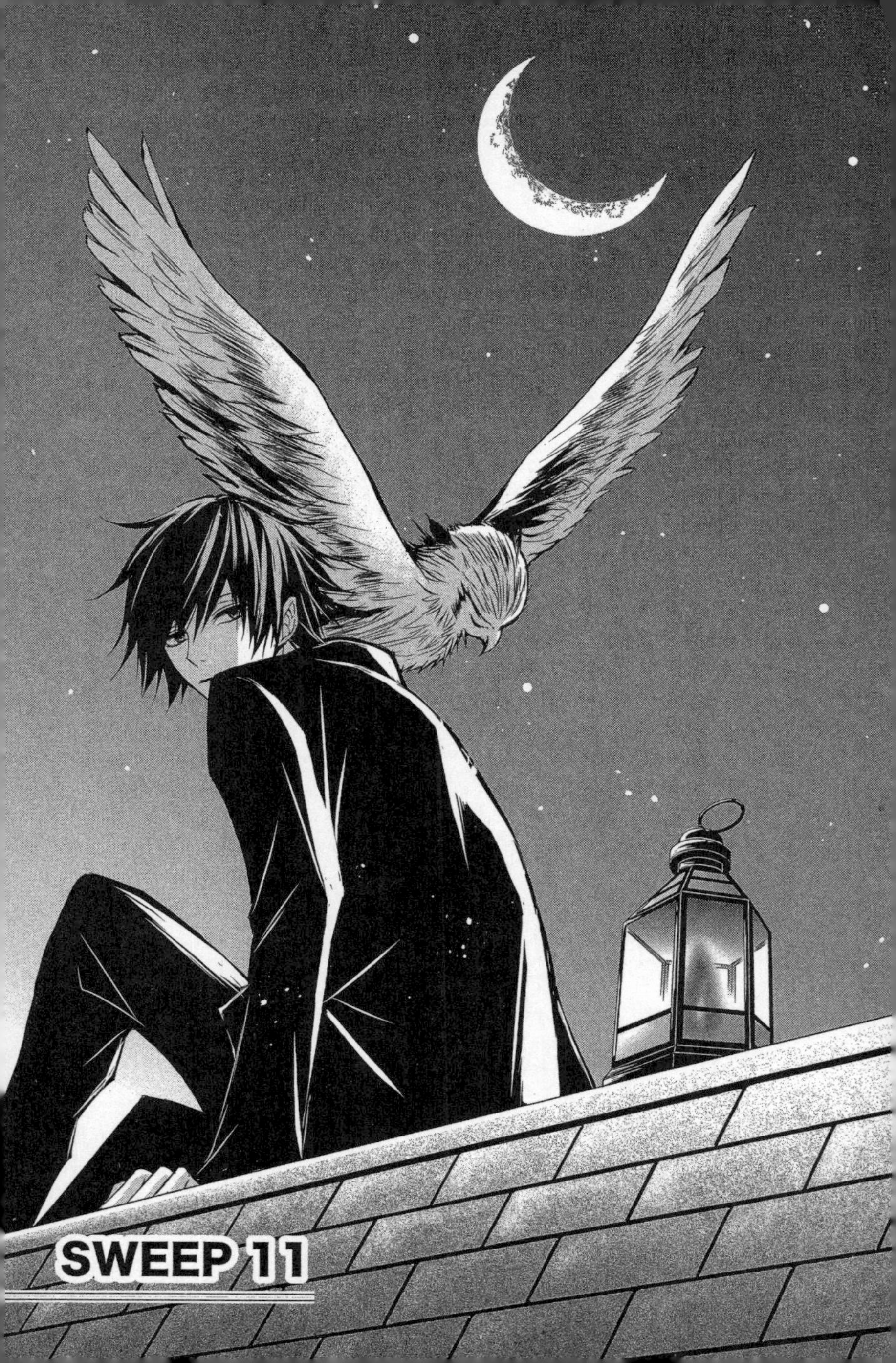
SWEEP 11

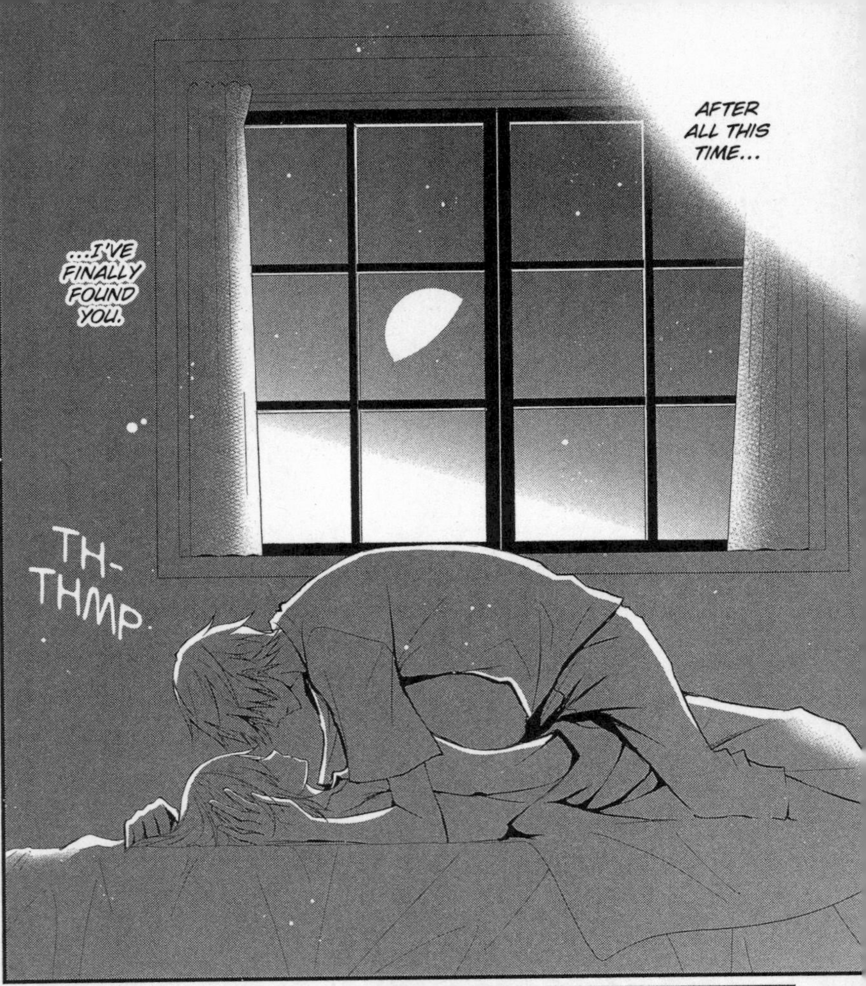
AFTER ALL THIS TIME...
...I'VE FINALLY FOUND YOU.
TH-THMP

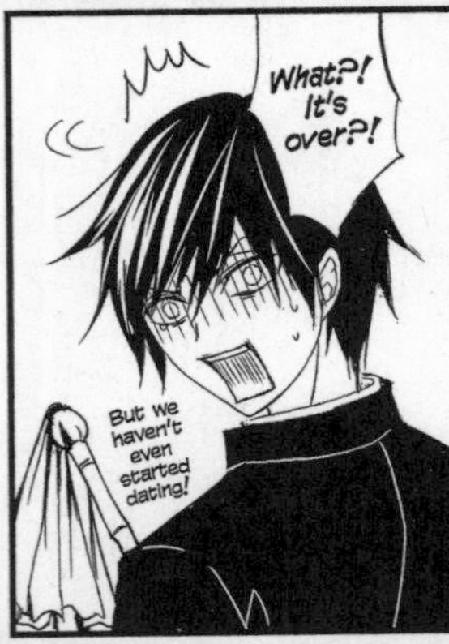
What?! It's over?!
But we haven't even started dating!

Hello, everyone!
Kyousuke Motomi here.

Thank you for picking up volume 3 of QQ Sweeper.

Actually, this is the final volume of this story.
I really hope you read it right to the end!

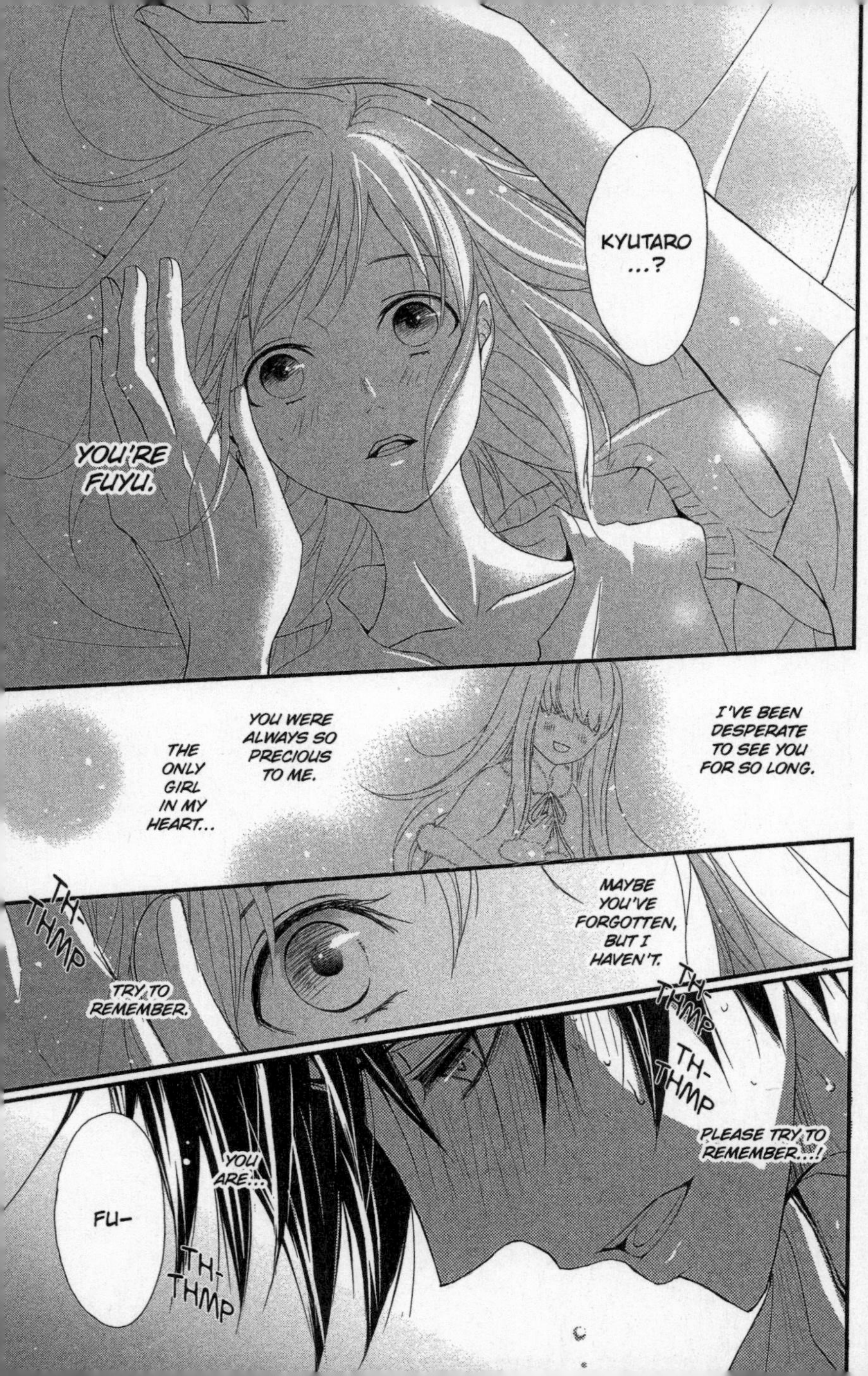
KYUTARO ...?
YOU'RE FUYU.
I'VE BEEN DESPERATE TO SEE YOU FOR SO LONG.
YOU WERE ALWAYS SO PRECIOUS TO ME.
THE ONLY GIRL IN MY HEART...
MAYBE YOU'VE FORGOTTEN, BUT I HAVEN'T.
TH-THMP
TRY TO REMEMBER.
TH-THMP
TH-THMP
PLEASE TRY TO REMEMBER...!
YOU ARE...
FU-
TH-THMP

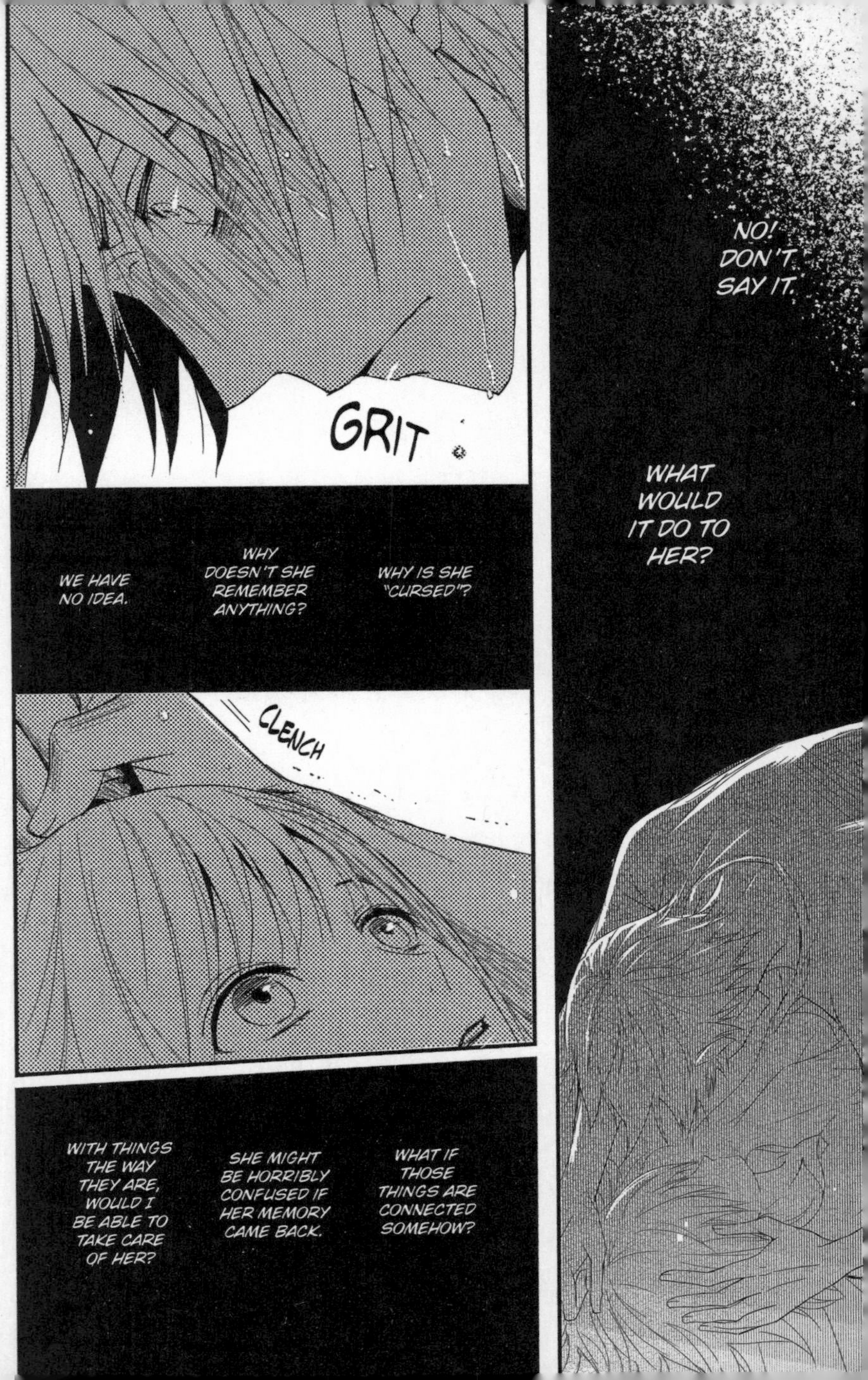
NO! DON'T SAY IT.
WHAT WOULD IT DO TO HER?
GRIT
WHY IS SHE "CURSED"?
WHY DOESN'T SHE REMEMBER ANYTHING?
WE HAVE NO IDEA.
CLENCH
WHAT IF THOSE THINGS ARE CONNECTED SOMEHOW?
SHE MIGHT BE HORRIBLY CONFUSED IF HER MEMORY CAME BACK.
WITH THINGS THE WAY THEY ARE, WOULD I BE ABLE TO TAKE CARE OF HER?

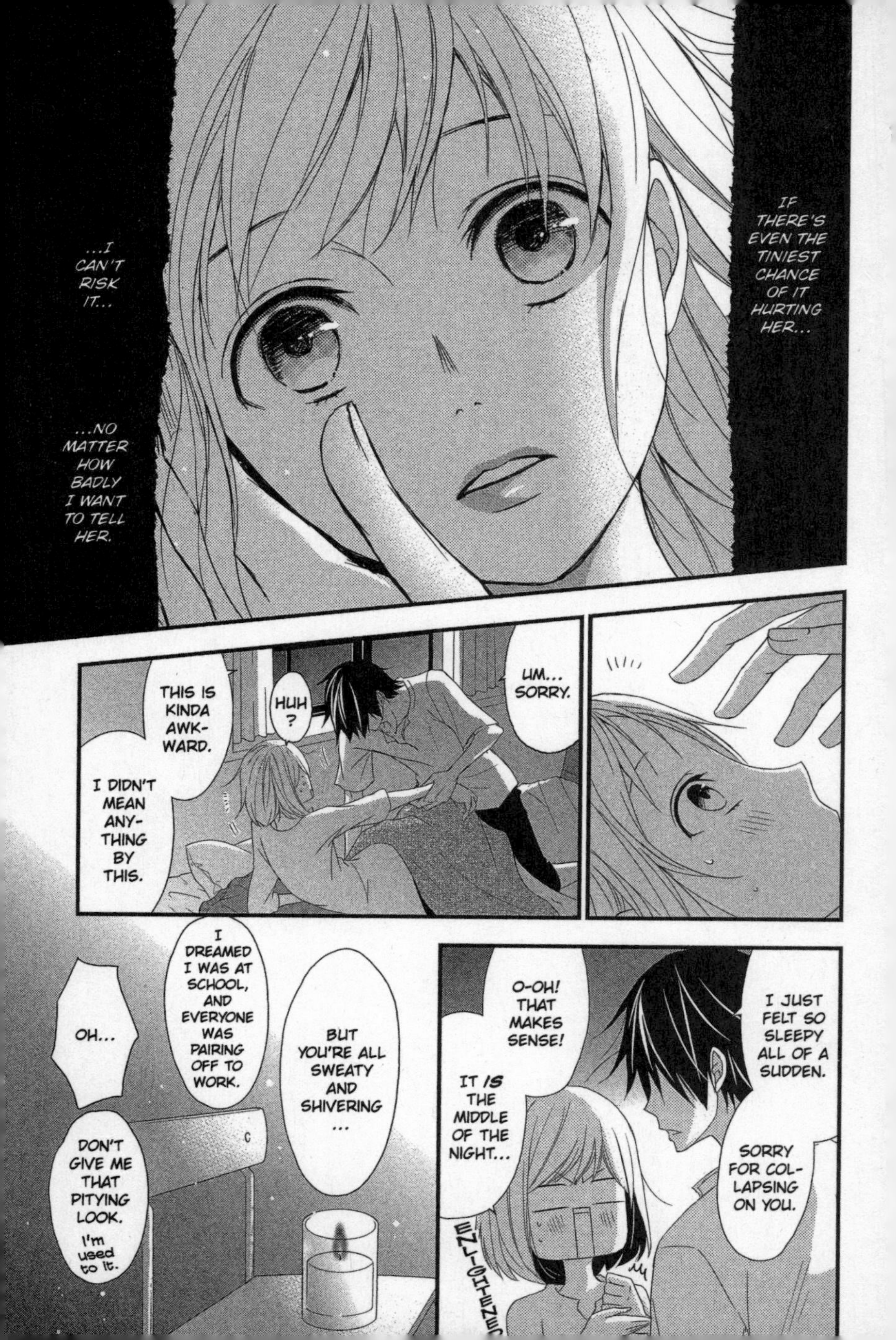
IF THERE'S EVEN THE TINIEST CHANCE OF IT HURTING HER...
...I CAN'T RISK IT...
...NO MATTER HOW BADLY I WANT TO TELL HER.
UM... SORRY.
HUH?
THIS IS KINDA AWK-WARD.
I DIDN'T MEAN ANY-THING BY THIS.
I JUST FELT SO SLEEPY ALL OF A SUDDEN.
O-OH! THAT MAKES SENSE!
SORRY FOR COL-LAPSING ON YOU.
IT IS THE MIDDLE OF THE NIGHT...
ENLIGHTENE
BUT YOU'RE ALL SWEATY AND SHIVERING...
I DREAMED I WAS AT SCHOOL, AND EVERYONE WAS PAIRING OFF TO WORK.
OH...
DON'T GIVE ME THAT PITYING LOOK.
I'm used to it.

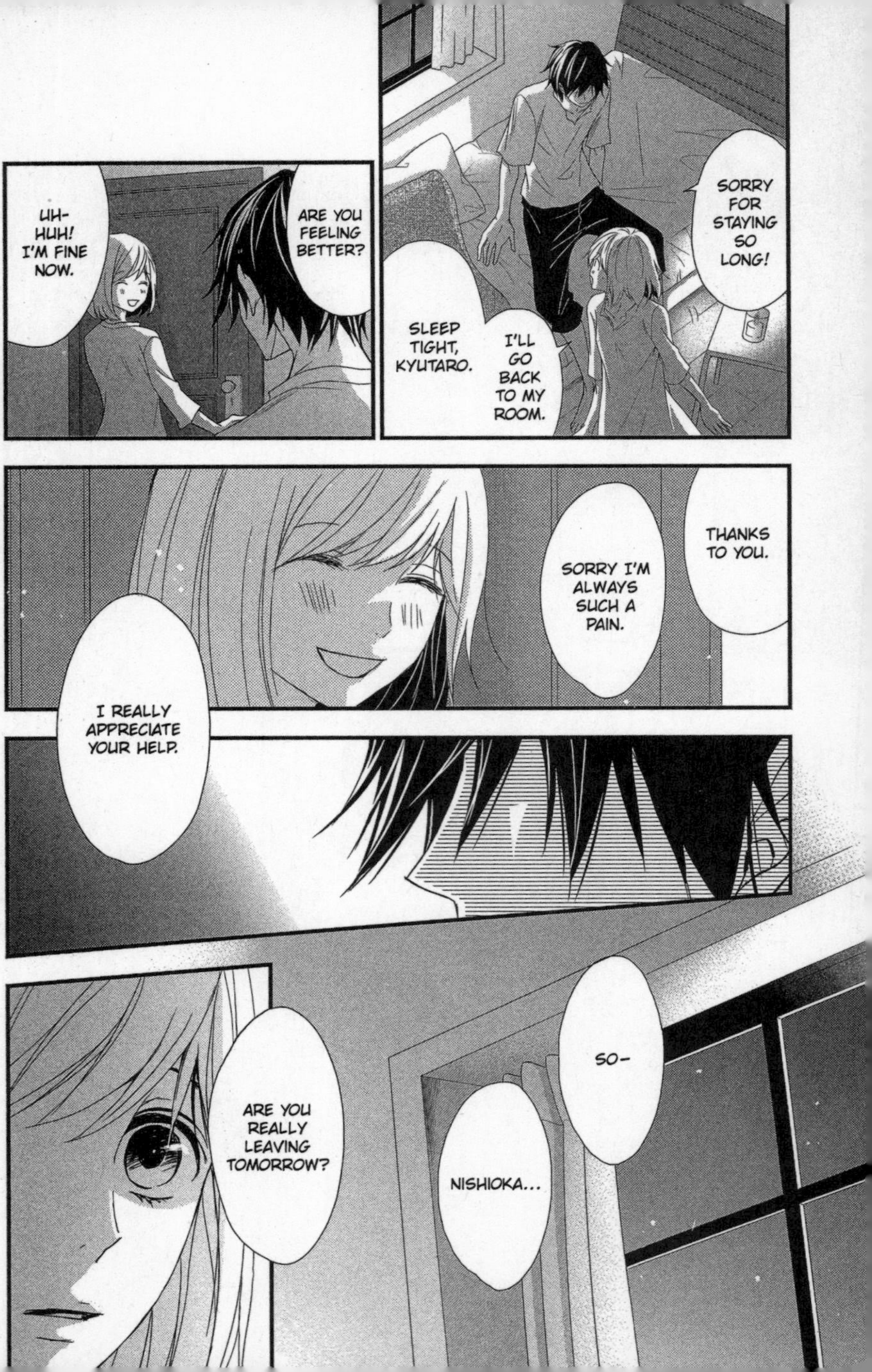
SORRY FOR STAYING SO LONG!
I'LL GO BACK TO MY ROOM.
SLEEP TIGHT, KYUTARO.
ARE YOU FEELING BETTER?
UH-HUH! I'M FINE NOW.
THANKS TO YOU.
SORRY I'M ALWAYS SUCH A PAIN.
I REALLY APPRECIATE YOUR HELP.
SO-
NISHIOKA...
ARE YOU REALLY LEAVING TOMORROW?

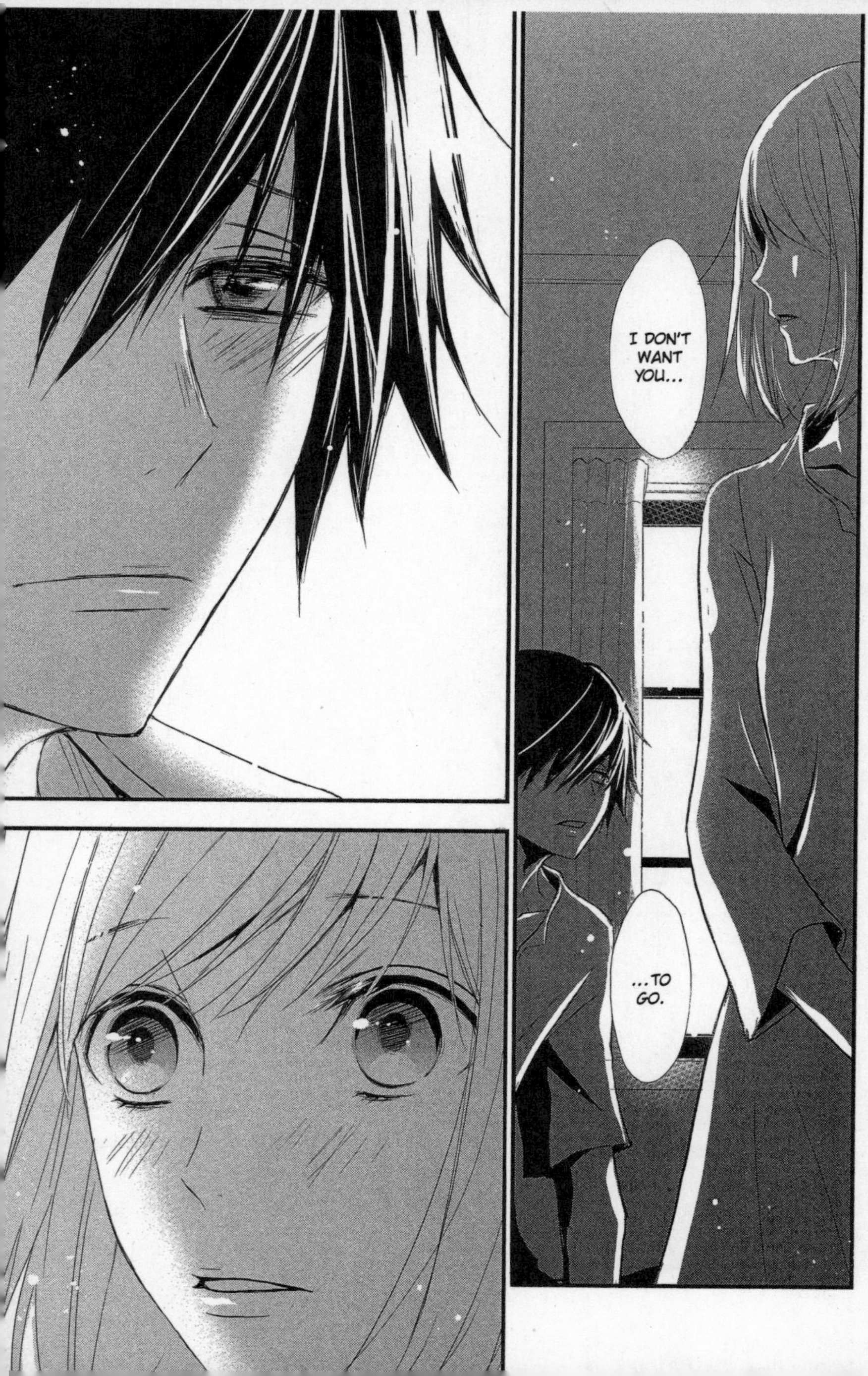
I DON'T WANT YOU...
...TO GO.

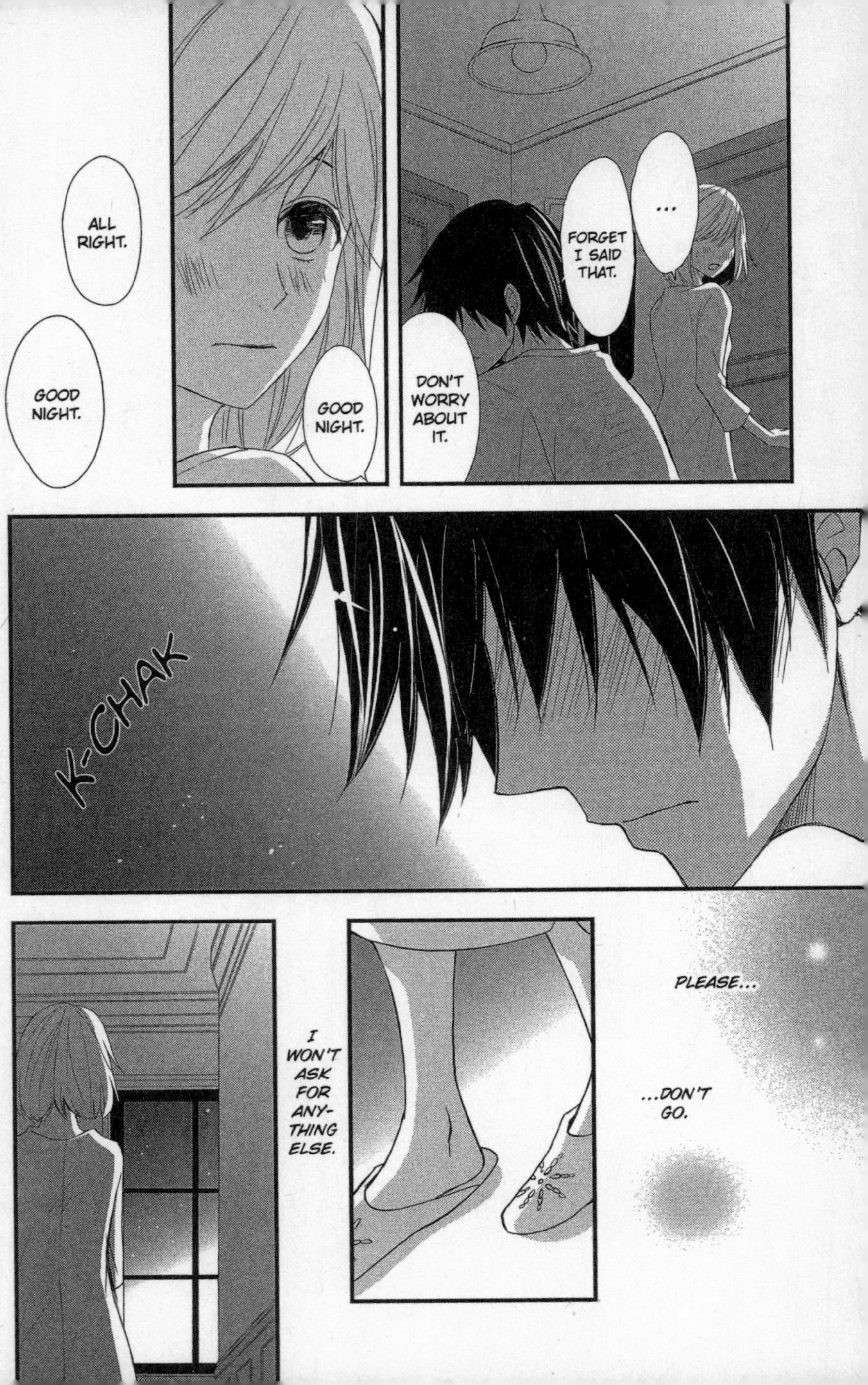
...
FORGET I SAID THAT.
DON'T WORRY ABOUT IT.
GOOD NIGHT.
ALL RIGHT.
GOOD NIGHT.
K-CHAK
PLEASE...
...DON'T GO.
I WON'T ASK FOR ANY-THING ELSE.

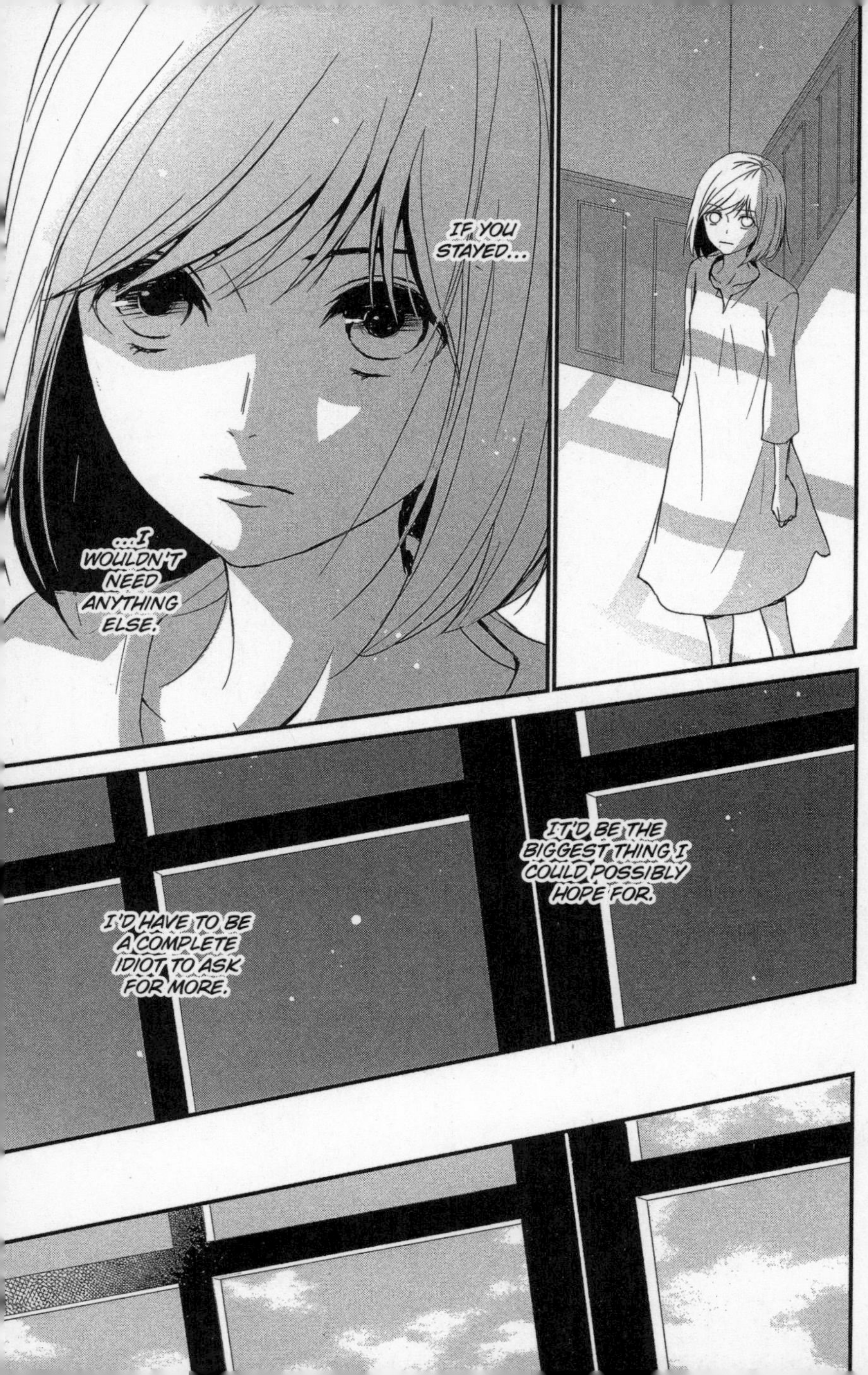
IF YOU STAYED...
...I WOULDN'T NEED ANYTHING ELSE.
IT'D BE THE BIGGEST THING I COULD POSSIBLY HOPE FOR.
I'D HAVE TO BE A COMPLETE IDIOT TO ASK FOR MORE.

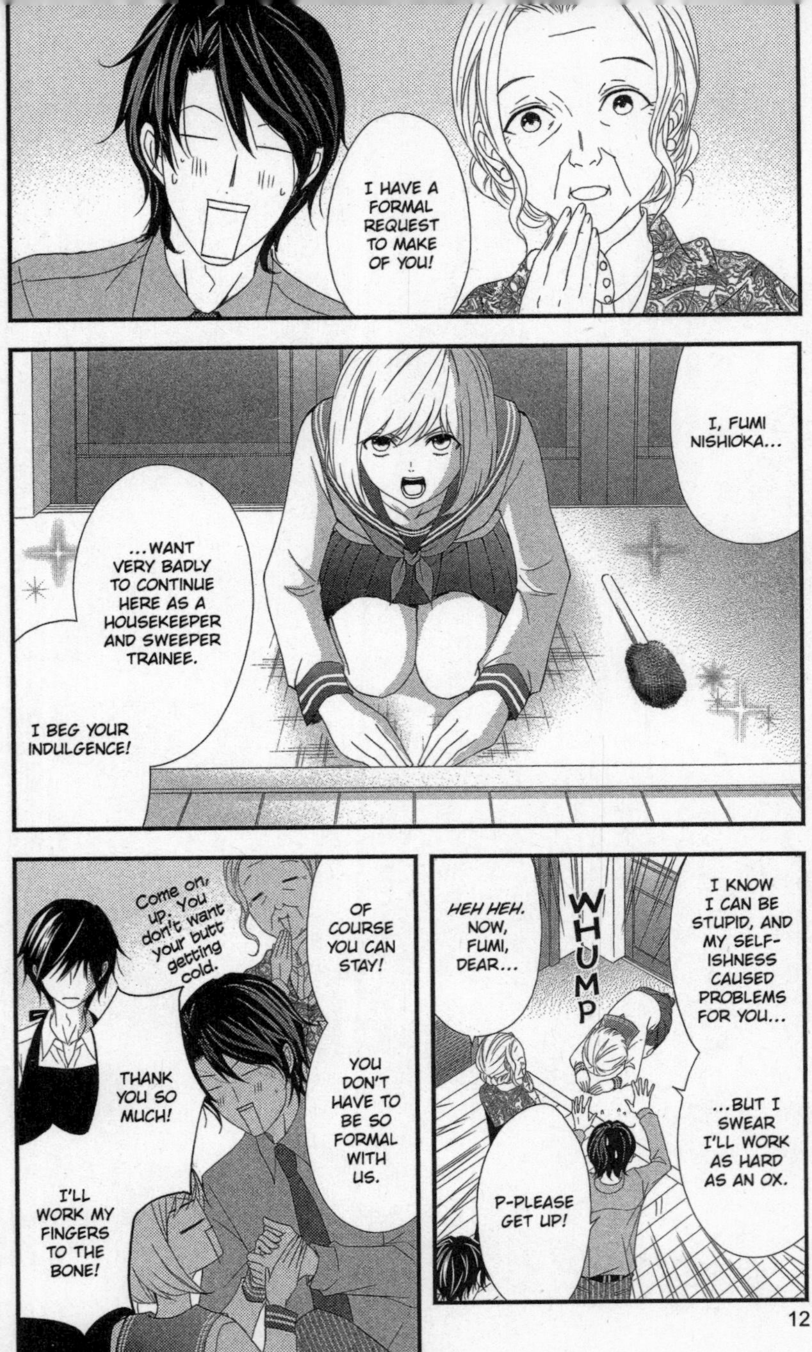
I HAVE A FORMAL REQUEST TO MAKE OF YOU!
I, FUMI NISHIOKA...
...WANT VERY BADLY TO CONTINUE HERE AS A HOUSEKEEPER AND SWEEPER TRAINEE.
I BEG YOUR INDULGENCE!
I KNOW I CAN BE STUPID, AND MY SELF-ISHNESS CAUSED PROBLEMS FOR YOU...
WHUMP
HEH HEH. NOW, FUMI, DEAR...
...BUT I SWEAR I'LL WORK AS HARD AS AN OX.
P-PLEASE GET UP!
OF COURSE YOU CAN STAY!
YOU DON'T HAVE TO BE SO FORMAL WITH US.
Come on, up. You don't want your butt getting cold.
THANK YOU SO MUCH!
I'LL WORK MY FINGERS TO THE BONE!

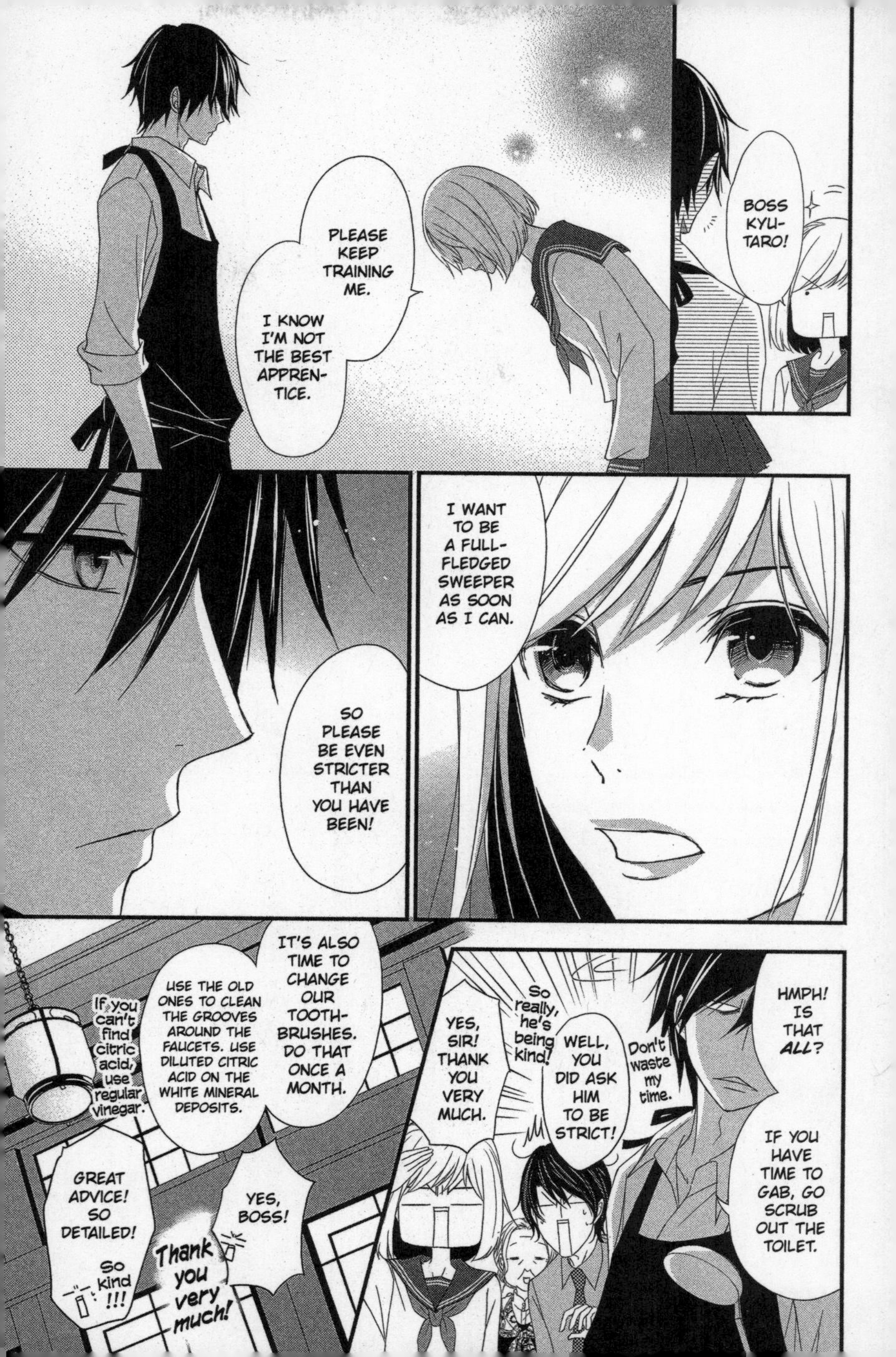
BOSS KYUTARO!
PLEASE KEEP TRAINING ME.
I KNOW I'M NOT THE BEST APPRENTICE.
I WANT TO BE A FULL-FLEDGED SWEEPER AS SOON AS I CAN.
SO PLEASE BE EVEN STRICTER THAN YOU HAVE BEEN!
HMPH! IS THAT ALL?
IF YOU HAVE TIME TO GAB, GO SCRUB OUT THE TOILET.
Don't waste my time.
WELL, YOU DID ASK HIM TO BE STRICT!
So really, he's being kind!
YES, SIR! THANK YOU VERY MUCH.
IT'S ALSO TIME TO CHANGE OUR TOOTHBRUSHES. DO THAT ONCE A MONTH.
USE THE OLD ONES TO CLEAN THE GROOVES AROUND THE FAUCETS. USE DILUTED CITRIC ACID ON THE WHITE MINERAL DEPOSITS.
If you can't find citric acid, use regular vinegar.
YES, BOSS!
GREAT ADVICE! SO DETAILED!
So kind!!!
Thank you very much!

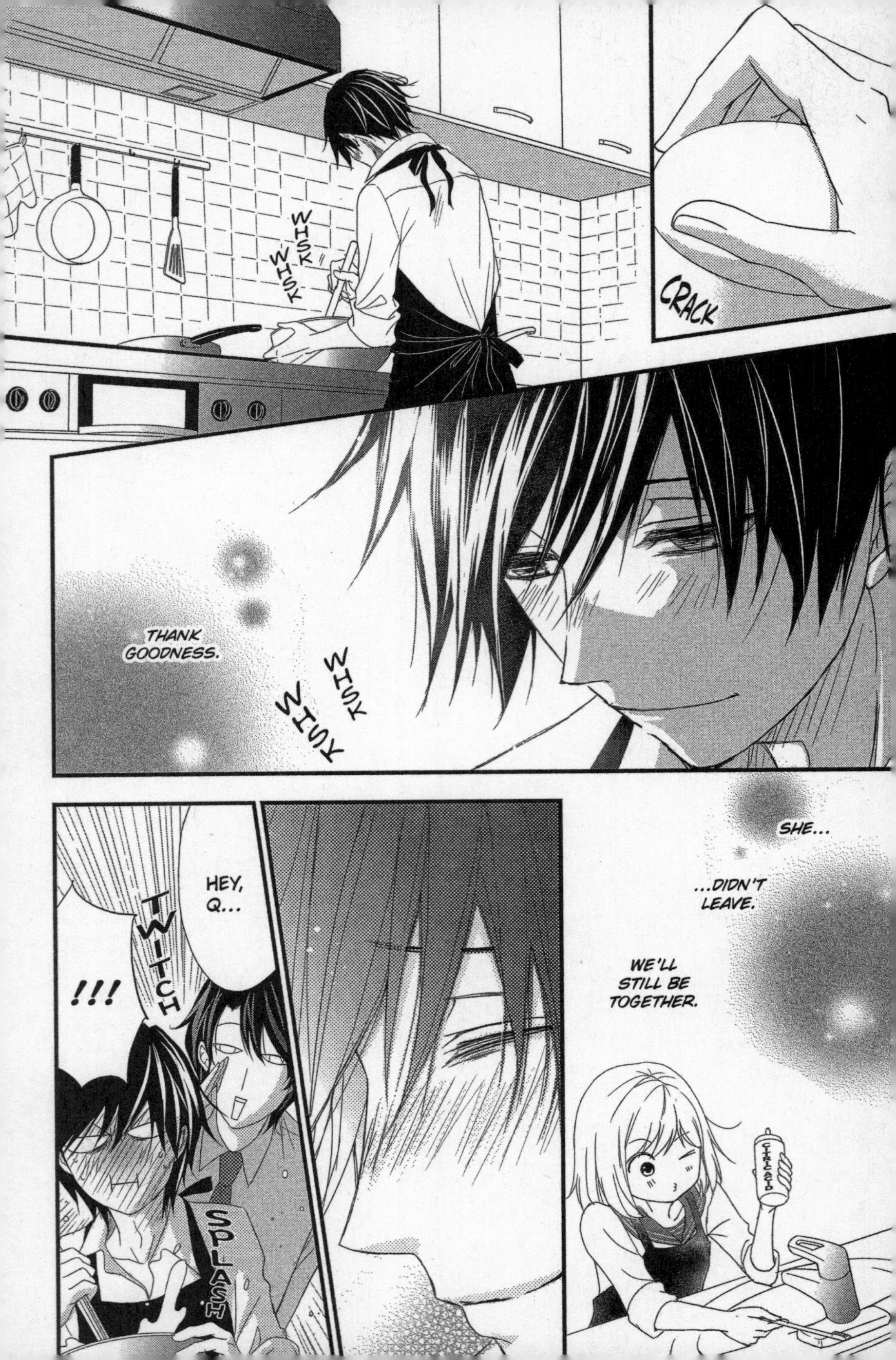
CRACK
WHSK WHSK
THANK GOODNESS.
WHSK WHSK
SHE...
...DIDN'T LEAVE.
WE'LL STILL BE TOGETHER.
HEY, Q...
TWITCH
!!!
SPLASH

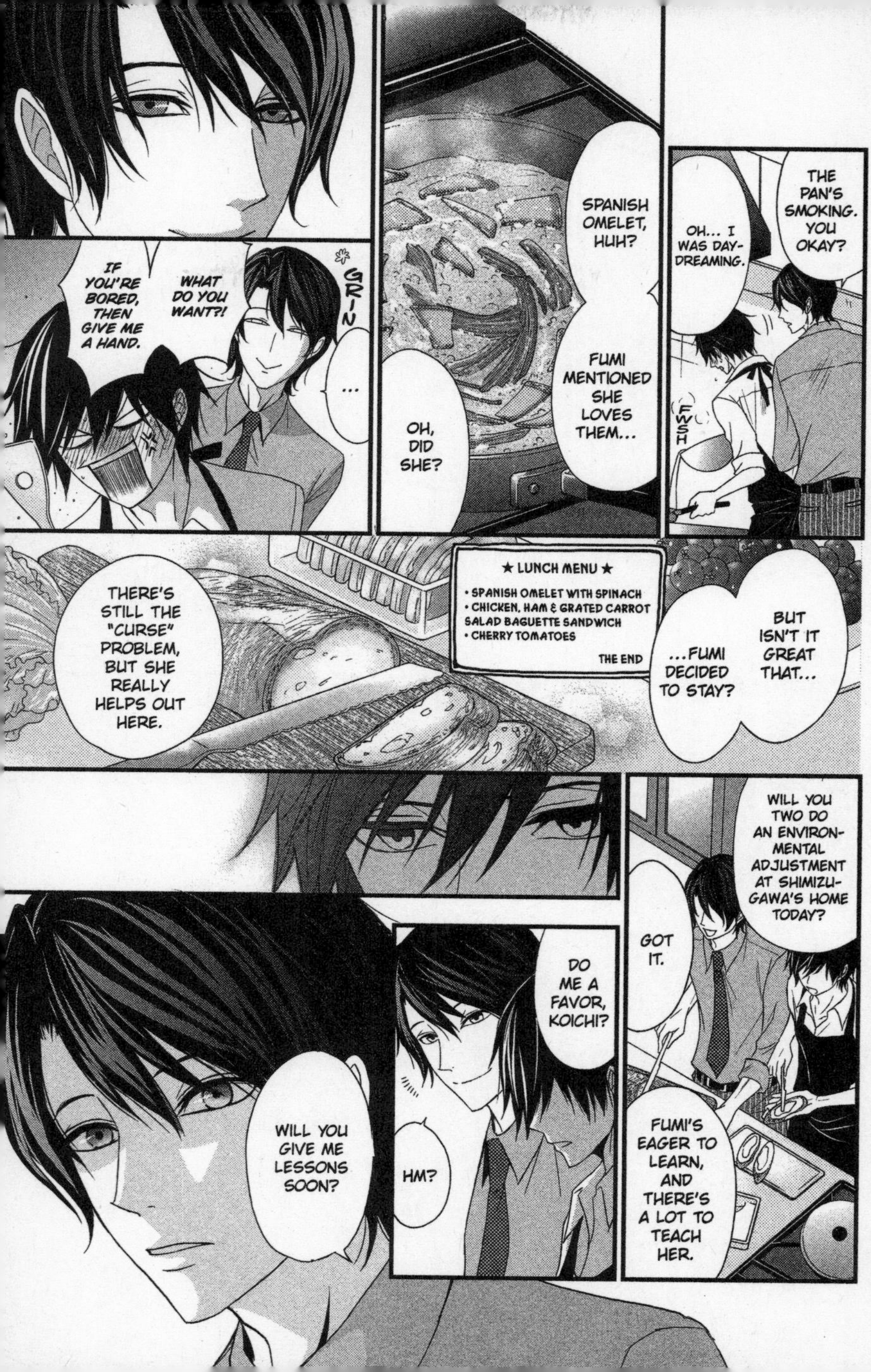
THE PAN'S SMOKING. YOU OKAY?
OH... I WAS DAY-DREAMING.
FWSH
SPANISH OMELET, HUH?
FUMI MENTIONED SHE LOVES THEM...
OH, DID SHE?
GRIN
...
WHAT DO YOU WANT?!
IF YOU'RE BORED, THEN GIVE ME A HAND.
BUT ISN'T IT GREAT THAT...
...FUMI DECIDED TO STAY?
★ LUNCH MENU ★
• SPANISH OMELET WITH SPINACH
• CHICKEN, HAM & GRATED CARROT SALAD BAGUETTE SANDWICH
• CHERRY TOMATOES
THE END
THERE'S STILL THE "CURSE" PROBLEM, BUT SHE REALLY HELPS OUT HERE.
WILL YOU TWO DO AN ENVIRON-MENTAL ADJUSTMENT AT SHIMIZU-GAWA'S HOME TODAY?
GOT IT.
FUMI'S EAGER TO LEARN, AND THERE'S A LOT TO TEACH HER.
DO ME A FAVOR, KOICHI?
HM?
WILL YOU GIVE ME LESSONS SOON?

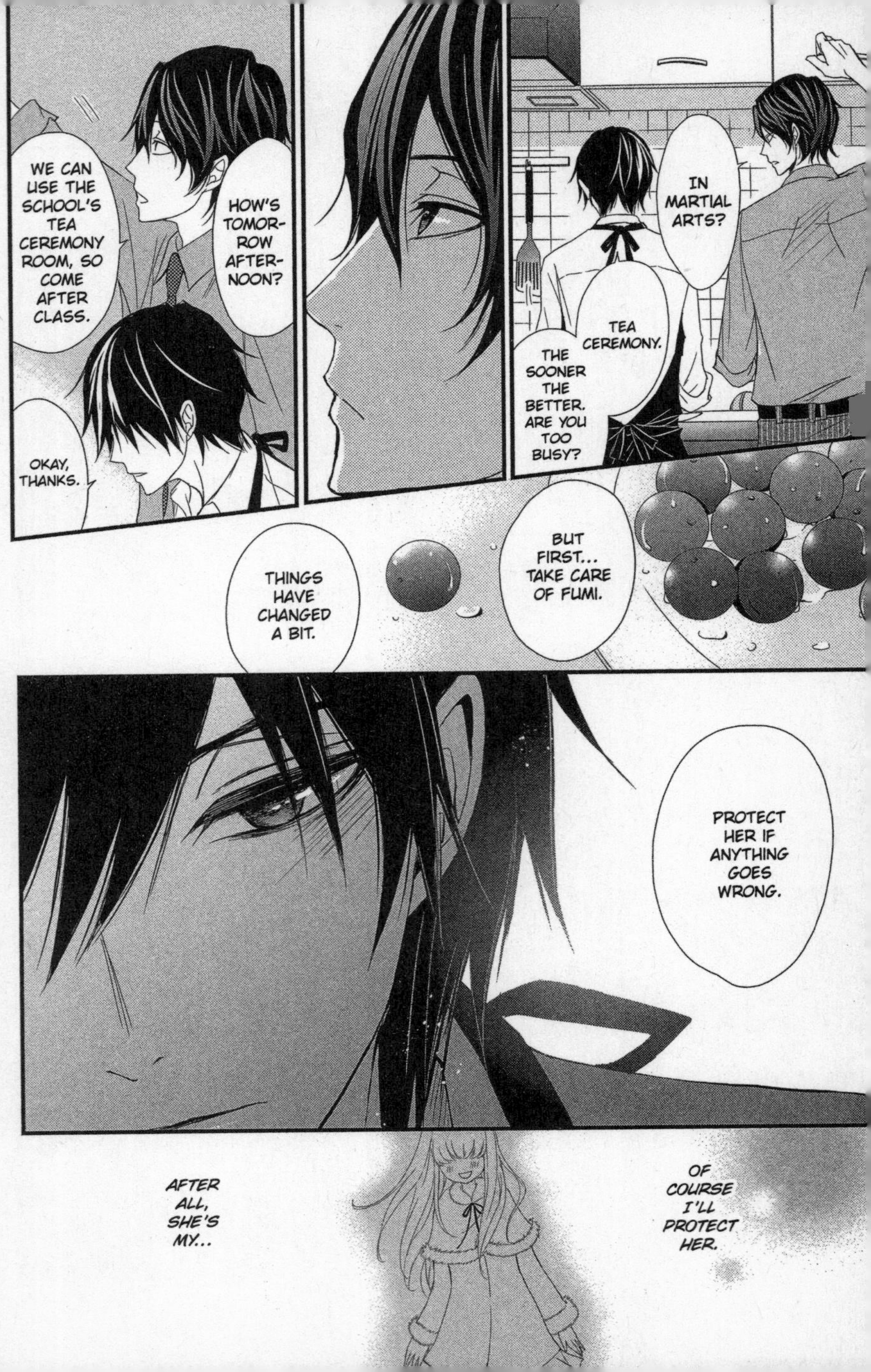
IN MARTIAL ARTS?
TEA CEREMONY.
THE SOONER THE BETTER. ARE YOU TOO BUSY?
HOW'S TOMORROW AFTERNOON?
WE CAN USE THE SCHOOL'S TEA CEREMONY ROOM, SO COME AFTER CLASS.
OKAY, THANKS.
BUT FIRST... TAKE CARE OF FUMI.
THINGS HAVE CHANGED A BIT.
PROTECT HER IF ANYTHING GOES WRONG.
OF COURSE I'LL PROTECT HER.
AFTER ALL, SHE'S MY...

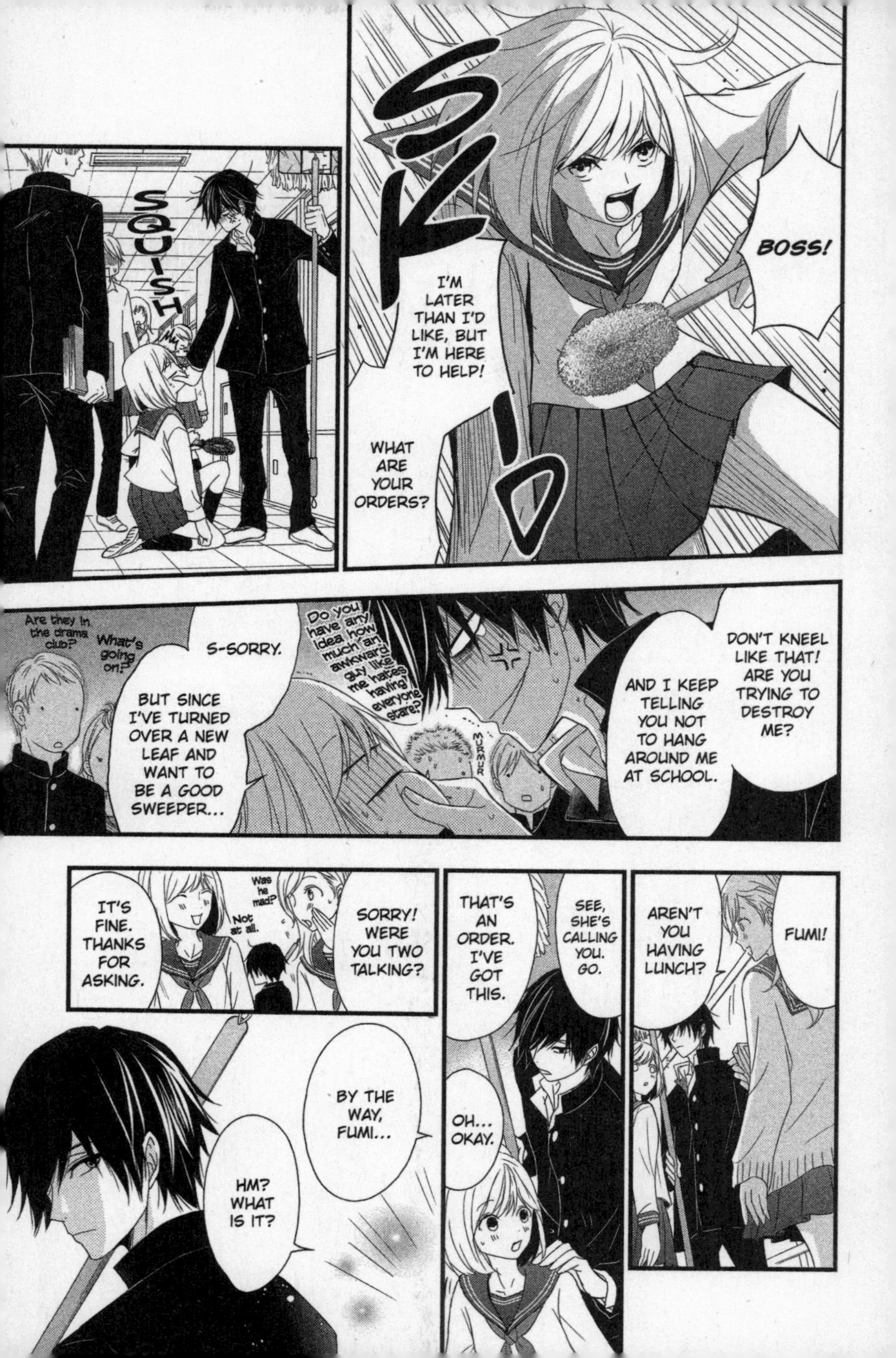
SKID
BOSS!
I'M LATER THAN I'D LIKE, BUT I'M HERE TO HELP!
WHAT ARE YOUR ORDERS?
SQUISH
DON'T KNEEL LIKE THAT! ARE YOU TRYING TO DESTROY ME?
AND I KEEP TELLING YOU NOT TO HANG AROUND ME AT SCHOOL.
MURMUR
Do you have any idea how much an awkward guy like me hates having everyone stare?
S-SORRY.
BUT SINCE I'VE TURNED OVER A NEW LEAF AND WANT TO BE A GOOD SWEEPER...
What's going on?
Are they in the drama club?
FUMI!
AREN'T YOU HAVING LUNCH?
SEE, SHE'S CALLING YOU. GO.
THAT'S AN ORDER. I'VE GOT THIS.
OH... OKAY.
SORRY! WERE YOU TWO TALKING?
Was he mad?
Not at all.
IT'S FINE. THANKS FOR ASKING.
BY THE WAY, FUMI...
HM? WHAT IS IT?

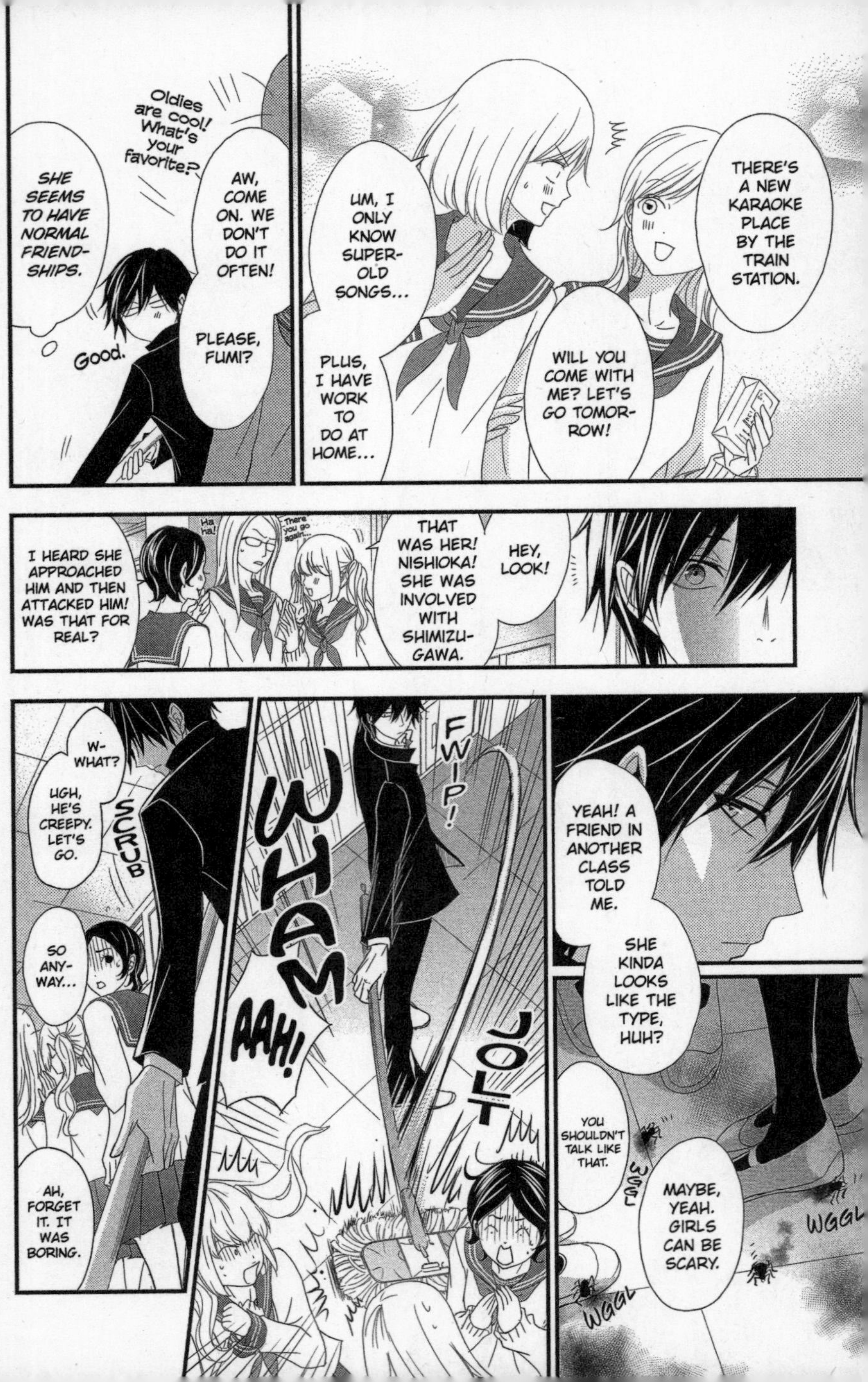
THERE'S A NEW KARAOKE PLACE BY THE TRAIN STATION.
WILL YOU COME WITH ME? LET'S GO TOMORROW!
UM, I ONLY KNOW SUPER-OLD SONGS...
PLUS, I HAVE WORK TO DO AT HOME...
Oldies are cool! What's your favorite?
AW, COME ON. WE DON'T DO IT OFTEN!
PLEASE, FUMI?
SHE SEEMS TO HAVE NORMAL FRIENDSHIPS.
Good.
HEY, LOOK!
THAT WAS HER! NISHIOKA! SHE WAS INVOLVED WITH SHIMIZUGAWA.
There you go again...
Ha ha!
I HEARD SHE APPROACHED HIM AND THEN ATTACKED HIM! WAS THAT FOR REAL?
YEAH! A FRIEND IN ANOTHER CLASS TOLD ME.
SHE KINDA LOOKS LIKE THE TYPE, HUH?
YOU SHOULDN'T TALK LIKE THAT.
MAYBE, YEAH. GIRLS CAN BE SCARY.
WGGL
WGGL
WGGL
FWIP!
WHAM
AAH!
JOLT
W-WHAT?
SCRUB
UGH, HE'S CREEPY. LET'S GO.
SO ANYWAY...
AH, FORGET IT. IT WAS BORING.

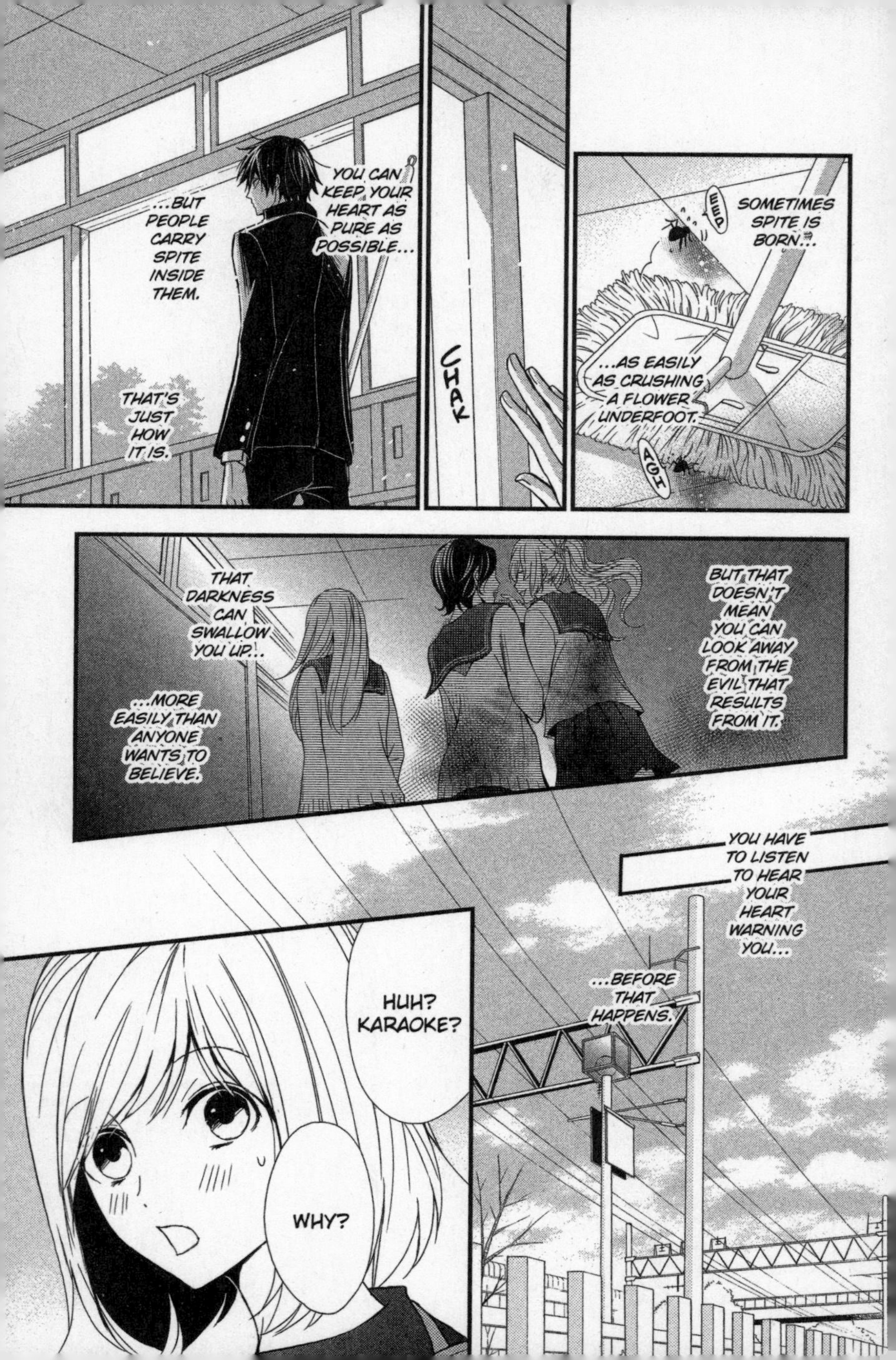
SOMETIMES SPITE IS BORN...
EEP
...AS EASILY AS CRUSHING A FLOWER UNDERFOOT.
AGH
CHAK
YOU CAN KEEP YOUR HEART AS PURE AS POSSIBLE...
...BUT PEOPLE CARRY SPITE INSIDE THEM.
THAT'S JUST HOW IT IS.
BUT THAT DOESN'T MEAN YOU CAN LOOK AWAY FROM THE EVIL THAT RESULTS FROM IT.
THAT DARKNESS CAN SWALLOW YOU UP...
...MORE EASILY THAN ANYONE WANTS TO BELIEVE.
YOU HAVE TO LISTEN TO HEAR YOUR HEART WARNING YOU...
...BEFORE THAT HAPPENS.
HUH? KARAOKE?
WHY?

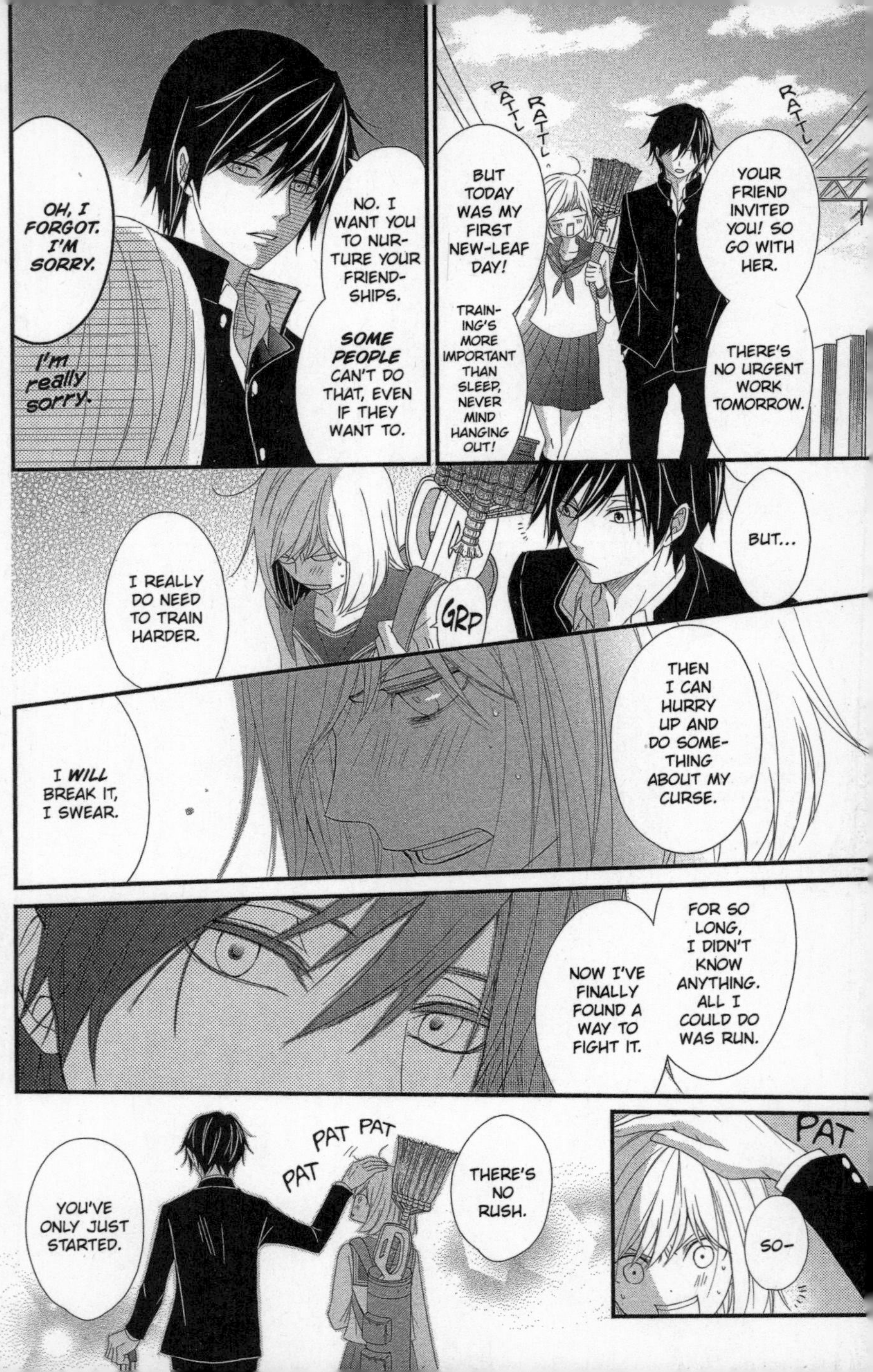
RATTL
YOUR FRIEND INVITED YOU! SO GO WITH HER.
THERE'S NO URGENT WORK TOMORROW.
RATTL RATTL
BUT TODAY WAS MY FIRST NEW-LEAF DAY!
TRAINING'S MORE IMPORTANT THAN SLEEP, NEVER MIND HANGING OUT!
NO. I WANT YOU TO NURTURE YOUR FRIENDSHIPS.
SOME PEOPLE CAN'T DO THAT, EVEN IF THEY WANT TO.
OH, I FORGOT. I'M SORRY.
I'm really sorry.
BUT...
GRP
I REALLY DO NEED TO TRAIN HARDER.
THEN I CAN HURRY UP AND DO SOMETHING ABOUT MY CURSE.
I ***WILL*** BREAK IT, I SWEAR.
FOR SO LONG, I DIDN'T KNOW ANYTHING. ALL I COULD DO WAS RUN.
NOW I'VE FINALLY FOUND A WAY TO FIGHT IT.
PAT
SO-
THERE'S NO RUSH.
PAT PAT PAT
YOU'VE ONLY JUST STARTED.

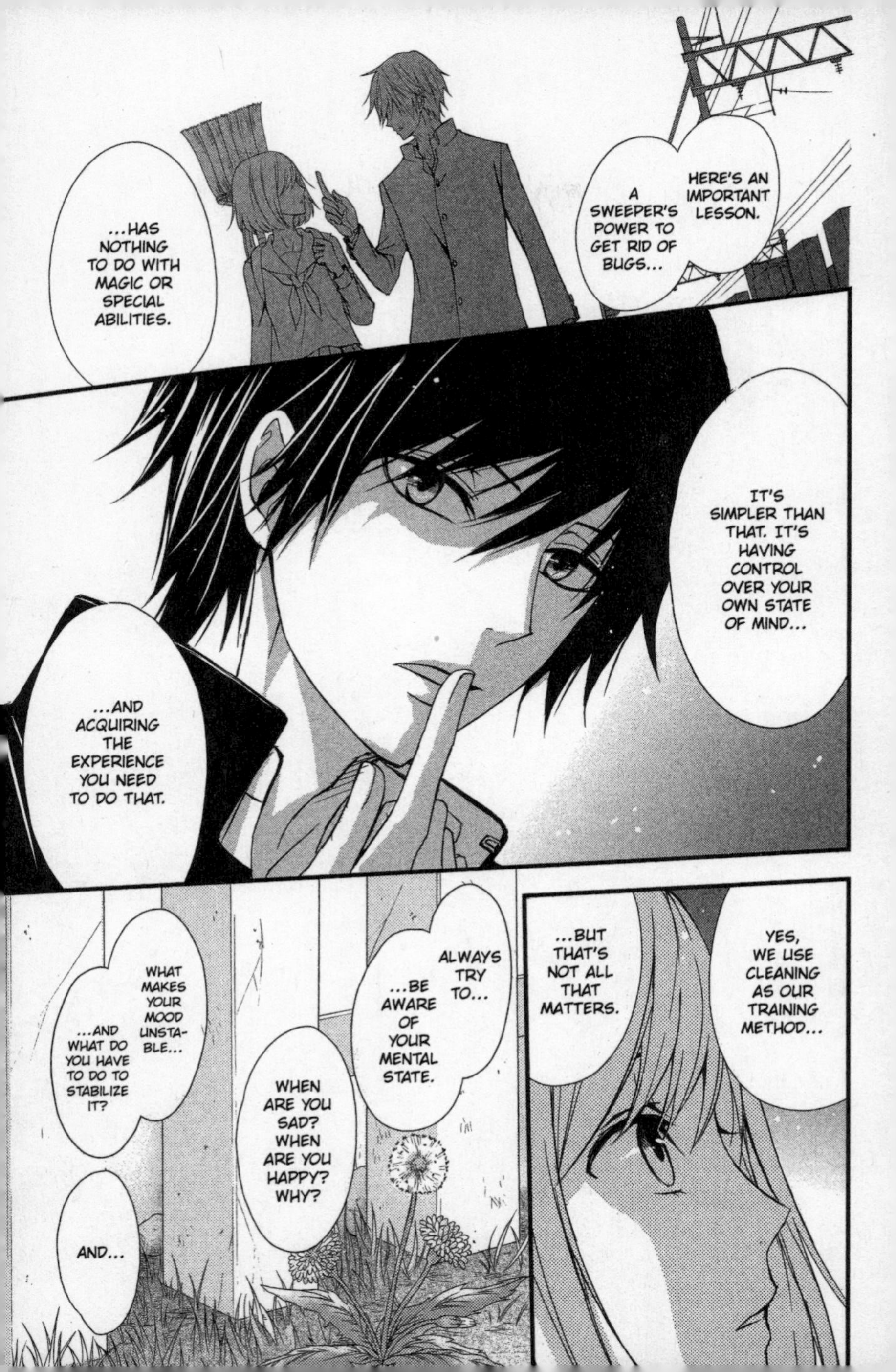
HERE'S AN IMPORTANT LESSON.
A SWEEPER'S POWER TO GET RID OF BUGS...
...HAS NOTHING TO DO WITH MAGIC OR SPECIAL ABILITIES.
IT'S SIMPLER THAN THAT. IT'S HAVING CONTROL OVER YOUR OWN STATE OF MIND...
...AND ACQUIRING THE EXPERIENCE YOU NEED TO DO THAT.
YES, WE USE CLEANING AS OUR TRAINING METHOD...
...BUT THAT'S NOT ALL THAT MATTERS.
ALWAYS TRY TO...
...BE AWARE OF YOUR MENTAL STATE.
WHEN ARE YOU SAD? WHEN ARE YOU HAPPY? WHY?
WHAT MAKES YOUR MOOD UNSTA-BLE...
...AND WHAT DO YOU HAVE TO DO TO STABILIZE IT?
AND...

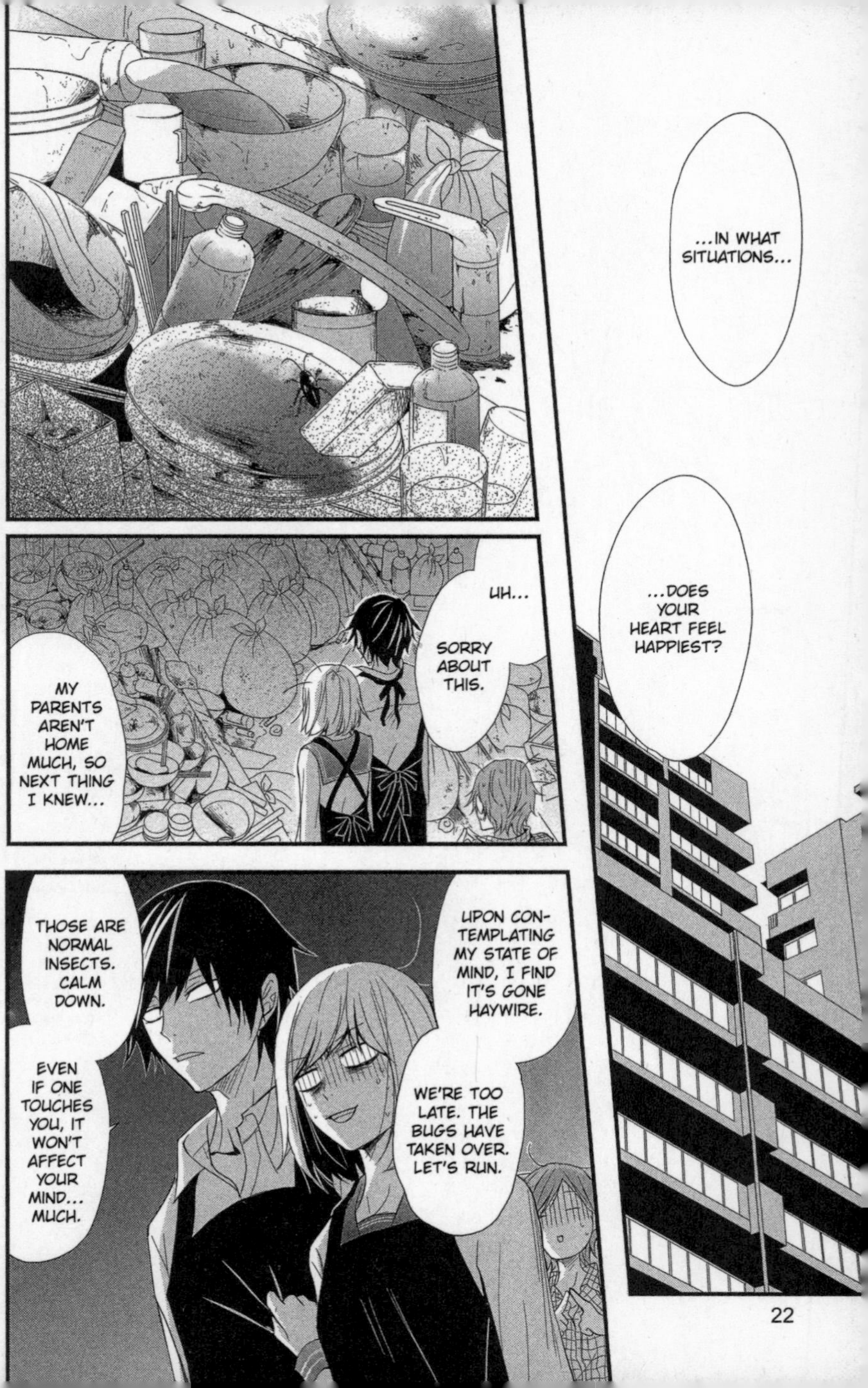
...IN WHAT SITUATIONS...
...DOES YOUR HEART FEEL HAPPIEST?
UH...
SORRY ABOUT THIS.
MY PARENTS AREN'T HOME MUCH, SO NEXT THING I KNEW...
UPON CON-TEMPLATING MY STATE OF MIND, I FIND IT'S GONE HAYWIRE.
WE'RE TOO LATE. THE BUGS HAVE TAKEN OVER. LET'S RUN.
THOSE ARE NORMAL INSECTS. CALM DOWN.
EVEN IF ONE TOUCHES YOU, IT WON'T AFFECT YOUR MIND... MUCH.

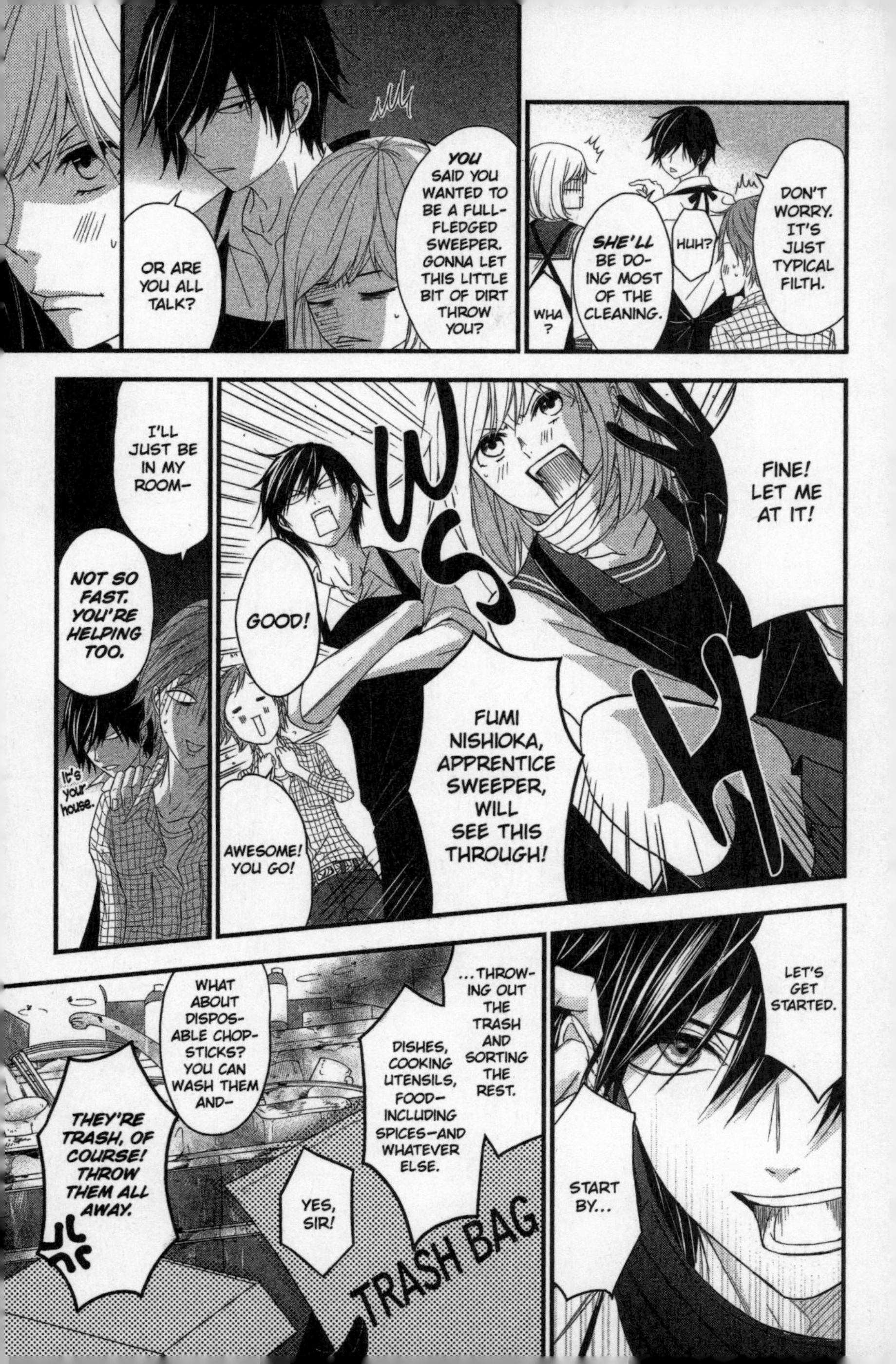
DON'T WORRY. IT'S JUST TYPICAL FILTH.
HUH?
SHE'LL BE DOING MOST OF THE CLEANING.
WHA?
YOU SAID YOU WANTED TO BE A FULL-FLEDGED SWEEPER. GONNA LET THIS LITTLE BIT OF DIRT THROW YOU?
OR ARE YOU ALL TALK?
FINE! LET ME AT IT!
FUMI NISHIOKA, APPRENTICE SWEEPER, WILL SEE THIS THROUGH!
GOOD!
AWESOME! YOU GO!
I'LL JUST BE IN MY ROOM-
NOT SO FAST. YOU'RE HELPING TOO.
It's your house.
LET'S GET STARTED.
START BY...
...THROWING OUT THE TRASH AND SORTING THE REST.
DISHES, COOKING UTENSILS, FOOD—INCLUDING SPICES—AND WHATEVER ELSE.
WHAT ABOUT DISPOSABLE CHOPSTICKS? YOU CAN WASH THEM AND-
YES, SIR!
TRASH BAG
THEY'RE TRASH, OF COURSE! THROW THEM ALL AWAY.

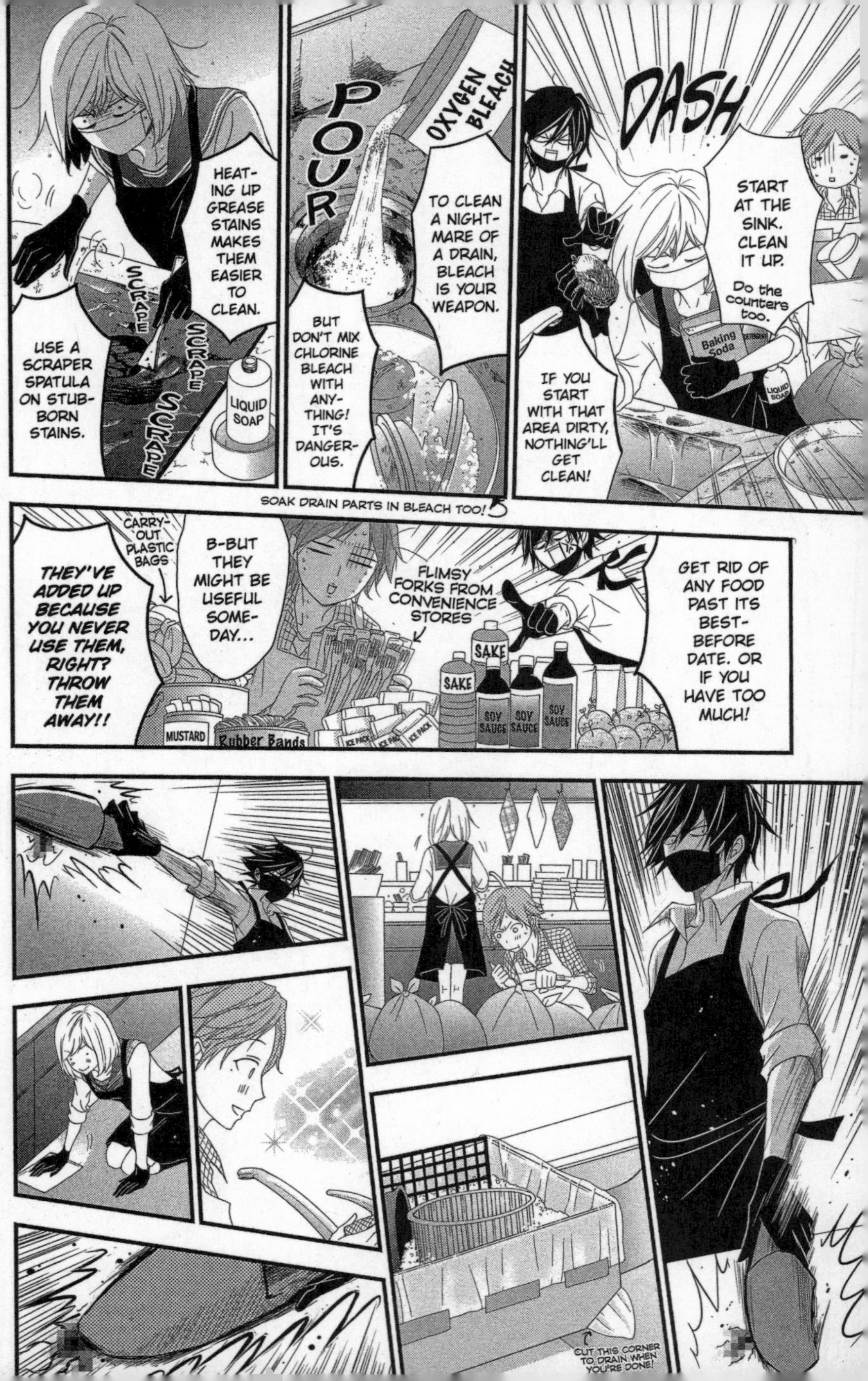
DASH
START AT THE SINK. CLEAN IT UP.
Do the counters too.
Baking Soda
DETERGENT
LIQUID SOAP
IF YOU START WITH THAT AREA DIRTY, NOTHING'LL GET CLEAN!
OXYGEN BLEACH
POUR
TO CLEAN A NIGHTMARE OF A DRAIN, BLEACH IS YOUR WEAPON.
BUT DON'T MIX CHLORINE BLEACH WITH ANYTHING! IT'S DANGEROUS.
SOAK DRAIN PARTS IN BLEACH TOO!
HEATING UP GREASE STAINS MAKES THEM EASIER TO CLEAN.
SCRAPE
SCRAPE
SCRAPE
LIQUID SOAP
USE A SCRAPER SPATULA ON STUBBORN STAINS.
GET RID OF ANY FOOD PAST ITS BEST-BEFORE DATE. OR IF YOU HAVE TOO MUCH!
SAKE
SAKE
SOY SAUCE
SOY SAUCE
SOY SAUCE
FLIMSY FORKS FROM CONVENIENCE STORES
B-BUT THEY MIGHT BE USEFUL SOMEDAY...
CARRY-OUT PLASTIC BAGS
THEY'VE ADDED UP BECAUSE YOU NEVER USE THEM, RIGHT? THROW THEM AWAY!!
MUSTARD
Rubber Bands
ICE PACK
CUT THIS CORNER TO DRAIN WHEN YOU'RE DONE!

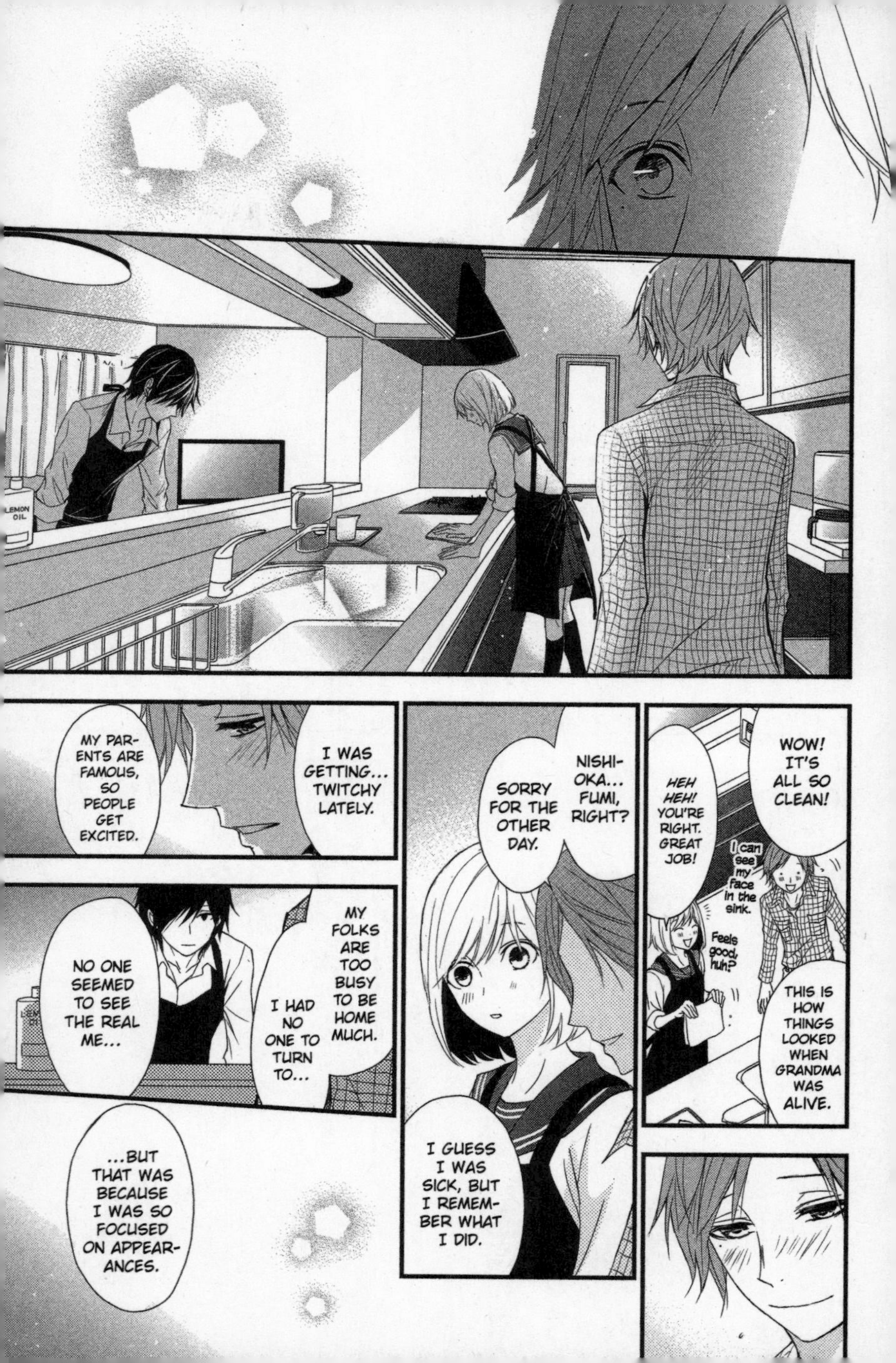
LEMON OIL
WOW! IT'S ALL SO CLEAN!
HEH HEH! YOU'RE RIGHT. GREAT JOB!
I can see my face in the sink.
Feels good, huh?
THIS IS HOW THINGS LOOKED WHEN GRANDMA WAS ALIVE.
NISHI-OKA... FUMI, RIGHT?
SORRY FOR THE OTHER DAY.
I GUESS I WAS SICK, BUT I REMEM-BER WHAT I DID.
I WAS GETTING... TWITCHY LATELY.
MY PAR-ENTS ARE FAMOUS, SO PEOPLE GET EXCITED.
MY FOLKS ARE TOO BUSY TO BE HOME MUCH.
I HAD NO ONE TO TURN TO...
NO ONE SEEMED TO SEE THE REAL ME...
...BUT THAT WAS BECAUSE I WAS SO FOCUSED ON APPEAR-ANCES.

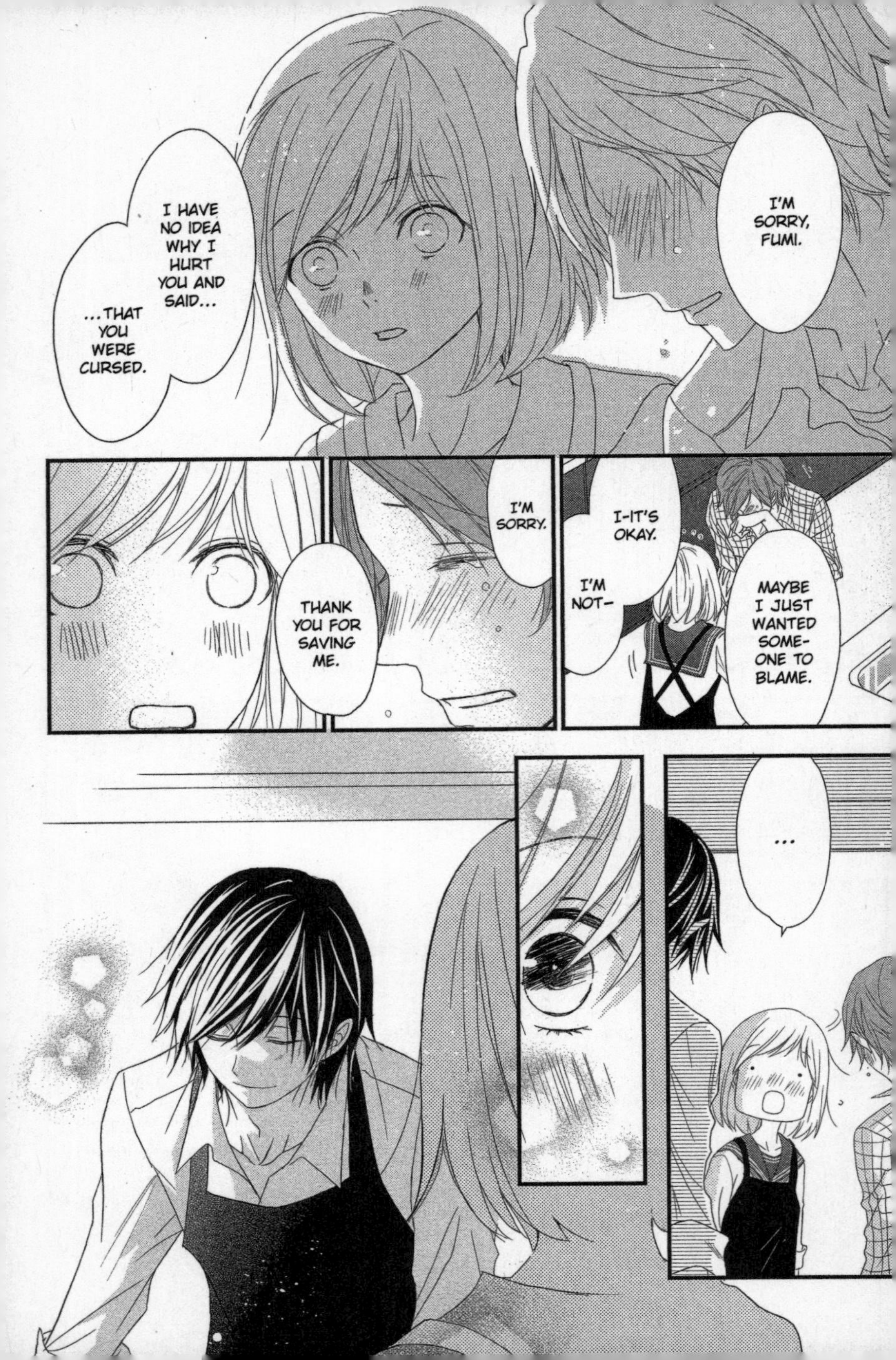

I'M SORRY, FUMI.
I HAVE NO IDEA WHY I HURT YOU AND SAID...
...THAT YOU WERE CURSED.
I-IT'S OKAY.
I'M NOT-
MAYBE I JUST WANTED SOME-ONE TO BLAME.
I'M SORRY.
THANK YOU FOR SAVING ME.
...

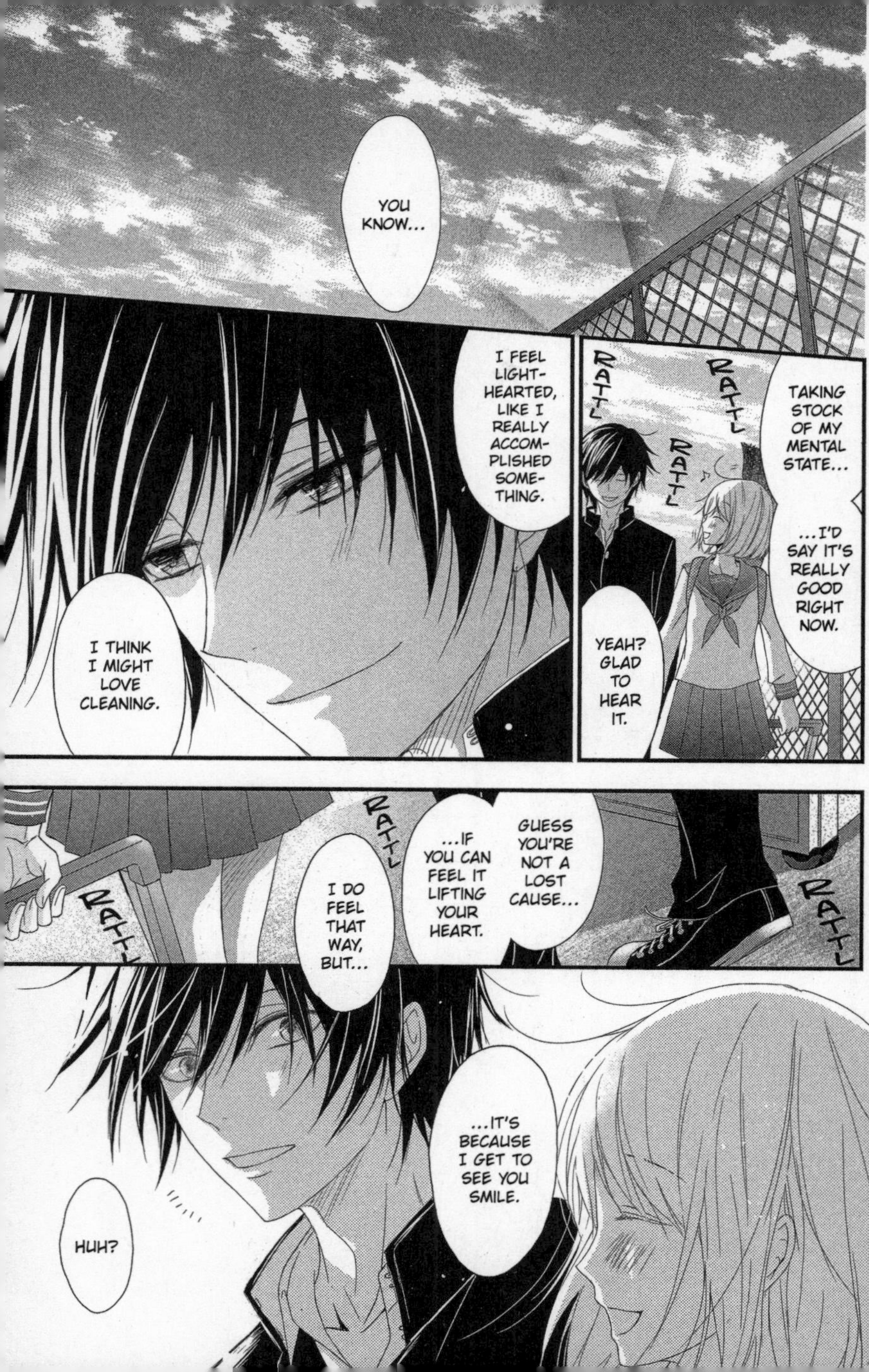
YOU KNOW...
TAKING STOCK OF MY MENTAL STATE...
RATTL
RATTL
RATTL
...I'D SAY IT'S REALLY GOOD RIGHT NOW.
YEAH? GLAD TO HEAR IT.
I FEEL LIGHT-HEARTED, LIKE I REALLY ACCOMPLISHED SOMETHING.
I THINK I MIGHT LOVE CLEANING.
RATTL
GUESS YOU'RE NOT A LOST CAUSE...
...IF YOU CAN FEEL IT LIFTING YOUR HEART.
RATTL
I DO FEEL THAT WAY, BUT...
RATTL
...IT'S BECAUSE I GET TO SEE YOU SMILE.
HUH?

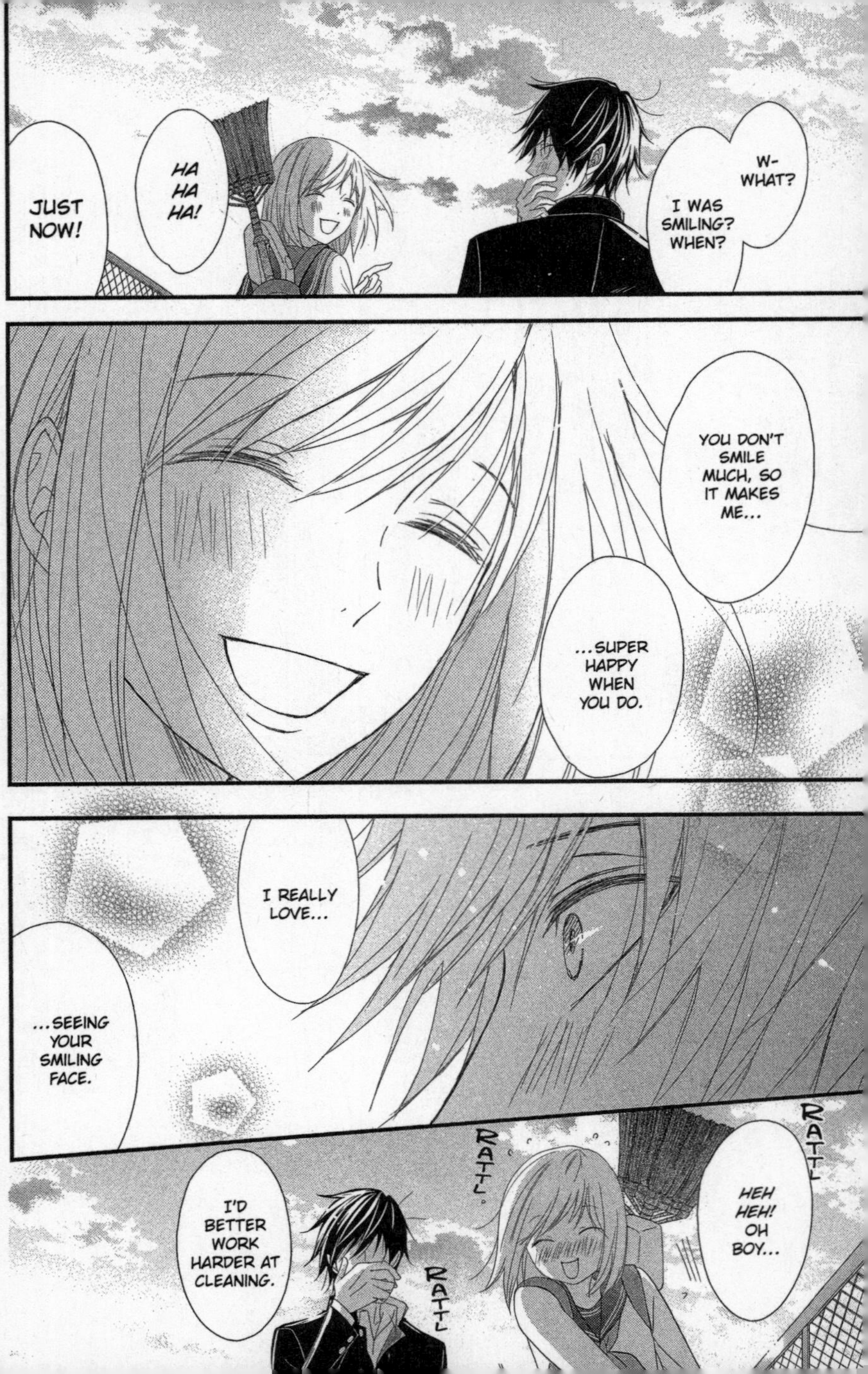
W-
WHAT?
I WAS SMILING? WHEN?
HA HA HA!
JUST NOW!
YOU DON'T SMILE MUCH, SO IT MAKES ME...
...SUPER HAPPY WHEN YOU DO.
I REALLY LOVE...
...SEEING YOUR SMILING FACE.
RATTL
HEH HEH! OH BOY...
RATTL
I'D BETTER WORK HARDER AT CLEANING.
RATTL

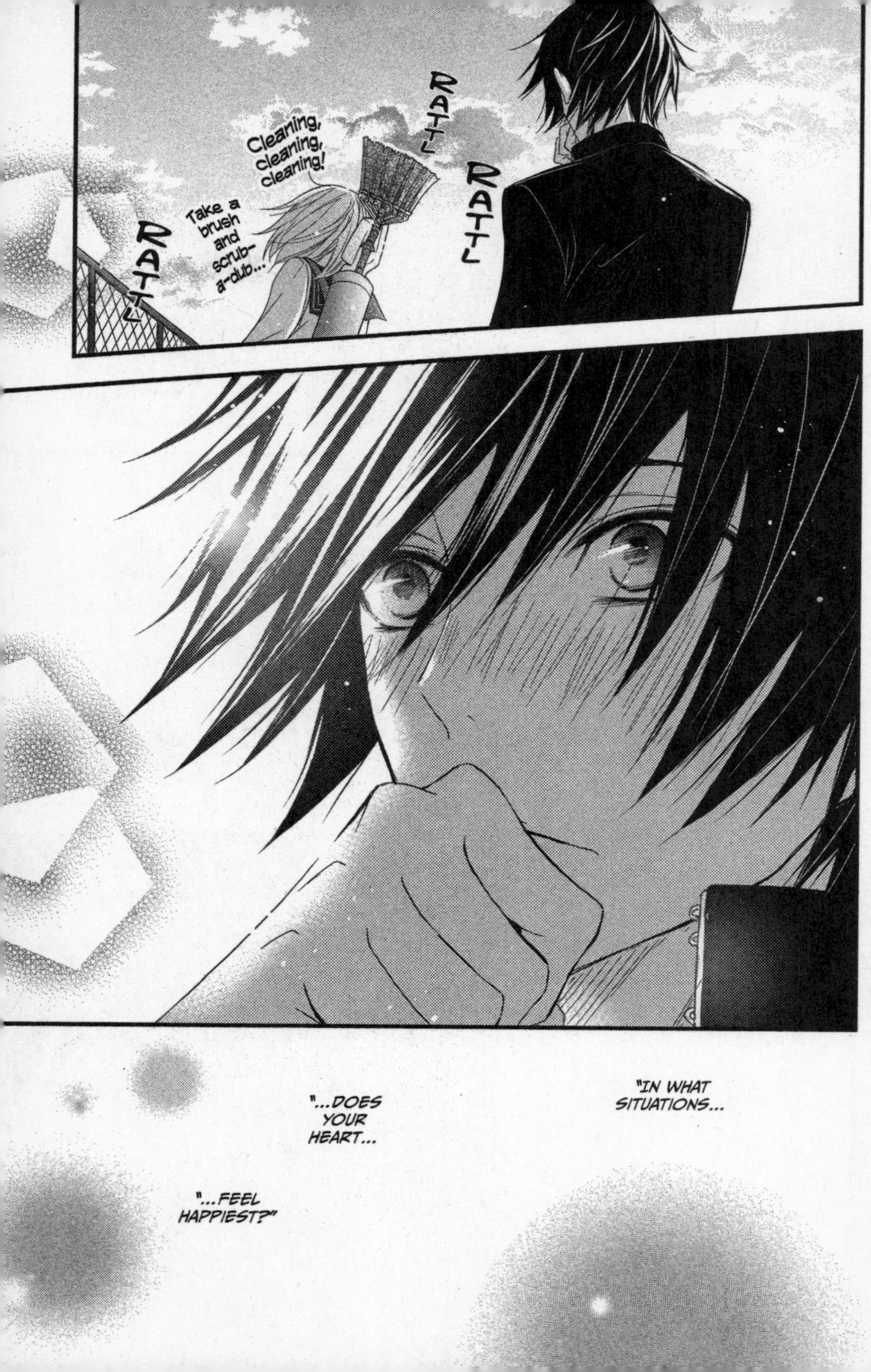

RATTL
RATTL
Cleaning, cleaning, cleaning!
Take a brush and scrub-a-dub...
RATTL
"IN WHAT SITUATIONS...
"...DOES YOUR HEART...
"...FEEL HAPPIEST?"

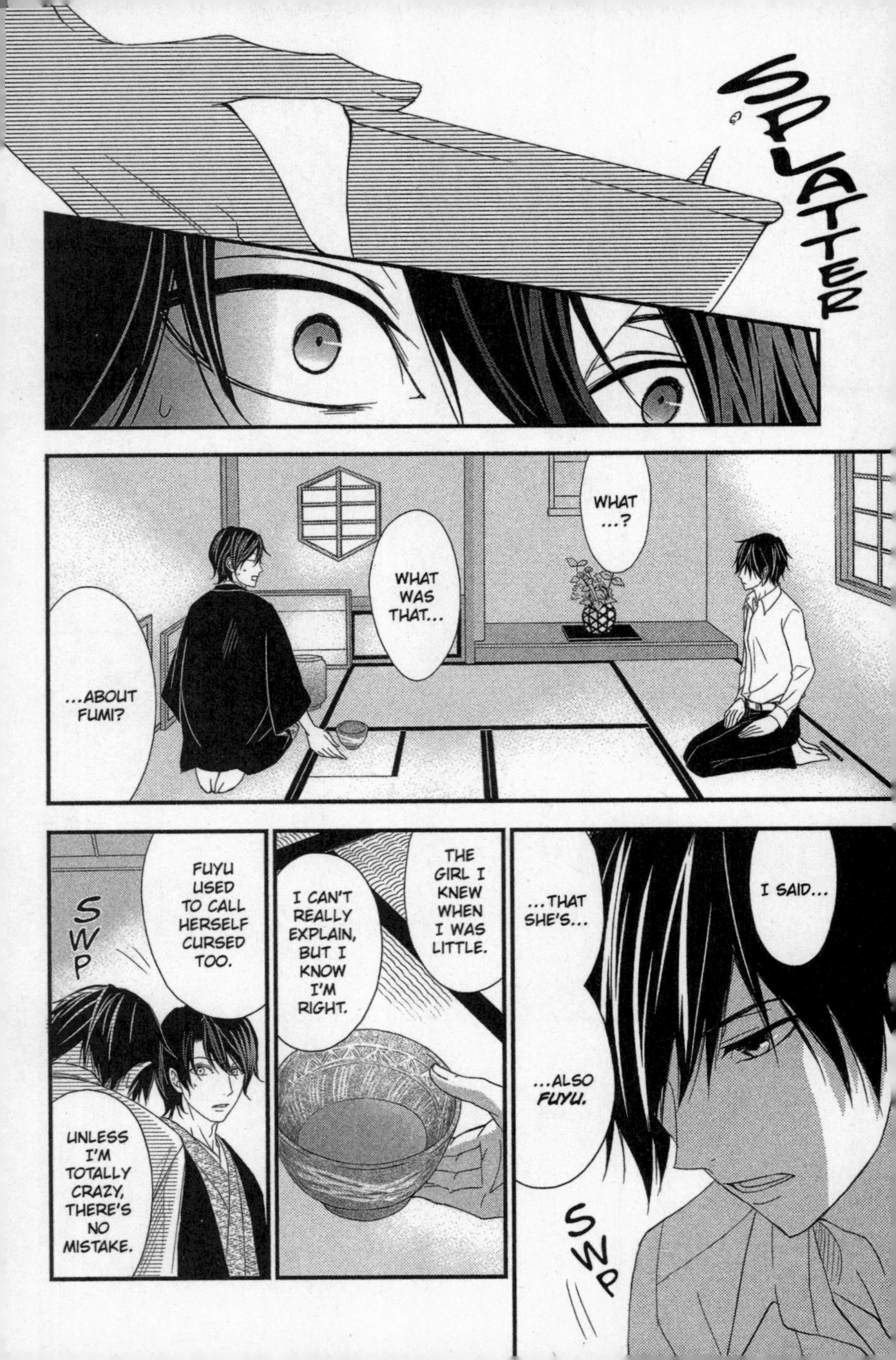
SPLATTER
WHAT ...?
WHAT WAS THAT...
...ABOUT FUMI?
I SAID...
...THAT SHE'S...
...ALSO FUYU.
SWP
THE GIRL I KNEW WHEN I WAS LITTLE.
I CAN'T REALLY EXPLAIN, BUT I KNOW I'M RIGHT.
FUYU USED TO CALL HERSELF CURSED TOO.
SWP
UNLESS I'M TOTALLY CRAZY, THERE'S NO MISTAKE.

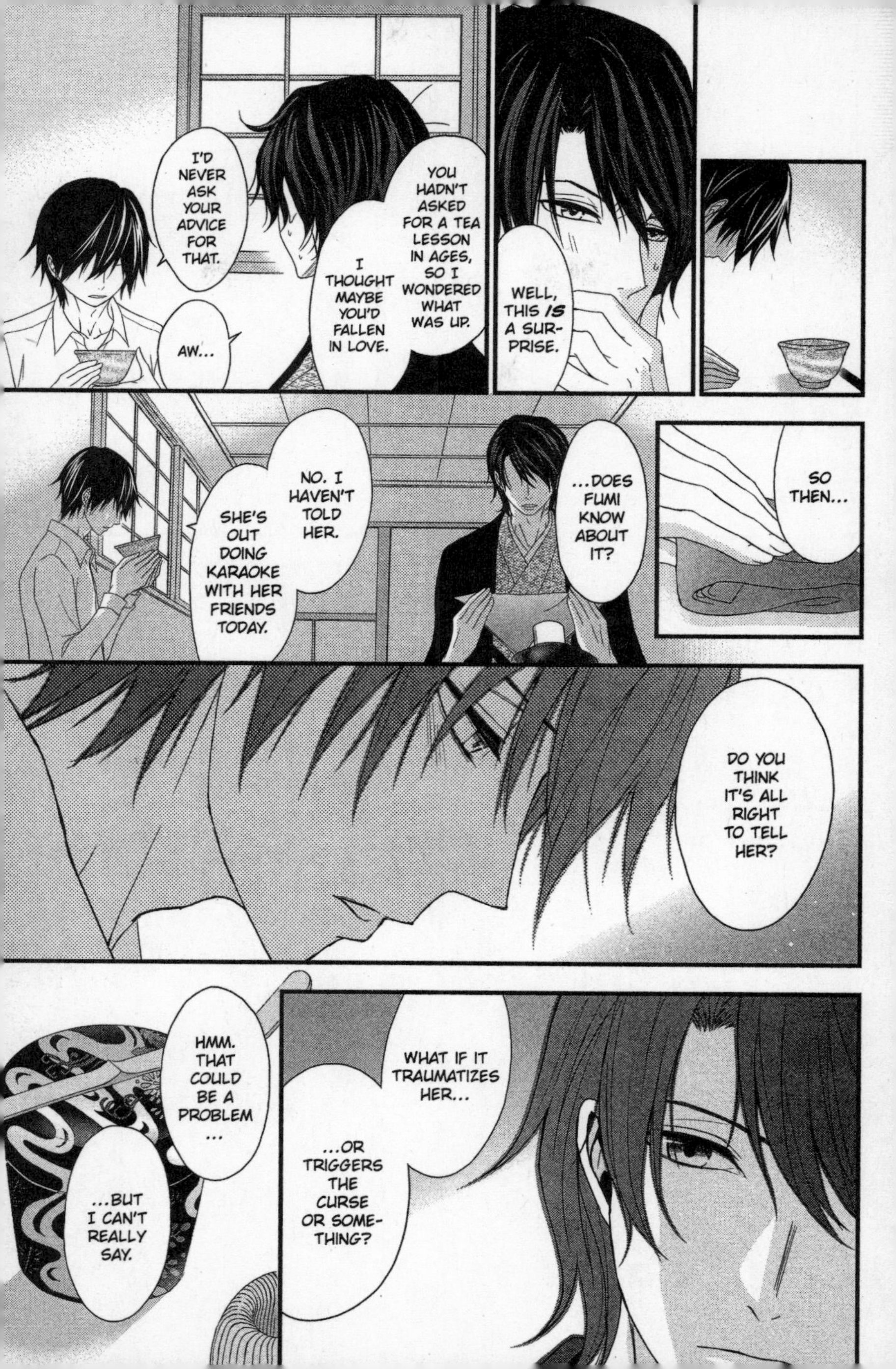
WELL, THIS *IS* A SURPRISE.
YOU HADN'T ASKED FOR A TEA LESSON IN AGES, SO I WONDERED WHAT WAS UP.
I THOUGHT MAYBE YOU'D FALLEN IN LOVE.
I'D NEVER ASK YOUR ADVICE FOR THAT.
AW...
SO THEN...
...DOES FUMI KNOW ABOUT IT?
NO. I HAVEN'T TOLD HER.
SHE'S OUT DOING KARAOKE WITH HER FRIENDS TODAY.
DO YOU THINK IT'S ALL RIGHT TO TELL HER?
WHAT IF IT TRAUMATIZES HER...
...OR TRIGGERS THE CURSE OR SOMETHING?
HMM. THAT COULD BE A PROBLEM...
...BUT I CAN'T REALLY SAY.

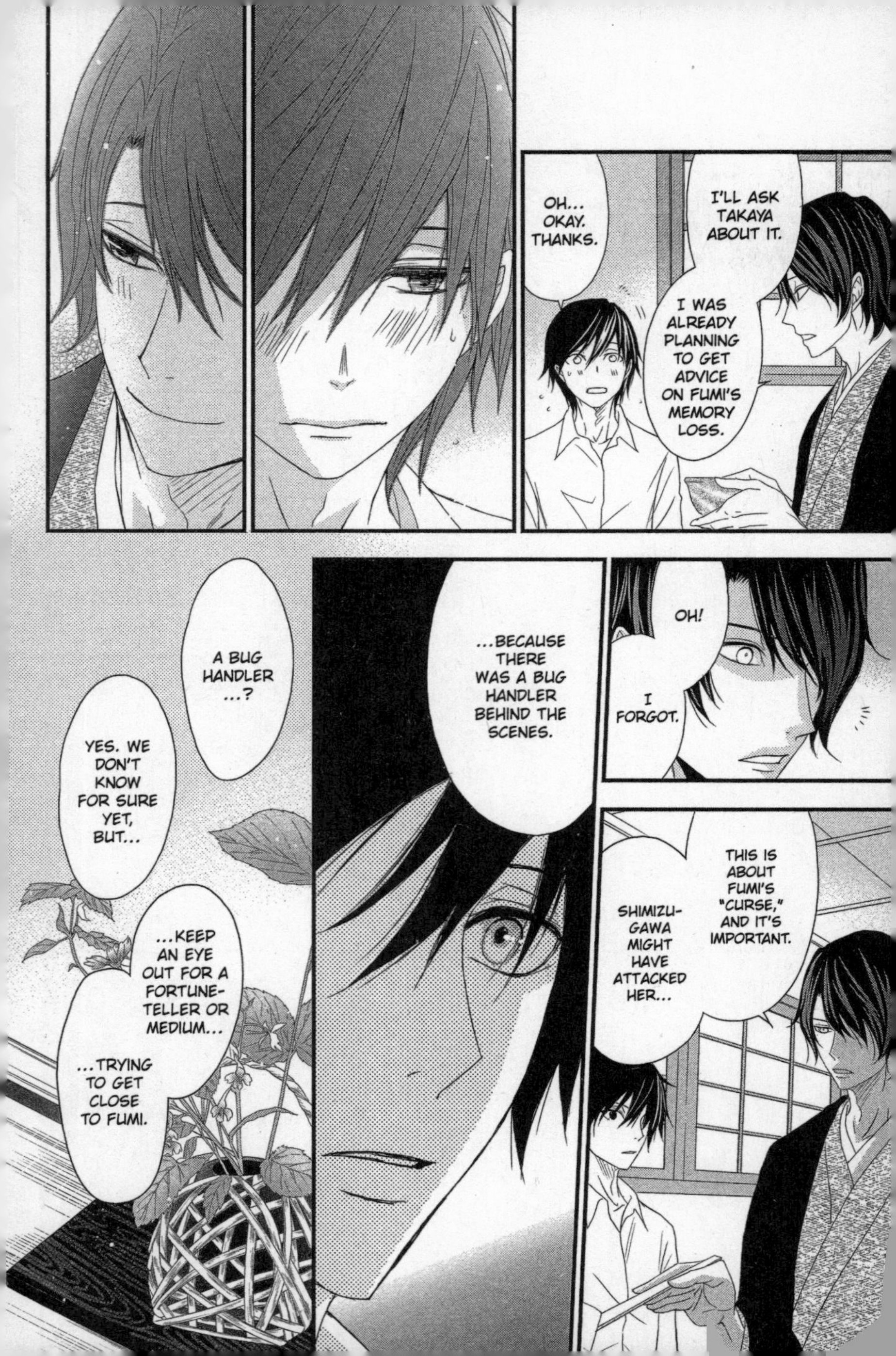
I'LL ASK TAKAYA ABOUT IT.
I WAS ALREADY PLANNING TO GET ADVICE ON FUMI'S MEMORY LOSS.
OH... OKAY. THANKS.
OH!
I FORGOT.
THIS IS ABOUT FUMI'S "CURSE," AND IT'S IMPORTANT.
SHIMIZUGAWA MIGHT HAVE ATTACKED HER...
...BECAUSE THERE WAS A BUG HANDLER BEHIND THE SCENES.
A BUG HANDLER ...?
YES. WE DON'T KNOW FOR SURE YET, BUT...
...KEEP AN EYE OUT FOR A FORTUNE-TELLER OR MEDIUM...
...TRYING TO GET CLOSE TO FUMI.

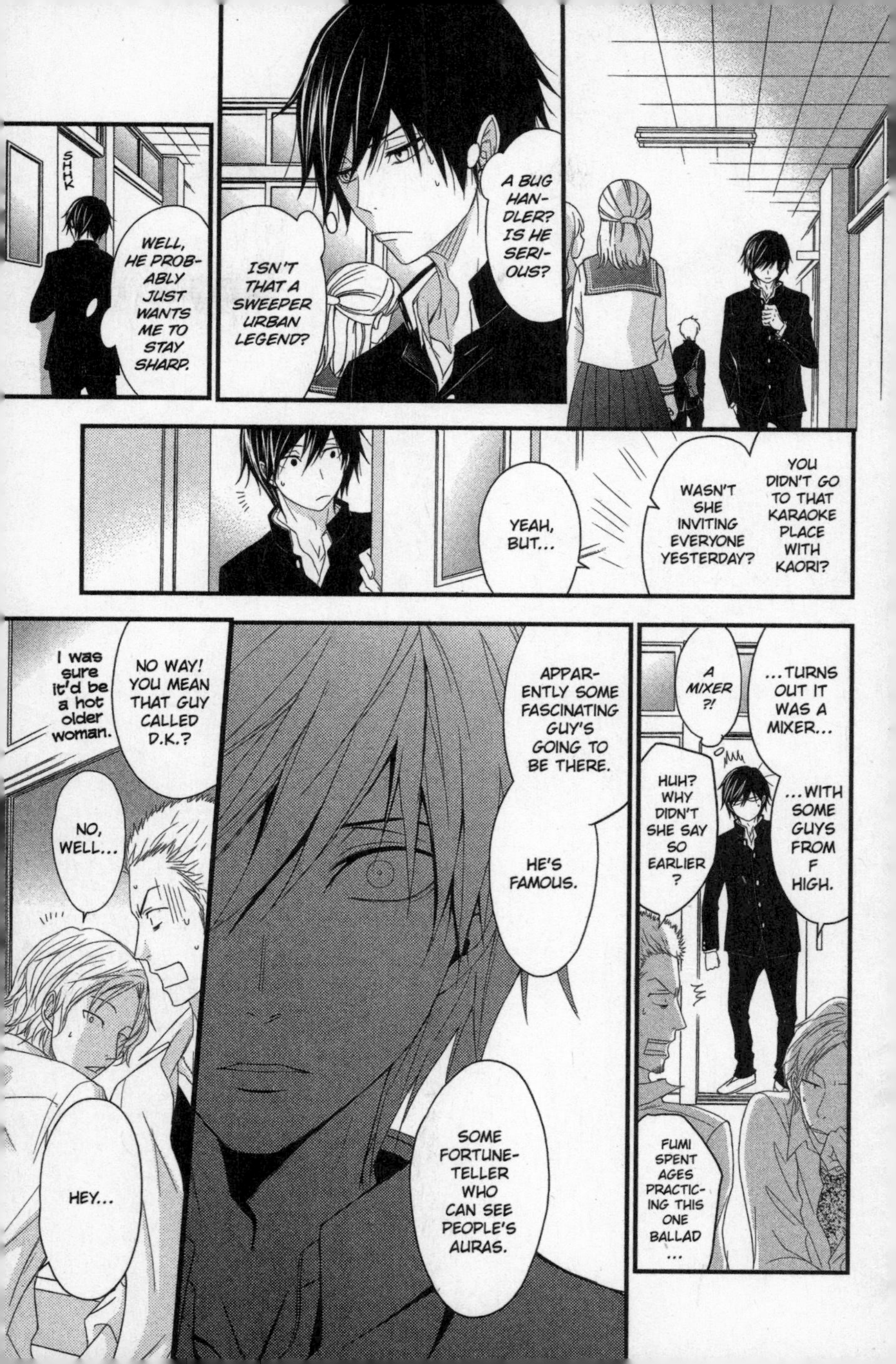
A BUG HANDLER? IS HE SERIOUS?
ISN'T THAT A SWEEPER URBAN LEGEND?
SHHK
WELL, HE PROBABLY JUST WANTS ME TO STAY SHARP.
YOU DIDN'T GO TO THAT KARAOKE PLACE WITH KAORI?
WASN'T SHE INVITING EVERYONE YESTERDAY?
YEAH, BUT...
...TURNS OUT IT WAS A MIXER...
A MIXER?!
...WITH SOME GUYS FROM F HIGH.
HUH? WHY DIDN'T SHE SAY SO EARLIER?
FUMI SPENT AGES PRACTICING THIS ONE BALLAD...
APPARENTLY SOME FASCINATING GUY'S GOING TO BE THERE.
HE'S FAMOUS.
SOME FORTUNE-TELLER WHO CAN SEE PEOPLE'S AURAS.
NO WAY! YOU MEAN THAT GUY CALLED D.K.?
I was sure it'd be a hot older woman.
NO, WELL...
HEY...

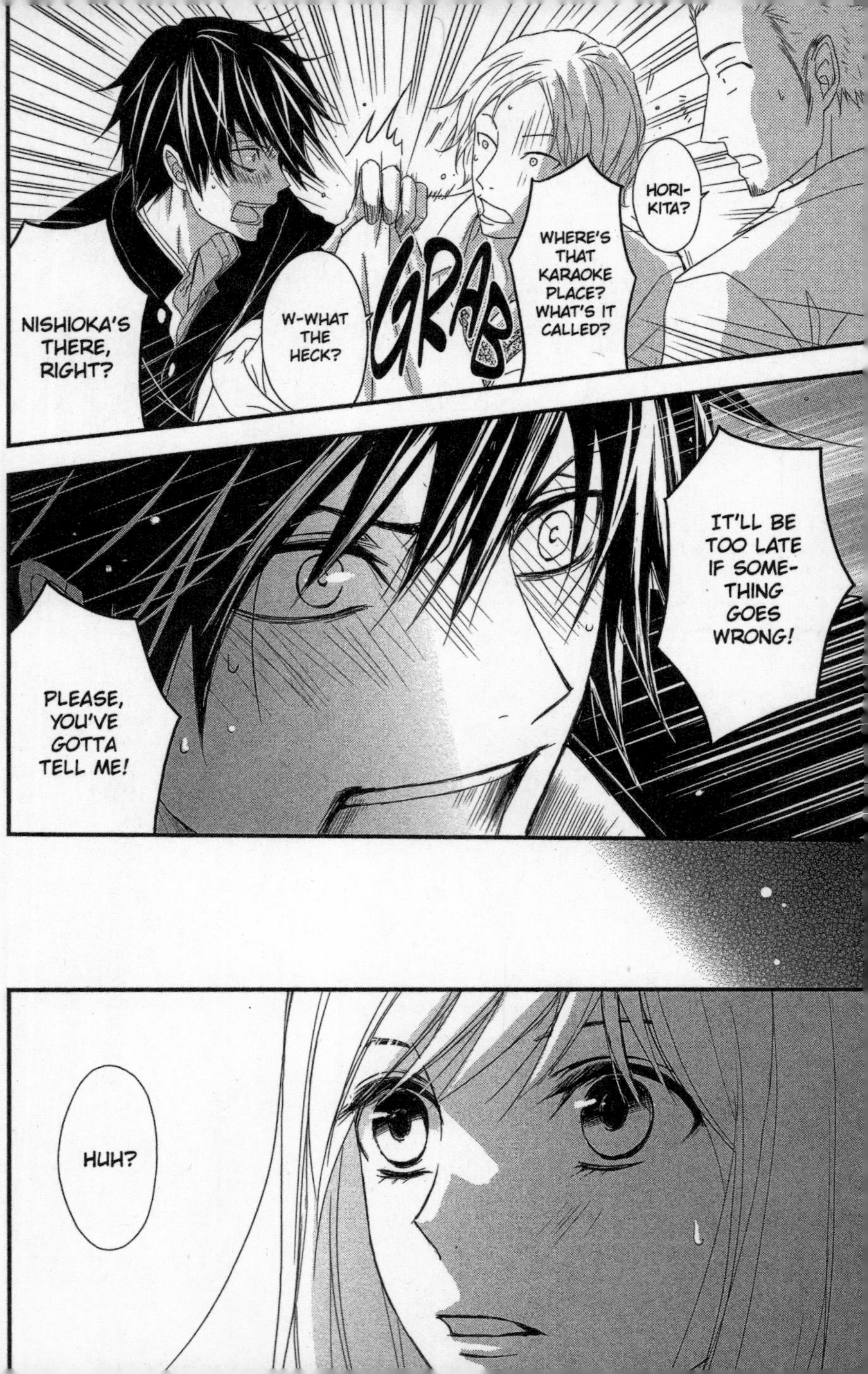
HORI-KITA?
WHERE'S THAT KARAOKE PLACE? WHAT'S IT CALLED?
GRAB
W-WHAT THE HECK?
NISHIOKA'S THERE, RIGHT?
IT'LL BE TOO LATE IF SOME-THING GOES WRONG!
PLEASE, YOU'VE GOTTA TELL ME!
HUH?

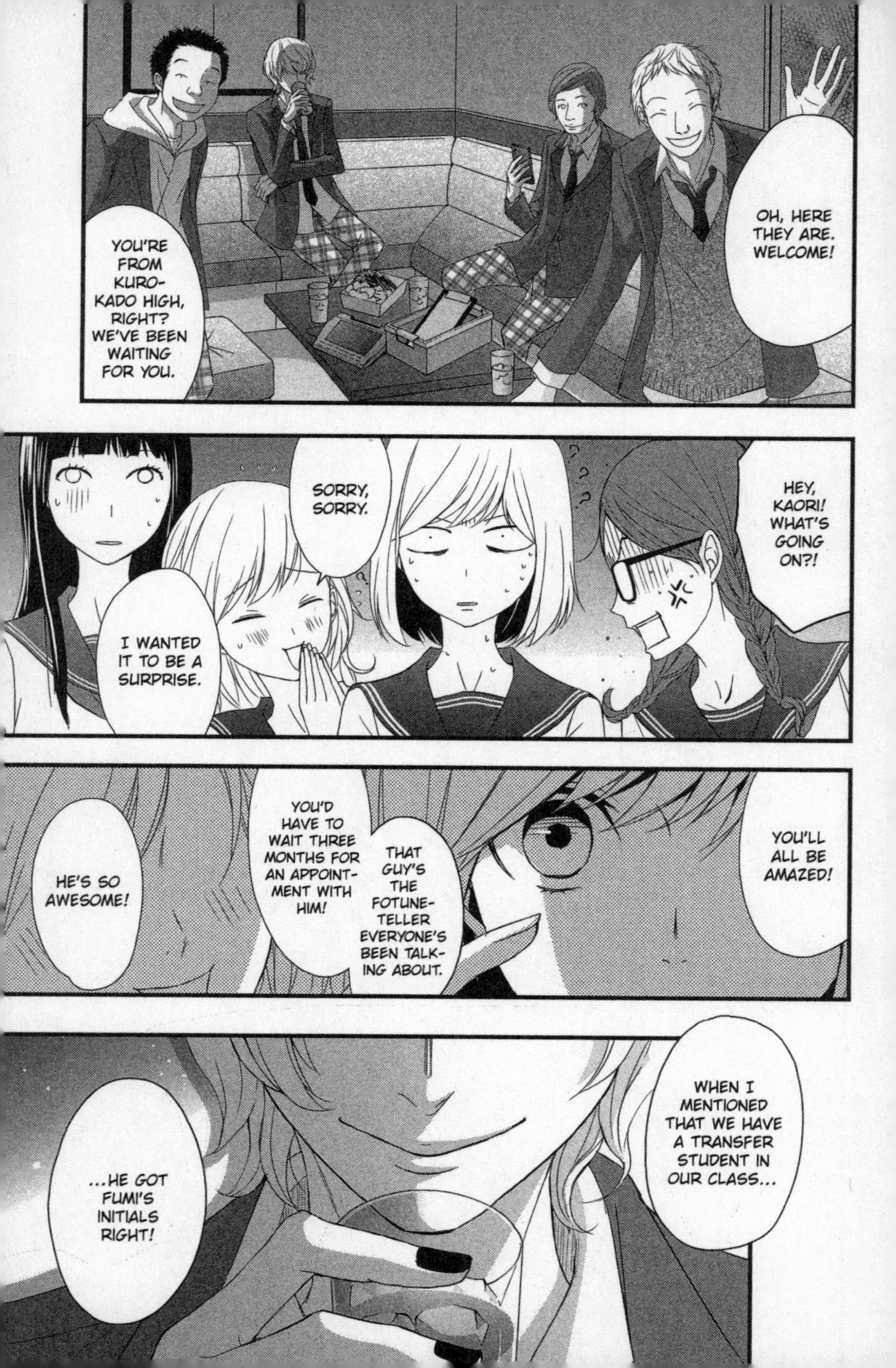
OH, HERE THEY ARE. WELCOME!
YOU'RE FROM KURO-KADO HIGH, RIGHT? WE'VE BEEN WAITING FOR YOU.
HEY, KAORI! WHAT'S GOING ON?!
SORRY, SORRY.
I WANTED IT TO BE A SURPRISE.
YOU'LL ALL BE AMAZED!
THAT GUY'S THE FOTUNE-TELLER EVERYONE'S BEEN TALK-ING ABOUT.
YOU'D HAVE TO WAIT THREE MONTHS FOR AN APPOINT-MENT WITH HIM!
HE'S SO AWESOME!
WHEN I MENTIONED THAT WE HAVE A TRANSFER STUDENT IN OUR CLASS...
...HE GOT FUMI'S INITIALS RIGHT!

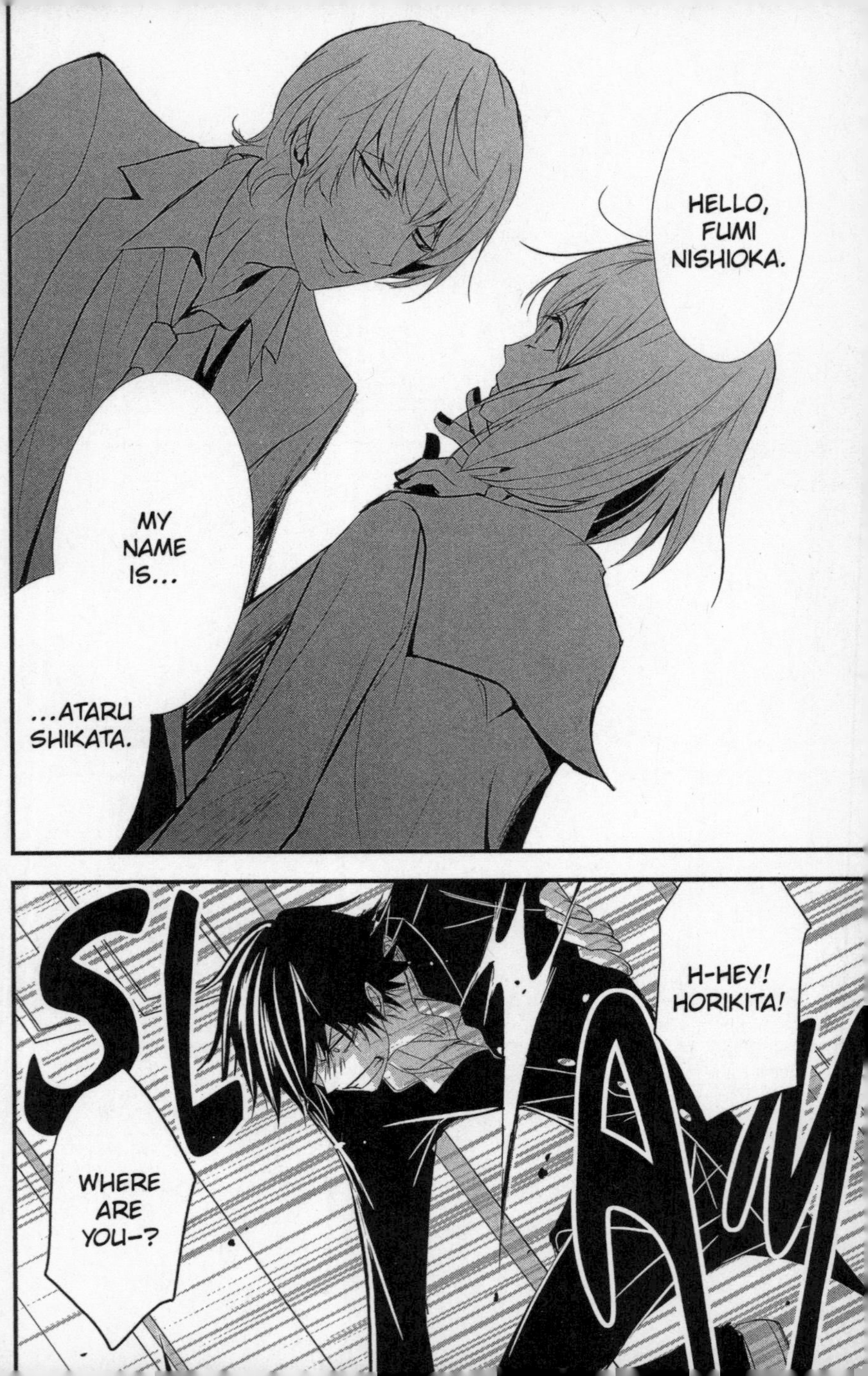
HELLO, FUMI NISHIOKA.
MY NAME IS...
...ATARU SHIKATA.
H-HEY! HORIKITA!
SLAM
WHERE ARE YOU-?

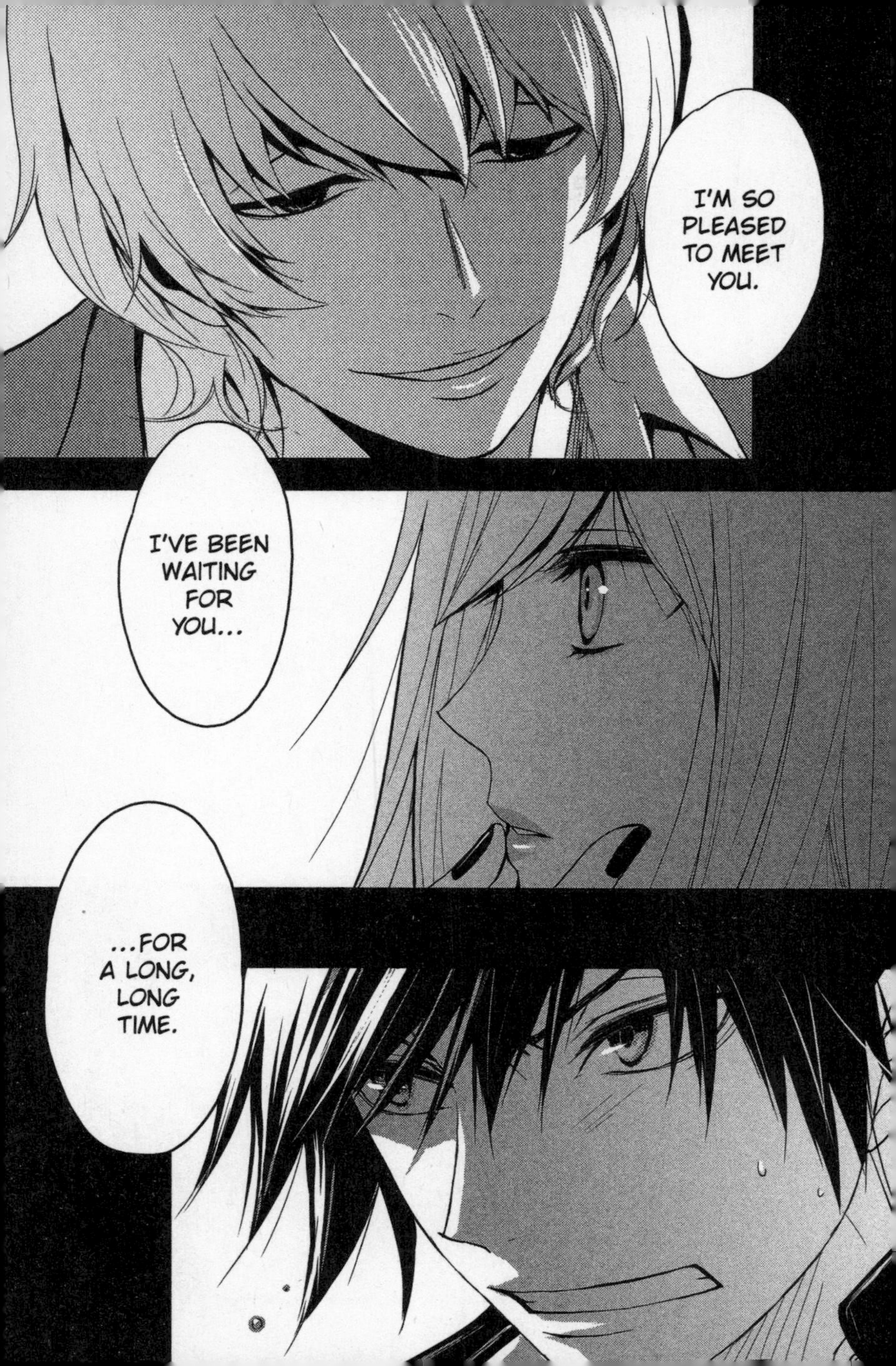
I'M SO PLEASED TO MEET YOU.
I'VE BEEN WAITING FOR YOU...
...FOR A LONG, LONG TIME.

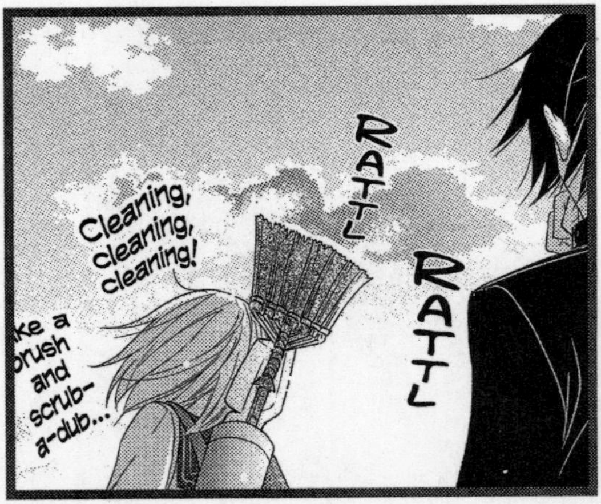
RATTL
RATTL
Cleaning, cleaning, cleaning!
ke a brush and scrub-a-dub...

SWEEP 12

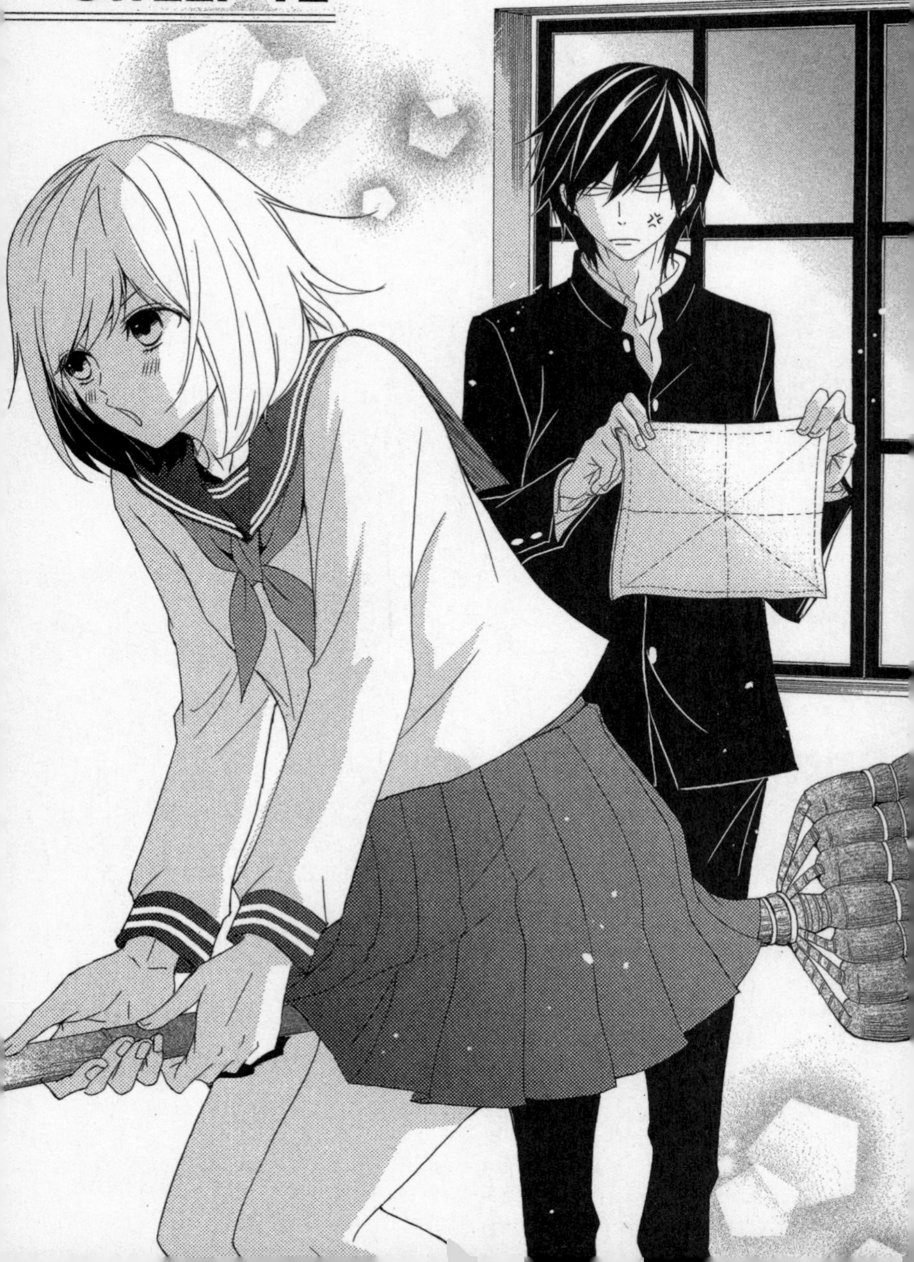

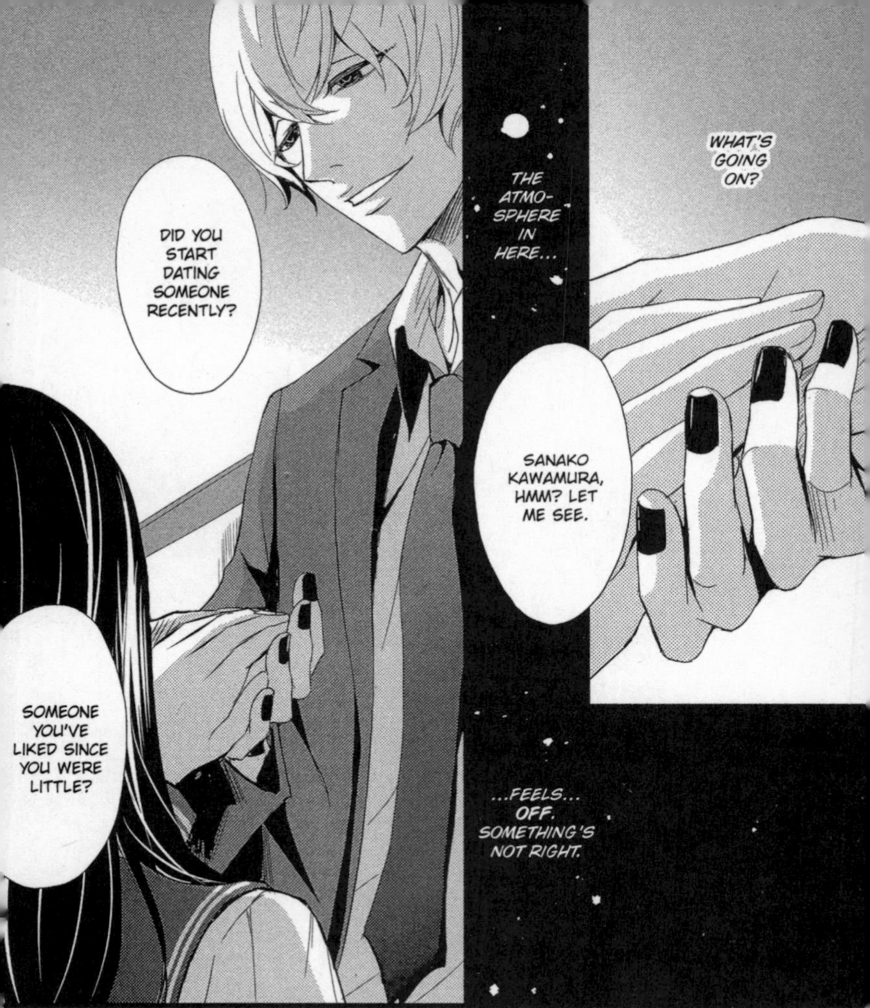
WHAT'S GOING ON?
SANAKO KAWAMURA, HMM? LET ME SEE.
THE ATMOSPHERE IN HERE...
DID YOU START DATING SOMEONE RECENTLY?
SOMEONE YOU'VE LIKED SINCE YOU WERE LITTLE?
...FEELS... OFF. SOMETHING'S NOT RIGHT.

We had another round of cleaning in Sweep 11! I used to save old ice packs and rubber bands like we see Shimizugawa doing, but I've stopped doing that.

I've switched to using aluminum clothespins instead of rubber bands to seal open packages of food. It's much more convenient! And if I need to tie something up, I just use string or plain masking tape.

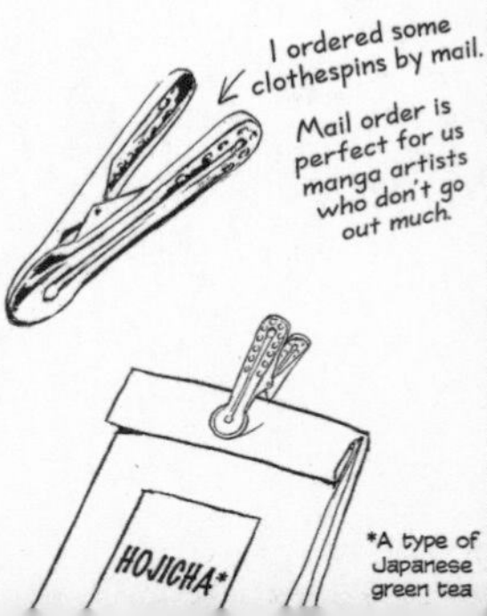
I ordered some clothespins by mail.
Mail order is perfect for us manga artists who don't go out much.
HOJICHA*
*A type of Japanese green tea

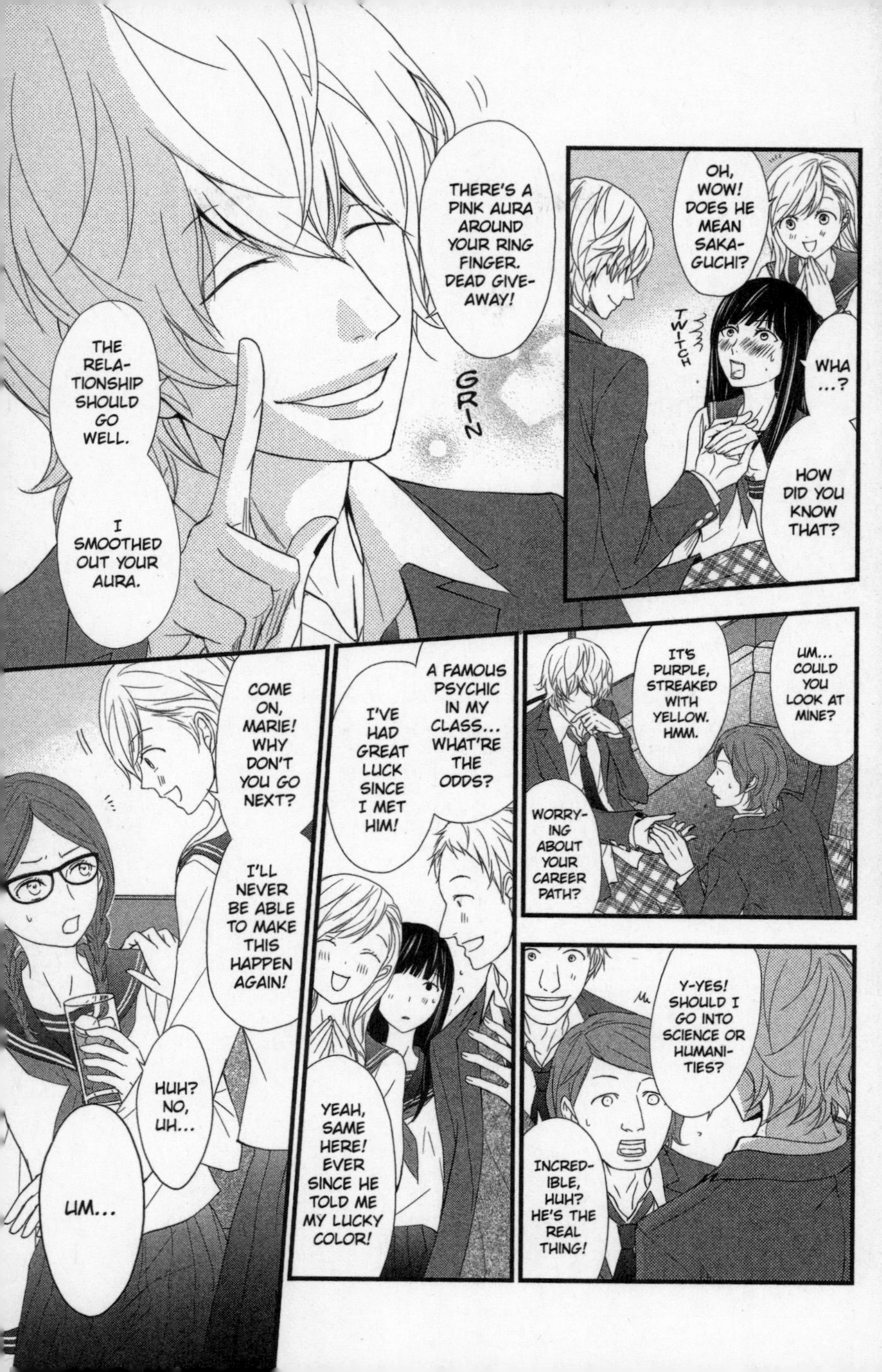
THERE'S A PINK AURA AROUND YOUR RING FINGER. DEAD GIVE-AWAY!
OH, WOW! DOES HE MEAN SAKA-GUCHI?
TWITCH
WHA ...?
HOW DID YOU KNOW THAT?
GR-IN
THE RELA-TIONSHIP SHOULD GO WELL.
I SMOOTHED OUT YOUR AURA.
UM... COULD YOU LOOK AT MINE?
IT'S PURPLE, STREAKED WITH YELLOW. HMM.
WORRY-ING ABOUT YOUR CAREER PATH?
Y-YES! SHOULD I GO INTO SCIENCE OR HUMANI-TIES?
INCRED-IBLE, HUH? HE'S THE REAL THING!
A FAMOUS PSYCHIC IN MY CLASS... WHAT'RE THE ODDS?
I'VE HAD GREAT LUCK SINCE I MET HIM!
YEAH, SAME HERE! EVER SINCE HE TOLD ME MY LUCKY COLOR!
COME ON, MARIE! WHY DON'T YOU GO NEXT?
I'LL NEVER BE ABLE TO MAKE THIS HAPPEN AGAIN!
HUH? NO, UH...
UM...

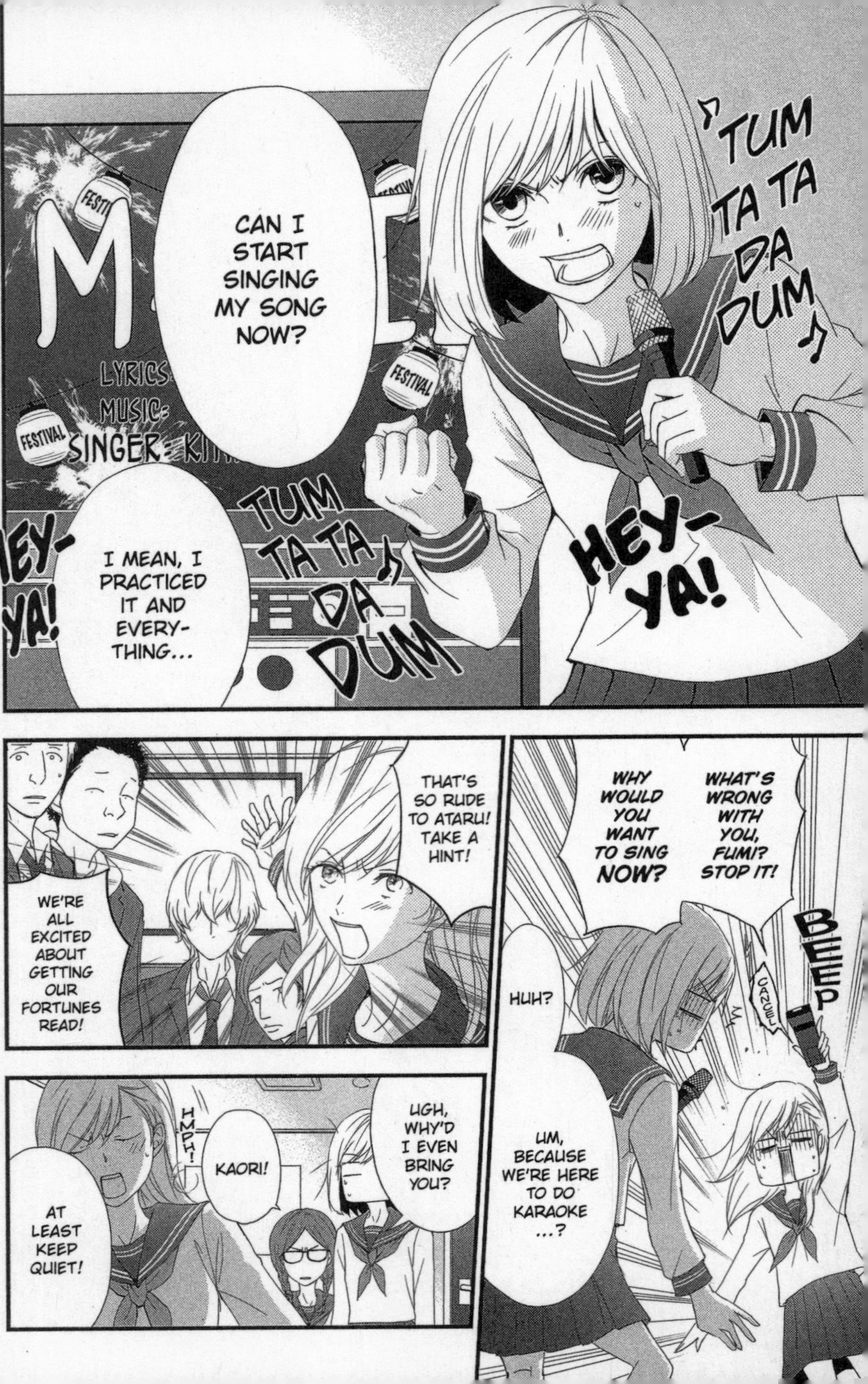

♪TUM TA TA DA DUM♪
CAN I START SINGING MY SONG NOW?
FESTIVAL
LYRICS:
MUSIC:
SINGER:
HEY-YA!
TUM TA TA♪ DA DUM
I MEAN, I PRACTICED IT AND EVERY-THING...
HEY-YA!
WHAT'S WRONG WITH YOU, FUMI? STOP IT!
WHY WOULD YOU WANT TO SING NOW?
BEEP
CANCEL
HUH?
UM, BECAUSE WE'RE HERE TO DO KARAOKE ...?
THAT'S SO RUDE TO ATARU! TAKE A HINT!
WE'RE ALL EXCITED ABOUT GETTING OUR FORTUNES READ!
UGH, WHY'D I EVEN BRING YOU?
KAORI!
HMPH!
AT LEAST KEEP QUIET!

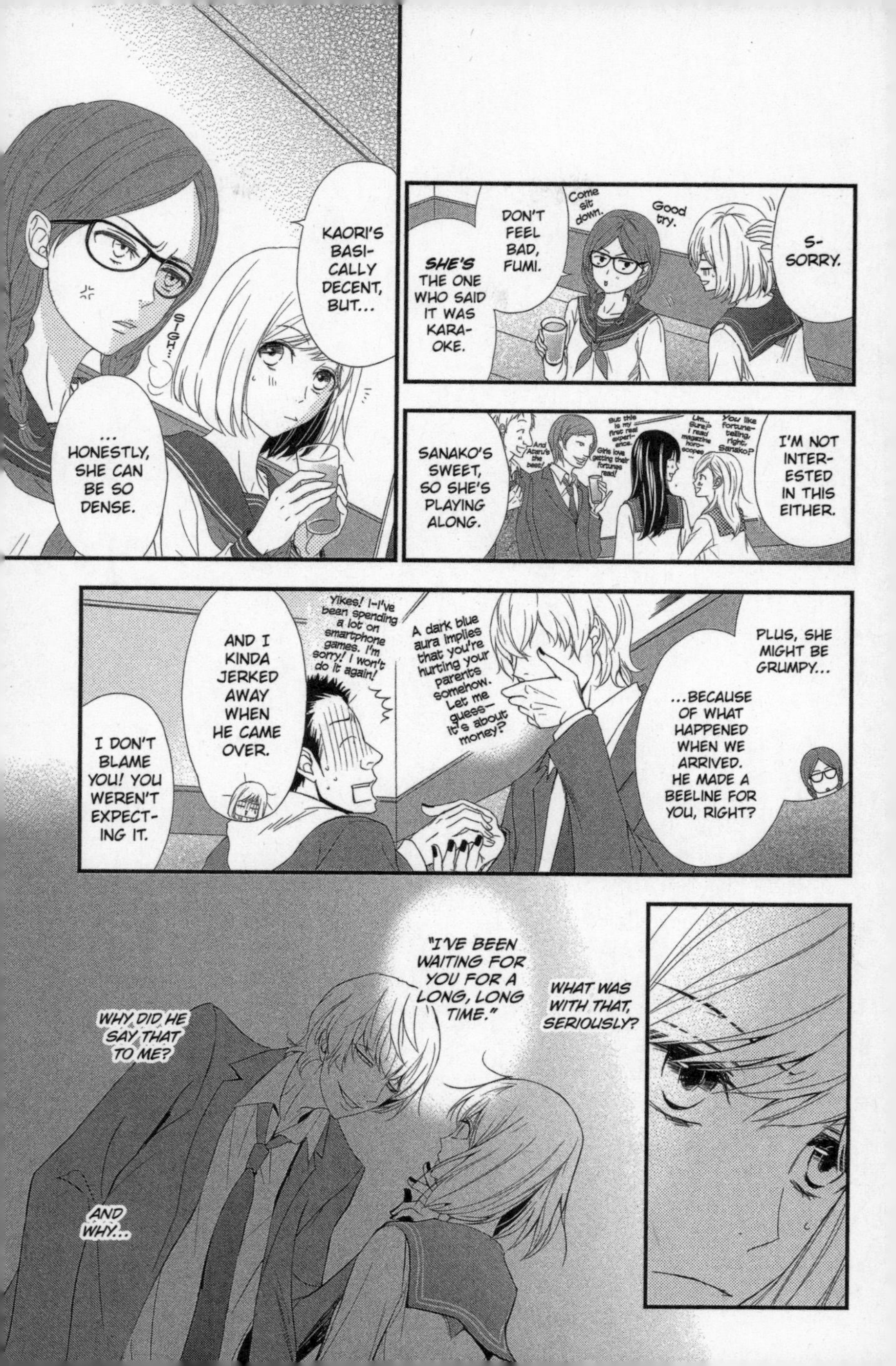
S-SORRY.
Good try.
Come sit down.
DON'T FEEL BAD, FUMI.
SHE'S THE ONE WHO SAID IT WAS KARAOKE.
I'M NOT INTERESTED IN THIS EITHER.
You like fortune-telling, right, Sanako?
Um... Sure? I read magazine horoscopes...
But this is my first real experience.
Girls love getting their fortunes read!
And Ataru's the best!
SANAKO'S SWEET, SO SHE'S PLAYING ALONG.
KAORI'S BASICALLY DECENT, BUT...
SIGH...
...HONESTLY, SHE CAN BE SO DENSE.
PLUS, SHE MIGHT BE GRUMPY...
...BECAUSE OF WHAT HAPPENED WHEN WE ARRIVED. HE MADE A BEELINE FOR YOU, RIGHT?
A dark blue aura implies that you're hurting your parents somehow. Let me guess—it's about money?
Yikes! I-I've been spending a lot on smartphone games. I'm sorry! I won't do it again!
AND I KINDA JERKED AWAY WHEN HE CAME OVER.
I DON'T BLAME YOU! YOU WEREN'T EXPECTING IT.
"I'VE BEEN WAITING FOR YOU FOR A LONG, LONG TIME."
WHAT WAS WITH THAT, SERIOUSLY?
WHY DID HE SAY THAT TO ME?
AND WHY...

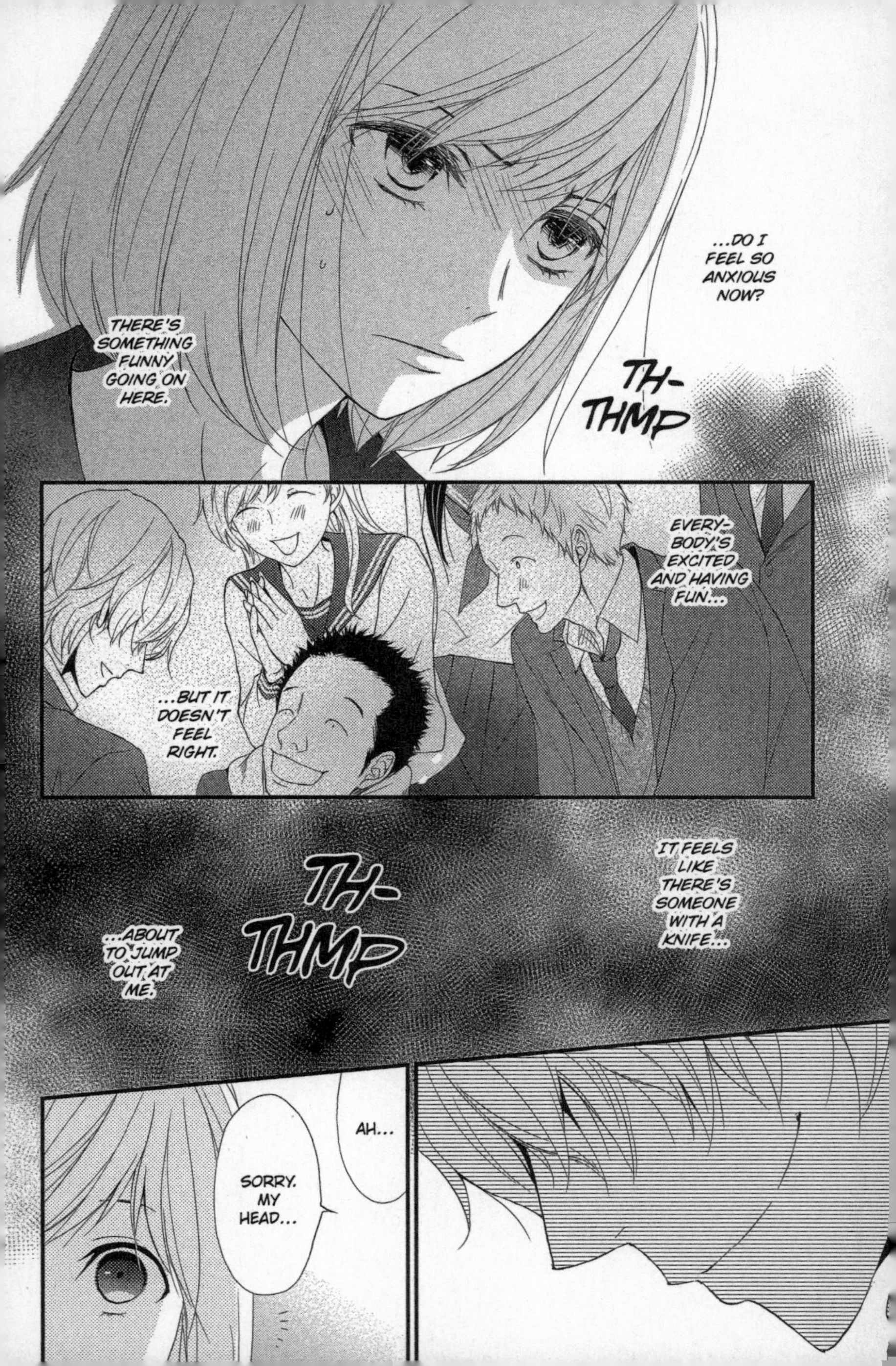
...DO I FEEL SO ANXIOUS NOW?
TH-THMP
THERE'S SOMETHING FUNNY GOING ON HERE.
EVERY-BODY'S EXCITED AND HAVING FUN...
...BUT IT DOESN'T FEEL RIGHT.
IT FEELS LIKE THERE'S SOMEONE WITH A KNIFE...
TH-THMP
...ABOUT TO JUMP OUT AT ME.
AH...
SORRY. MY HEAD...

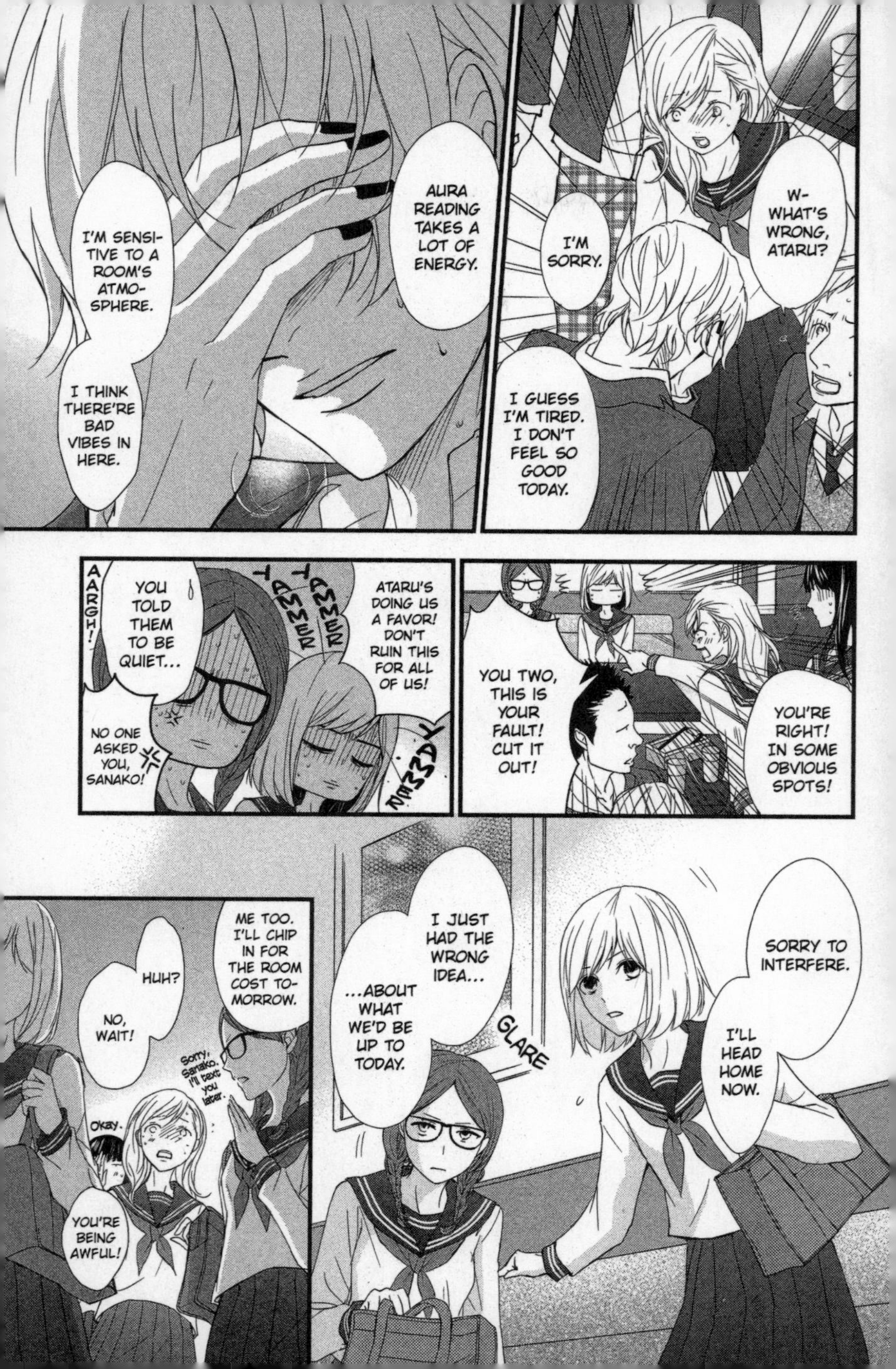

W-WHAT'S WRONG, ATARU?
I'M SORRY.
I GUESS I'M TIRED. I DON'T FEEL SO GOOD TODAY.
AURA READING TAKES A LOT OF ENERGY.
I'M SENSITIVE TO A ROOM'S ATMOSPHERE.
I THINK THERE'RE BAD VIBES IN HERE.
YOU'RE RIGHT! IN SOME OBVIOUS SPOTS!
YOU TWO, THIS IS YOUR FAULT! CUT IT OUT!
ATARU'S DOING US A FAVOR! DON'T RUIN THIS FOR ALL OF US!
YAMMER YAMMER
YOU TOLD THEM TO BE QUIET...
AARGH!
YAMMER
NO ONE ASKED YOU, SANAKO!
SORRY TO INTERFERE.
I'LL HEAD HOME NOW.
GLARE
I JUST HAD THE WRONG IDEA...
...ABOUT WHAT WE'D BE UP TO TODAY.
ME TOO. I'LL CHIP IN FOR THE ROOM COST TOMORROW.
HUH?
NO, WAIT!
Sorry, Sanako. I'll text you later.
Okay.
YOU'RE BEING AWFUL!

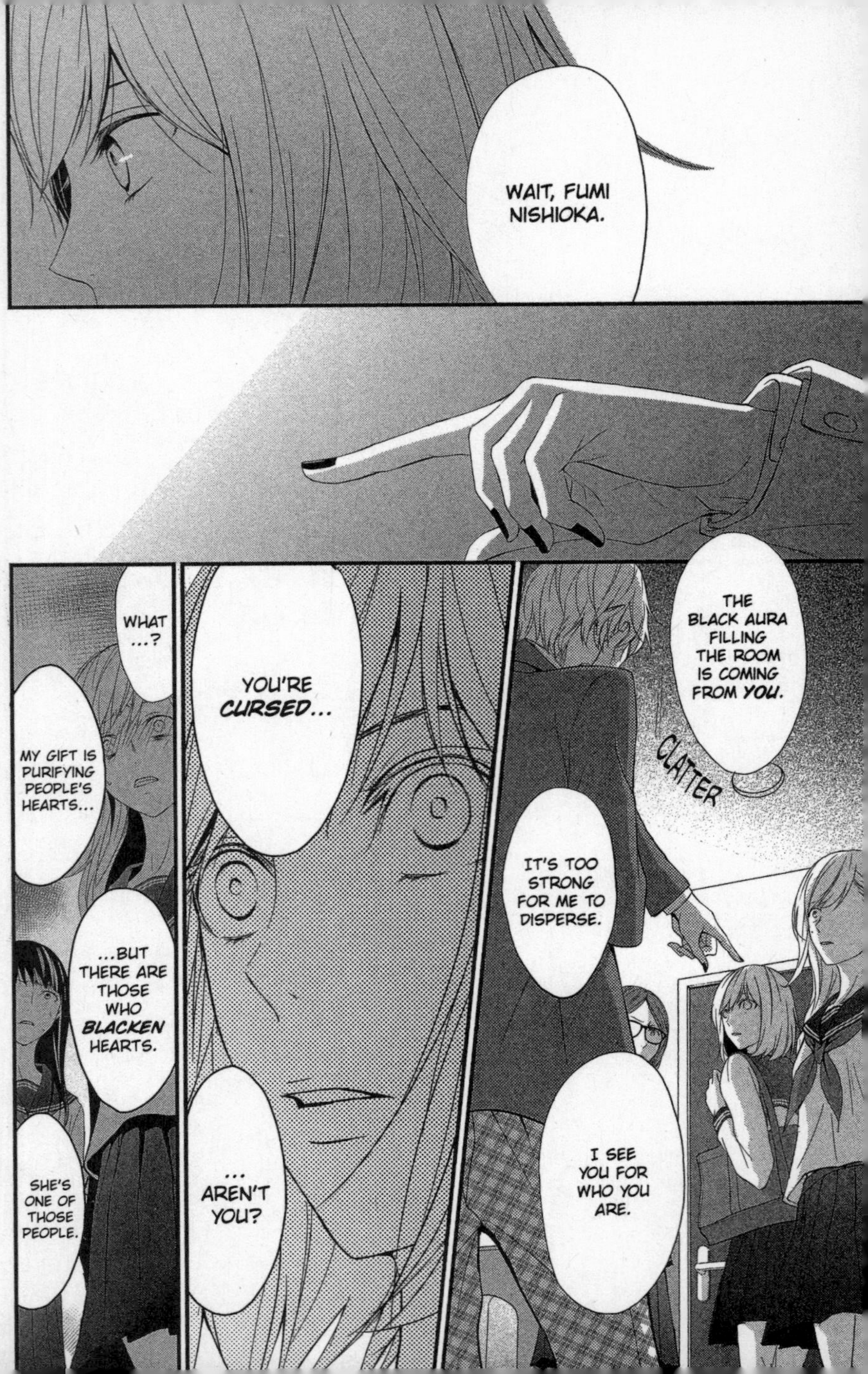
WAIT, FUMI NISHIOKA.
THE BLACK AURA FILLING THE ROOM IS COMING FROM *YOU*.
CLATTER
IT'S TOO STRONG FOR ME TO DISPERSE.
I SEE YOU FOR WHO YOU ARE.
YOU'RE *CURSED*...
...AREN'T YOU?
WHAT...?
MY GIFT IS PURIFYING PEOPLE'S HEARTS...
...BUT THERE ARE THOSE WHO *BLACKEN* HEARTS.
SHE'S ONE OF THOSE PEOPLE.

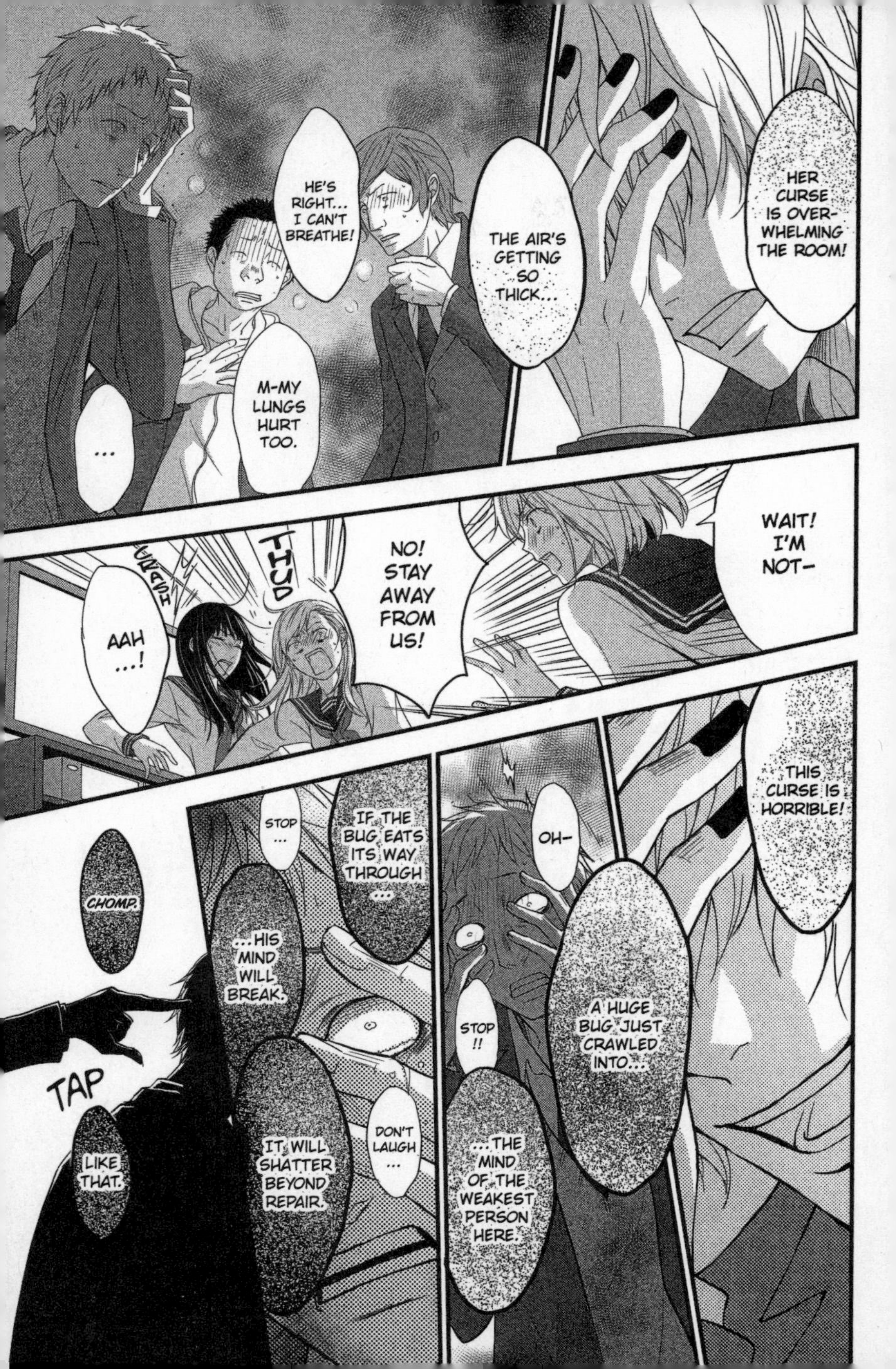
HER CURSE IS OVER-WHELMING THE ROOM!
THE AIR'S GETTING SO THICK...
HE'S RIGHT... I CAN'T BREATHE!
M-MY LUNGS HURT TOO.
...
WAIT! I'M NOT-
NO! STAY AWAY FROM US!
THUD
CRASH
AAH ...!
THIS CURSE IS HORRIBLE!
A HUGE BUG JUST CRAWLED INTO...
...THE MIND OF THE WEAKEST PERSON HERE.
OH-
STOP !!
STOP ...
IF THE BUG EATS ITS WAY THROUGH ...
...HIS MIND WILL BREAK.
DON'T LAUGH ...
IT WILL SHATTER BEYOND REPAIR.
CHOMP.
TAP
LIKE THAT.

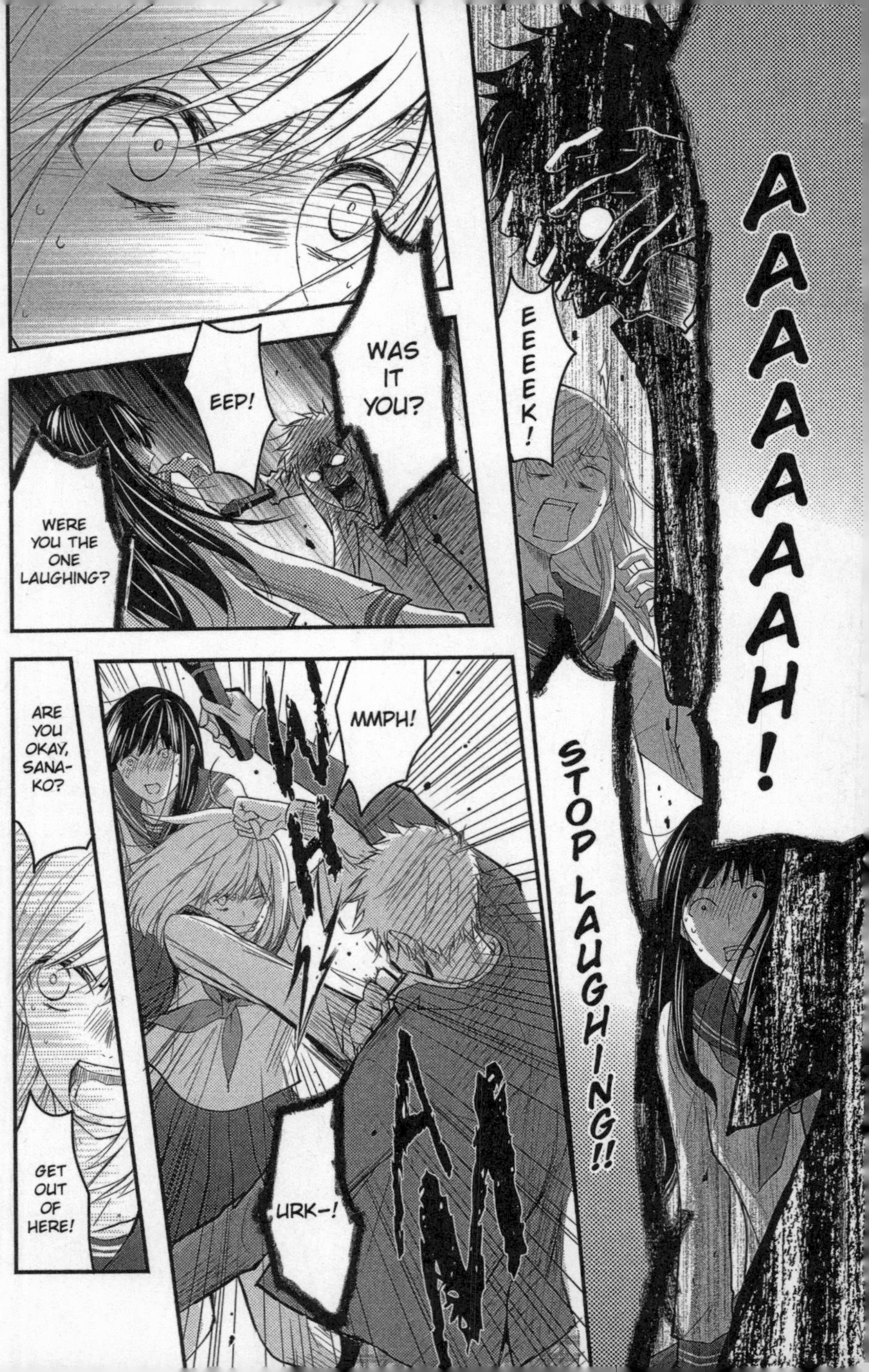
AAAAAAH!
EEEEEK!
STOP LAUGHING!!
WAS IT YOU?
EEP!
WERE YOU THE ONE LAUGHING?
MMPH!
WHAM
ARE YOU OKAY, SANAKO?
URK-!
GET OUT OF HERE!

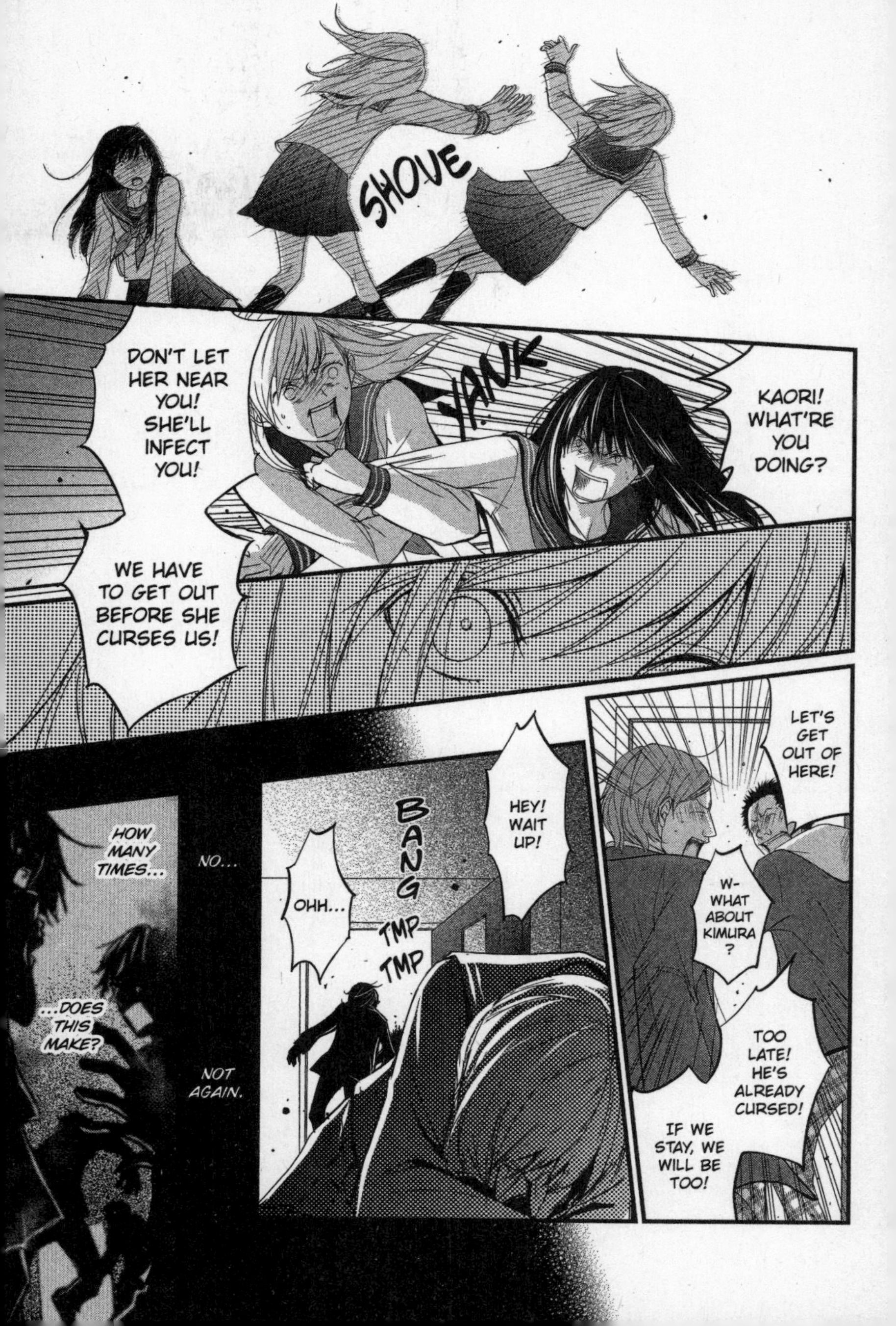
SHOVE
YANK
KAORI! WHAT'RE YOU DOING?
DON'T LET HER NEAR YOU! SHE'LL INFECT YOU!
WE HAVE TO GET OUT BEFORE SHE CURSES US!
LET'S GET OUT OF HERE!
W-WHAT ABOUT KIMURA?
TOO LATE! HE'S ALREADY CURSED!
IF WE STAY, WE WILL BE TOO!
HEY! WAIT UP!
BANG
OHH...
TMP TMP
NO...
HOW MANY TIMES...
...DOES THIS MAKE?
NOT AGAIN.

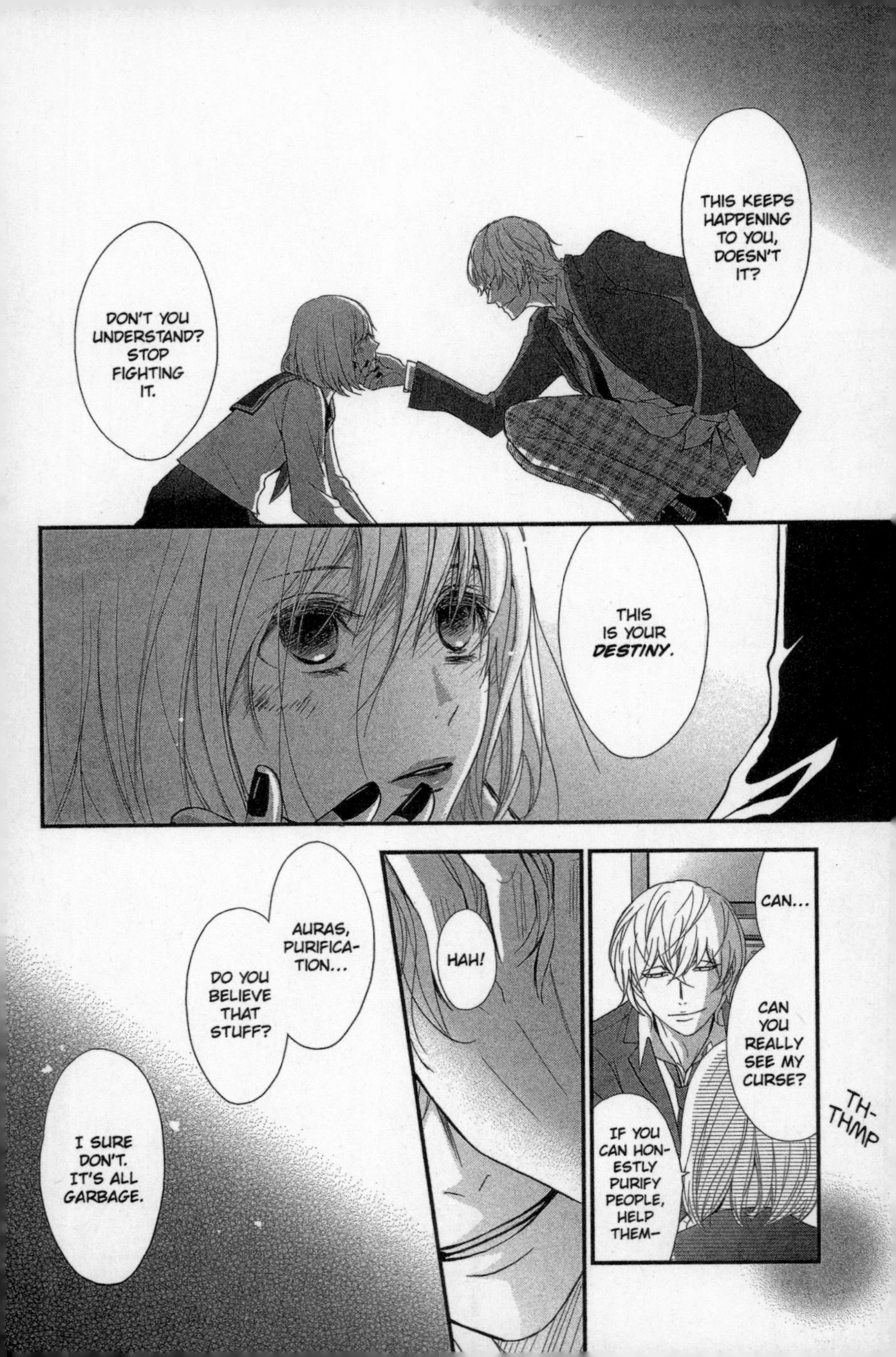
THIS KEEPS HAPPENING TO YOU, DOESN'T IT?
DON'T YOU UNDERSTAND? STOP FIGHTING IT.
THIS IS YOUR *DESTINY*.
CAN...
CAN YOU REALLY SEE MY CURSE?
TH-THMP
IF YOU CAN HONESTLY PURIFY PEOPLE, HELP THEM—
HAH!
AURAS, PURIFICATION...
DO YOU BELIEVE THAT STUFF?
I SURE DON'T. IT'S ALL GARBAGE.

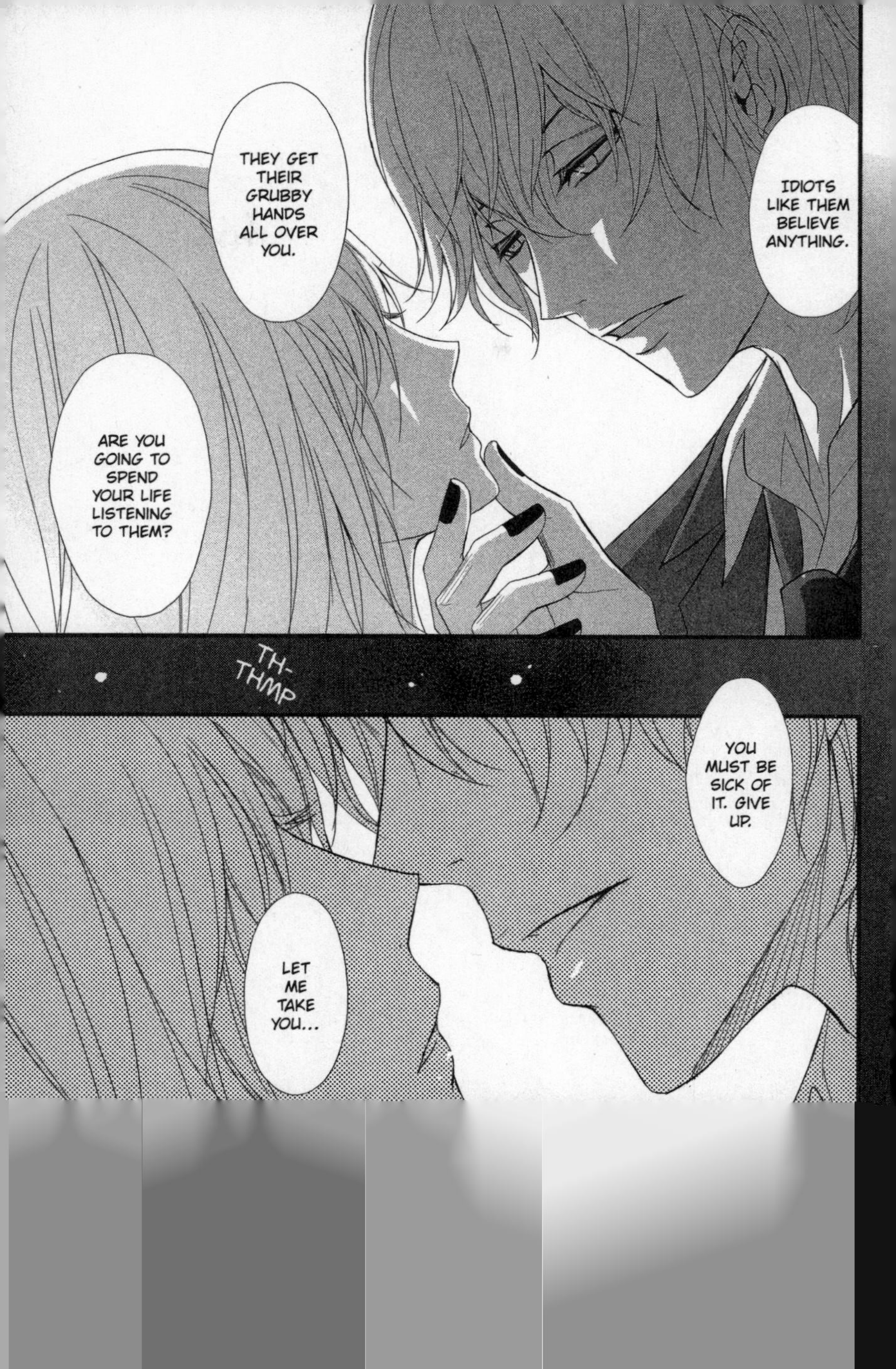
IDIOTS LIKE THEM BELIEVE ANYTHING.
THEY GET THEIR GRUBBY HANDS ALL OVER YOU.
ARE YOU GOING TO SPEND YOUR LIFE LISTENING TO THEM?
TH-THMP
YOU MUST BE SICK OF IT. GIVE UP.
LET ME TAKE YOU...

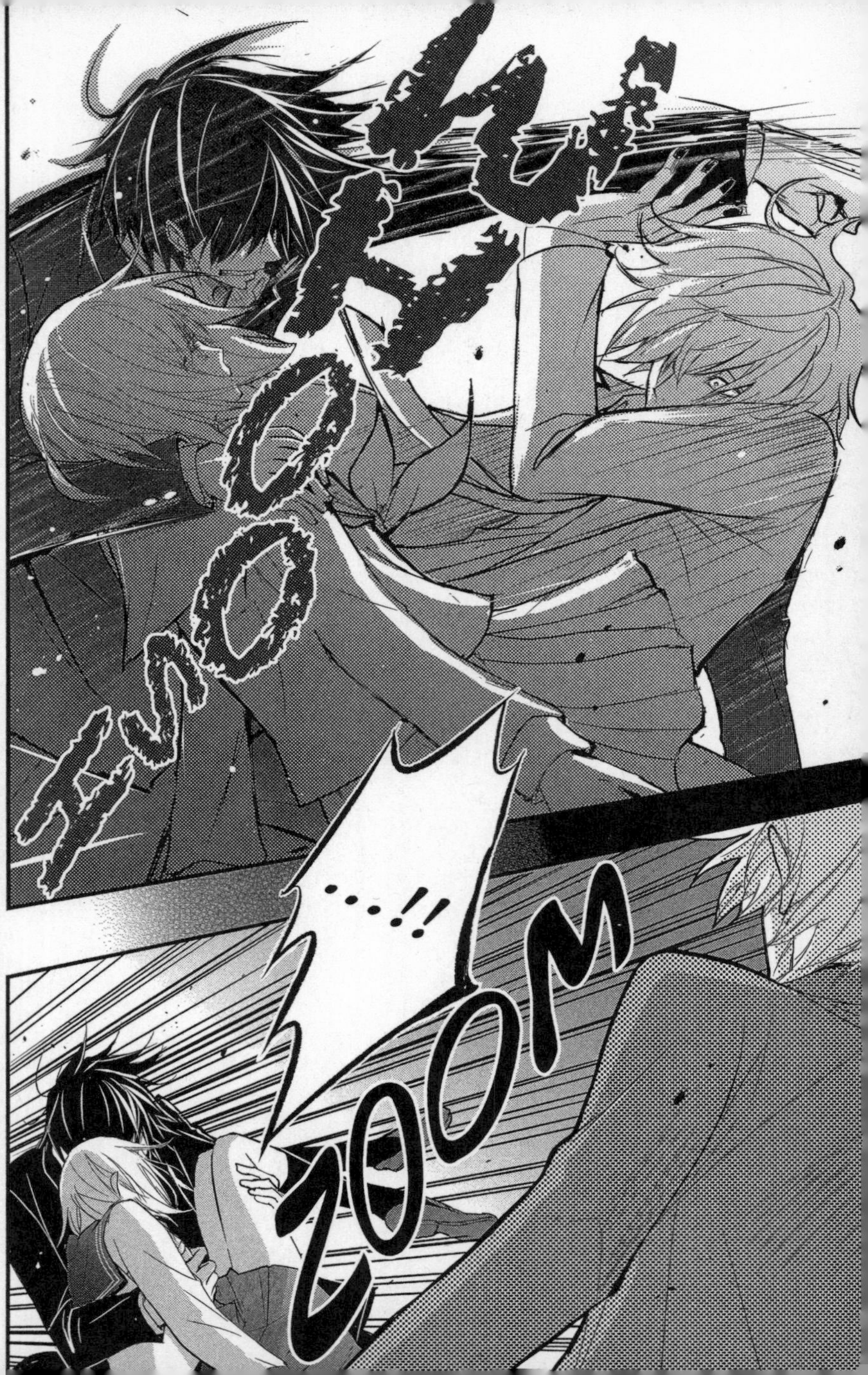
...!!
ZOOM

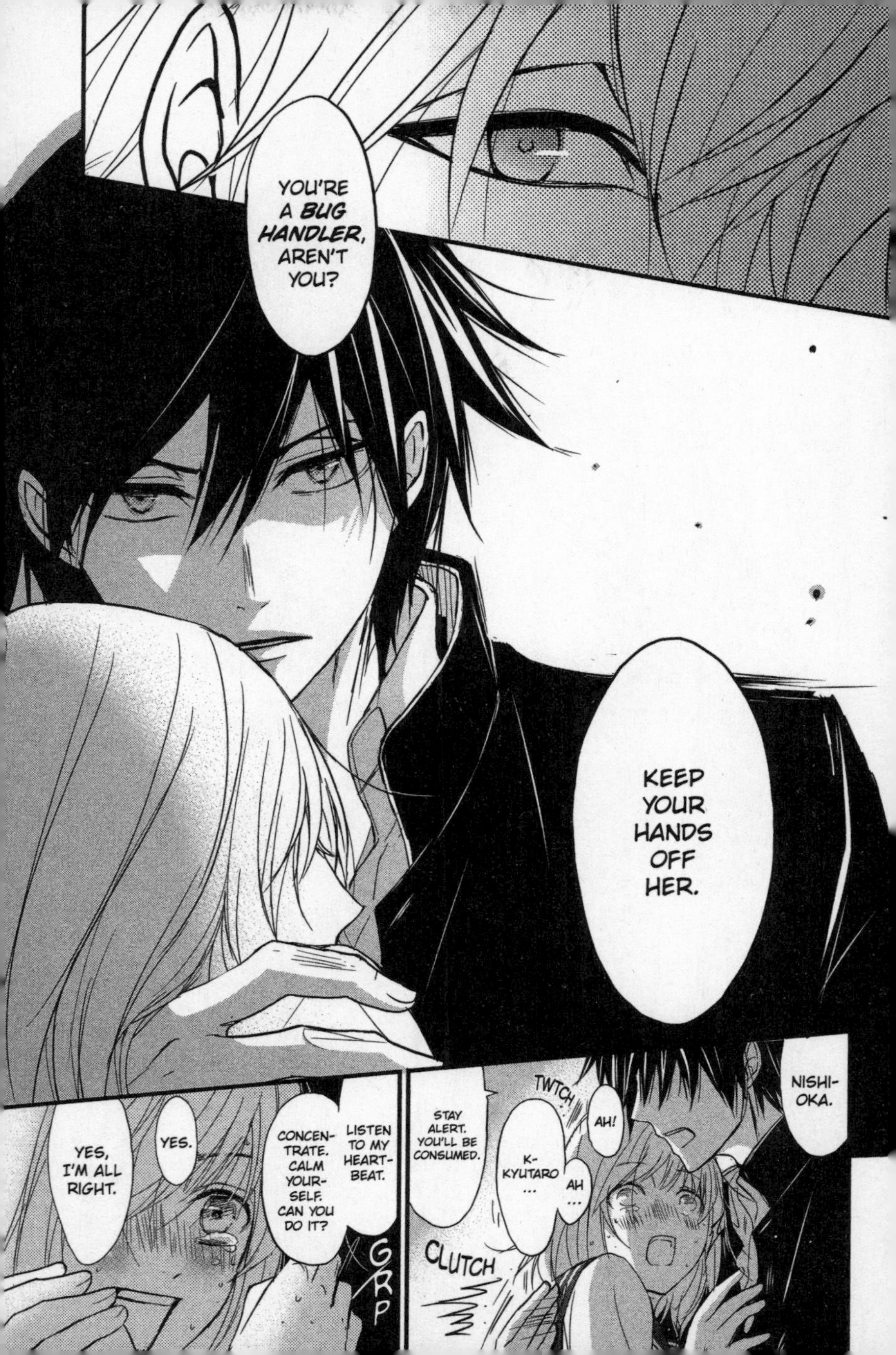
YOU'RE A *BUG HANDLER*, AREN'T YOU?
KEEP YOUR HANDS OFF HER.
NISHI-OKA.
TWTCH
AH!
K-KYUTARO ...
AH ...
STAY ALERT. YOU'LL BE CONSUMED.
CLUTCH
LISTEN TO MY HEART-BEAT.
CONCEN-TRATE. CALM YOUR-SELF. CAN YOU DO IT?
GRP
YES.
YES, I'M ALL RIGHT.

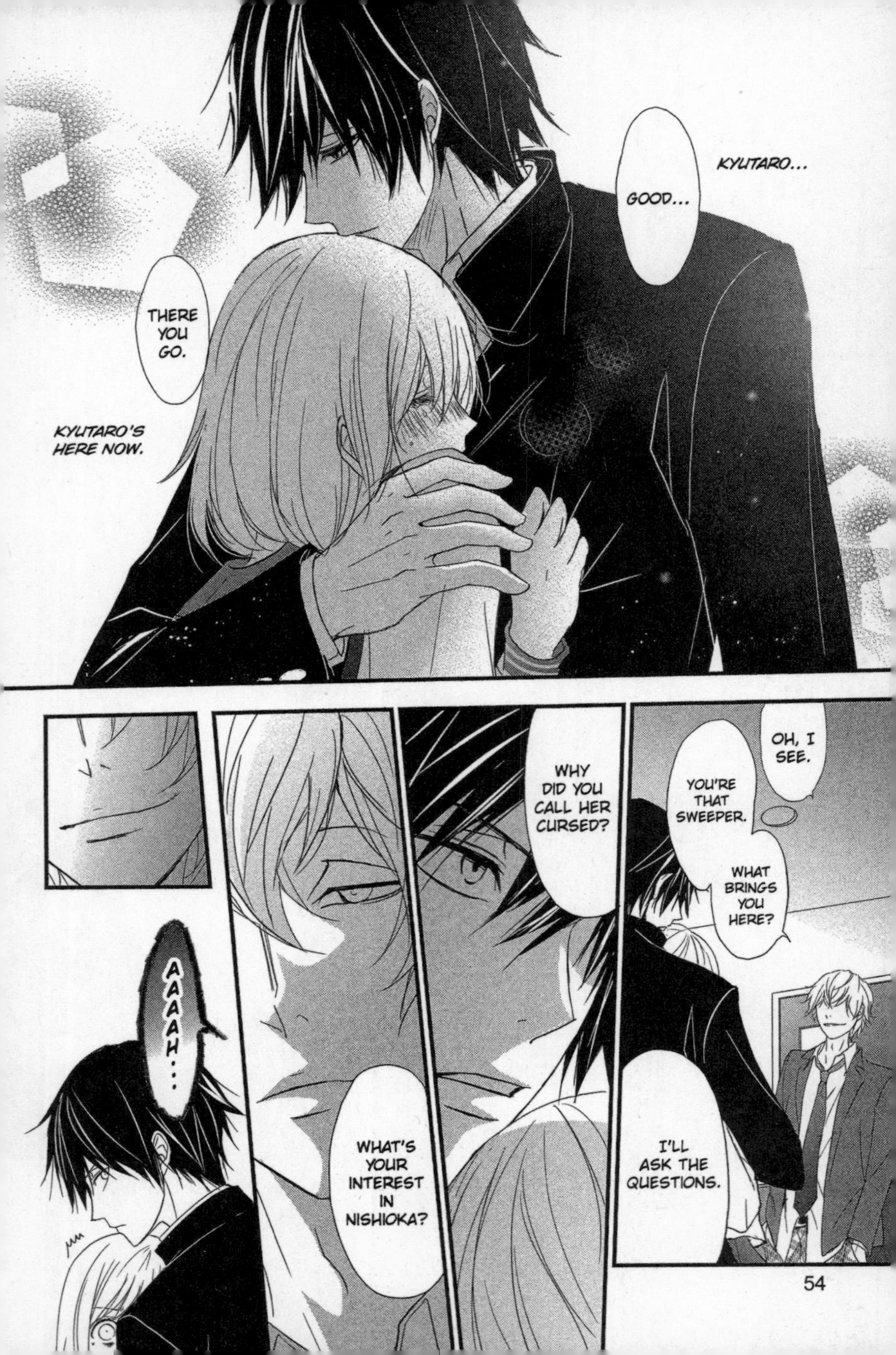
KYUTARO...
GOOD...
THERE YOU GO.
KYUTARO'S HERE NOW.
OH, I SEE.
YOU'RE THAT SWEEPER.
WHAT BRINGS YOU HERE?
I'LL ASK THE QUESTIONS.
WHY DID YOU CALL HER CURSED?
WHAT'S YOUR INTEREST IN NISHIOKA?
AAAAH...

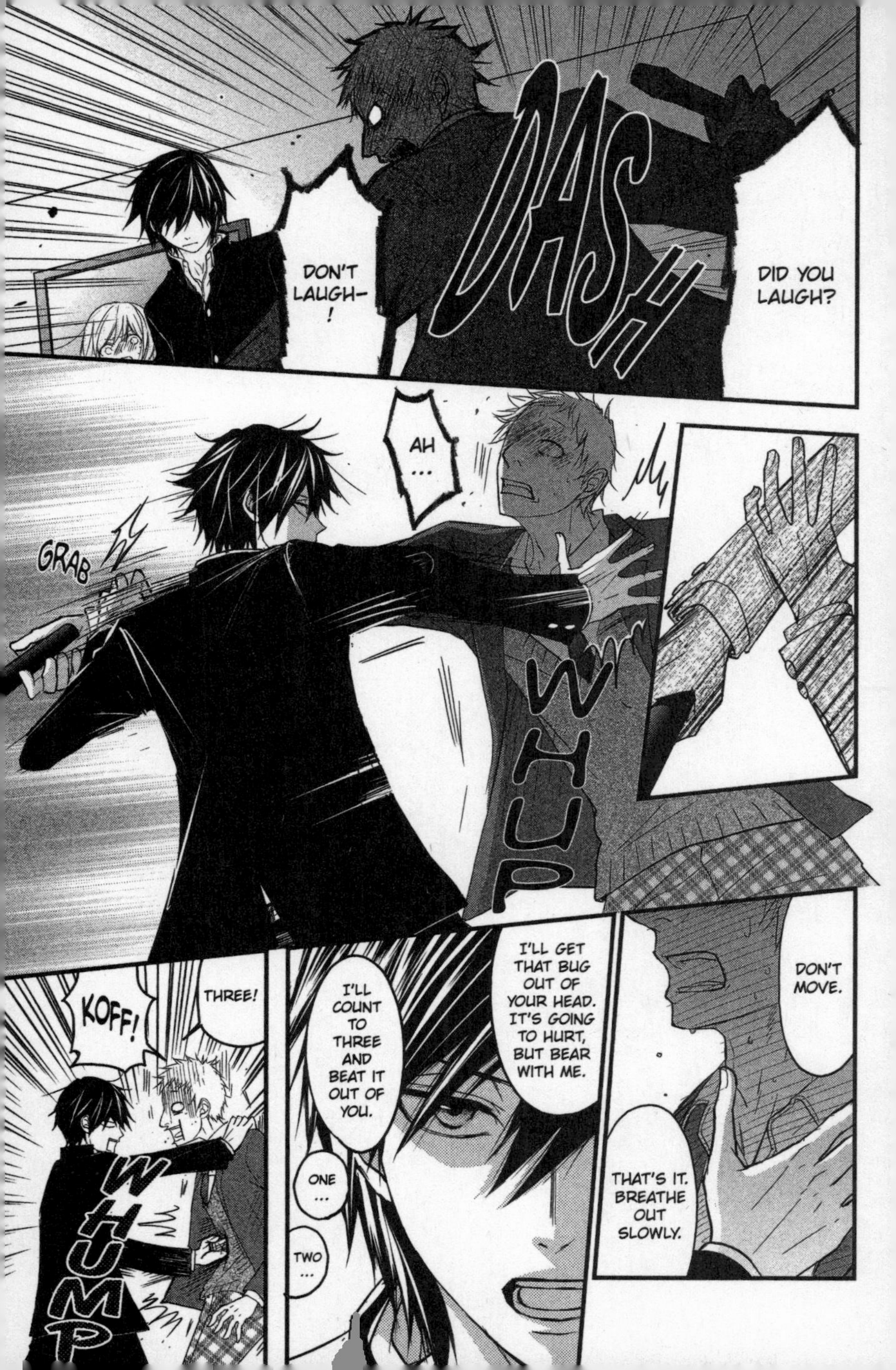
DID YOU LAUGH?
DASH
DON'T LAUGH—!
AH ...
GRAB
WHUP
DON'T MOVE.
THAT'S IT. BREATHE OUT SLOWLY.
I'LL GET THAT BUG OUT OF YOUR HEAD. IT'S GOING TO HURT, BUT BEAR WITH ME.
I'LL COUNT TO THREE AND BEAT IT OUT OF YOU.
ONE ...
TWO ...
THREE!
KOFF!
WHUMP

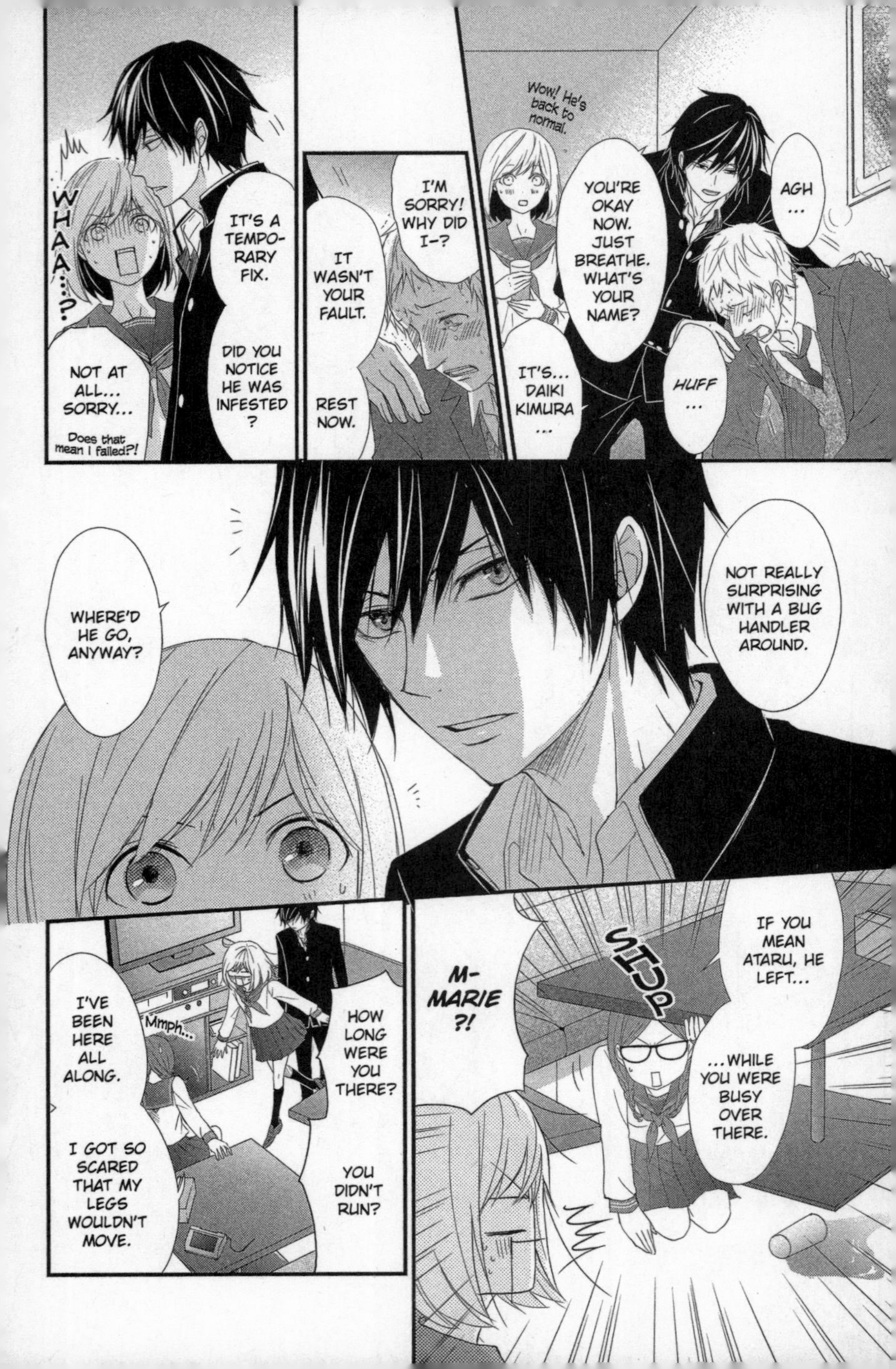
AGH ...
Wow! He's back to normal.
YOU'RE OKAY NOW. JUST BREATHE. WHAT'S YOUR NAME?
HUFF ...
IT'S... DAIKI KIMURA ...
I'M SORRY! WHY DID I-?
IT WASN'T YOUR FAULT.
REST NOW.
IT'S A TEMPORARY FIX.
DID YOU NOTICE HE WAS INFESTED?
WHAA...?
NOT AT ALL... SORRY...
Does that mean I failed?!
NOT REALLY SURPRISING WITH A BUG HANDLER AROUND.
WHERE'D HE GO, ANYWAY?
IF YOU MEAN ATARU, HE LEFT...
M-MARIE?!
...WHILE YOU WERE BUSY OVER THERE.
HOW LONG WERE YOU THERE?
I'VE BEEN HERE ALL ALONG.
Mmph...
YOU DIDN'T RUN?
I GOT SO SCARED THAT MY LEGS WOULDN'T MOVE.

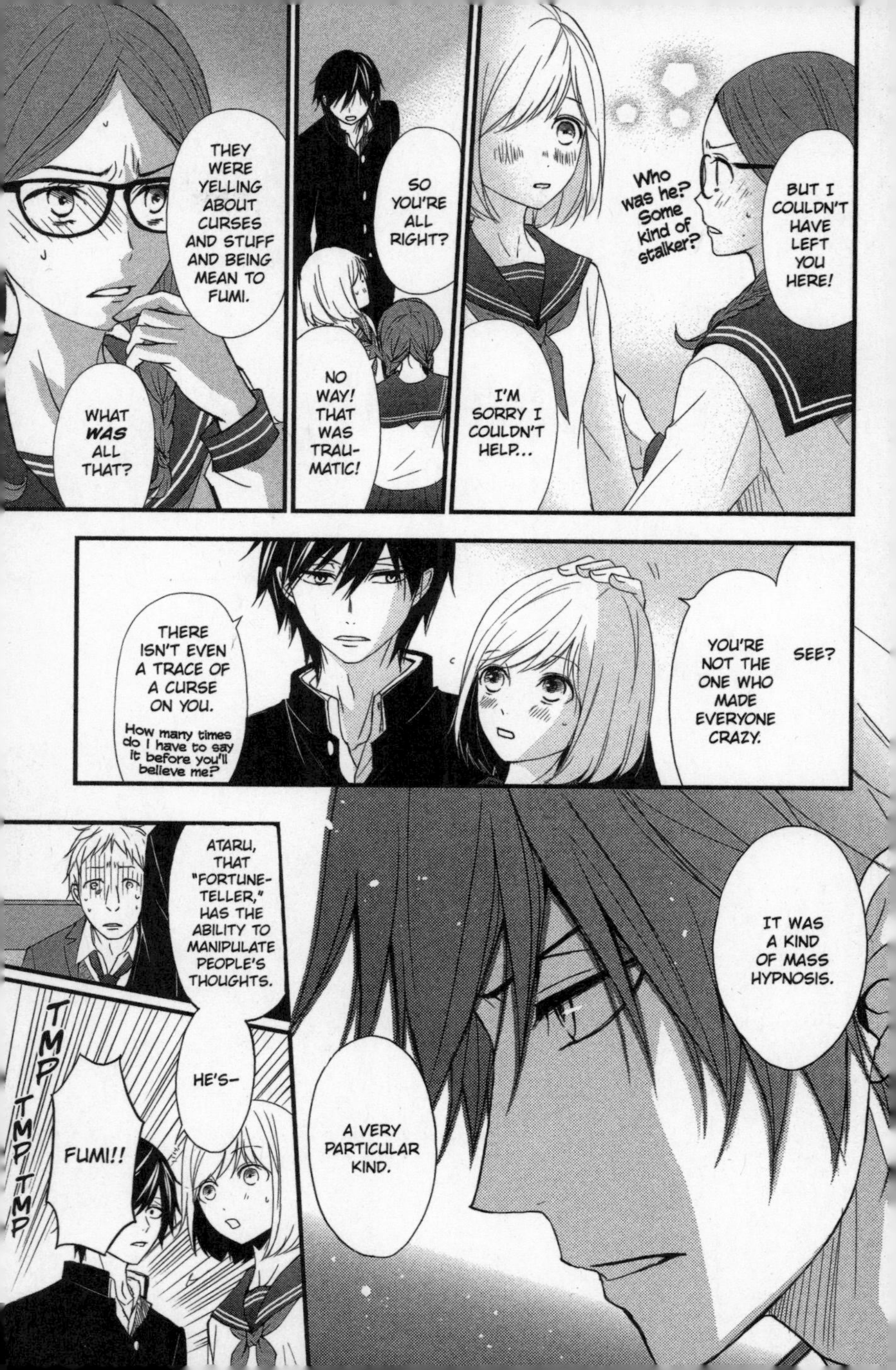
BUT I COULDN'T HAVE LEFT YOU HERE!
Who was he? Some kind of stalker?
I'M SORRY I COULDN'T HELP...
SO YOU'RE ALL RIGHT?
NO WAY! THAT WAS TRAU-MATIC!
THEY WERE YELLING ABOUT CURSES AND STUFF AND BEING MEAN TO FUMI.
WHAT *WAS* ALL THAT?
SEE?
YOU'RE NOT THE ONE WHO MADE EVERYONE CRAZY.
THERE ISN'T EVEN A TRACE OF A CURSE ON YOU.
How many times do I have to say it before you'll believe me?
IT WAS A KIND OF MASS HYPNOSIS.
A VERY PARTICULAR KIND.
ATARU, THAT "FORTUNE-TELLER," HAS THE ABILITY TO MANIPULATE PEOPLE'S THOUGHTS.
HE'S—
TMP TMP TMP TMP
FUMI!!

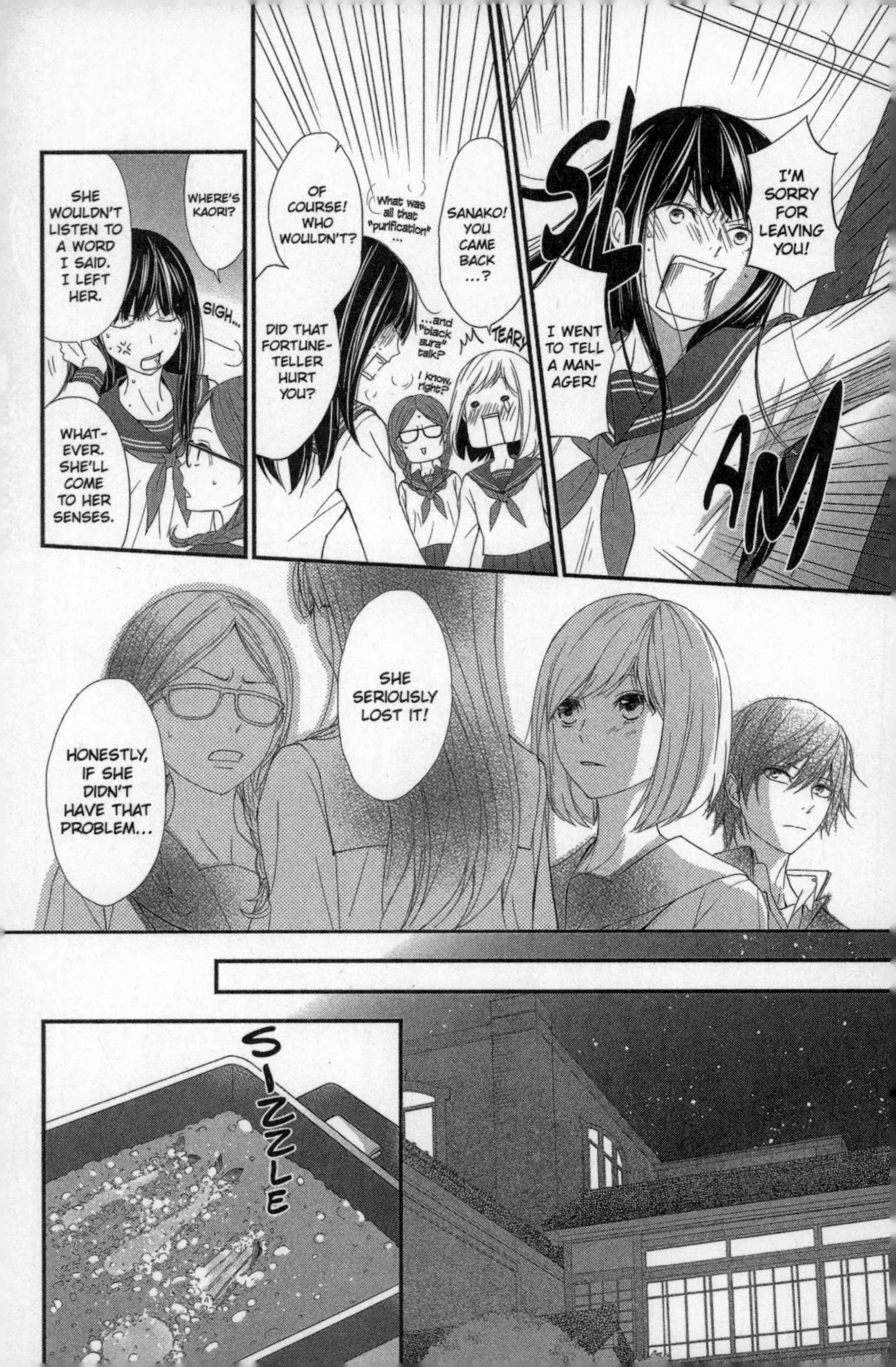
SLAM
I'M SORRY FOR LEAVING YOU!
I WENT TO TELL A MANAGER!
SANAKO! YOU CAME BACK ...?
TEARY
OF COURSE! WHO WOULDN'T?
What was all that "purification" ...
...and "black aura" talk?
I know, right?
DID THAT FORTUNE-TELLER HURT YOU?
WHERE'S KAORI?
SHE WOULDN'T LISTEN TO A WORD I SAID. I LEFT HER.
SIGH...
WHATEVER. SHE'LL COME TO HER SENSES.
SHE SERIOUSLY LOST IT!
HONESTLY, IF SHE DIDN'T HAVE THAT PROBLEM...
SIZZLE

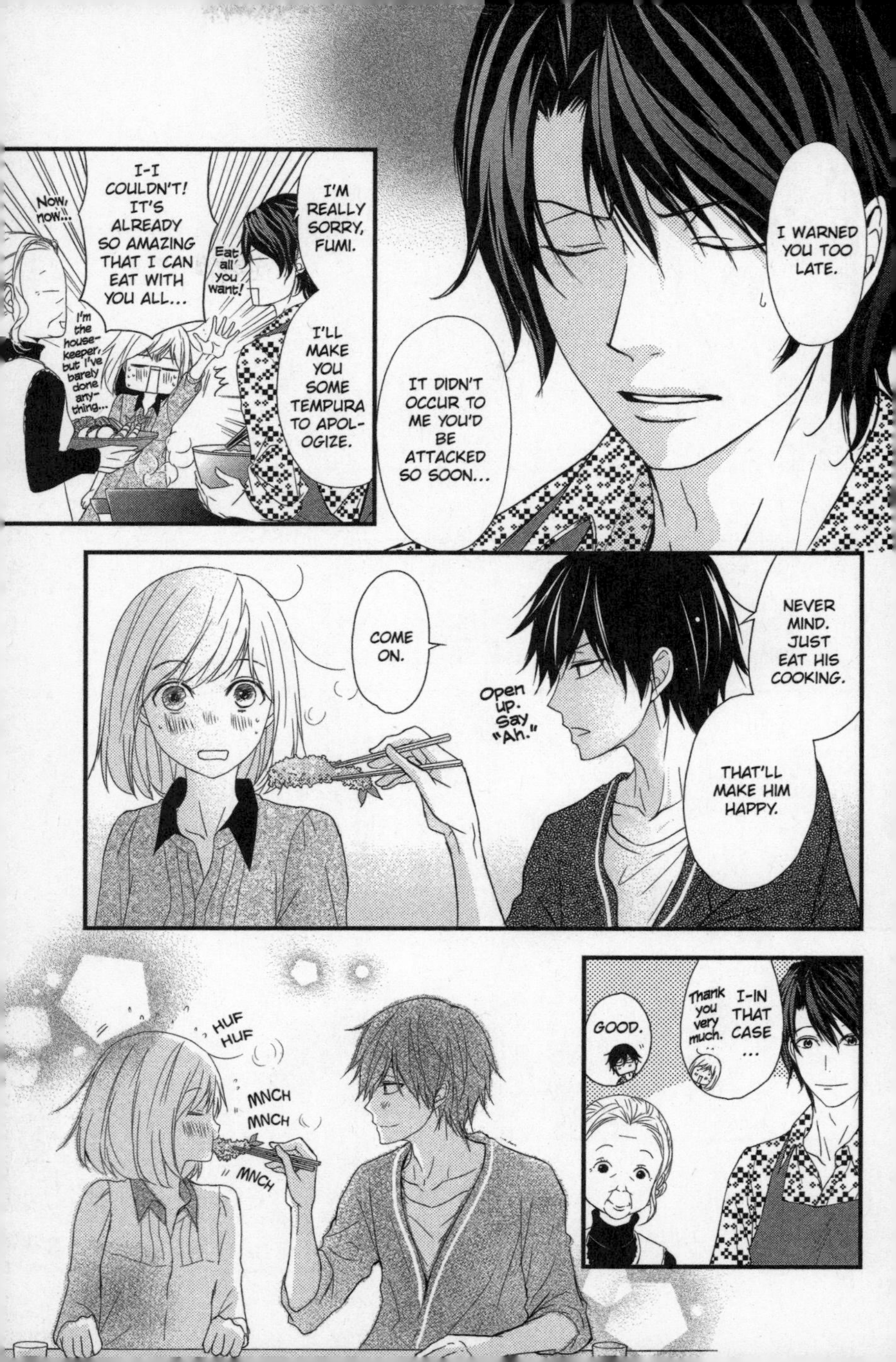

I WARNED YOU TOO LATE.
IT DIDN'T OCCUR TO ME YOU'D BE ATTACKED SO SOON...
I'M REALLY SORRY, FUMI.
I'LL MAKE YOU SOME TEMPURA TO APOLOGIZE.
Eat all you want!
I-I COULDN'T! IT'S ALREADY SO AMAZING THAT I CAN EAT WITH YOU ALL...
Now, now...
I'm the housekeeper, but I've barely done anything...
NEVER MIND. JUST EAT HIS COOKING.
THAT'LL MAKE HIM HAPPY.
Open up. Say "Ah."
COME ON.
I-IN THAT CASE ...
Thank you very much.
GOOD.
HUF HUF
MNCH MNCH
MNCH

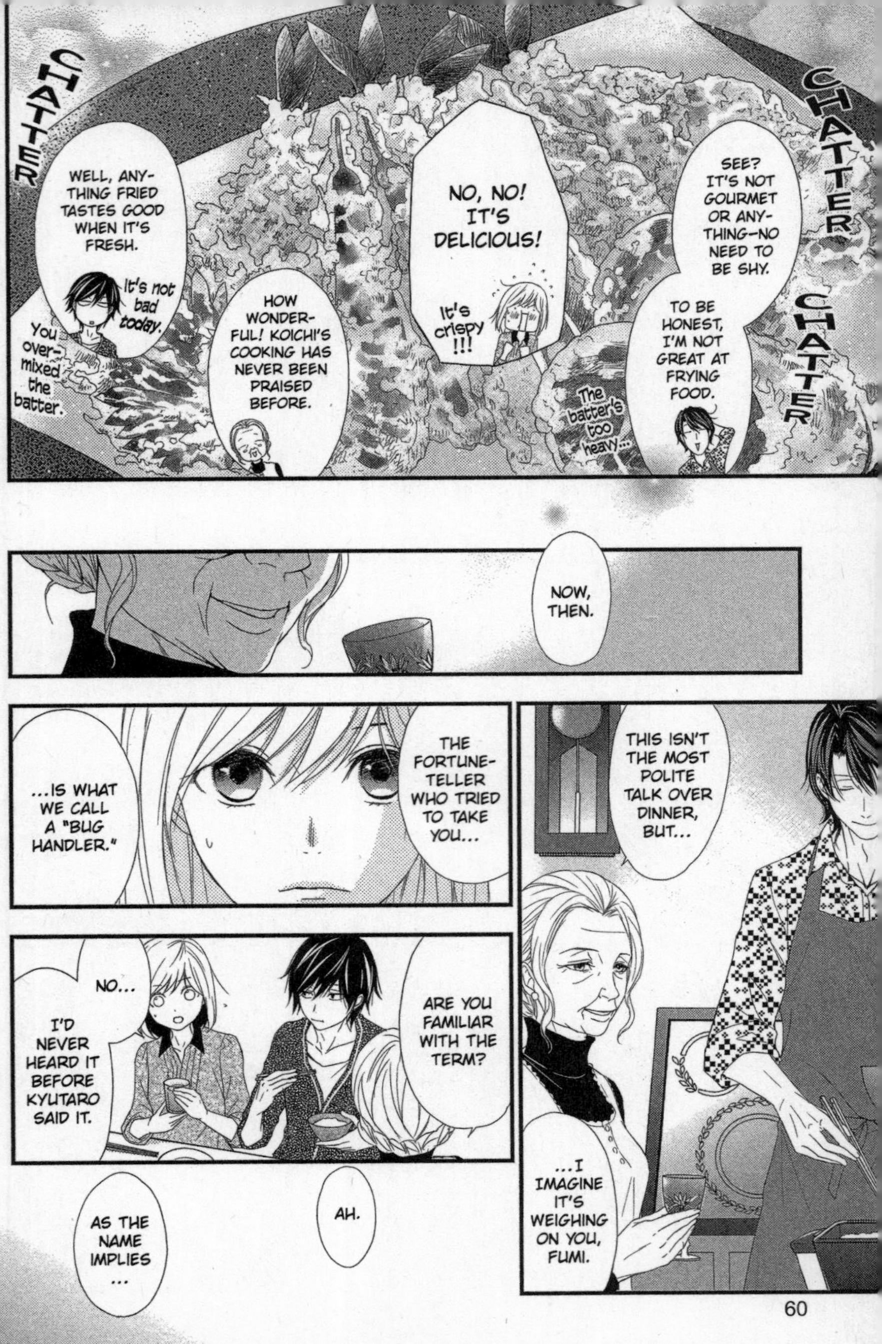
CHATTER
SEE? IT'S NOT GOURMET OR ANYTHING—NO NEED TO BE SHY.
CHATTER
TO BE HONEST, I'M NOT GREAT AT FRYING FOOD.
The batter's too heavy...
NO, NO! IT'S DELICIOUS!
It's crispy!!!
HOW WONDERFUL! KOICHI'S COOKING HAS NEVER BEEN PRAISED BEFORE.
WELL, ANYTHING FRIED TASTES GOOD WHEN IT'S FRESH.
It's not bad today.
You overmixed the batter.
CHATTER
NOW, THEN.
THIS ISN'T THE MOST POLITE TALK OVER DINNER, BUT...
...I IMAGINE IT'S WEIGHING ON YOU, FUMI.
THE FORTUNE-TELLER WHO TRIED TO TAKE YOU...
...IS WHAT WE CALL A "BUG HANDLER."
ARE YOU FAMILIAR WITH THE TERM?
NO...
I'D NEVER HEARD IT BEFORE KYUTARO SAID IT.
AH.
AS THE NAME IMPLIES ...

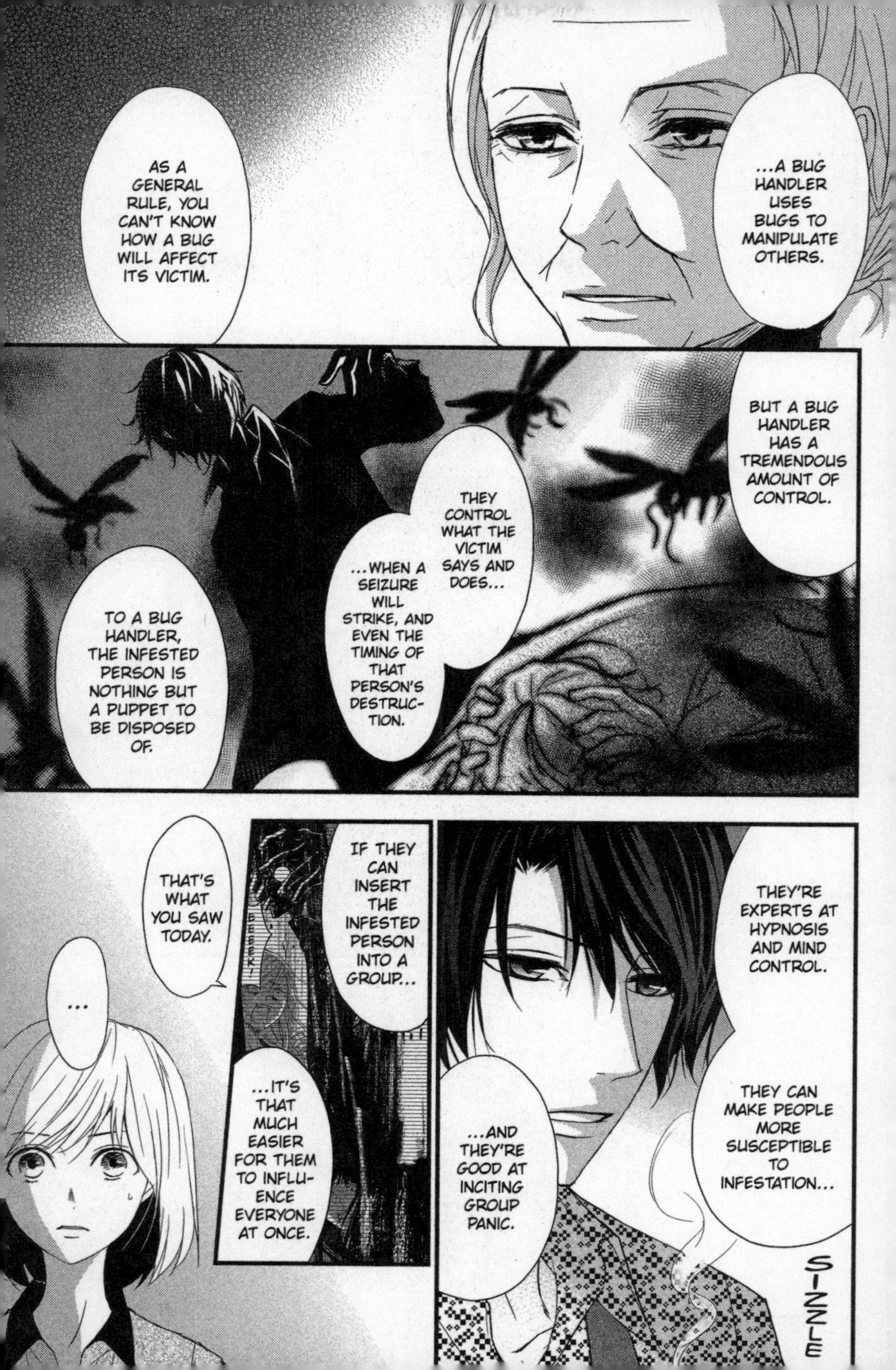
...A BUG HANDLER USES BUGS TO MANIPULATE OTHERS.
AS A GENERAL RULE, YOU CAN'T KNOW HOW A BUG WILL AFFECT ITS VICTIM.
BUT A BUG HANDLER HAS A TREMENDOUS AMOUNT OF CONTROL.
THEY CONTROL WHAT THE VICTIM SAYS AND DOES...
...WHEN A SEIZURE WILL STRIKE, AND EVEN THE TIMING OF THAT PERSON'S DESTRUC-TION.
TO A BUG HANDLER, THE INFESTED PERSON IS NOTHING BUT A PUPPET TO BE DISPOSED OF.
THEY'RE EXPERTS AT HYPNOSIS AND MIND CONTROL.
THEY CAN MAKE PEOPLE MORE SUSCEPTIBLE TO INFESTATION...
...AND THEY'RE GOOD AT INCITING GROUP PANIC.
SIZZLE
IF THEY CAN INSERT THE INFESTED PERSON INTO A GROUP...
...IT'S THAT MUCH EASIER FOR THEM TO INFLU-ENCE EVERYONE AT ONCE.
THAT'S WHAT YOU SAW TODAY.
...

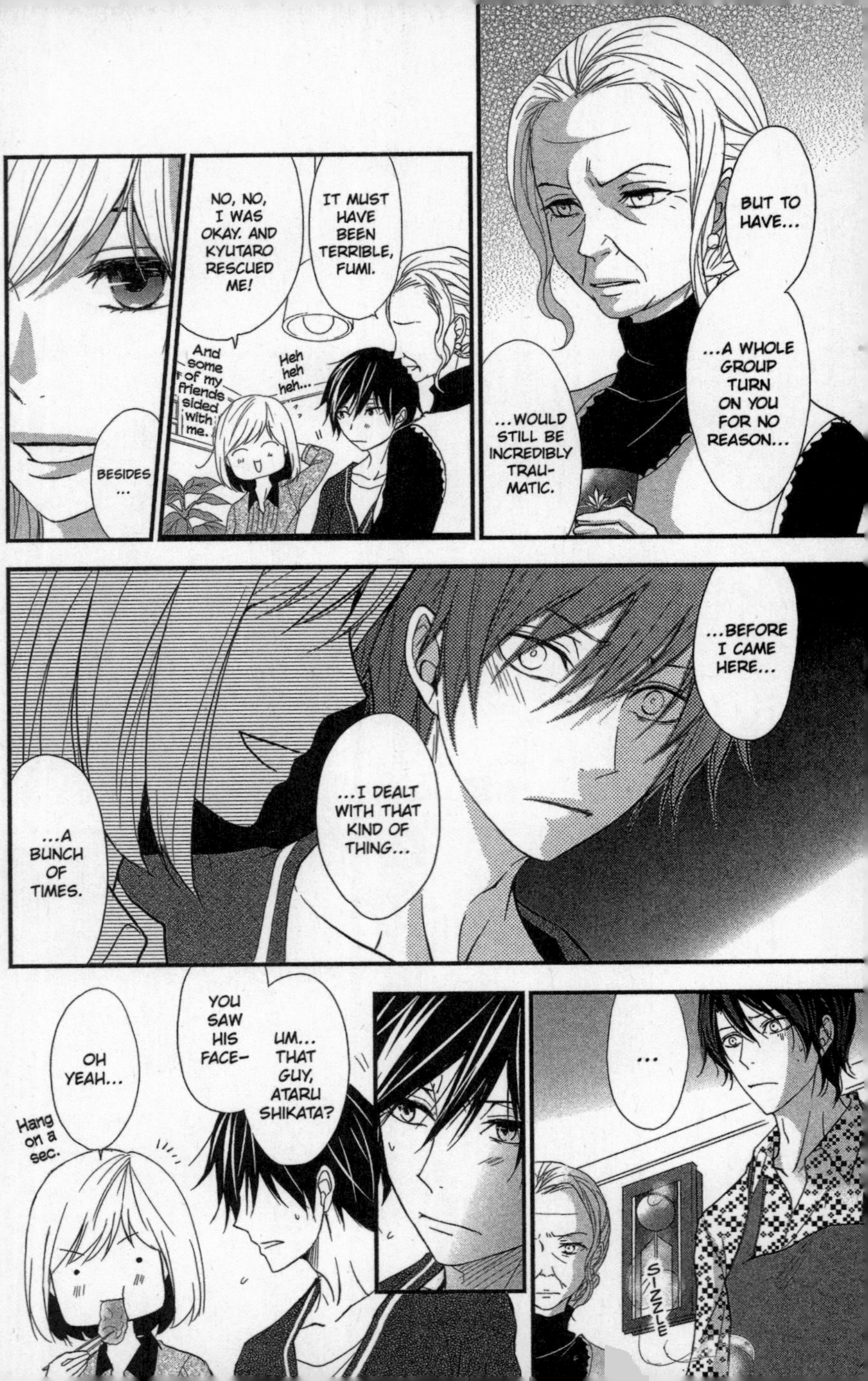
BUT TO HAVE...
...A WHOLE GROUP TURN ON YOU FOR NO REASON...
...WOULD STILL BE INCREDIBLY TRAU-MATIC.
IT MUST HAVE BEEN TERRIBLE, FUMI.
NO, NO, I WAS OKAY. AND KYUTARO RESCUED ME!
Heh heh heh...
And some of my friends sided with me.
BESIDES...
...BEFORE I CAME HERE...
...I DEALT WITH THAT KIND OF THING...
...A BUNCH OF TIMES.
...
SIZZLE
UM... THAT GUY, ATARU SHIKATA?
YOU SAW HIS FACE—
OH YEAH...
Hang on a sec.

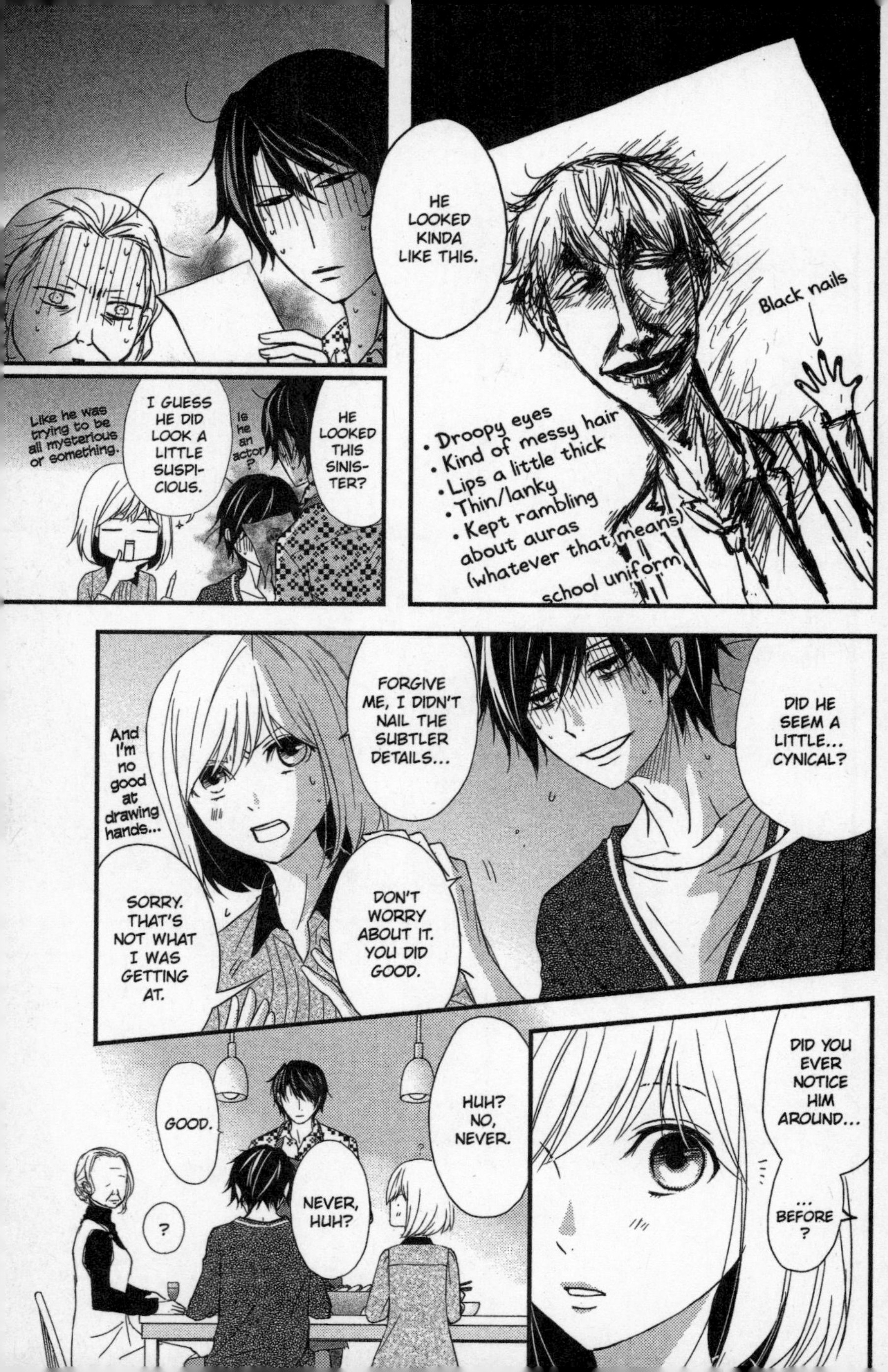
HE LOOKED KINDA LIKE THIS.
Black nails
• Droopy eyes
• Kind of messy hair
• Lips a little thick
• Thin/lanky
• Kept rambling about auras (whatever that means)
school uniform
HE LOOKED THIS SINISTER?
Is he an actor?
I GUESS HE DID LOOK A LITTLE SUSPICIOUS.
Like he was trying to be all mysterious or something.
DID HE SEEM A LITTLE... CYNICAL?
FORGIVE ME, I DIDN'T NAIL THE SUBTLER DETAILS...
And I'm no good at drawing hands...
DON'T WORRY ABOUT IT. YOU DID GOOD.
SORRY. THAT'S NOT WHAT I WAS GETTING AT.
DID YOU EVER NOTICE HIM AROUND...
...BEFORE?
HUH? NO, NEVER.
GOOD.
NEVER, HUH?
?

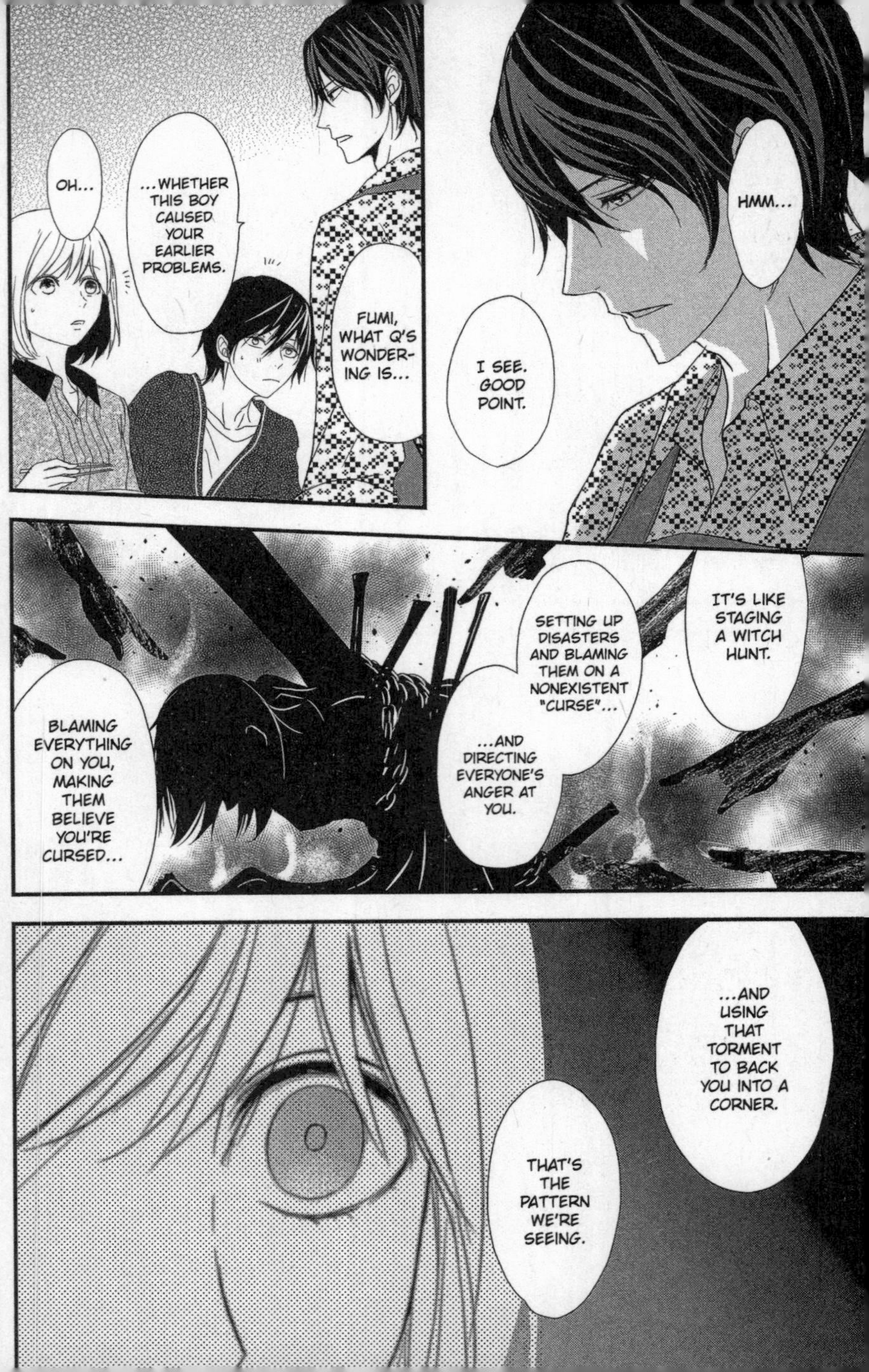
HMM...
I SEE. GOOD POINT.
FUMI, WHAT Q'S WONDERING IS...
...WHETHER THIS BOY CAUSED YOUR EARLIER PROBLEMS.
OH...
IT'S LIKE STAGING A WITCH HUNT.
SETTING UP DISASTERS AND BLAMING THEM ON A NONEXISTENT "CURSE"...
...AND DIRECTING EVERYONE'S ANGER AT YOU.
BLAMING EVERYTHING ON YOU, MAKING THEM BELIEVE YOU'RE CURSED...
...AND USING THAT TORMENT TO BACK YOU INTO A CORNER.
THAT'S THE PATTERN WE'RE SEEING.

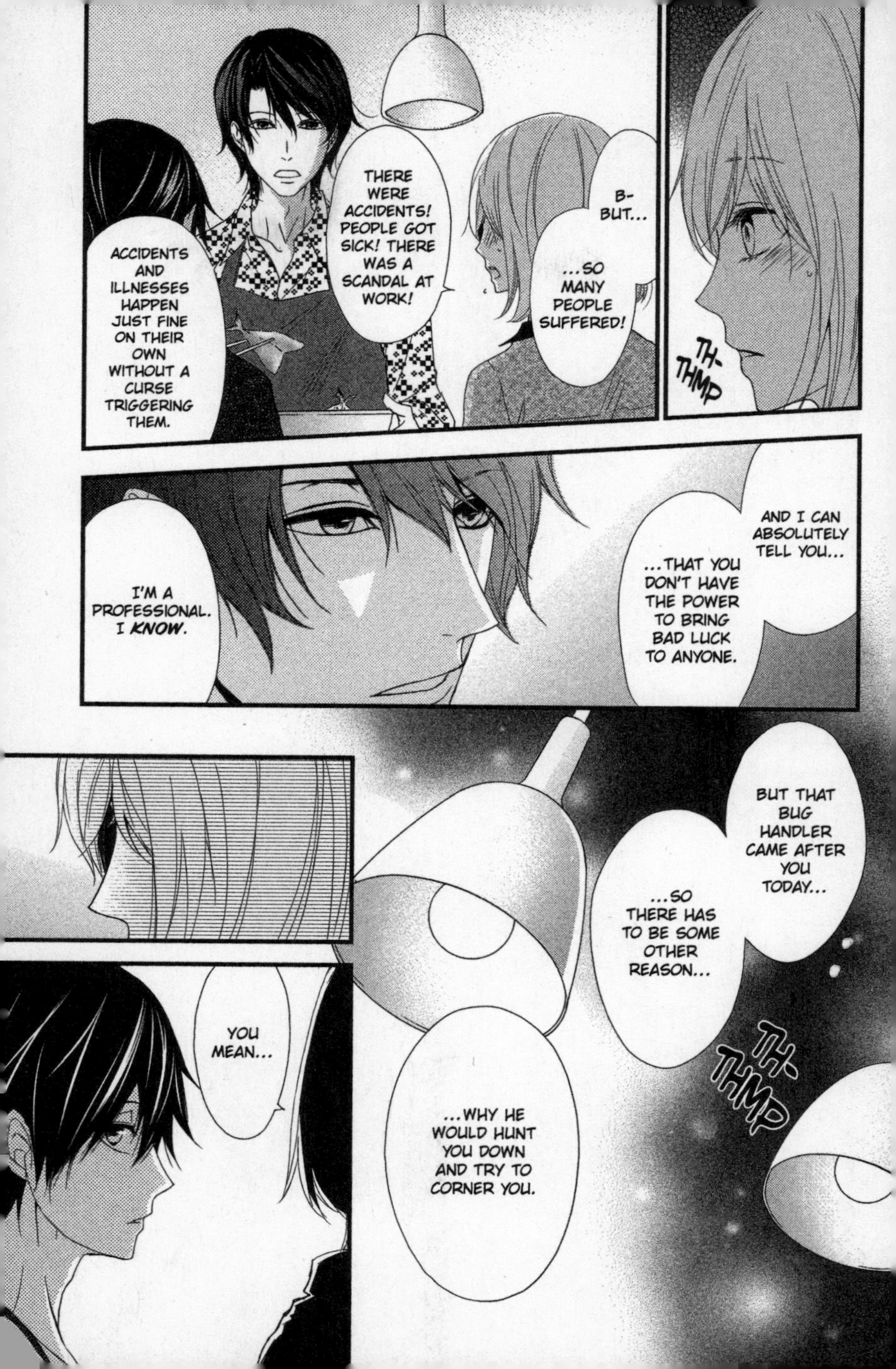
TH-THMP
B-BUT...
...SO MANY PEOPLE SUFFERED!
THERE WERE ACCIDENTS! PEOPLE GOT SICK! THERE WAS A SCANDAL AT WORK!
ACCIDENTS AND ILLNESSES HAPPEN JUST FINE ON THEIR OWN WITHOUT A CURSE TRIGGERING THEM.
AND I CAN ABSOLUTELY TELL YOU...
...THAT YOU DON'T HAVE THE POWER TO BRING BAD LUCK TO ANYONE.
I'M A PROFESSIONAL. I *KNOW*.
BUT THAT BUG HANDLER CAME AFTER YOU TODAY...
...SO THERE HAS TO BE SOME OTHER REASON...
TH-THMP
YOU MEAN...
...WHY HE WOULD HUNT YOU DOWN AND TRY TO CORNER YOU.

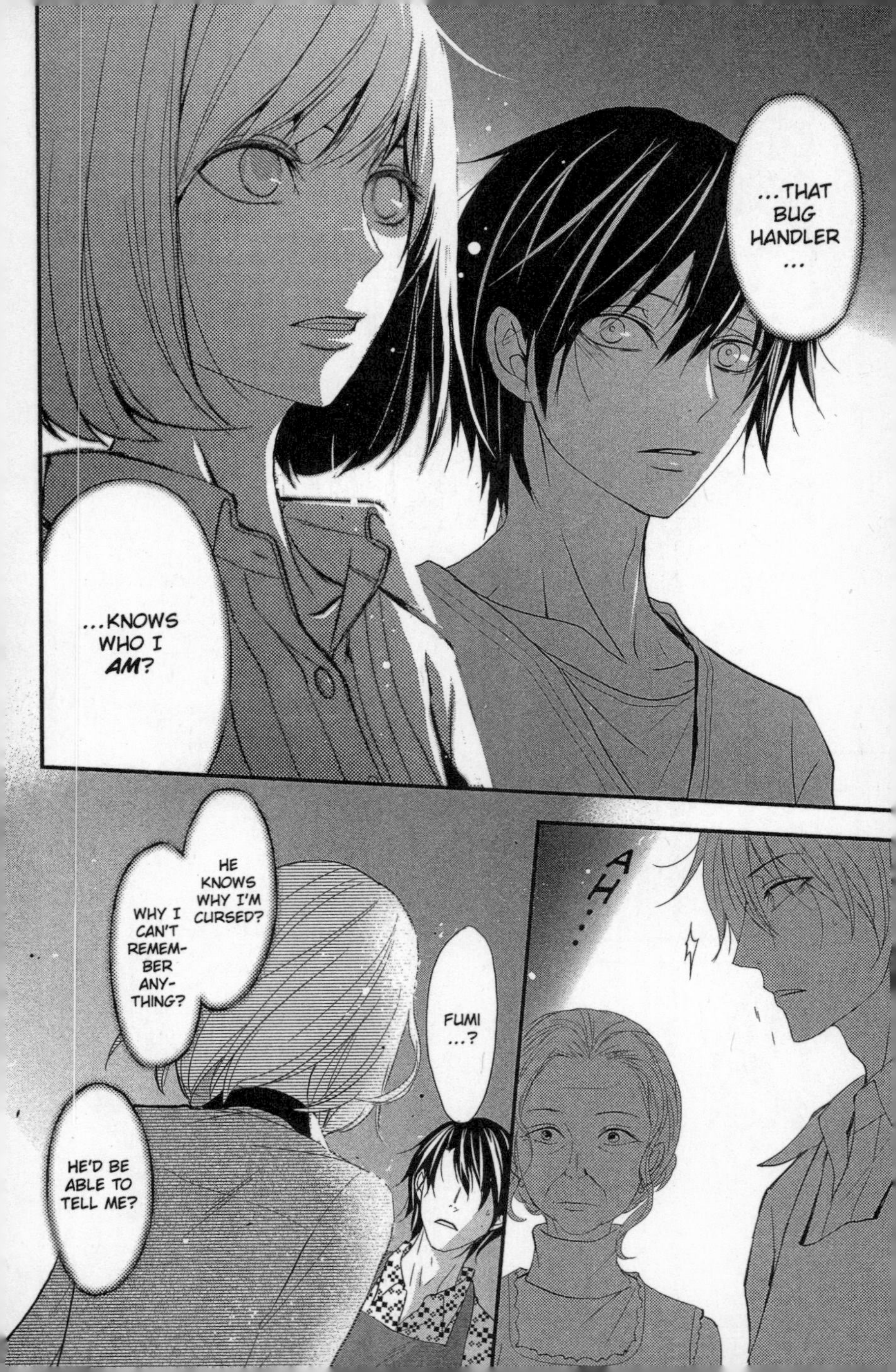
...THAT BUG HANDLER ...
...KNOWS WHO I AM?
AH...
FUMI ...?
HE KNOWS WHY I'M CURSED?
WHY I CAN'T REMEMBER ANYTHING?
HE'D BE ABLE TO TELL ME?

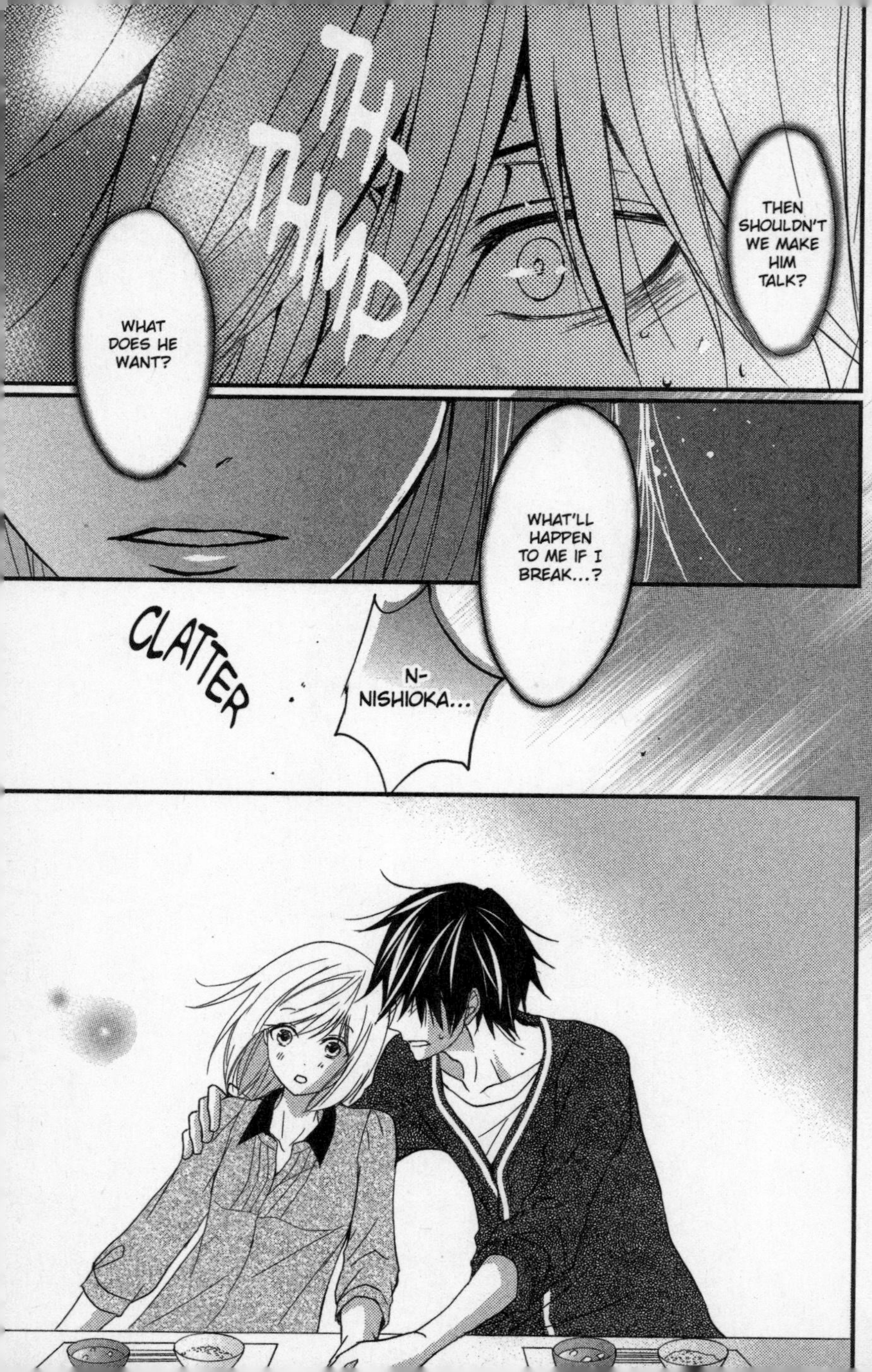
THEN SHOULDN'T WE MAKE HIM TALK?
TH-THMP
WHAT DOES HE WANT?
WHAT'LL HAPPEN TO ME IF I BREAK...?
N-NISHIOKA...
CLATTER

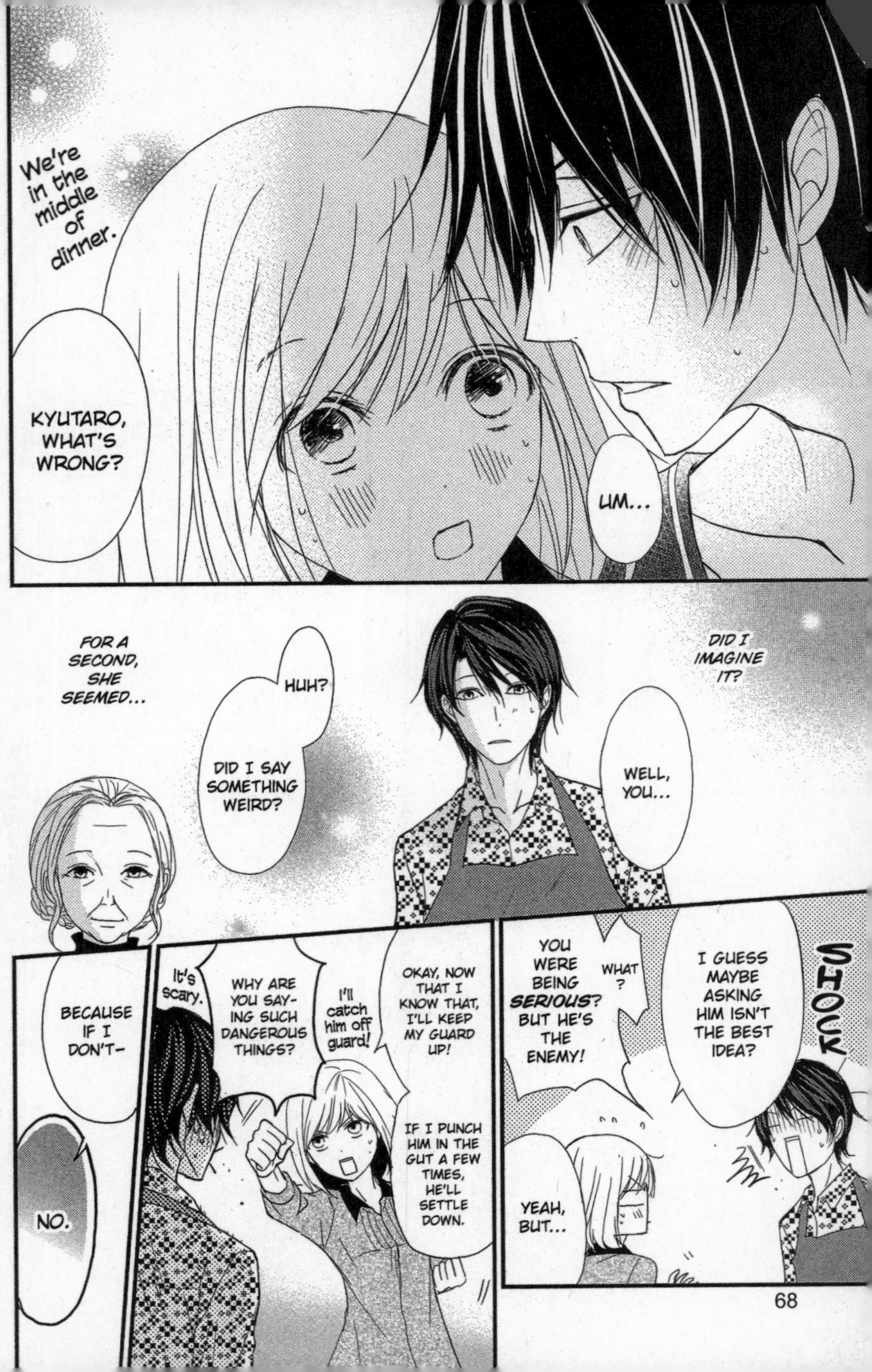
We're in the middle of dinner.
KYUTARO, WHAT'S WRONG?
UM...
WELL, YOU...
HUH?
DID I SAY SOMETHING WEIRD?
FOR A SECOND, SHE SEEMED...
DID I IMAGINE IT?
I GUESS MAYBE ASKING HIM ISN'T THE BEST IDEA?
SHOCK
WHAT?
YOU WERE BEING *SERIOUS*? BUT HE'S THE ENEMY!
YEAH, BUT...
OKAY, NOW THAT I KNOW THAT, I'LL KEEP MY GUARD UP!
I'll catch him off guard!
IF I PUNCH HIM IN THE GUT A FEW TIMES, HE'LL SETTLE DOWN.
WHY ARE YOU SAY-ING SUCH DANGEROUS THINGS?
It's scary.
BECAUSE IF I DON'T-
NO.

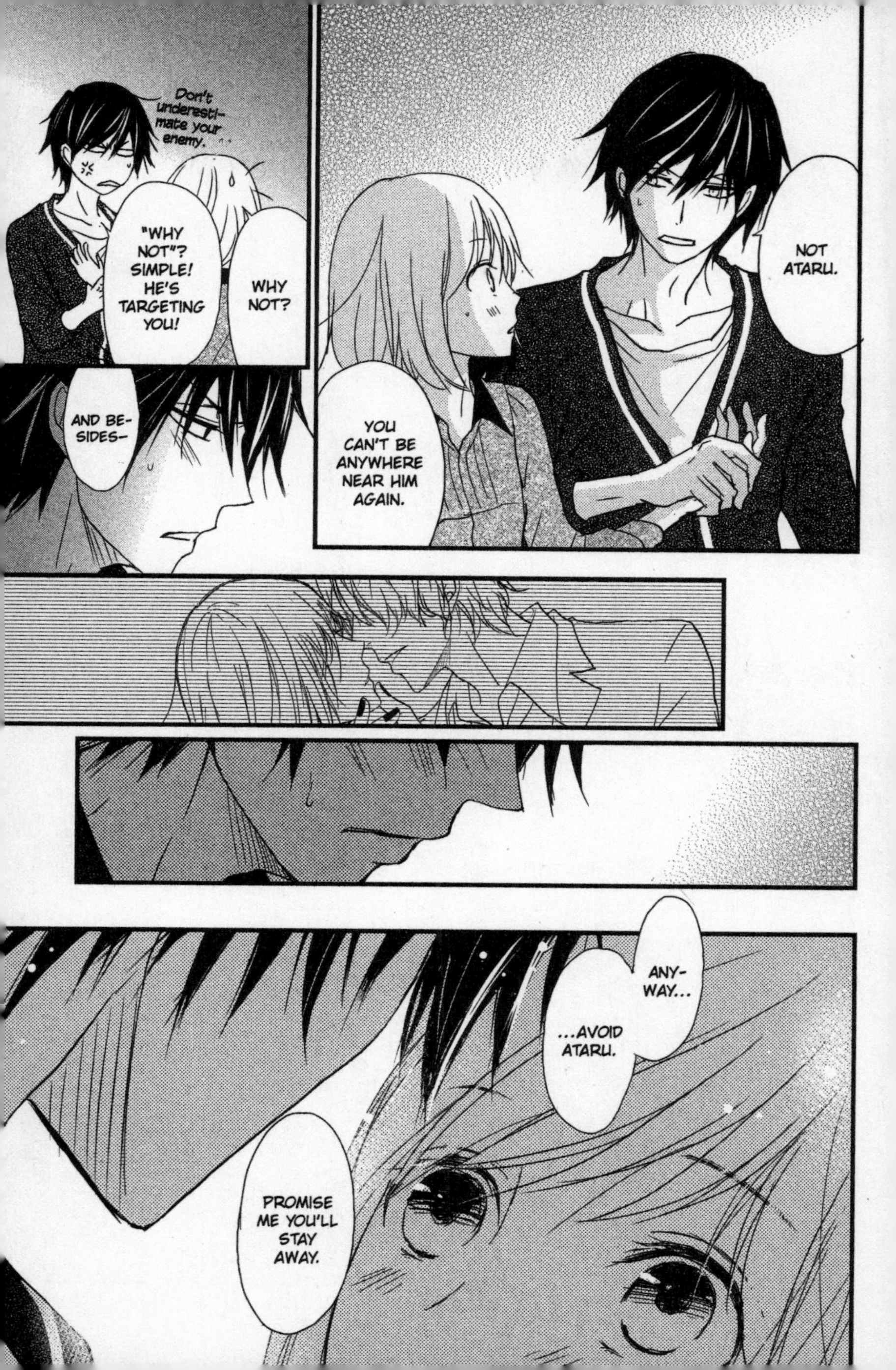
NOT ATARU.
YOU CAN'T BE ANYWHERE NEAR HIM AGAIN.
WHY NOT?
"WHY NOT"? SIMPLE! HE'S TARGETING YOU!
Don't underestimate your enemy.
AND BE-SIDES-
ANY-WAY...
...AVOID ATARU.
PROMISE ME YOU'LL STAY AWAY.

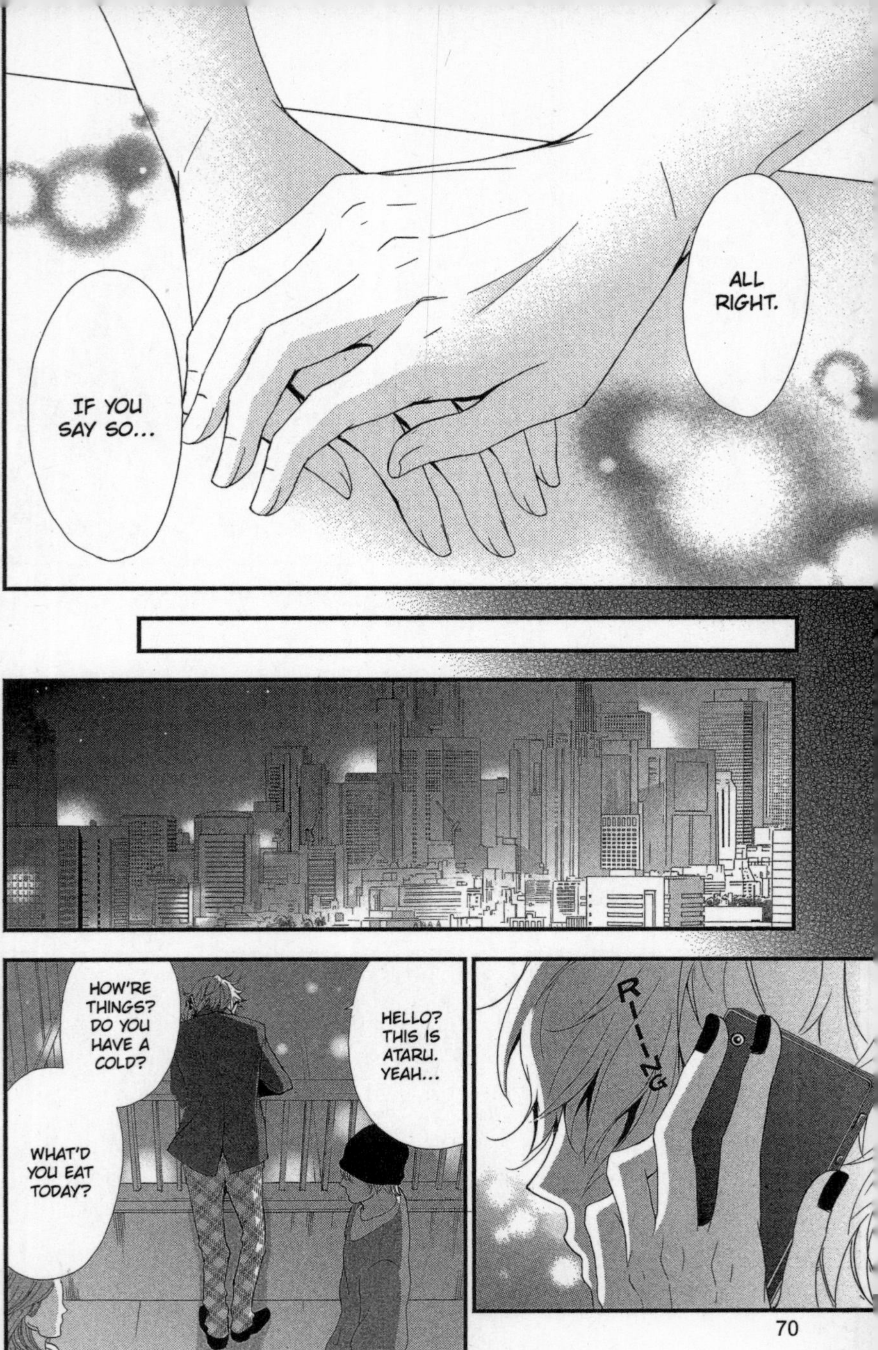
ALL RIGHT.
IF YOU SAY SO...
R-I-I-NG
HELLO? THIS IS ATARU. YEAH...
HOW'RE THINGS? DO YOU HAVE A COLD?
WHAT'D YOU EAT TODAY?

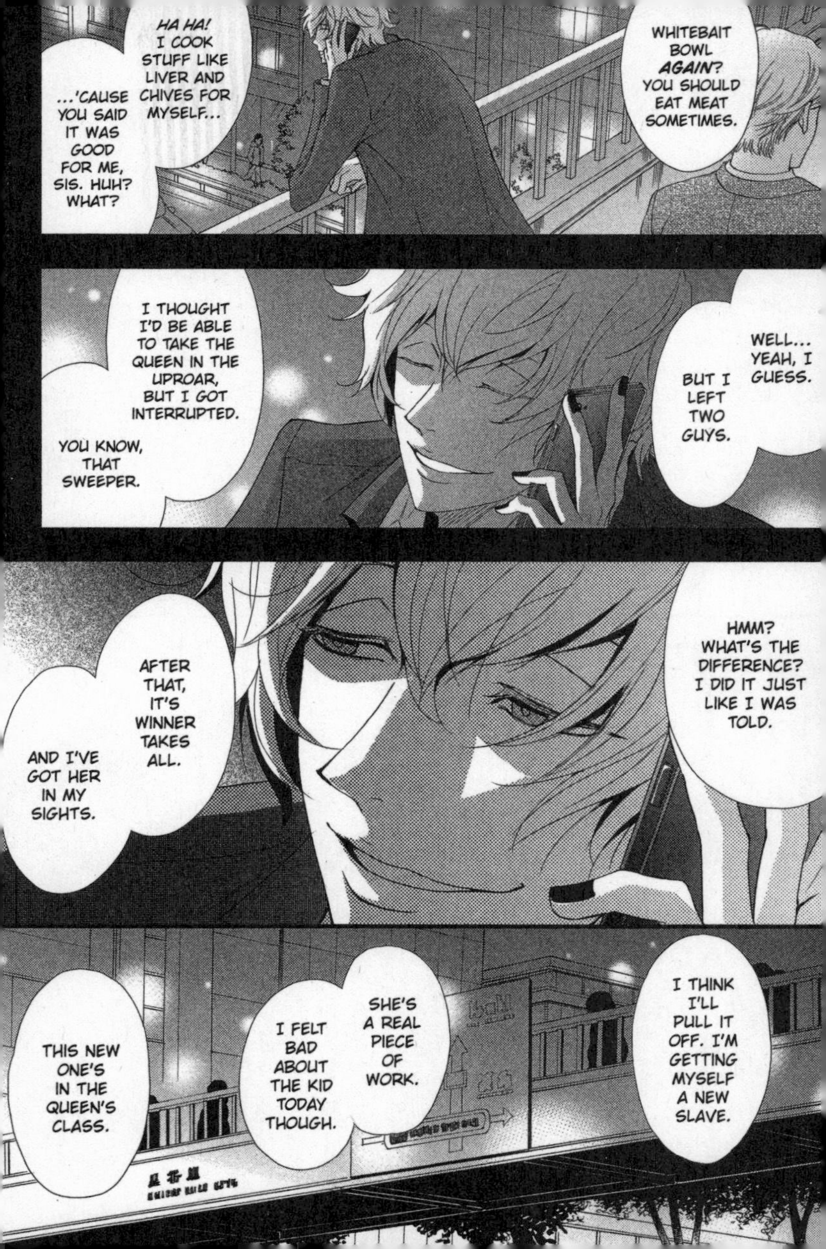
WHITEBAIT BOWL *AGAIN*? YOU SHOULD EAT MEAT SOMETIMES.
HA HA! I COOK STUFF LIKE LIVER AND CHIVES FOR MYSELF...
...'CAUSE YOU SAID IT WAS GOOD FOR ME, SIS. HUH? WHAT?
WELL... YEAH, I GUESS.
BUT I LEFT TWO GUYS.
I THOUGHT I'D BE ABLE TO TAKE THE QUEEN IN THE UPROAR, BUT I GOT INTERRUPTED.
YOU KNOW, THAT SWEEPER.
HMM? WHAT'S THE DIFFERENCE? I DID IT JUST LIKE I WAS TOLD.
AFTER THAT, IT'S WINNER TAKES ALL.
AND I'VE GOT HER IN MY SIGHTS.
I THINK I'LL PULL IT OFF. I'M GETTING MYSELF A NEW SLAVE.
SHE'S A REAL PIECE OF WORK.
I FELT BAD ABOUT THE KID TODAY THOUGH.
THIS NEW ONE'S IN THE QUEEN'S CLASS.

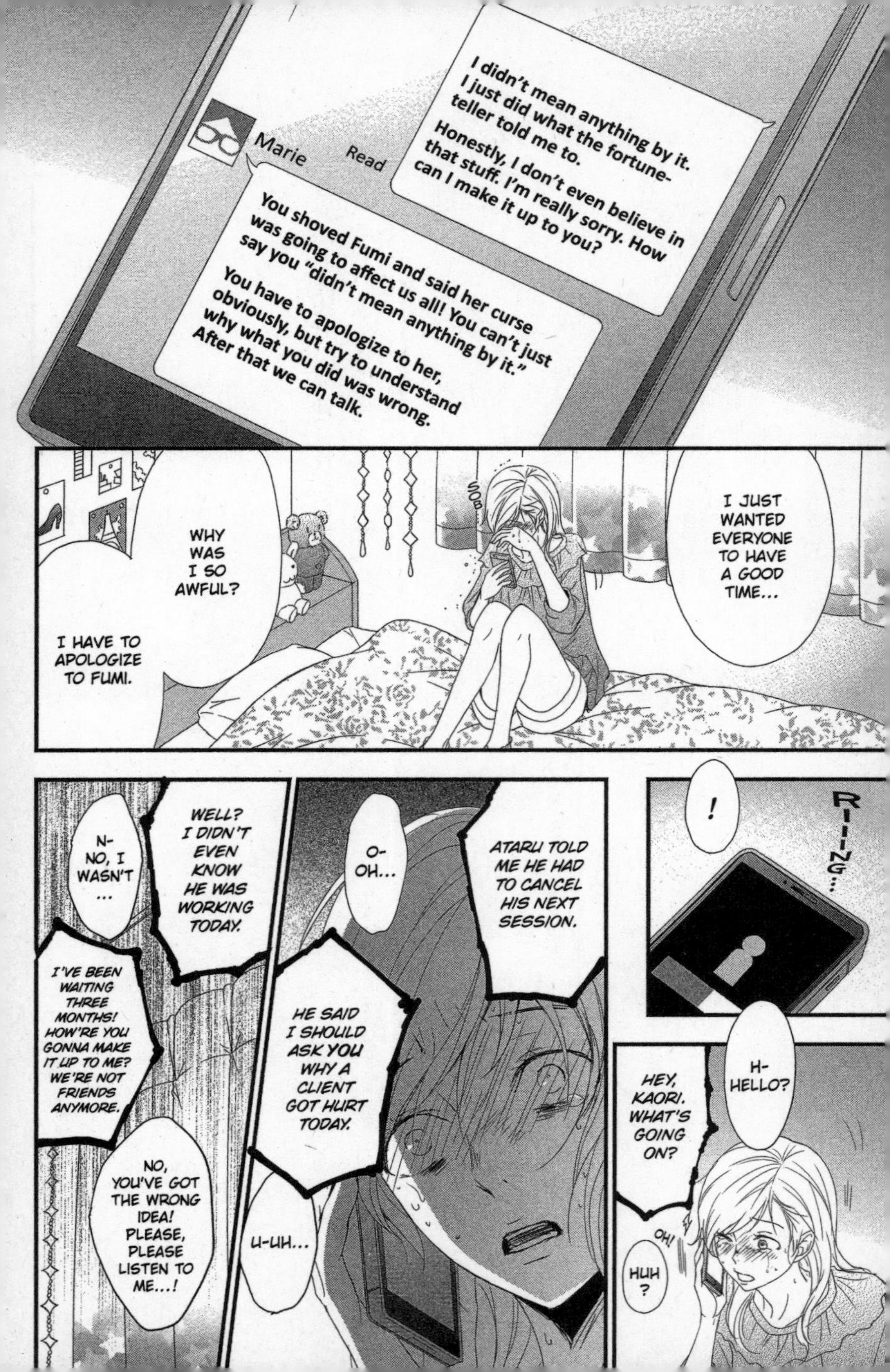
I didn't mean anything by it. I just did what the fortune-teller told me to.
Honestly, I don't even believe in that stuff. I'm really sorry. How can I make it up to you?
Read
Marie
You shoved Fumi and said her curse was going to affect us all! You can't just say you "didn't mean anything by it."
You have to apologize to her, obviously, but try to understand why what you did was wrong. After that we can talk.
I JUST WANTED EVERYONE TO HAVE A GOOD TIME...
SOB
WHY WAS I SO AWFUL?
I HAVE TO APOLOGIZE TO FUMI.
!
RIIING...
H-HELLO?
HEY, KAORI. WHAT'S GOING ON?
OH!
HUH?
ATARU TOLD ME HE HAD TO CANCEL HIS NEXT SESSION.
O-OH...
HE SAID I SHOULD ASK YOU WHY A CLIENT GOT HURT TODAY.
U-UH...
WELL? I DIDN'T EVEN KNOW HE WAS WORKING TODAY.
N-NO, I WASN'T ...
I'VE BEEN WAITING THREE MONTHS! HOW'RE YOU GONNA MAKE IT UP TO ME? WE'RE NOT FRIENDS ANYMORE.
NO, YOU'VE GOT THE WRONG IDEA! PLEASE, PLEASE LISTEN TO ME...!

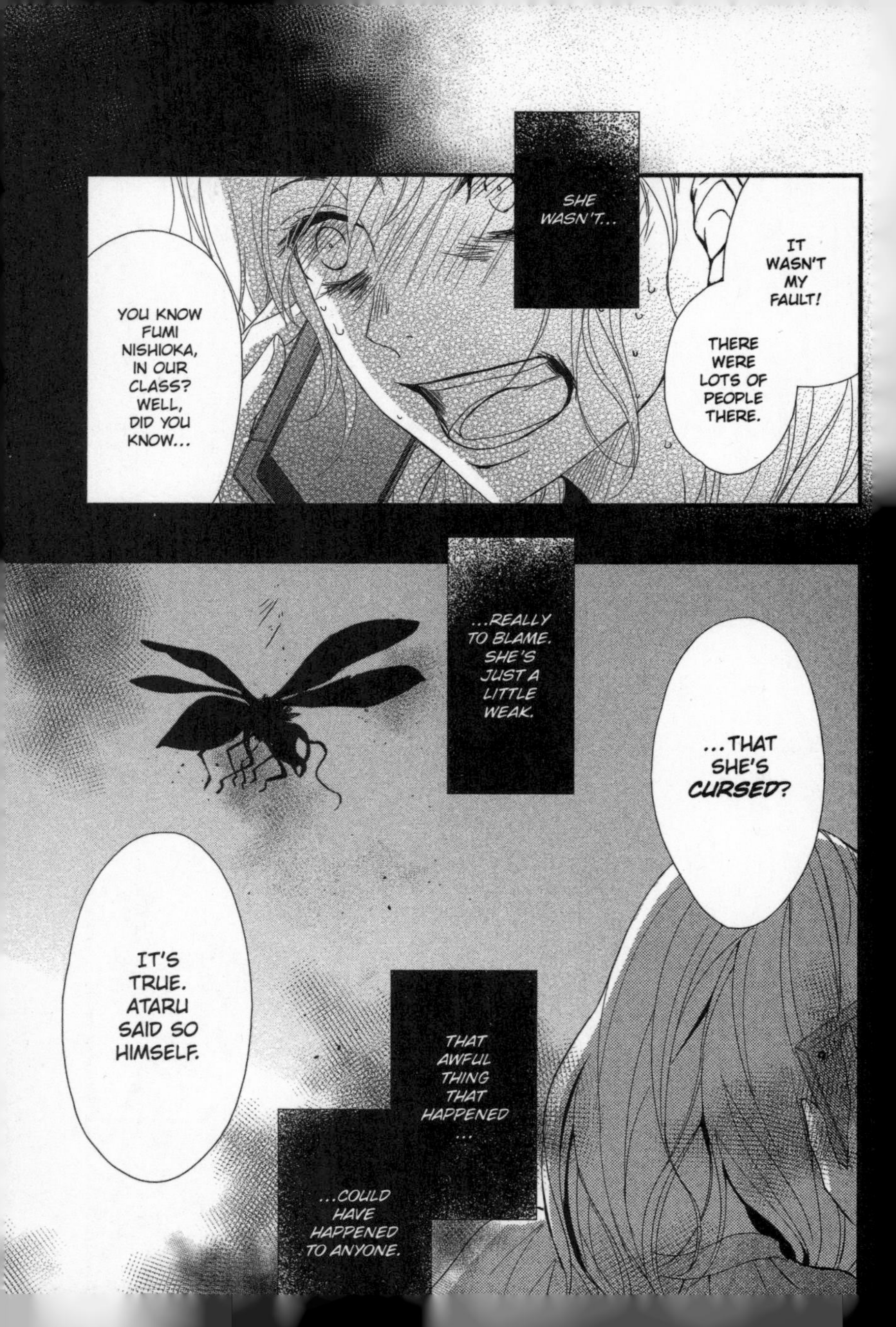
IT WASN'T MY FAULT! THERE WERE LOTS OF PEOPLE THERE.
SHE WASN'T...
YOU KNOW FUMI NISHIOKA, IN OUR CLASS? WELL, DID YOU KNOW...
...THAT SHE'S *CURSED?*
...REALLY TO BLAME. SHE'S JUST A LITTLE WEAK.
THAT AWFUL THING THAT HAPPENED...
IT'S TRUE. ATARU SAID SO HIMSELF.
...COULD HAVE HAPPENED TO ANYONE.

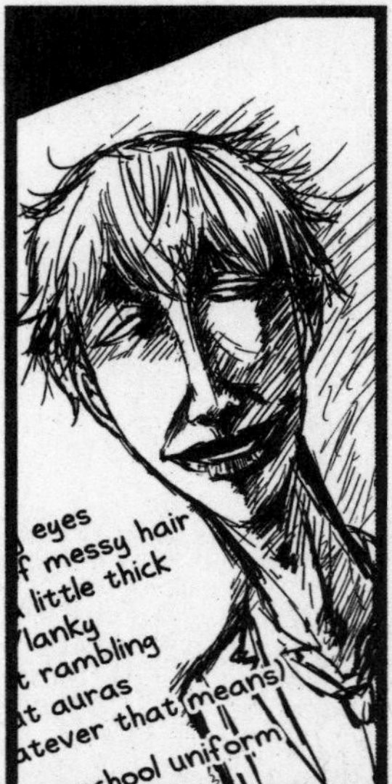
eyes
f messy hair
little thick
lanky
t rambling
t auras
atever that means)
school uniform

SWEEP 13

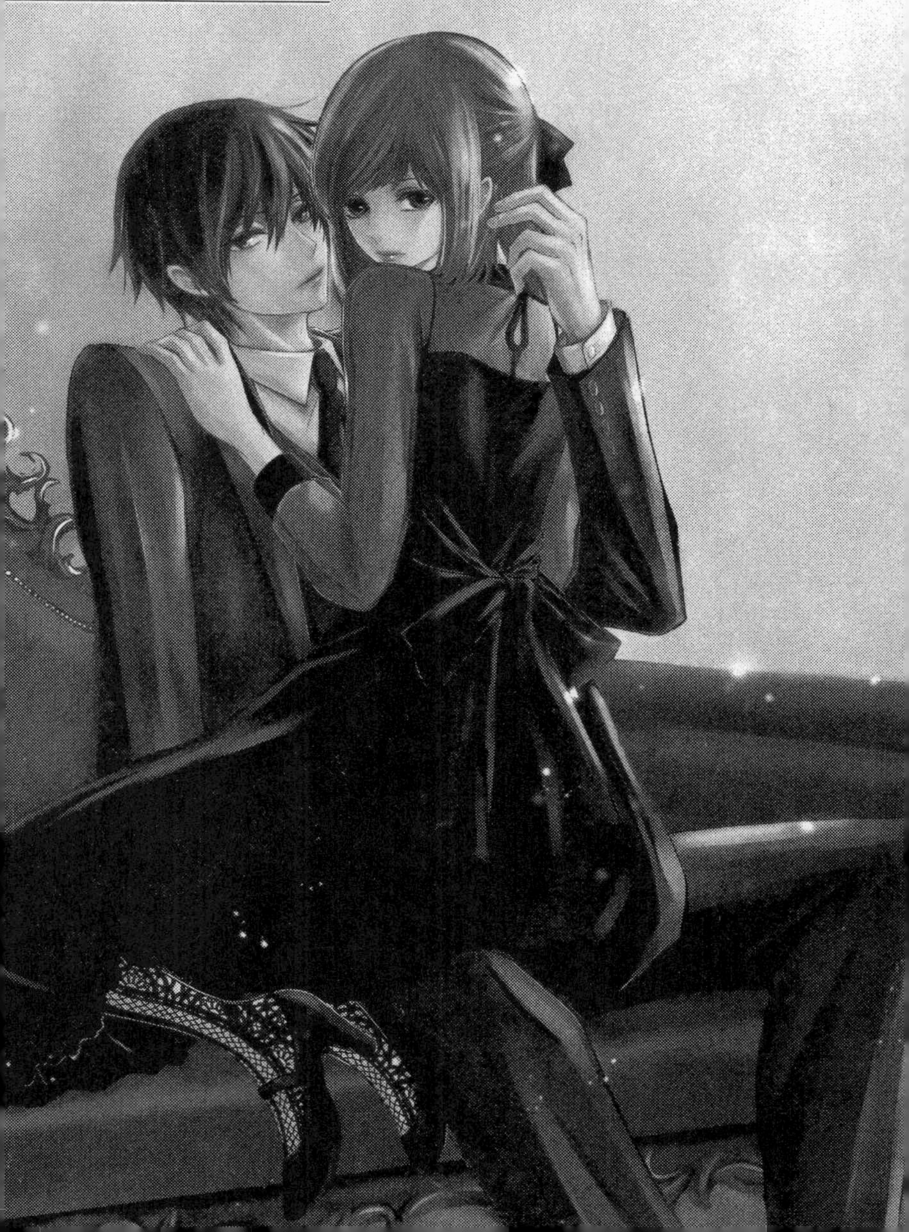

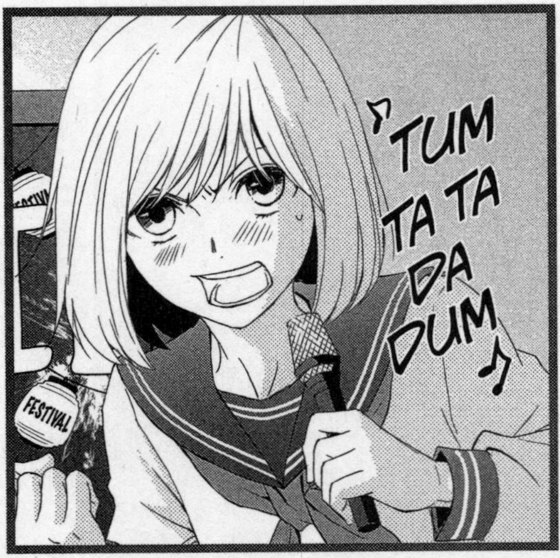
♪TUM TA TA DA DUM♪
FESTIVAL

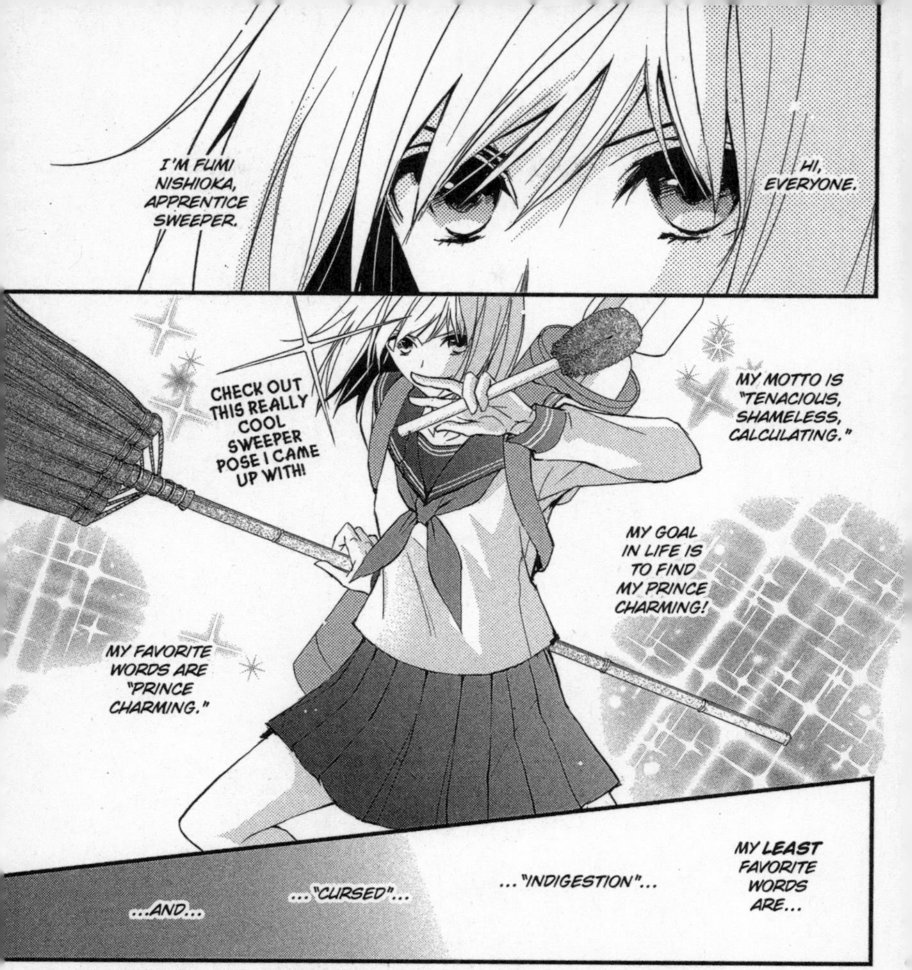
HI, EVERYONE.
I'M FUMI NISHIOKA, APPRENTICE SWEEPER.
MY MOTTO IS "TENACIOUS, SHAMELESS, CALCULATING."
MY GOAL IN LIFE IS TO FIND MY PRINCE CHARMING!
MY FAVORITE WORDS ARE "PRINCE CHARMING."
CHECK OUT THIS REALLY COOL SWEEPER POSE I CAME UP WITH!
MY LEAST FAVORITE WORDS ARE...
..."INDIGESTION"...
..."CURSED"...
...AND...

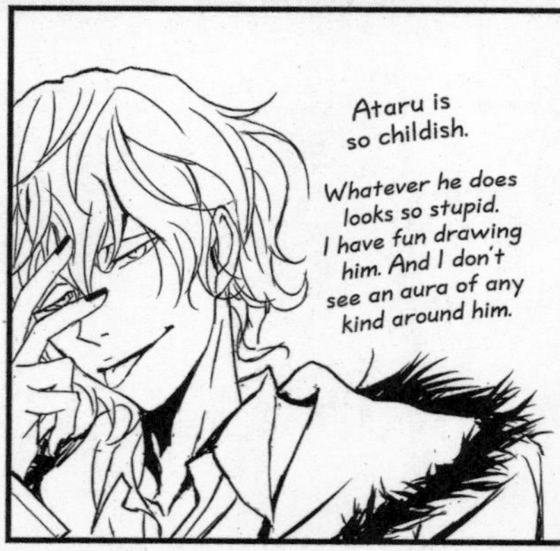
Ataru is so childish.
Whatever he does looks so stupid. I have fun drawing him. And I don't see an aura of any kind around him.

I kind of put aura reading down in Sweep 12, so I have to apologize. I can't see auras at all, so it's all foreign to me.

It must be terrible for people who really can see auras. When they're in a crowded train, all those colors must be dizzying! Am I wrong?

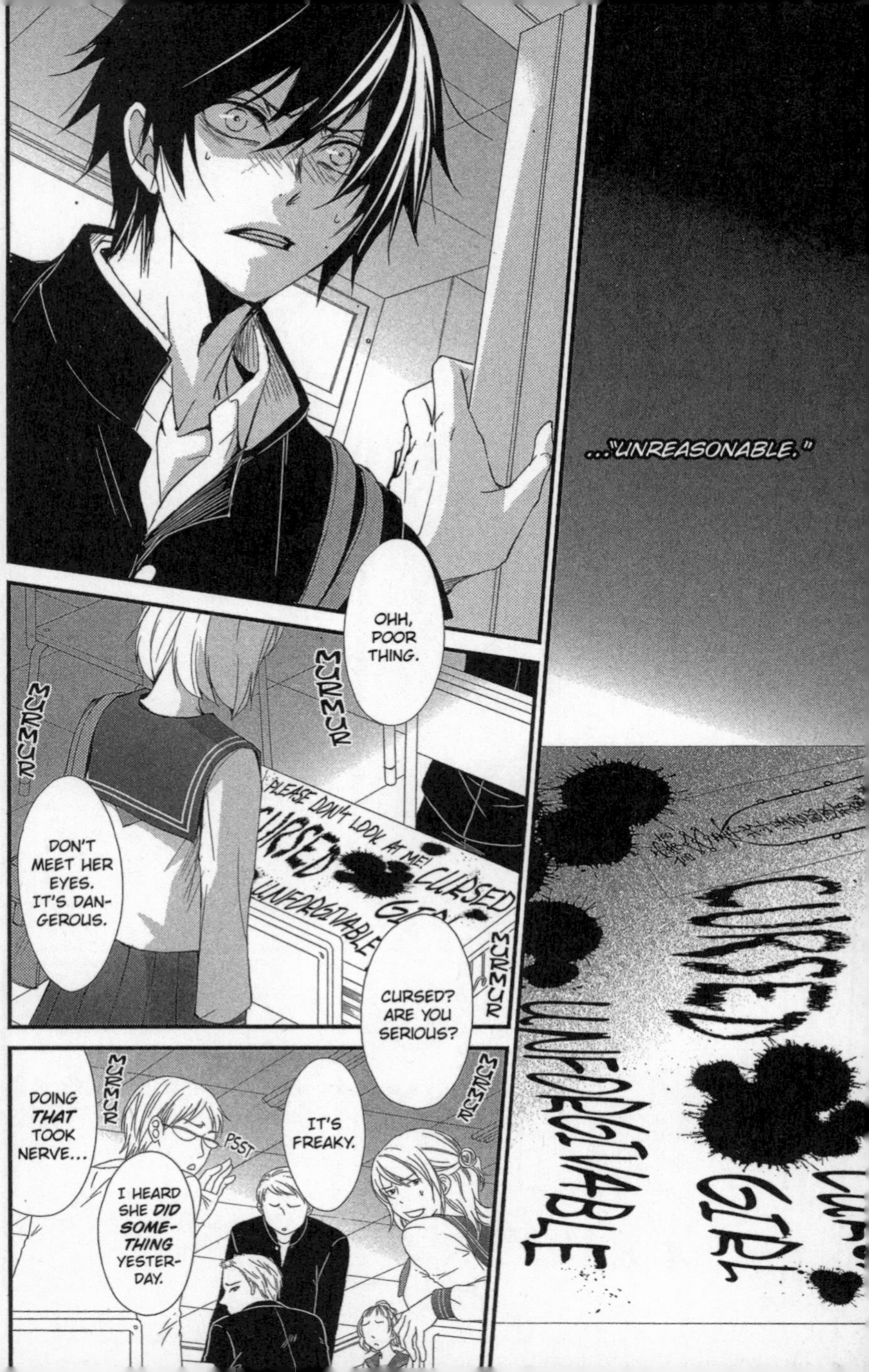
..."UNREASONABLE."
CURSED
GIRL
UNFORGIVABLE
OHH, POOR THING.
MURMUR
MURMUR
PLEASE DON'T LOOK AT ME!
CURSED
CURSED GIRL
UNFORGIVABLE
DON'T MEET HER EYES. IT'S DANGEROUS.
CURSED? ARE YOU SERIOUS?
MURMUR
MURMUR
IT'S FREAKY.
MURMUR
DOING *THAT* TOOK NERVE...
PSST
I HEARD SHE *DID SOMETHING* YESTERDAY.

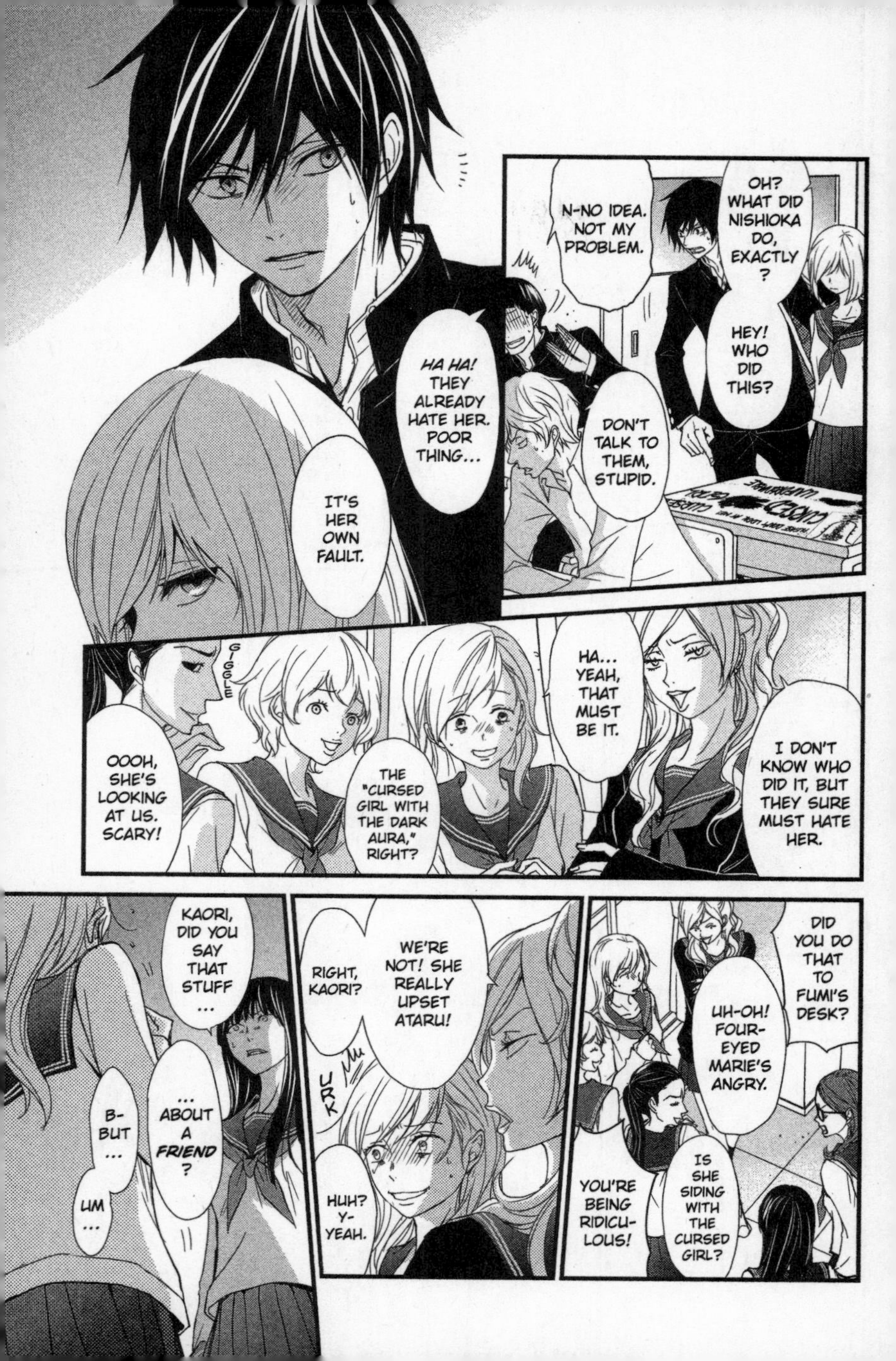
OH? WHAT DID NISHIOKA DO, EXACTLY?
N-NO IDEA. NOT MY PROBLEM.
HEY! WHO DID THIS?
DON'T TALK TO THEM, STUPID.
HA HA! THEY ALREADY HATE HER. POOR THING...
IT'S HER OWN FAULT.
I DON'T KNOW WHO DID IT, BUT THEY SURE MUST HATE HER.
HA... YEAH, THAT MUST BE IT.
THE "CURSED GIRL WITH THE DARK AURA," RIGHT?
GIGGLE
OOOH, SHE'S LOOKING AT US. SCARY!
DID YOU DO THAT TO FUMI'S DESK?
UH-OH! FOUR-EYED MARIE'S ANGRY.
IS SHE SIDING WITH THE CURSED GIRL?
YOU'RE BEING RIDICULOUS!
WE'RE NOT! SHE REALLY UPSET ATARU!
RIGHT, KAORI?
URK
HUH? Y-YEAH.
KAORI, DID YOU SAY THAT STUFF...
...ABOUT A *FRIEND*?
B-BUT...
UM...

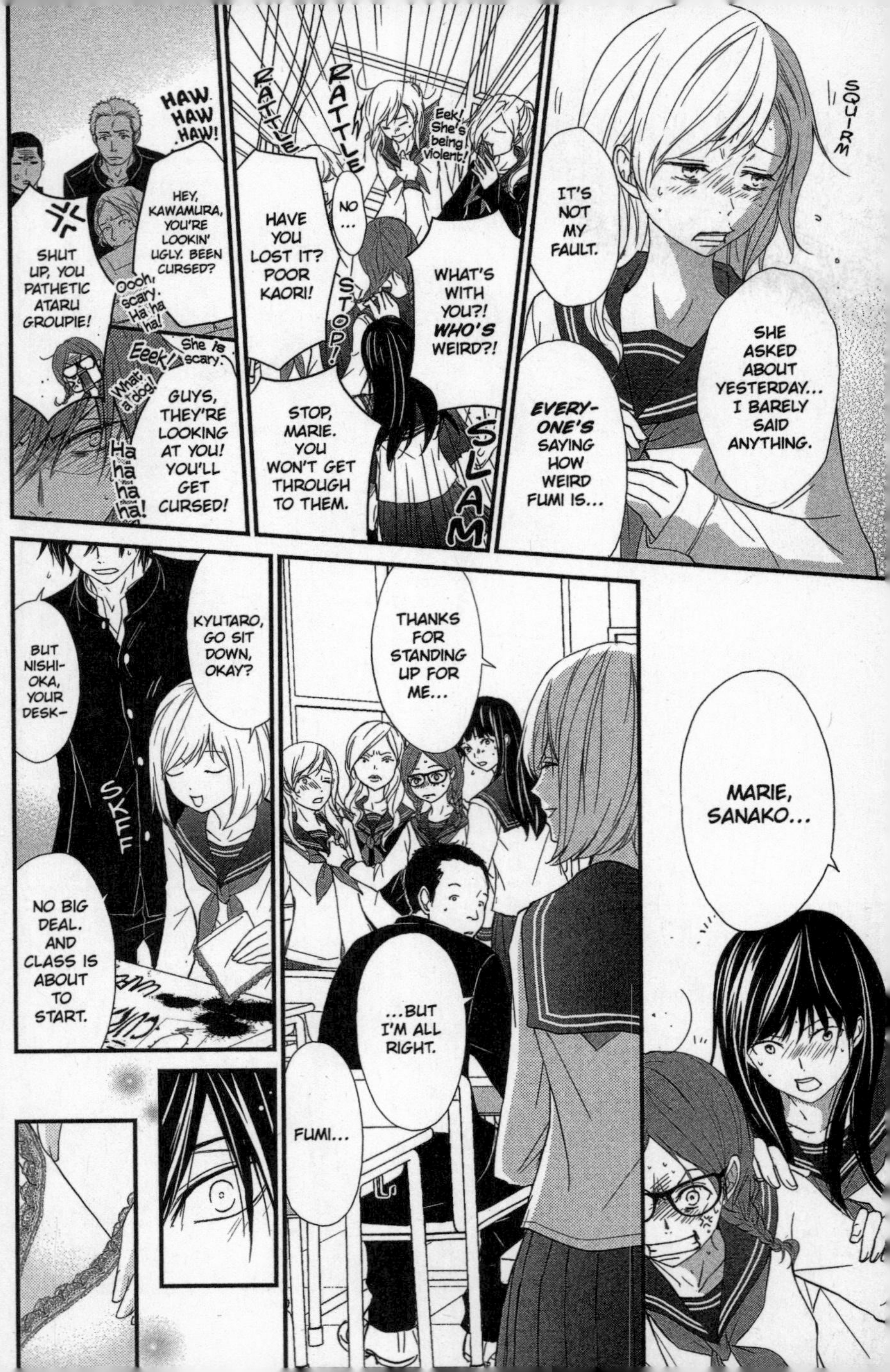
SQUIRM
IT'S NOT MY FAULT.
SHE ASKED ABOUT YESTERDAY... I BARELY SAID ANYTHING.
EVERY-ONE'S SAYING HOW WEIRD FUMI IS...
RATTLE
RATTLE
Eek! She's being violent!
WHAT'S WITH YOU?! WHO'S WEIRD?!
NO...
HAVE YOU LOST IT? POOR KAORI!
STOP!
STOP, MARIE. YOU WON'T GET THROUGH TO THEM.
SLAM
HAW HAW HAW!
HEY, KAWAMURA, YOU'RE LOOKIN' UGLY. BEEN CURSED?
SHUT UP, YOU PATHETIC ATARU GROUPIE!
Oook, scary. Ha ha ha!
She is scary.
Eeek!
What a dog!
GUYS, THEY'RE LOOKING AT YOU! YOU'LL GET CURSED!
Ha ha ha ha!
MARIE, SANAKO...
THANKS FOR STANDING UP FOR ME...
...BUT I'M ALL RIGHT.
FUMI...
KYUTARO, GO SIT DOWN, OKAY?
BUT NISHI-OKA, YOUR DESK—
SKFF
NO BIG DEAL. AND CLASS IS ABOUT TO START.

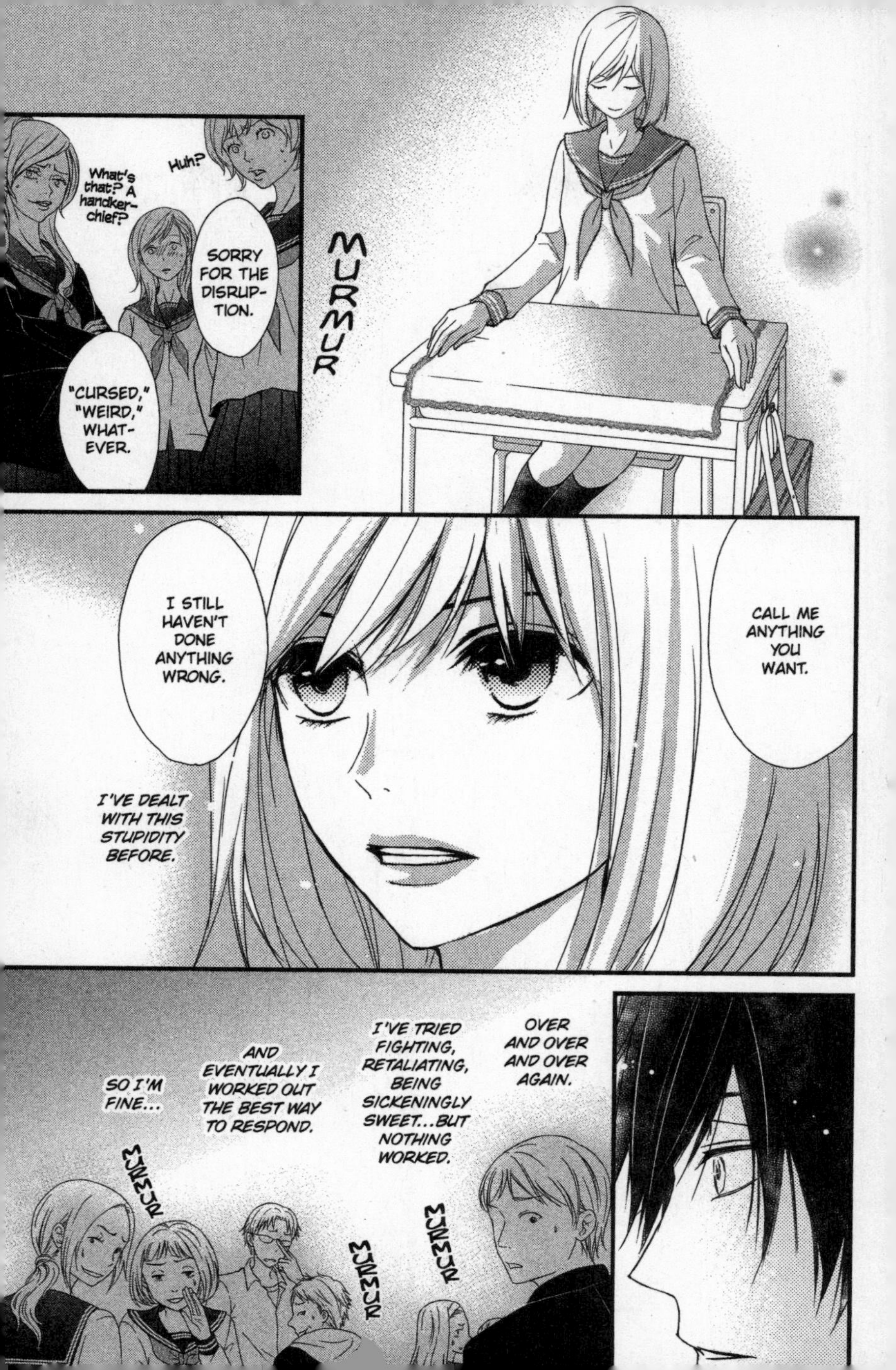
MURMUR
Huh?
SORRY FOR THE DISRUPTION.
What's that? A handkerchief?
"CURSED," "WEIRD," WHATEVER.
CALL ME ANYTHING YOU WANT.
I STILL HAVEN'T DONE ANYTHING WRONG.
I'VE DEALT WITH THIS STUPIDITY BEFORE.
OVER AND OVER AND OVER AGAIN.
I'VE TRIED FIGHTING, RETALIATING, BEING SICKENINGLY SWEET...BUT NOTHING WORKED.
AND EVENTUALLY I WORKED OUT THE BEST WAY TO RESPOND.
SO I'M FINE...
MURMUR
MURMUR
MURMUR

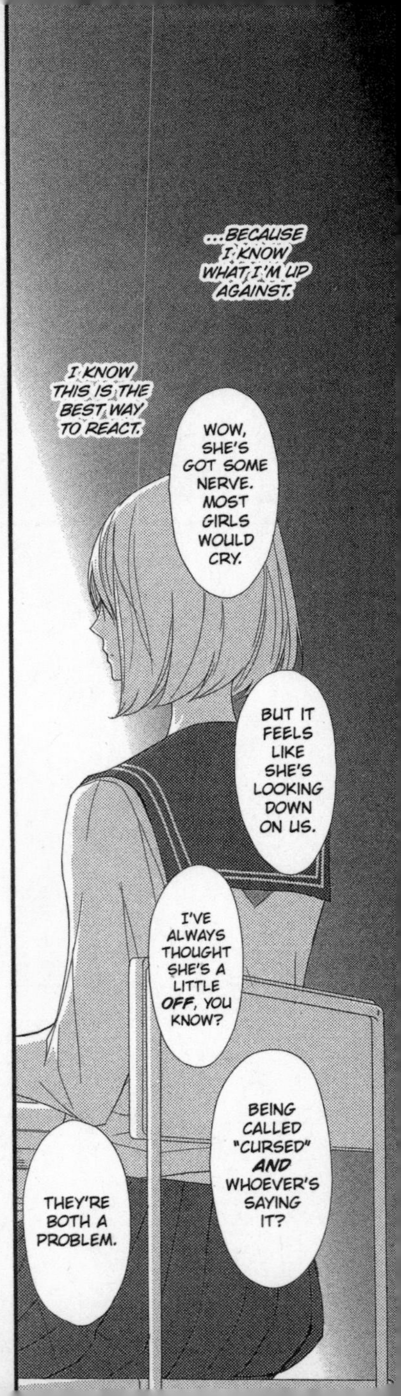
...BECAUSE I KNOW WHAT I'M UP AGAINST.
I KNOW THIS IS THE BEST WAY TO REACT.
WOW, SHE'S GOT SOME NERVE. MOST GIRLS WOULD CRY.
BUT IT FEELS LIKE SHE'S LOOKING DOWN ON US.
I'VE ALWAYS THOUGHT SHE'S A LITTLE **OFF**, YOU KNOW?
BEING CALLED "CURSED" **AND** WHOEVER'S SAYING IT?
THEY'RE BOTH A PROBLEM.
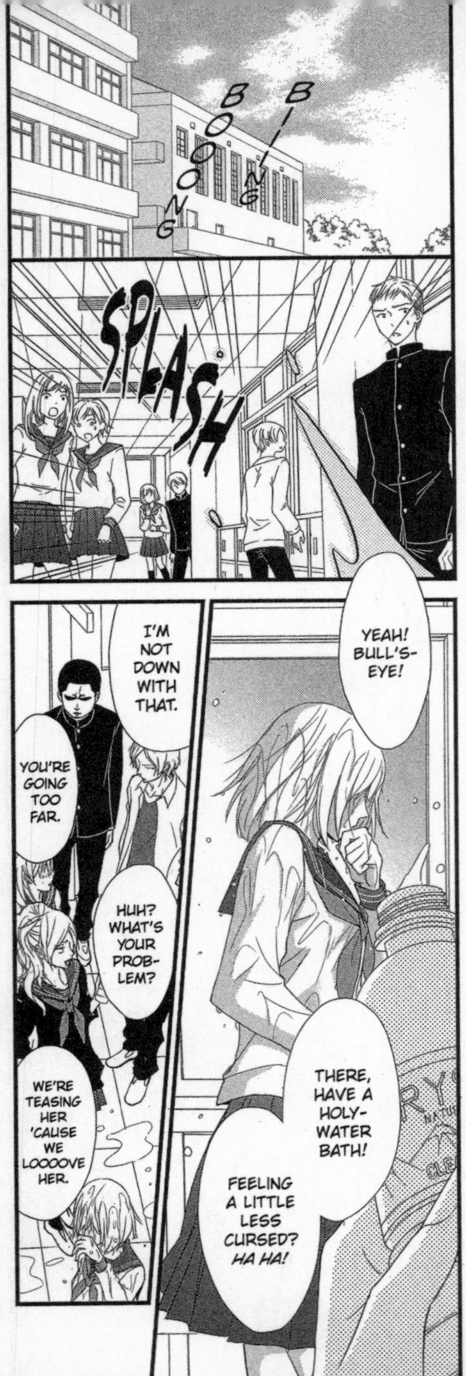
BIIING
BOOONG
SPLASH
YEAH! BULL'S-EYE!
THERE, HAVE A HOLY-WATER BATH!
FEELING A LITTLE LESS CURSED? *HA HA!*
I'M NOT DOWN WITH THAT.
YOU'RE GOING TOO FAR.
HUH? WHAT'S YOUR PROB-LEM?
WE'RE TEASING HER 'CAUSE WE LOOOOVE HER.

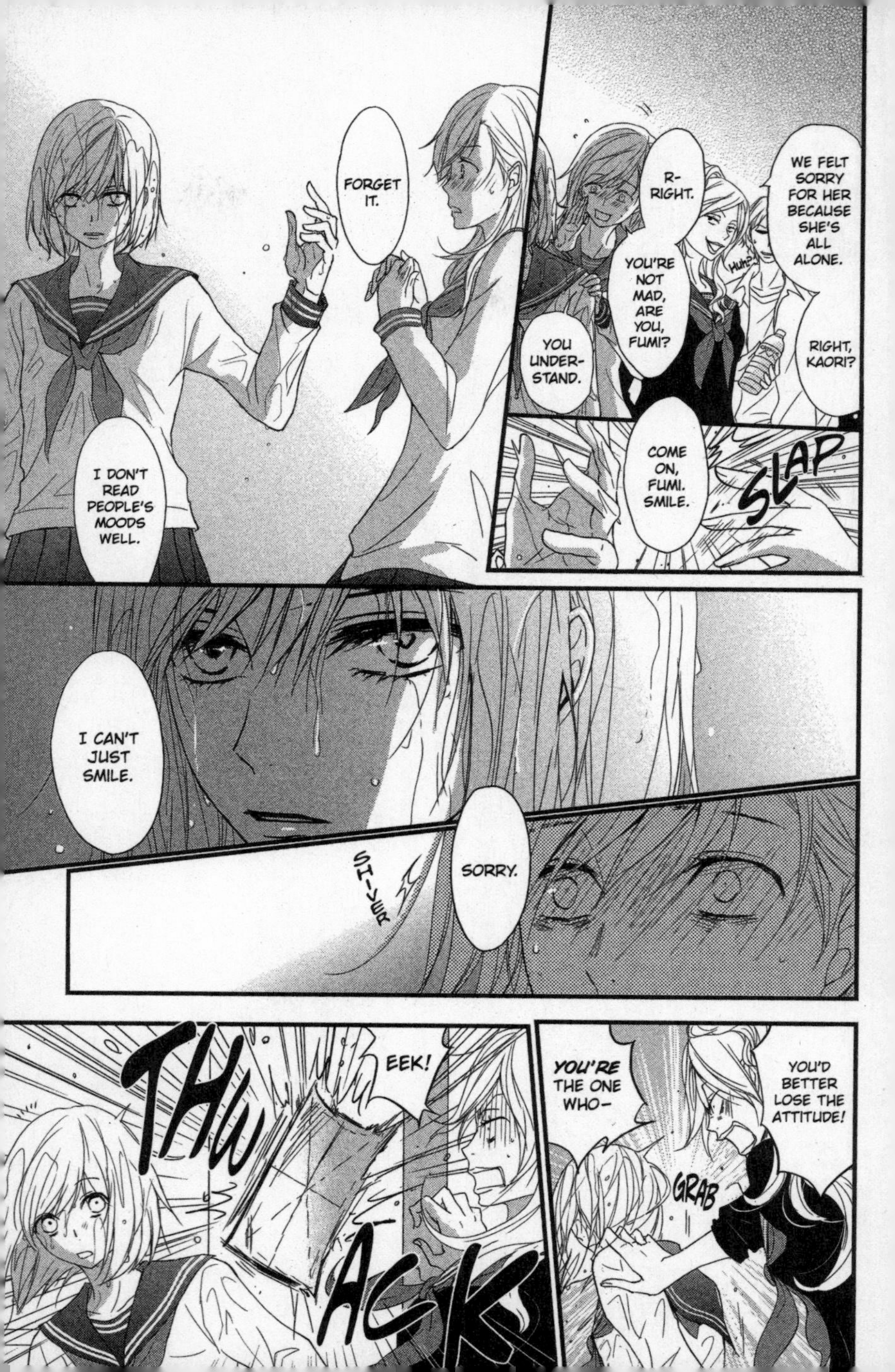

WE FELT SORRY FOR HER BECAUSE SHE'S ALL ALONE.
RIGHT, KAORI?
Huh?
R-RIGHT.
YOU'RE NOT MAD, ARE YOU, FUMI?
YOU UNDERSTAND.
COME ON, FUMI. SMILE.
SLAP
FORGET IT.
I DON'T READ PEOPLE'S MOODS WELL.
I CAN'T JUST SMILE.
SORRY.
SHIVER
YOU'D BETTER LOSE THE ATTITUDE!
YOU'RE THE ONE WHO-
GRAB
EEK!
THWACK

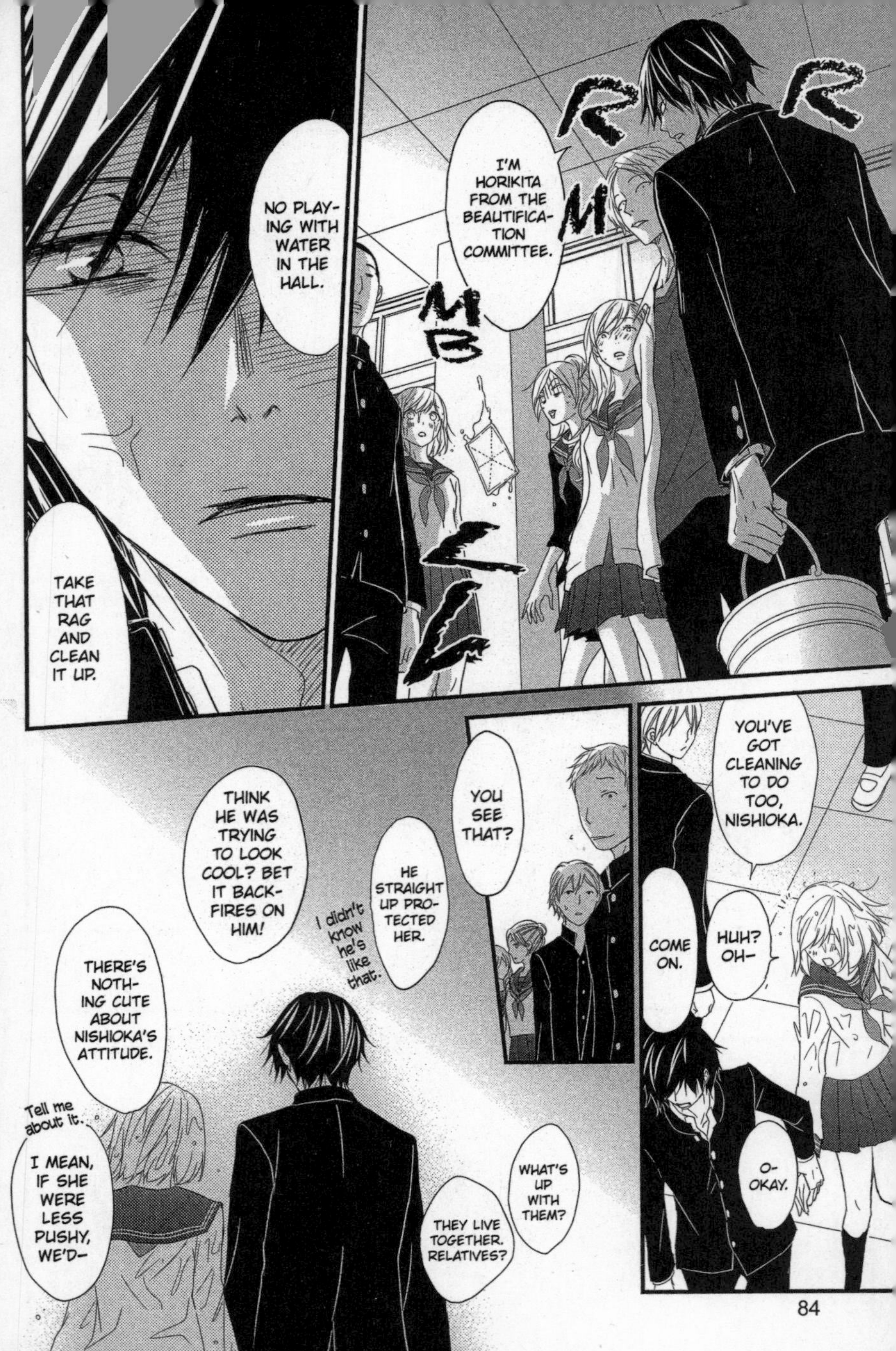
I'M HORIKITA FROM THE BEAUTIFICATION COMMITTEE.
NO PLAYING WITH WATER IN THE HALL.
TAKE THAT RAG AND CLEAN IT UP.
YOU'VE GOT CLEANING TO DO TOO, NISHIOKA.
HUH? OH-
COME ON.
O-OKAY.
YOU SEE THAT?
HE STRAIGHT UP PROTECTED HER.
I didn't know he's like that.
THINK HE WAS TRYING TO LOOK COOL? BET IT BACKFIRES ON HIM!
THERE'S NOTHING CUTE ABOUT NISHIOKA'S ATTITUDE.
WHAT'S UP WITH THEM?
THEY LIVE TOGETHER. RELATIVES?
Tell me about it.
I MEAN, IF SHE WERE LESS PUSHY, WE'D-

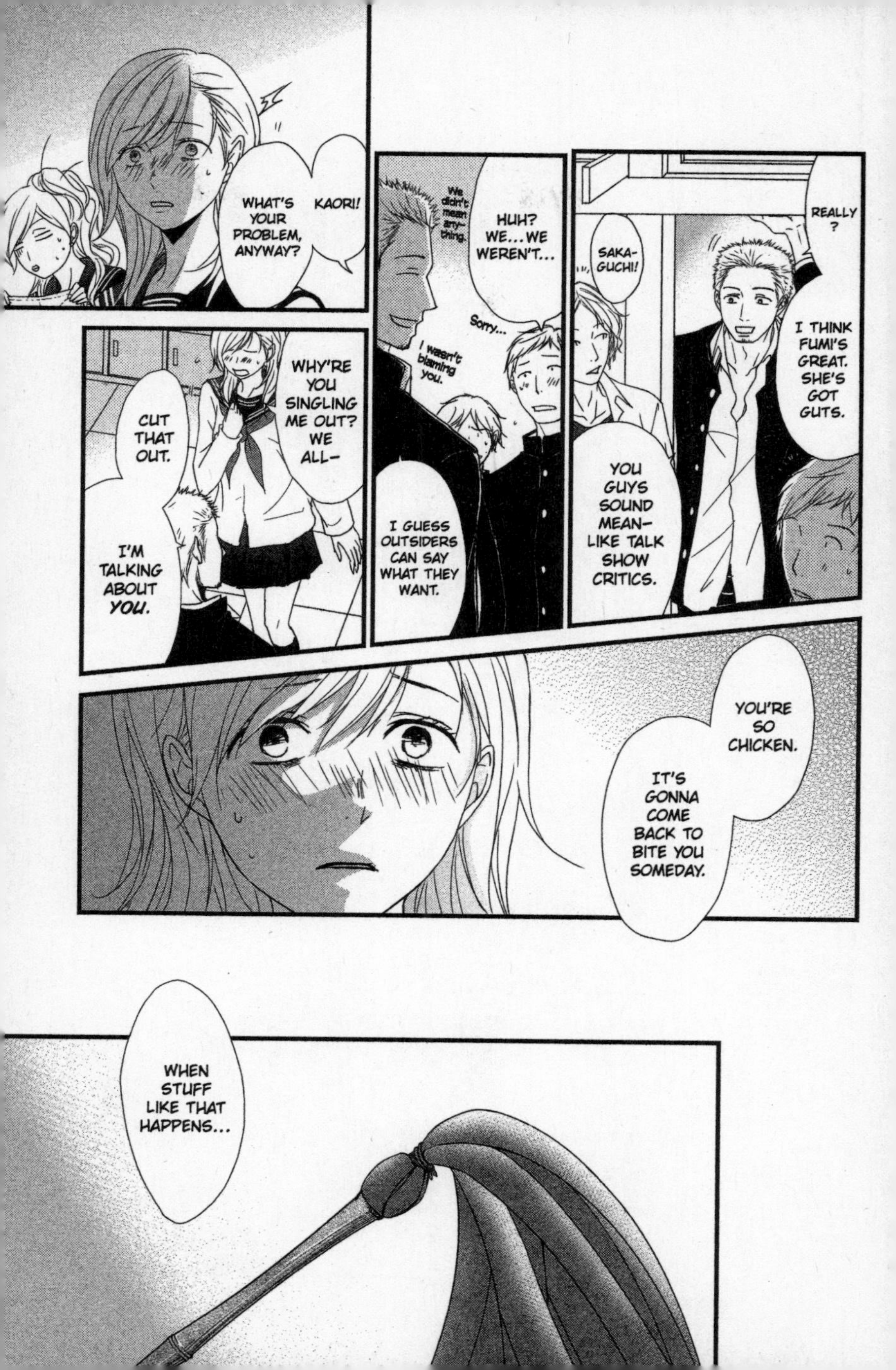

REALLY?
I THINK FUMI'S GREAT. SHE'S GOT GUTS.
SAKA-GUCHI!
YOU GUYS SOUND MEAN-LIKE TALK SHOW CRITICS.
HUH? WE...WE WEREN'T...
We didn't mean any-thing.
Sorry...
I wasn't blaming you.
I GUESS OUTSIDERS CAN SAY WHAT THEY WANT.
KAORI!
WHAT'S YOUR PROBLEM, ANYWAY?
WHY'RE YOU SINGLING ME OUT? WE ALL-
CUT THAT OUT.
I'M TALKING ABOUT *YOU*.
YOU'RE SO CHICKEN.
IT'S GONNA COME BACK TO BITE YOU SOMEDAY.
WHEN STUFF LIKE THAT HAPPENS...

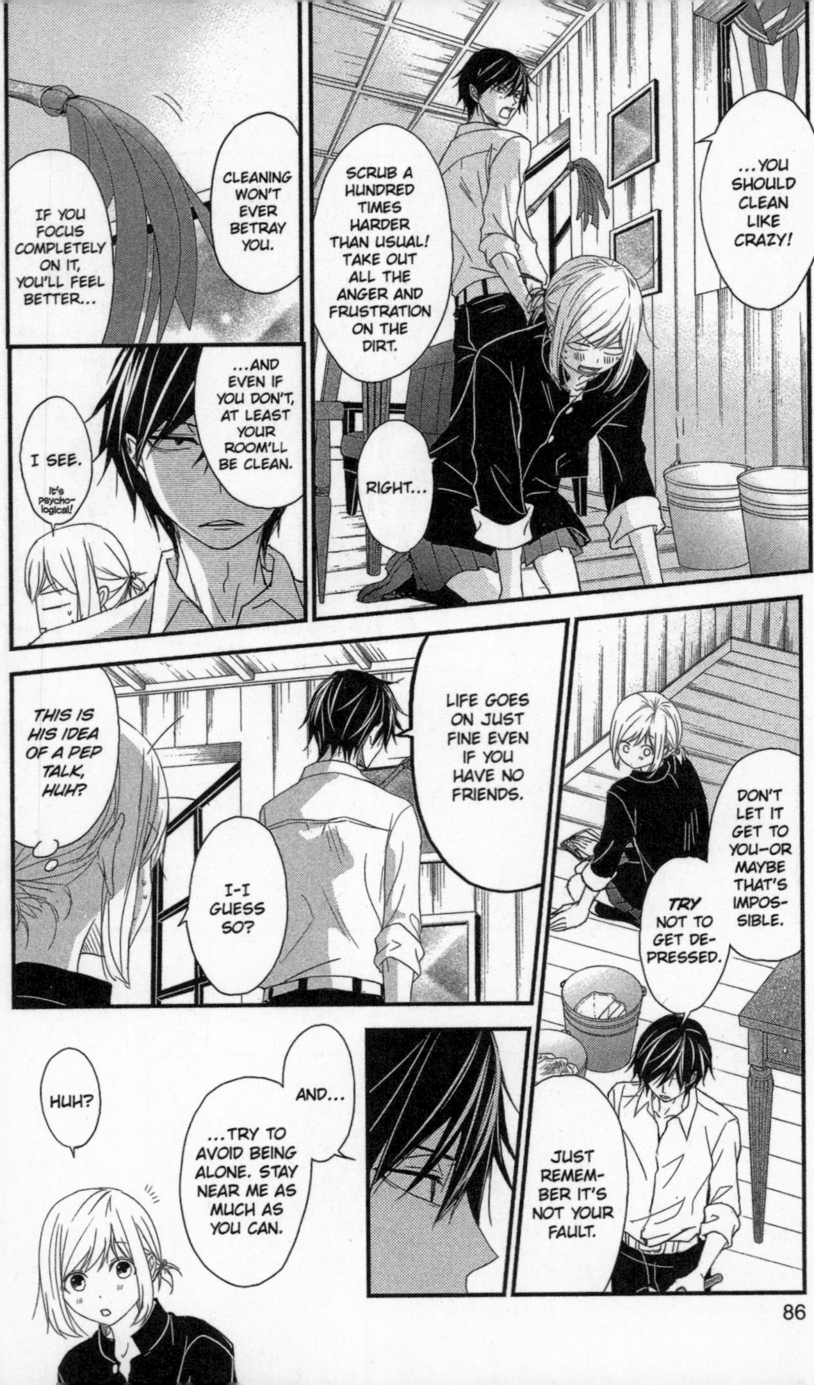
...YOU SHOULD CLEAN LIKE CRAZY!
SCRUB A HUNDRED TIMES HARDER THAN USUAL! TAKE OUT ALL THE ANGER AND FRUSTRATION ON THE DIRT.
RIGHT...
CLEANING WON'T EVER BETRAY YOU.
IF YOU FOCUS COMPLETELY ON IT, YOU'LL FEEL BETTER...
...AND EVEN IF YOU DON'T, AT LEAST YOUR ROOM'LL BE CLEAN.
I SEE.
It's psychological!
DON'T LET IT GET TO YOU—OR MAYBE THAT'S IMPOSSIBLE.
TRY NOT TO GET DEPRESSED.
JUST REMEMBER IT'S NOT YOUR FAULT.
LIFE GOES ON JUST FINE EVEN IF YOU HAVE NO FRIENDS.
I-I GUESS SO?
THIS IS HIS IDEA OF A PEP TALK, HUH?
AND...
...TRY TO AVOID BEING ALONE. STAY NEAR ME AS MUCH AS YOU CAN.
HUH?

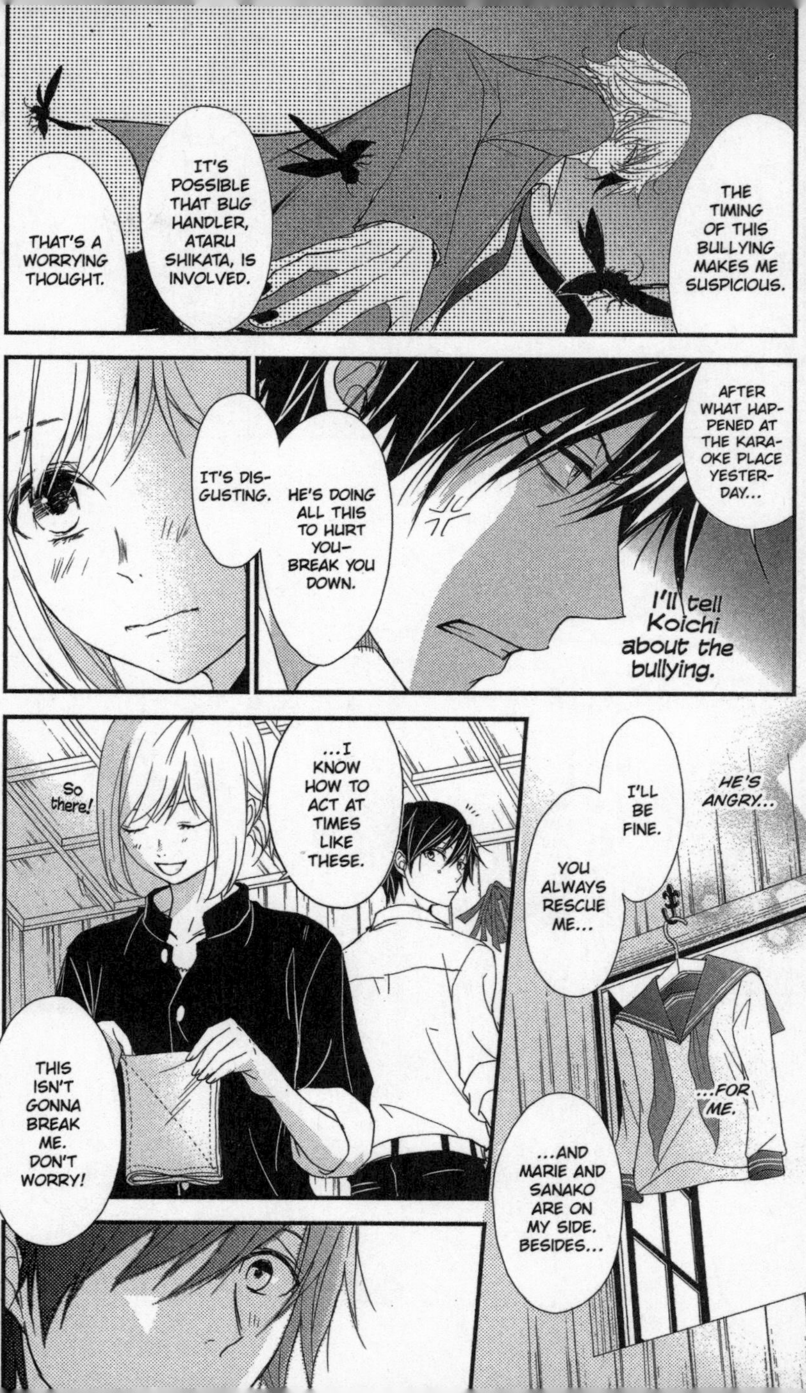

THE TIMING OF THIS BULLYING MAKES ME SUSPICIOUS.
IT'S POSSIBLE THAT BUG HANDLER, ATARU SHIKATA, IS INVOLVED.
THAT'S A WORRYING THOUGHT.
AFTER WHAT HAPPENED AT THE KARAOKE PLACE YESTERDAY...
I'll tell Koichi about the bullying.
HE'S DOING ALL THIS TO HURT YOU—BREAK YOU DOWN.
IT'S DISGUSTING.
HE'S ANGRY...
I'LL BE FINE.
YOU ALWAYS RESCUE ME...
...FOR ME.
...AND MARIE AND SANAKO ARE ON MY SIDE. BESIDES...
...I KNOW HOW TO ACT AT TIMES LIKE THESE.
So there!
THIS ISN'T GONNA BREAK ME. DON'T WORRY!

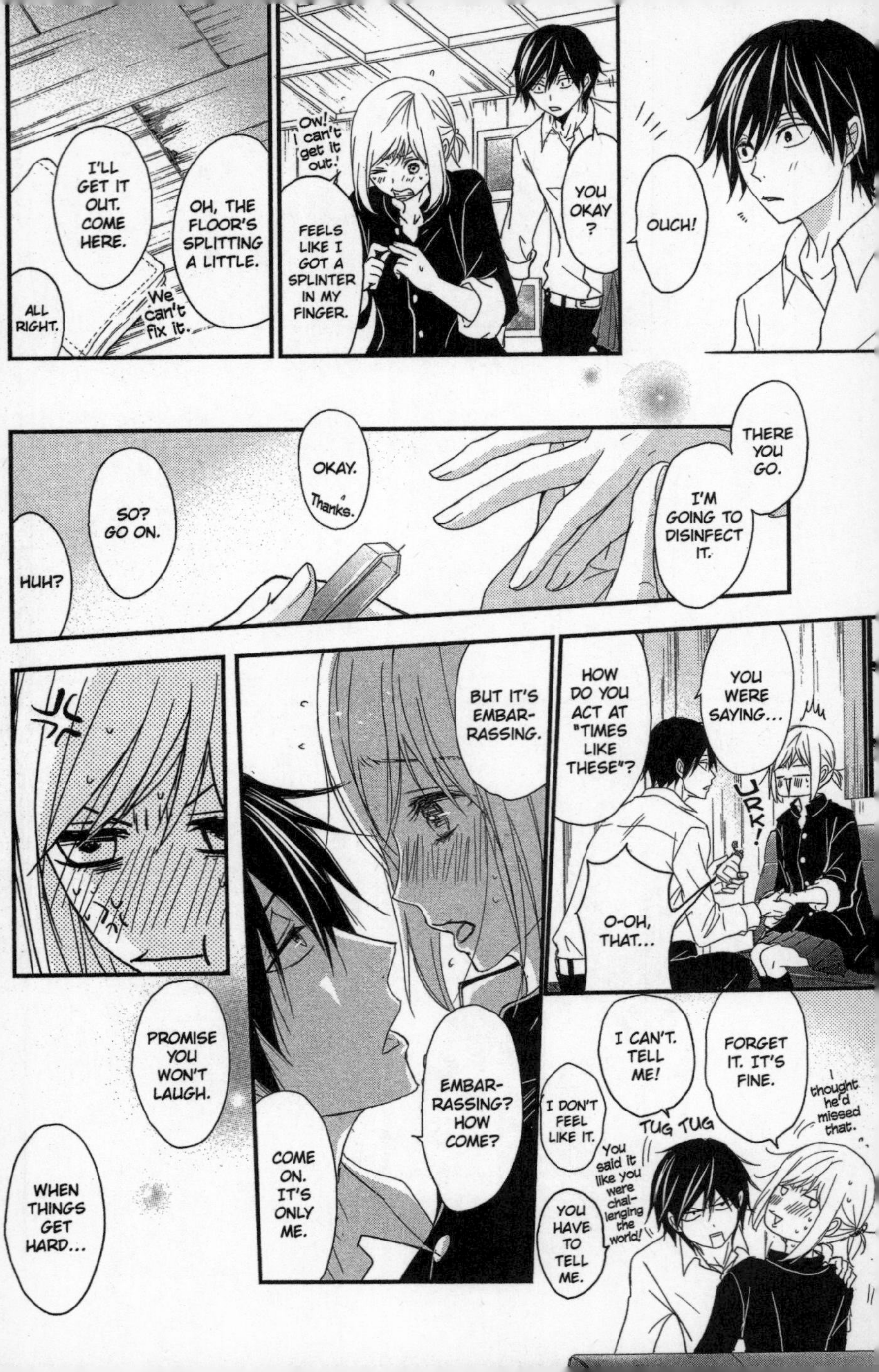
OUCH!
YOU OKAY?
Ow! I can't get it out!
FEELS LIKE I GOT A SPLINTER IN MY FINGER.
OH, THE FLOOR'S SPLITTING A LITTLE.
We can't fix it.
I'LL GET IT OUT. COME HERE.
ALL RIGHT.
THERE YOU GO.
I'M GOING TO DISINFECT IT.
OKAY.
Thanks.
SO? GO ON.
HUH?
YOU WERE SAYING...
URK!
HOW DO YOU ACT AT "TIMES LIKE THESE"?
O-OH, THAT...
FORGET IT. IT'S FINE.
I thought he'd missed that.
I CAN'T. TELL ME!
TUG TUG
I DON'T FEEL LIKE IT.
You said it like you were challenging the world!
YOU HAVE TO TELL ME.
BUT IT'S EMBARRASSING.
EMBARRASSING? HOW COME?
COME ON. IT'S ONLY ME.
PROMISE YOU WON'T LAUGH.
WHEN THINGS GET HARD...

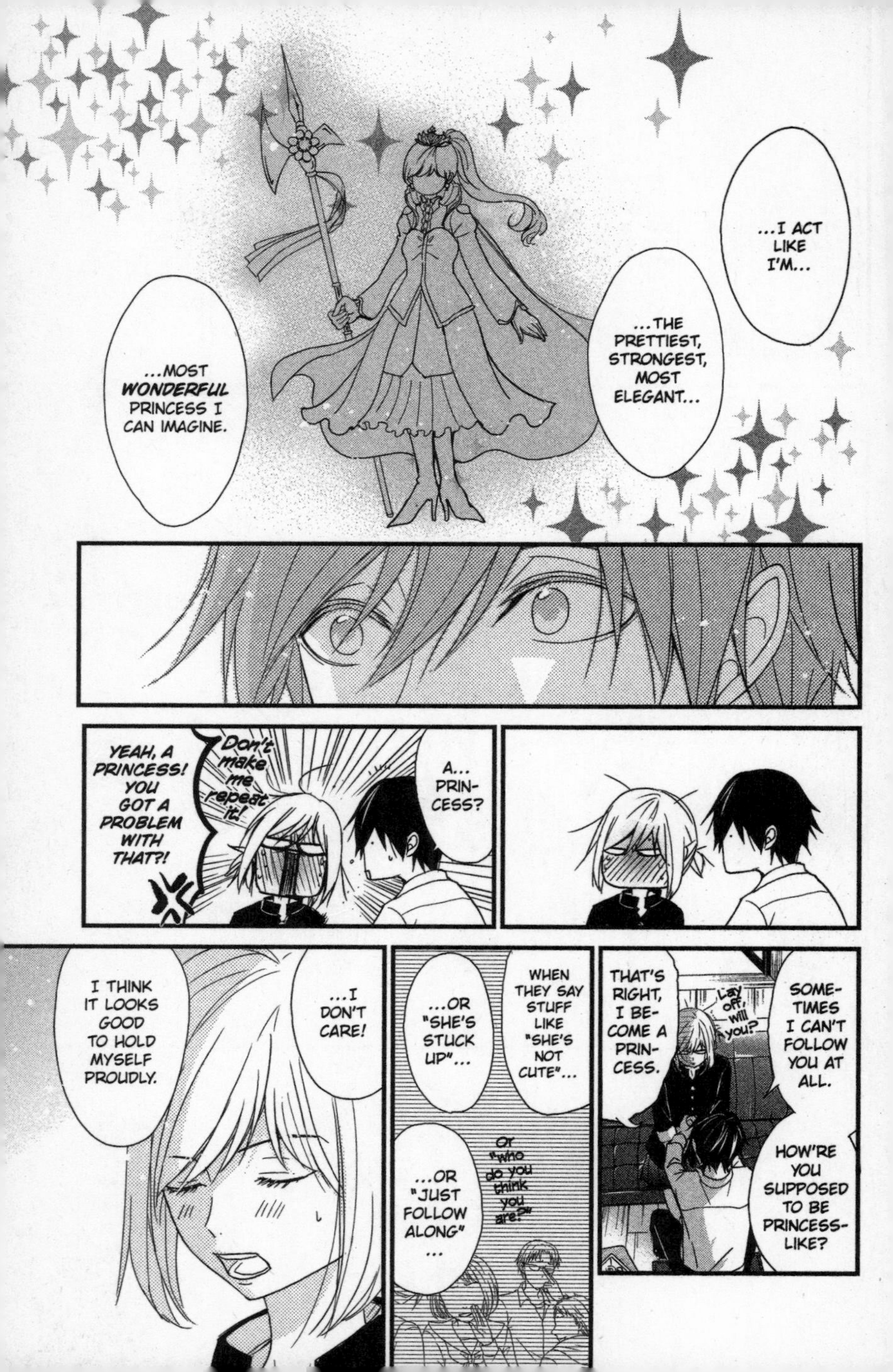
...I ACT LIKE I'M...
...THE PRETTIEST, STRONGEST, MOST ELEGANT...
...MOST WONDERFUL PRINCESS I CAN IMAGINE.
A... PRIN-CESS?
Don't make me repeat it!
YEAH, A PRINCESS! YOU GOT A PROBLEM WITH THAT?!
SOME-TIMES I CAN'T FOLLOW YOU AT ALL.
HOW'RE YOU SUPPOSED TO BE PRINCESS-LIKE?
Lay off, will you?
THAT'S RIGHT, I BE-COME A PRIN-CESS.
WHEN THEY SAY STUFF LIKE "SHE'S NOT CUTE"...
...OR "SHE'S STUCK UP"...
Or "who do you think you are?"
...OR "JUST FOLLOW ALONG"...
...I DON'T CARE!
I THINK IT LOOKS GOOD TO HOLD MYSELF PROUDLY.

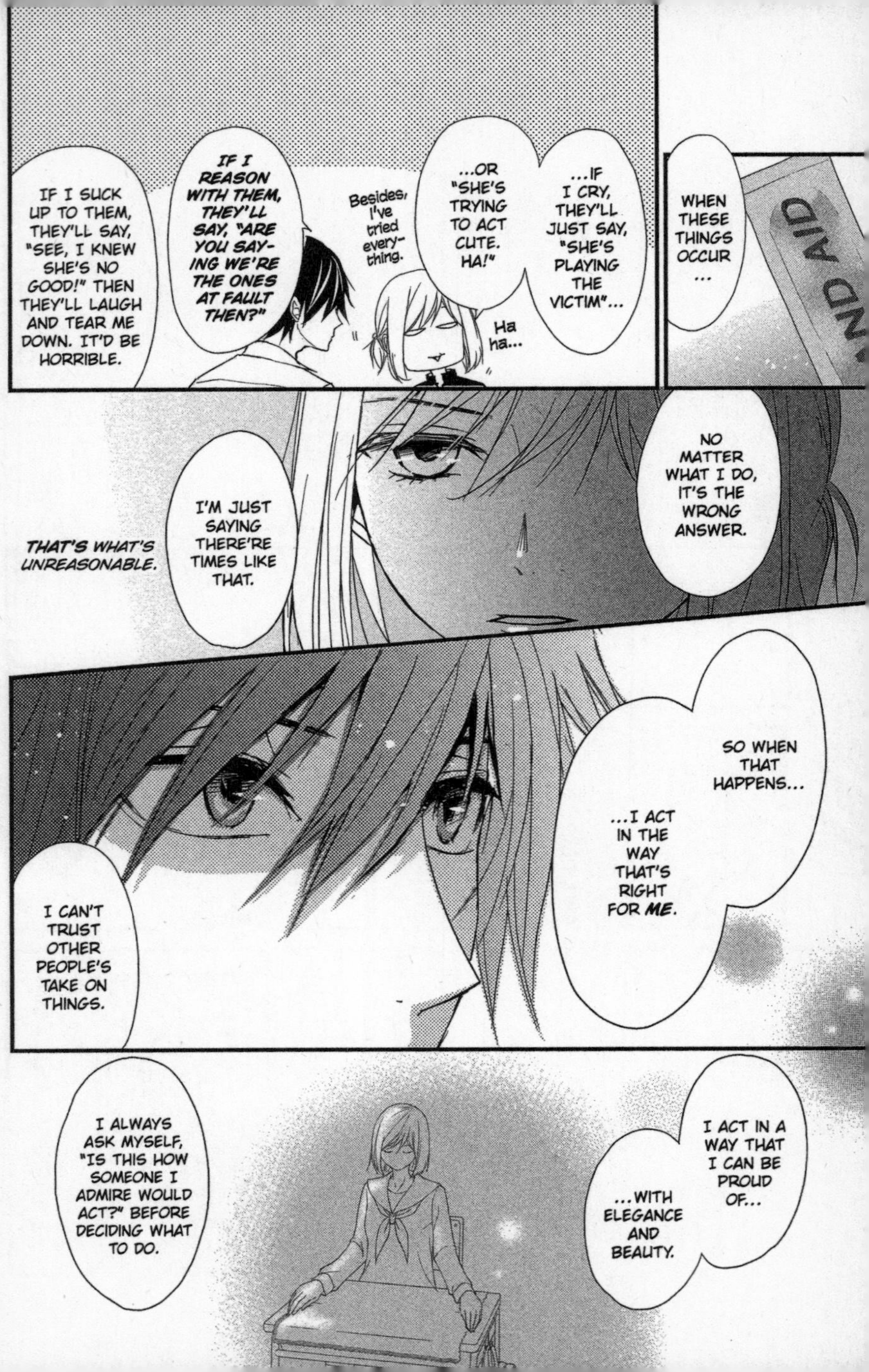
WHEN THESE THINGS OCCUR...
...IF I CRY, THEY'LL JUST SAY, "SHE'S PLAYING THE VICTIM"...
...OR "SHE'S TRYING TO ACT CUTE. HA!"
Ha ha...
Besides, I've tried every-thing.
IF I REASON WITH THEM, THEY'LL SAY, "ARE YOU SAY-ING WE'RE THE ONES AT FAULT THEN?"
IF I SUCK UP TO THEM, THEY'LL SAY, "SEE, I KNEW SHE'S NO GOOD!" THEN THEY'LL LAUGH AND TEAR ME DOWN. IT'D BE HORRIBLE.
NO MATTER WHAT I DO, IT'S THE WRONG ANSWER.
I'M JUST SAYING THERE'RE TIMES LIKE THAT.
THAT'S WHAT'S UNREASONABLE.
SO WHEN THAT HAPPENS...
...I ACT IN THE WAY THAT'S RIGHT FOR ME.
I CAN'T TRUST OTHER PEOPLE'S TAKE ON THINGS.
I ACT IN A WAY THAT I CAN BE PROUD OF...
...WITH ELEGANCE AND BEAUTY.
I ALWAYS ASK MYSELF, "IS THIS HOW SOMEONE I ADMIRE WOULD ACT?" BEFORE DECIDING WHAT TO DO.

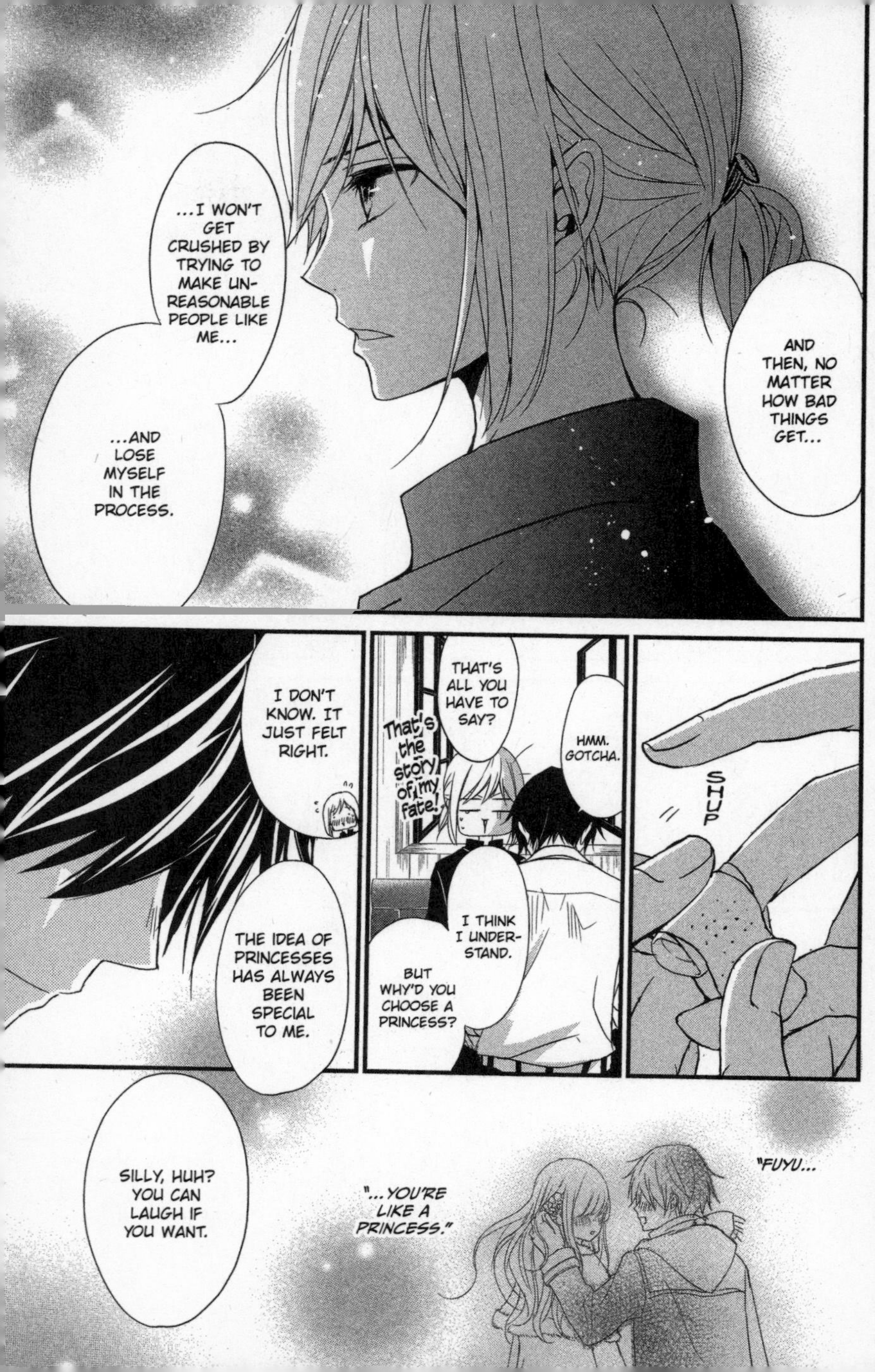
AND THEN, NO MATTER HOW BAD THINGS GET...
...I WON'T GET CRUSHED BY TRYING TO MAKE UN-REASONABLE PEOPLE LIKE ME...
...AND LOSE MYSELF IN THE PROCESS.
SHUP
HMM. GOTCHA.
THAT'S ALL YOU HAVE TO SAY?
That's the story of my fate!
I THINK I UNDER-STAND.
BUT WHY'D YOU CHOOSE A PRINCESS?
I DON'T KNOW. IT JUST FELT RIGHT.
THE IDEA OF PRINCESSES HAS ALWAYS BEEN SPECIAL TO ME.
"FUYU...
"...YOU'RE LIKE A PRINCESS."
SILLY, HUH? YOU CAN LAUGH IF YOU WANT.

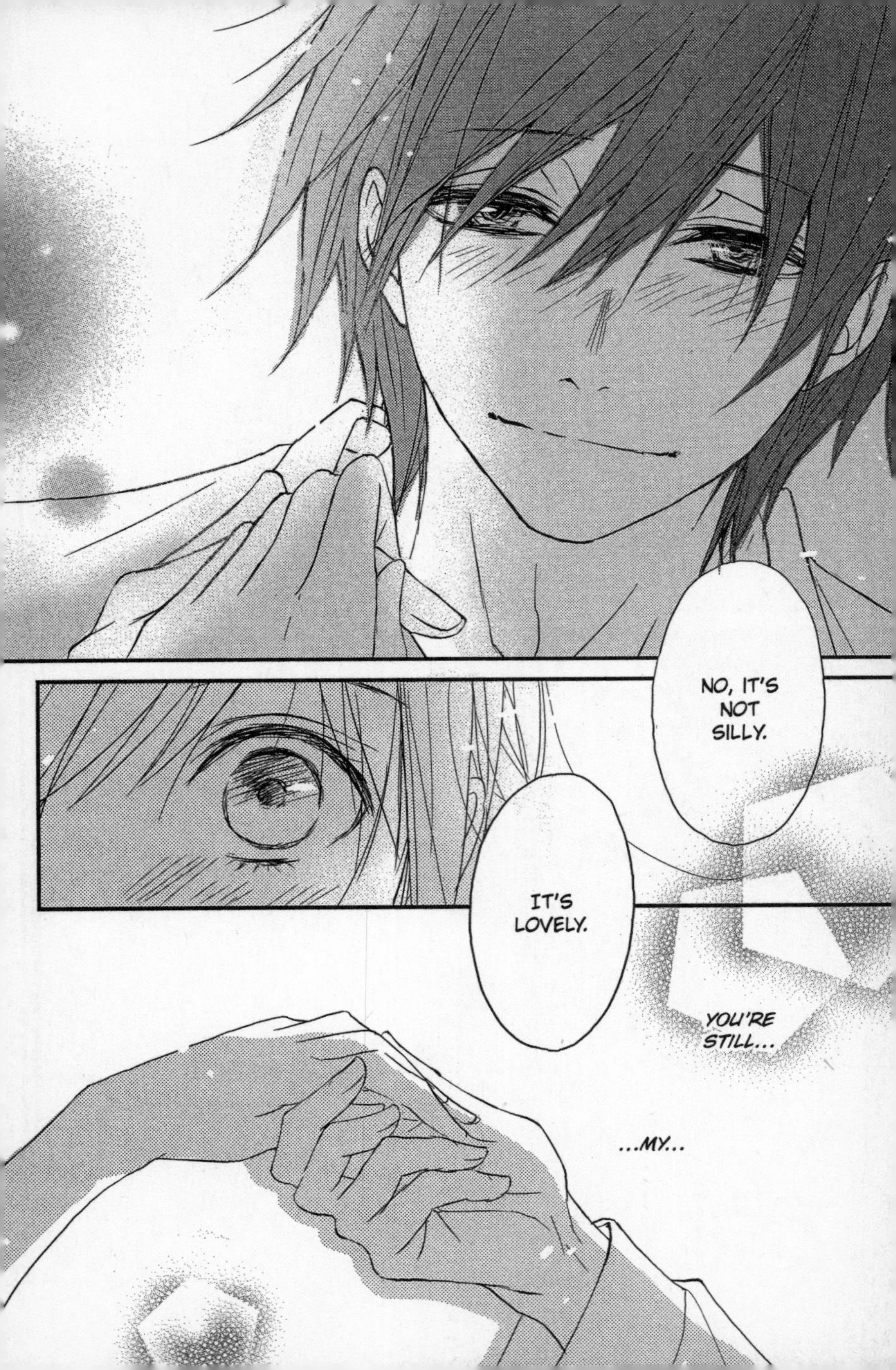
NO, IT'S NOT SILLY.
IT'S LOVELY.
YOU'RE STILL...
...MY...

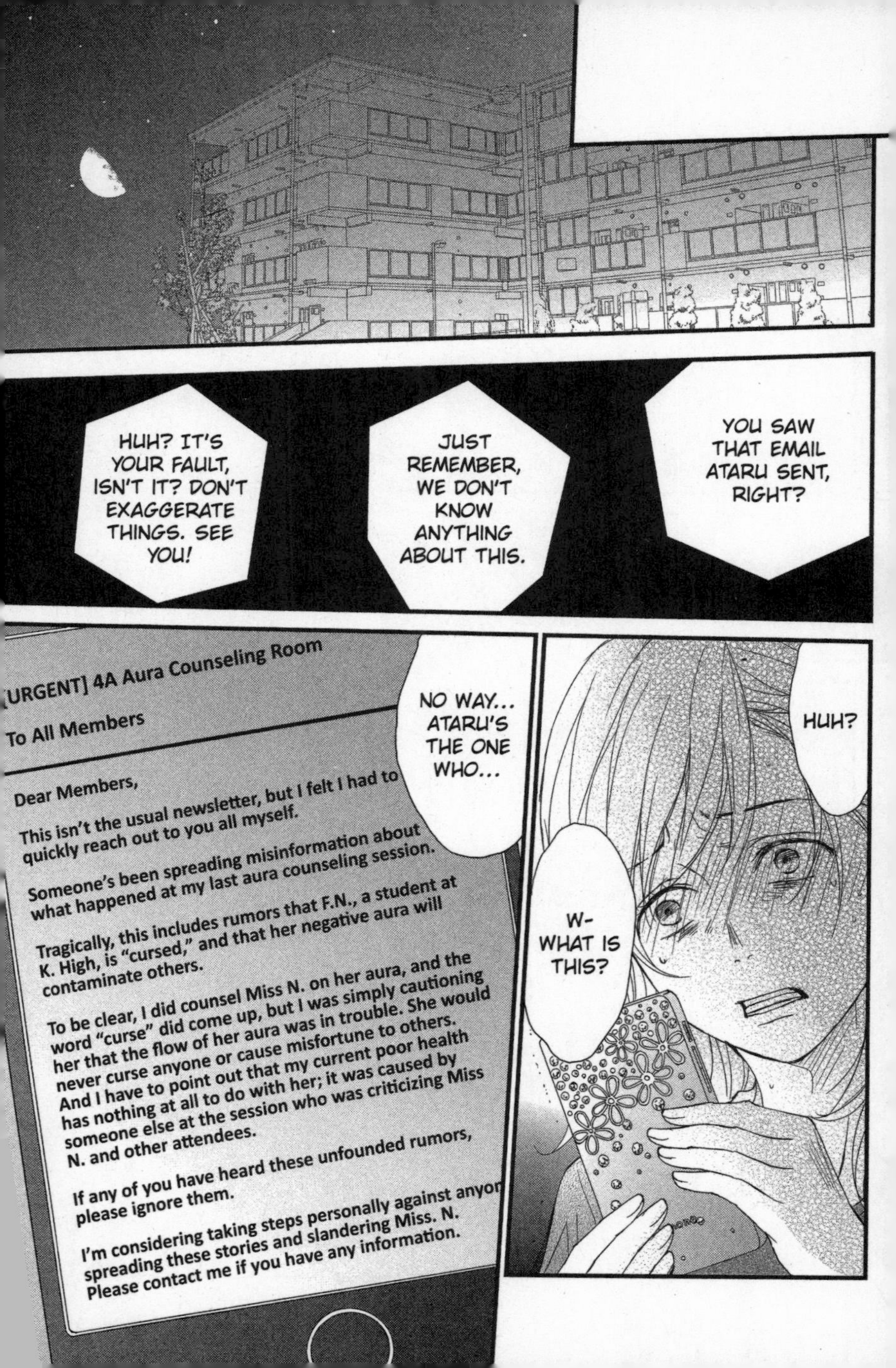
YOU SAW THAT EMAIL ATARU SENT, RIGHT?
JUST REMEMBER, WE DON'T KNOW ANYTHING ABOUT THIS.
HUH? IT'S YOUR FAULT, ISN'T IT? DON'T EXAGGERATE THINGS. SEE YOU!
HUH?
W- WHAT IS THIS?
URGENT] 4A Aura Counseling Room
To All Members
Dear Members,
This isn't the usual newsletter, but I felt I had to quickly reach out to you all myself.
Someone's been spreading misinformation about what happened at my last aura counseling session.
Tragically, this includes rumors that F.N., a student at K. High, is "cursed," and that her negative aura will contaminate others.
To be clear, I did counsel Miss N. on her aura, and the word "curse" did come up, but I was simply cautioning her that the flow of her aura was in trouble. She would never curse anyone or cause misfortune to others. And I have to point out that my current poor health has nothing at all to do with her; it was caused by someone else at the session who was criticizing Miss N. and other attendees.
If any of you have heard these unfounded rumors, please ignore them.
I'm considering taking steps personally against anyon spreading these stories and slandering Miss. N. Please contact me if you have any information.
NO WAY... ATARU'S THE ONE WHO...

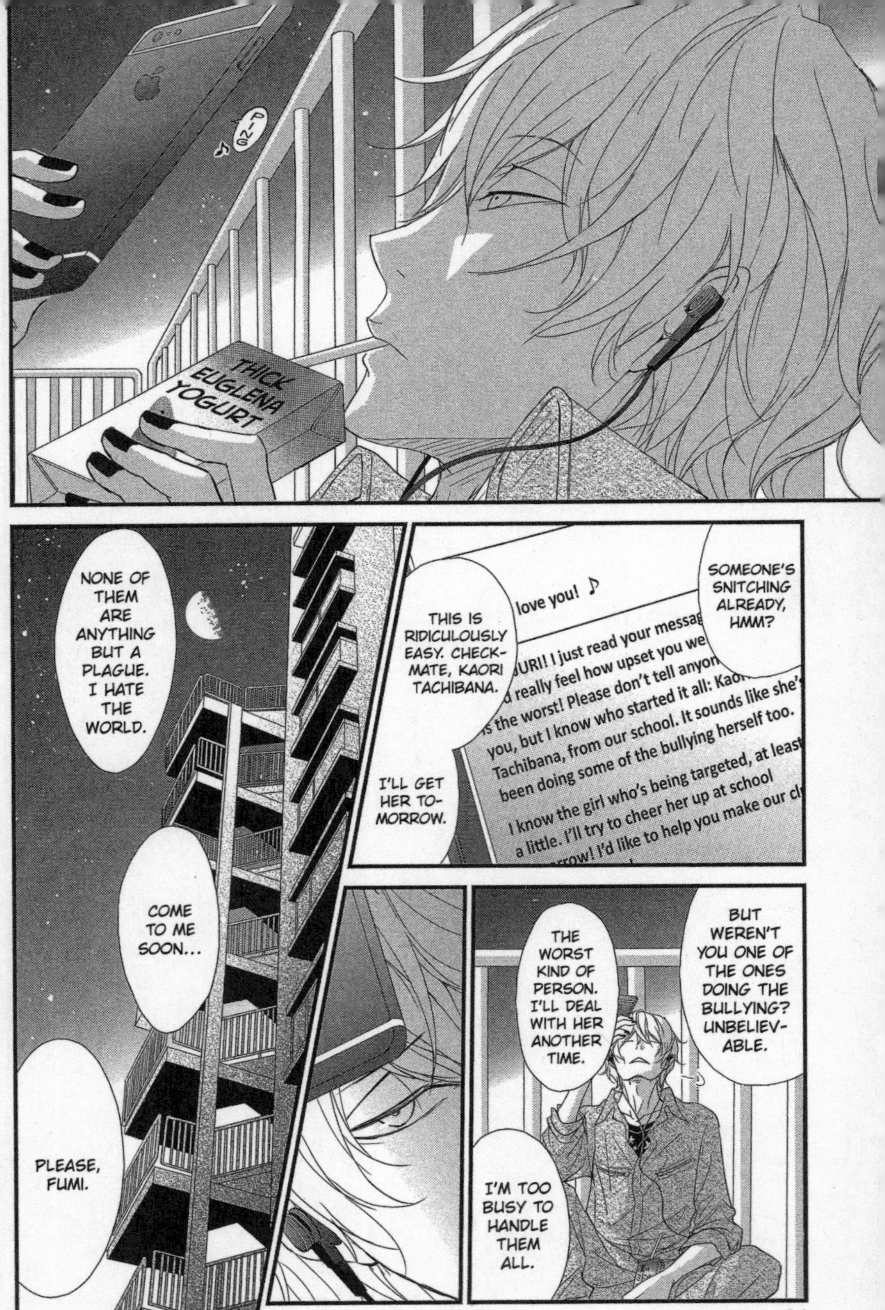
PING
THICK EUGLENA YOGURT
SOMEONE'S SNITCHING ALREADY, HMM?
love you! ♪
JURI! I just read your messag
d really feel how upset you we
is the worst! Please don't tell anyon
you, but I know who started it all: Kaor
Tachibana, from our school. It sounds like she's
been doing some of the bullying herself too.
I know the girl who's being targeted, at least
a little. I'll try to cheer her up at school
orrow! I'd like to help you make our cl
THIS IS RIDICULOUSLY EASY. CHECK-MATE, KAORI TACHIBANA.
I'LL GET HER TO-MORROW.
BUT WEREN'T YOU ONE OF THE ONES DOING THE BULLYING? UNBELIEV-ABLE.
THE WORST KIND OF PERSON. I'LL DEAL WITH HER ANOTHER TIME.
I'M TOO BUSY TO HANDLE THEM ALL.
NONE OF THEM ARE ANYTHING BUT A PLAGUE. I HATE THE WORLD.
COME TO ME SOON...
PLEASE, FUMI.

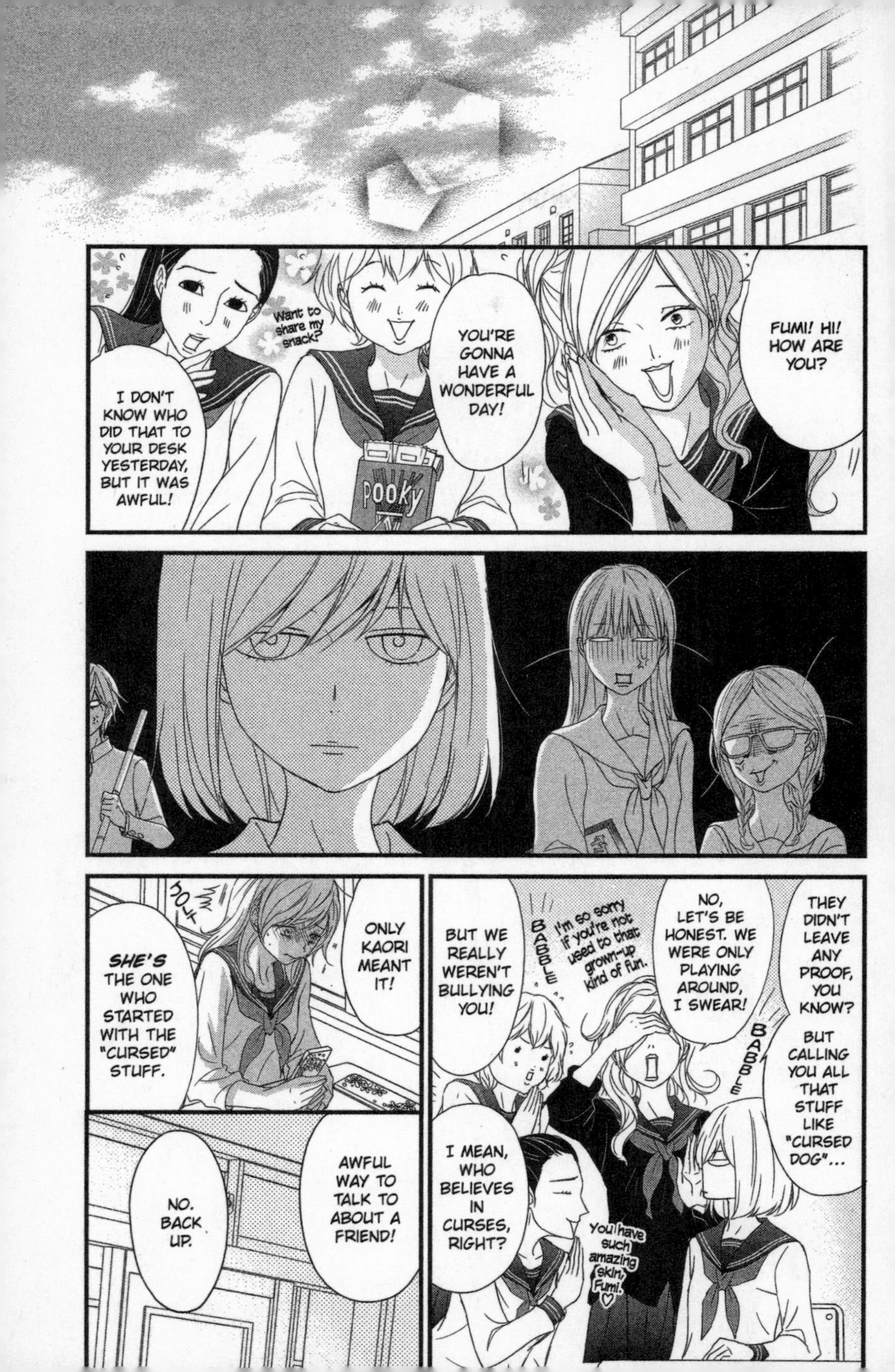
FUMI! HI! HOW ARE YOU?
YOU'RE GONNA HAVE A WONDERFUL DAY!
Want to share my snack?
pooky
I DON'T KNOW WHO DID THAT TO YOUR DESK YESTERDAY, BUT IT WAS AWFUL!
THEY DIDN'T LEAVE ANY PROOF, YOU KNOW?
BUT CALLING YOU ALL THAT STUFF LIKE "CURSED DOG"...
NO, LET'S BE HONEST. WE WERE ONLY PLAYING AROUND, I SWEAR!
BABBLE
I'm so sorry if you're not used to that grown-up kind of fun.
BABBLE
BUT WE REALLY WEREN'T BULLYING YOU!
I MEAN, WHO BELIEVES IN CURSES, RIGHT?
You have such amazing skin, Fumi. ♡
ONLY KAORI MEANT IT!
SHE'S THE ONE WHO STARTED WITH THE "CURSED" STUFF.
AWFUL WAY TO TALK TO ABOUT A FRIEND!
NO. BACK UP.

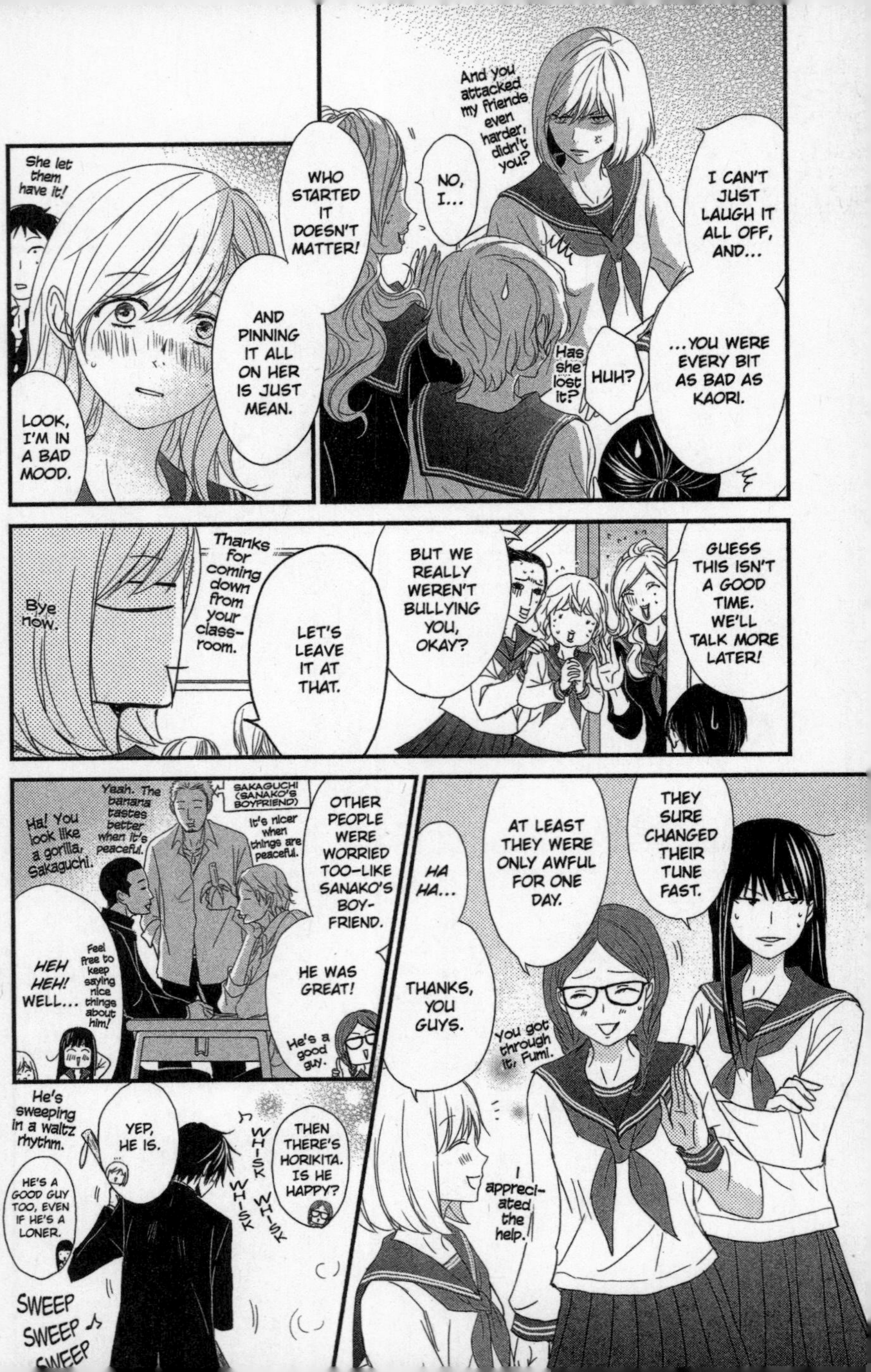

I CAN'T JUST LAUGH IT ALL OFF, AND...
And you attacked my friends even harder, didn't you?
NO, I...
...YOU WERE EVERY BIT AS BAD AS KAORI.
HUH?
Has she lost it?
WHO STARTED IT DOESN'T MATTER!
AND PINNING IT ALL ON HER IS JUST MEAN.
She let them have it!
LOOK, I'M IN A BAD MOOD.
GUESS THIS ISN'T A GOOD TIME. WE'LL TALK MORE LATER!
BUT WE REALLY WEREN'T BULLYING YOU, OKAY?
LET'S LEAVE IT AT THAT.
Thanks for coming down from your classroom.
Bye now.
THEY SURE CHANGED THEIR TUNE FAST.
AT LEAST THEY WERE ONLY AWFUL FOR ONE DAY.
HA HA...
THANKS, YOU GUYS.
You got through it, Fumi.
I appreciated the help.
OTHER PEOPLE WERE WORRIED TOO—LIKE SANAKO'S BOYFRIEND.
SAKAGUCHI (SANAKO'S BOYFRIEND)
It's nicer when things are peaceful.
Yeah. The banana tastes better when it's peaceful.
Ha! You look like a gorilla, Sakaguchi.
HE WAS GREAT!
He's a good guy.
Feel free to keep saying nice things about him!
HEH HEH! WELL...
THEN THERE'S HORIKITA. IS HE HAPPY?
WHISK WHISK
YEP, HE IS.
He's sweeping in a waltz rhythm.
HE'S A GOOD GUY TOO, EVEN IF HE'S A LONER.
SWEEP SWEEP SWEEP

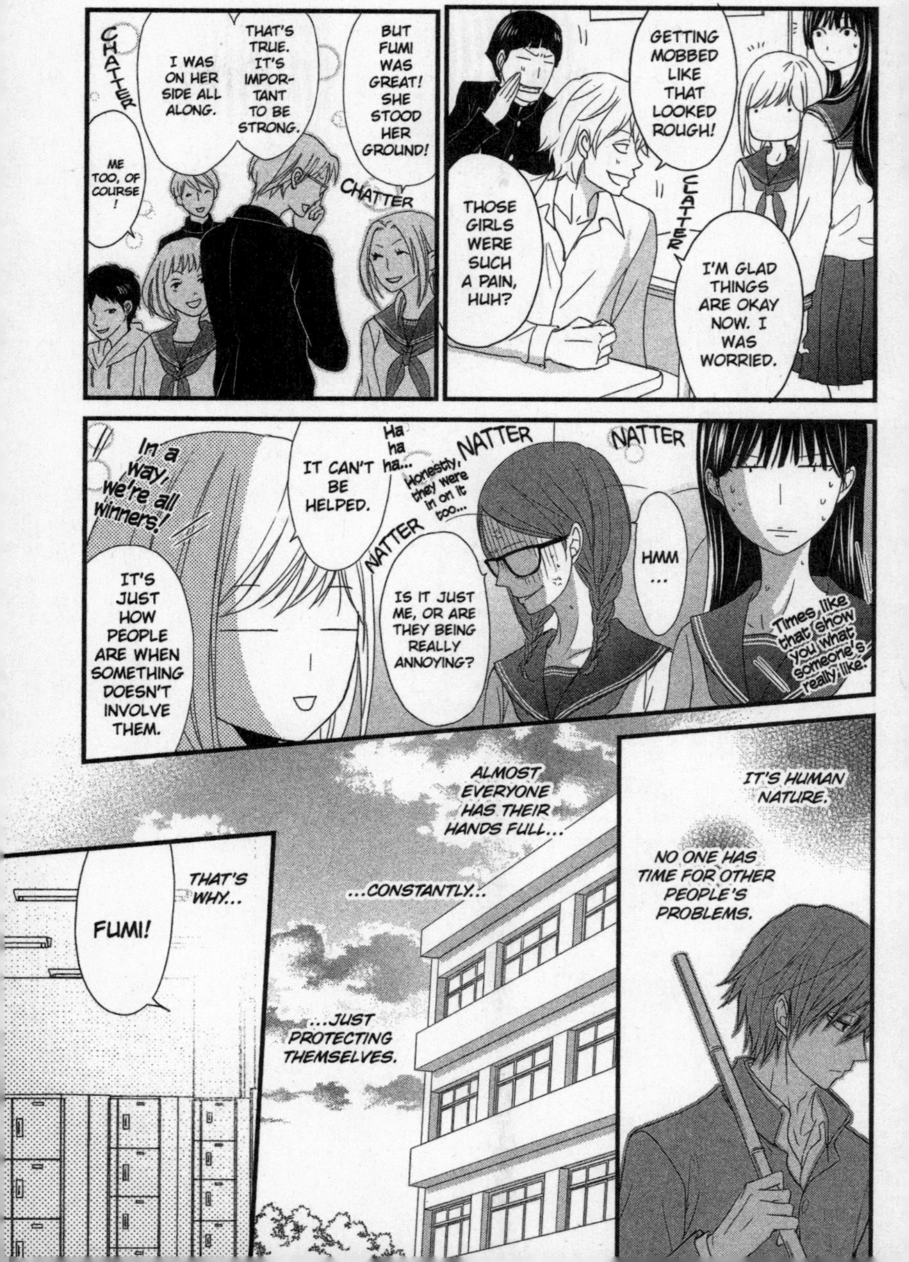
GETTING MOBBED LIKE THAT LOOKED ROUGH!
CLATTER
I'M GLAD THINGS ARE OKAY NOW. I WAS WORRIED.
THOSE GIRLS WERE SUCH A PAIN, HUH?
BUT FUMI WAS GREAT! SHE STOOD HER GROUND!
CHATTER
THAT'S TRUE. IT'S IMPORTANT TO BE STRONG.
I WAS ON HER SIDE ALL ALONG.
CHATTER
ME TOO, OF COURSE!
Times like that show you what someone's really like.
HMM...
NATTER
NATTER
IS IT JUST ME, OR ARE THEY BEING REALLY ANNOYING?
Honestly, they were in on it too...
NATTER
Ha ha ha...
IT CAN'T BE HELPED.
In a way, we're all winners!
IT'S JUST HOW PEOPLE ARE WHEN SOMETHING DOESN'T INVOLVE THEM.
IT'S HUMAN NATURE.
NO ONE HAS TIME FOR OTHER PEOPLE'S PROBLEMS.
ALMOST EVERYONE HAS THEIR HANDS FULL...
...CONSTANTLY...
...JUST PROTECTING THEMSELVES.
THAT'S WHY...
FUMI!

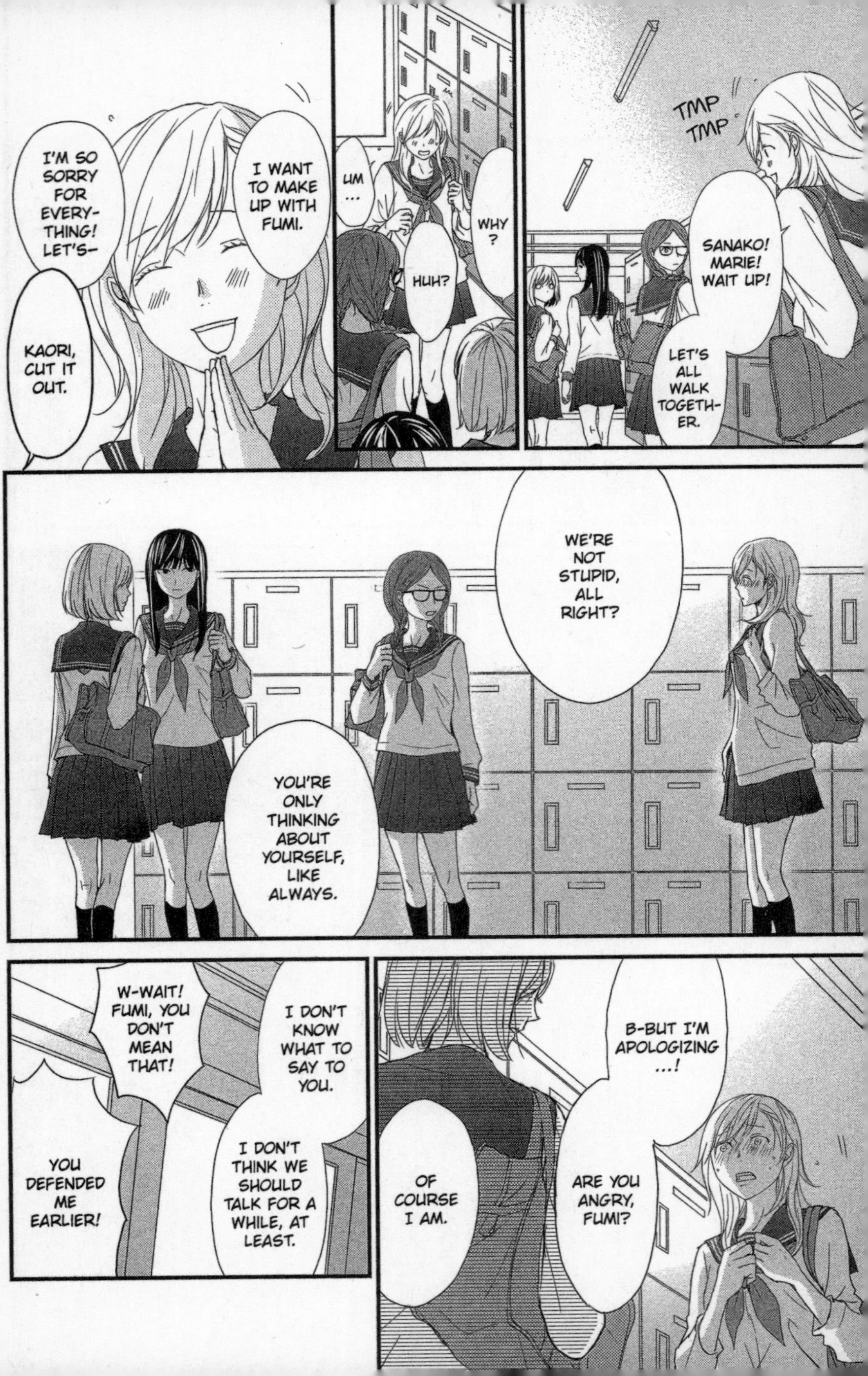
TMP TMP
SANAKO! MARIE! WAIT UP!
LET'S ALL WALK TOGETH-ER.
WHY?
UM ...
HUH?
I WANT TO MAKE UP WITH FUMI.
I'M SO SORRY FOR EVERY-THING! LET'S—
KAORI, CUT IT OUT.
WE'RE NOT STUPID, ALL RIGHT?
YOU'RE ONLY THINKING ABOUT YOURSELF, LIKE ALWAYS.
B-BUT I'M APOLOGIZING ...!
ARE YOU ANGRY, FUMI?
OF COURSE I AM.
I DON'T KNOW WHAT TO SAY TO YOU.
I DON'T THINK WE SHOULD TALK FOR A WHILE, AT LEAST.
W-WAIT! FUMI, YOU DON'T MEAN THAT!
YOU DEFENDED ME EARLIER!

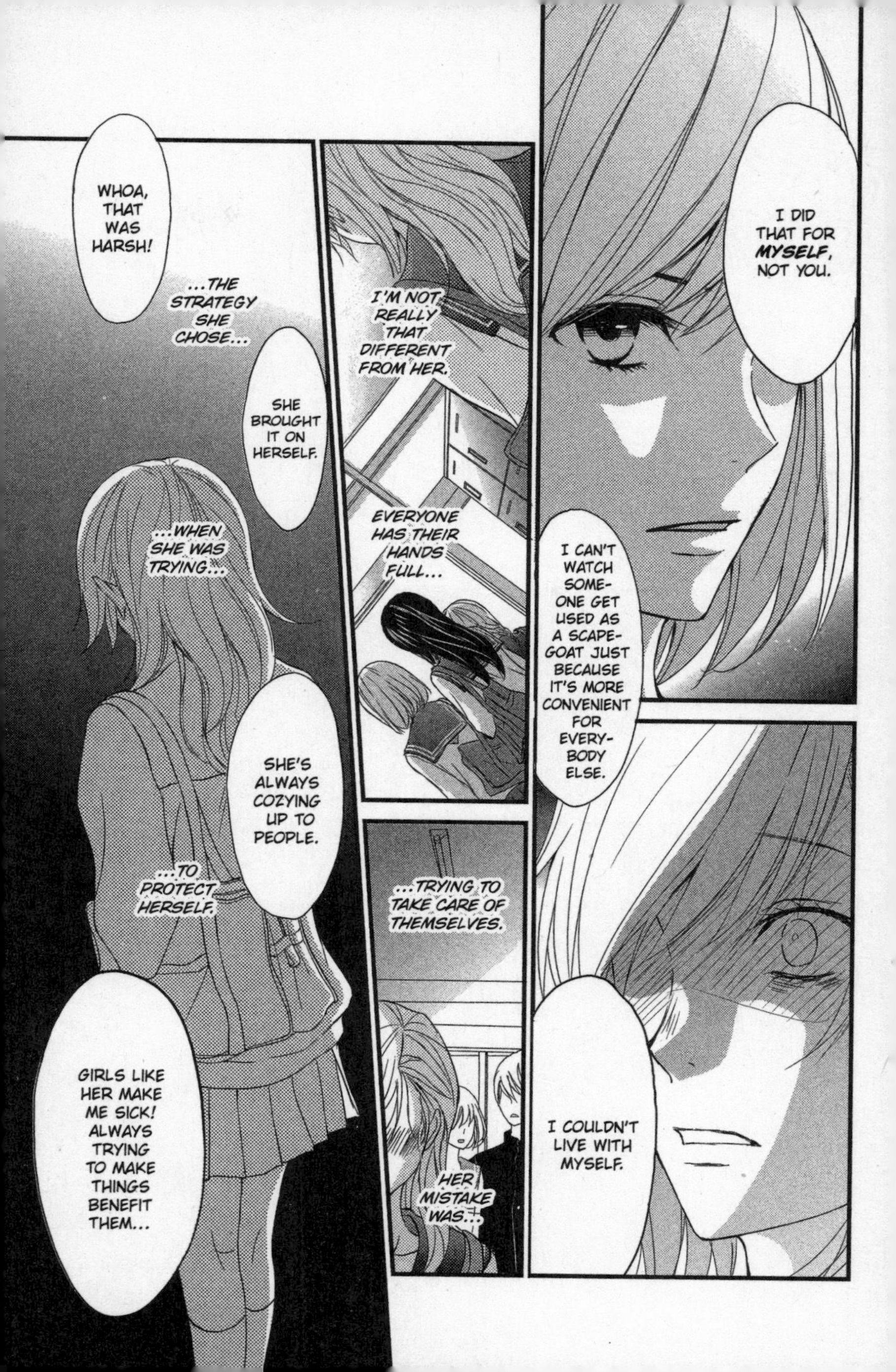
I DID THAT FOR **MYSELF**, NOT YOU.
I CAN'T WATCH SOME-ONE GET USED AS A SCAPE-GOAT JUST BECAUSE IT'S MORE CONVENIENT FOR EVERY-BODY ELSE.
I COULDN'T LIVE WITH MYSELF.
I'M NOT REALLY THAT DIFFERENT FROM HER.
EVERYONE HAS THEIR HANDS FULL...
...TRYING TO TAKE CARE OF THEMSELVES.
HER MISTAKE WAS...
WHOA, THAT WAS HARSH!
...THE STRATEGY SHE CHOSE...
SHE BROUGHT IT ON HERSELF.
...WHEN SHE WAS TRYING...
SHE'S ALWAYS COZYING UP TO PEOPLE.
...TO PROTECT HERSELF.
GIRLS LIKE HER MAKE ME SICK! ALWAYS TRYING TO MAKE THINGS BENEFIT THEM...

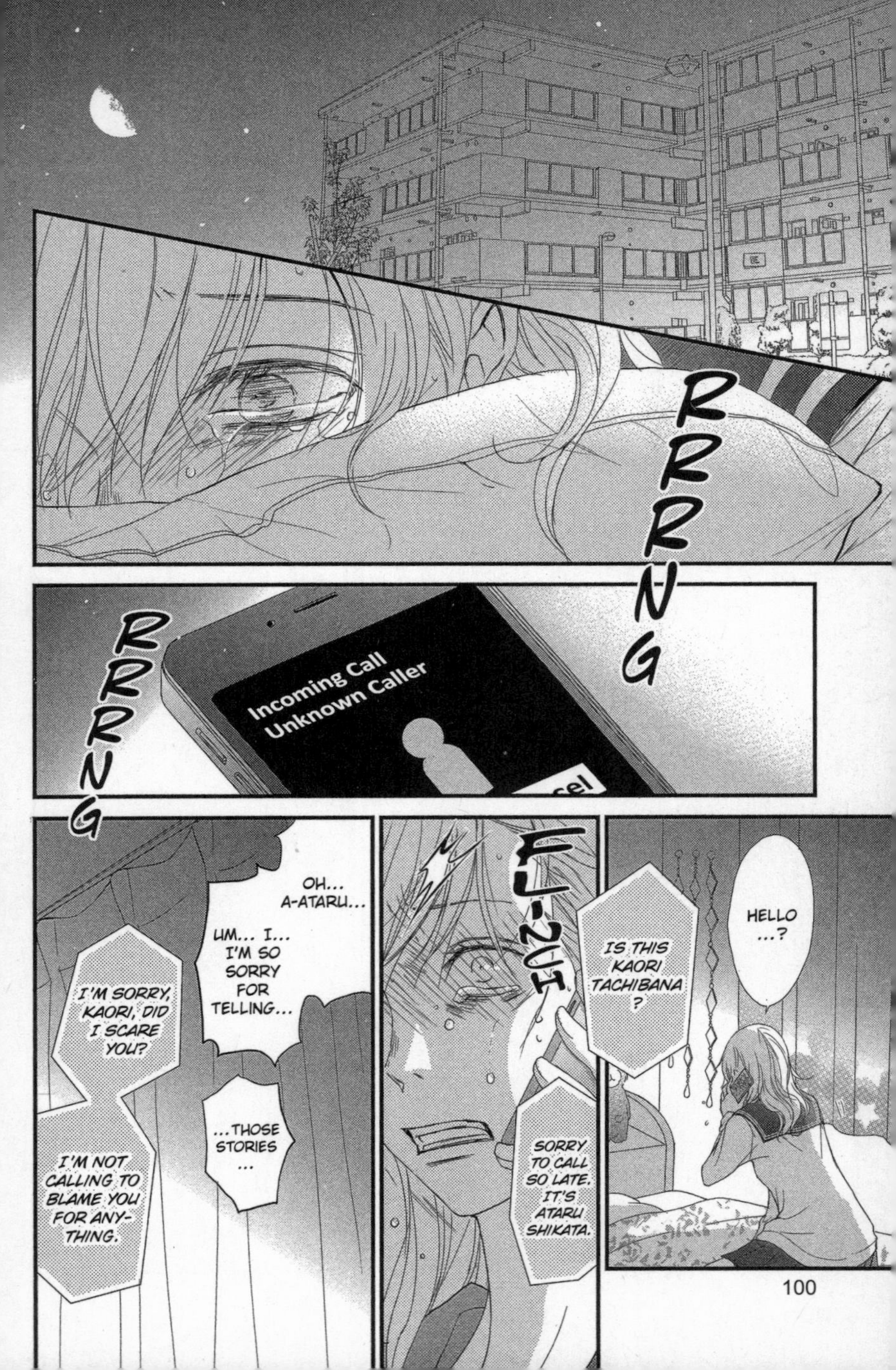
RRRNG
Incoming Call
Unknown Caller
RRRNG
HELLO ...?
IS THIS KAORI TACHIBANA ?
SORRY TO CALL SO LATE. IT'S ATARU SHIKATA.
FLINCH
OH... A-ATARU...
UM... I... I'M SO SORRY FOR TELLING...
...THOSE STORIES ...
I'M SORRY, KAORI, DID I SCARE YOU?
I'M NOT CALLING TO BLAME YOU FOR ANYTHING.

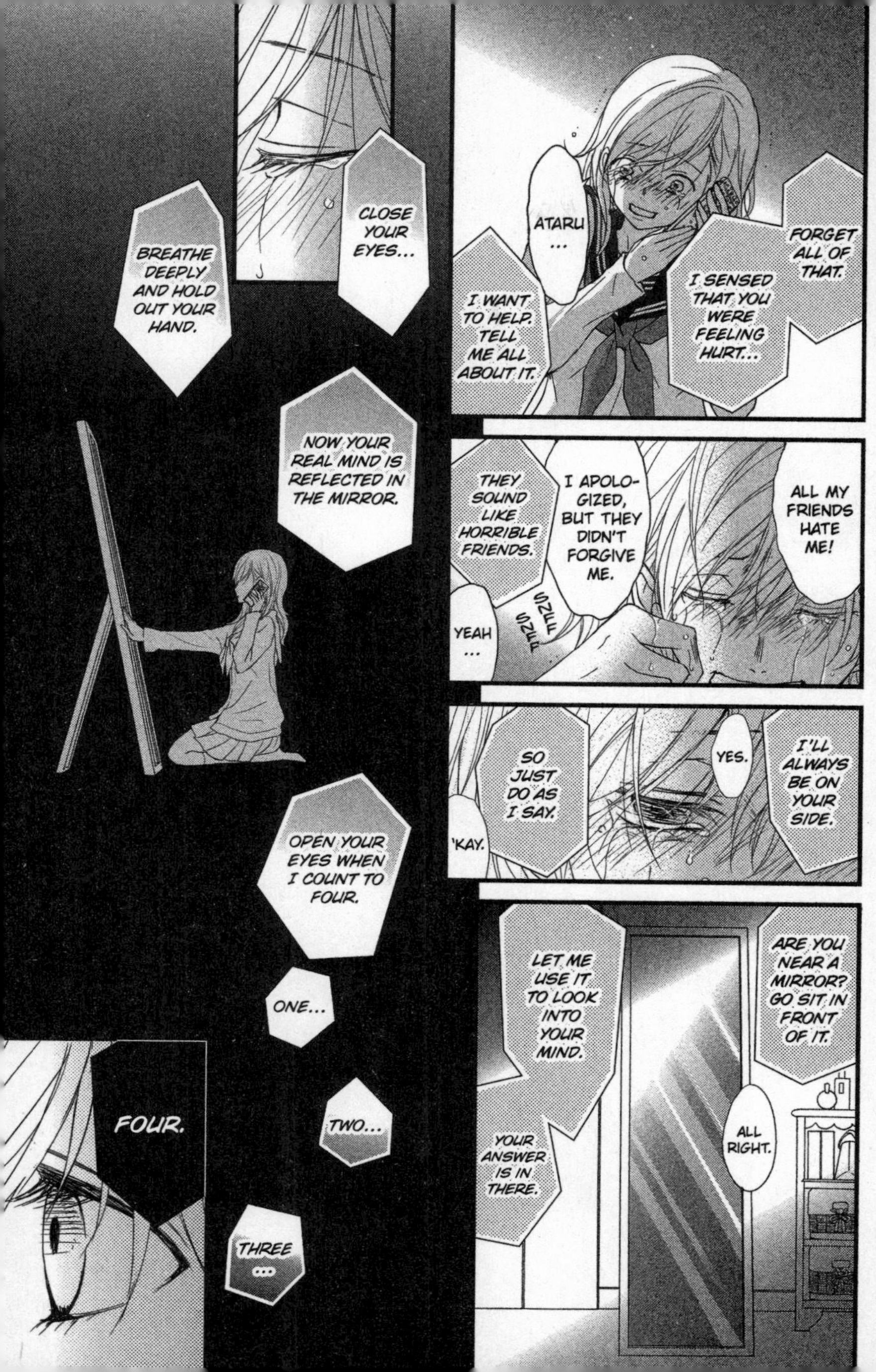
FORGET ALL OF THAT.
ATARU ...
I SENSED THAT YOU WERE FEELING HURT...
I WANT TO HELP. TELL ME ALL ABOUT IT.
ALL MY FRIENDS HATE ME!
I APOLO-GIZED, BUT THEY DIDN'T FORGIVE ME.
THEY SOUND LIKE HORRIBLE FRIENDS.
SNIFF SNIFF
YEAH ...
I'LL ALWAYS BE ON YOUR SIDE.
YES.
SO JUST DO AS I SAY.
'KAY.
ARE YOU NEAR A MIRROR? GO SIT IN FRONT OF IT.
LET ME USE IT TO LOOK INTO YOUR MIND.
ALL RIGHT.
YOUR ANSWER IS IN THERE.
CLOSE YOUR EYES...
BREATHE DEEPLY AND HOLD OUT YOUR HAND.
NOW YOUR REAL MIND IS REFLECTED IN THE MIRROR.
OPEN YOUR EYES WHEN I COUNT TO FOUR.
ONE...
TWO...
THREE ...
FOUR.

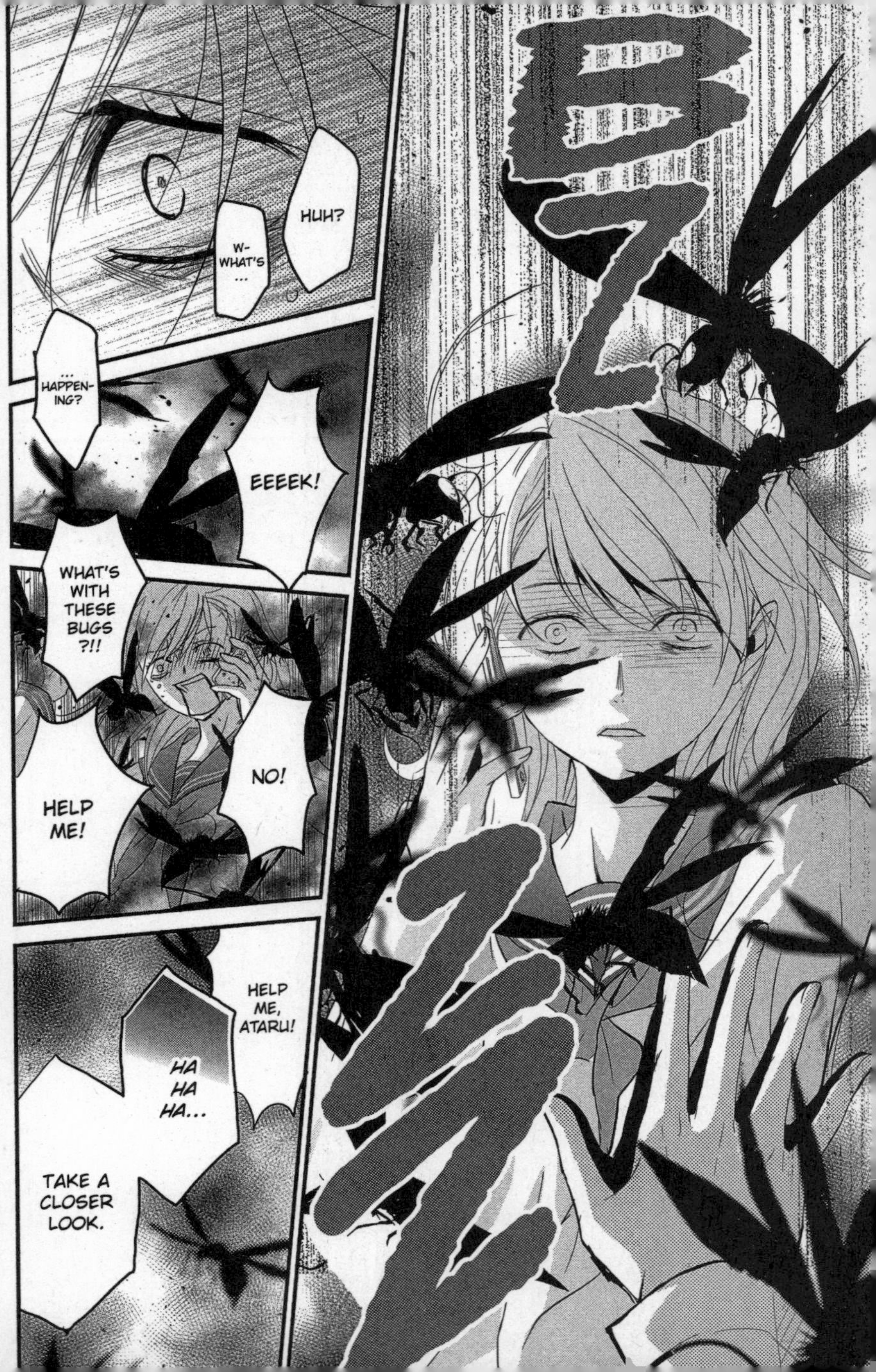
HUH?
W-WHAT'S...
...HAPPENING?
EEEEK!
WHAT'S WITH THESE BUGS?!!
NO!
HELP ME!
HELP ME, ATARU!
HA HA HA...
TAKE A CLOSER LOOK.

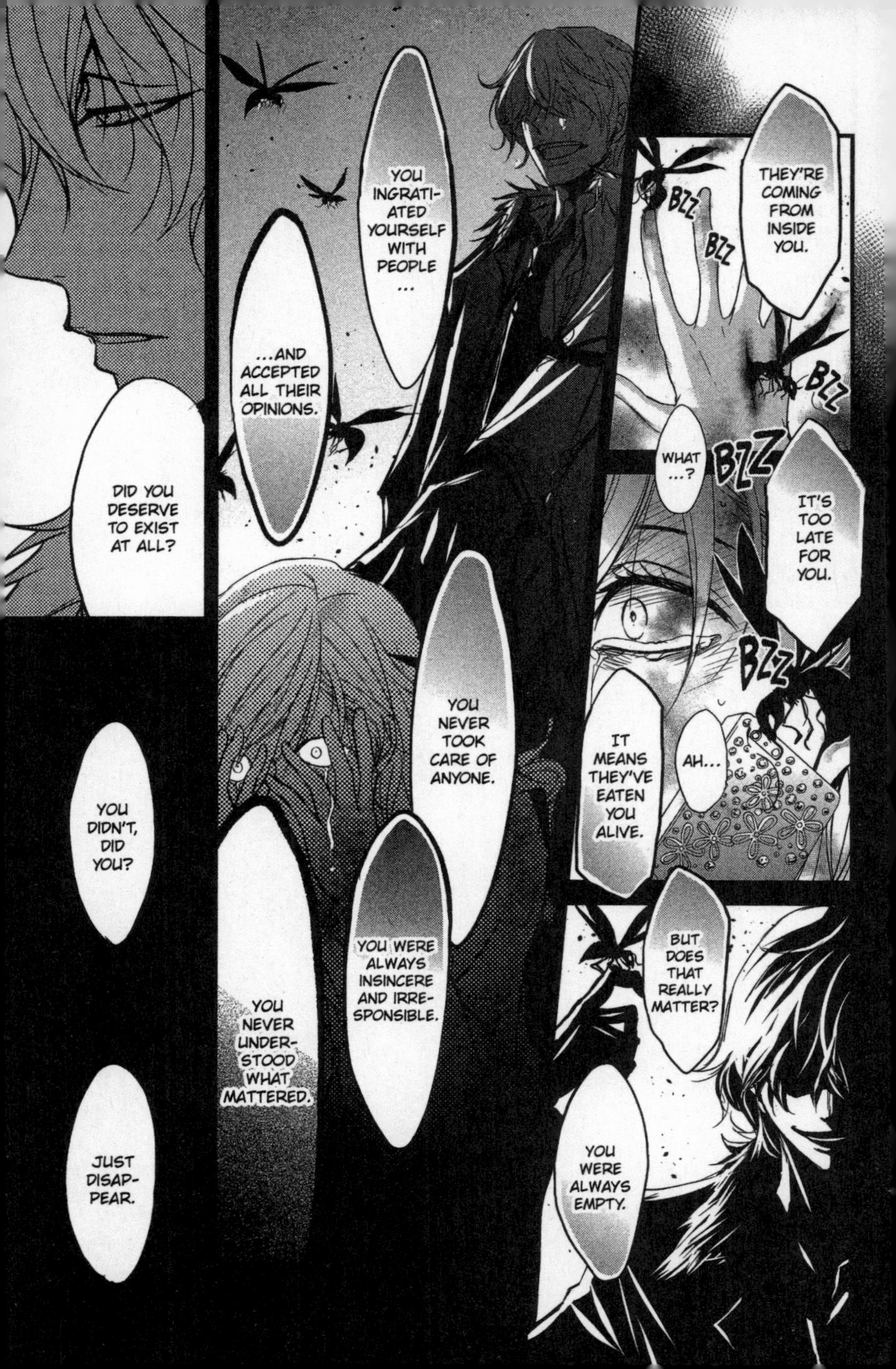
THEY'RE COMING FROM INSIDE YOU.
BZZ
BZZ
BZZ
WHAT...?
BZZ
IT'S TOO LATE FOR YOU.
BZZ
AH...
IT MEANS THEY'VE EATEN YOU ALIVE.
YOU INGRATIATED YOURSELF WITH PEOPLE...
...AND ACCEPTED ALL THEIR OPINIONS.
DID YOU DESERVE TO EXIST AT ALL?
BUT DOES THAT REALLY MATTER?
YOU WERE ALWAYS EMPTY.
YOU NEVER TOOK CARE OF ANYONE.
YOU WERE ALWAYS INSINCERE AND IRRESPONSIBLE.
YOU NEVER UNDERSTOOD WHAT MATTERED.
YOU DIDN'T, DID YOU?
JUST DISAPPEAR.

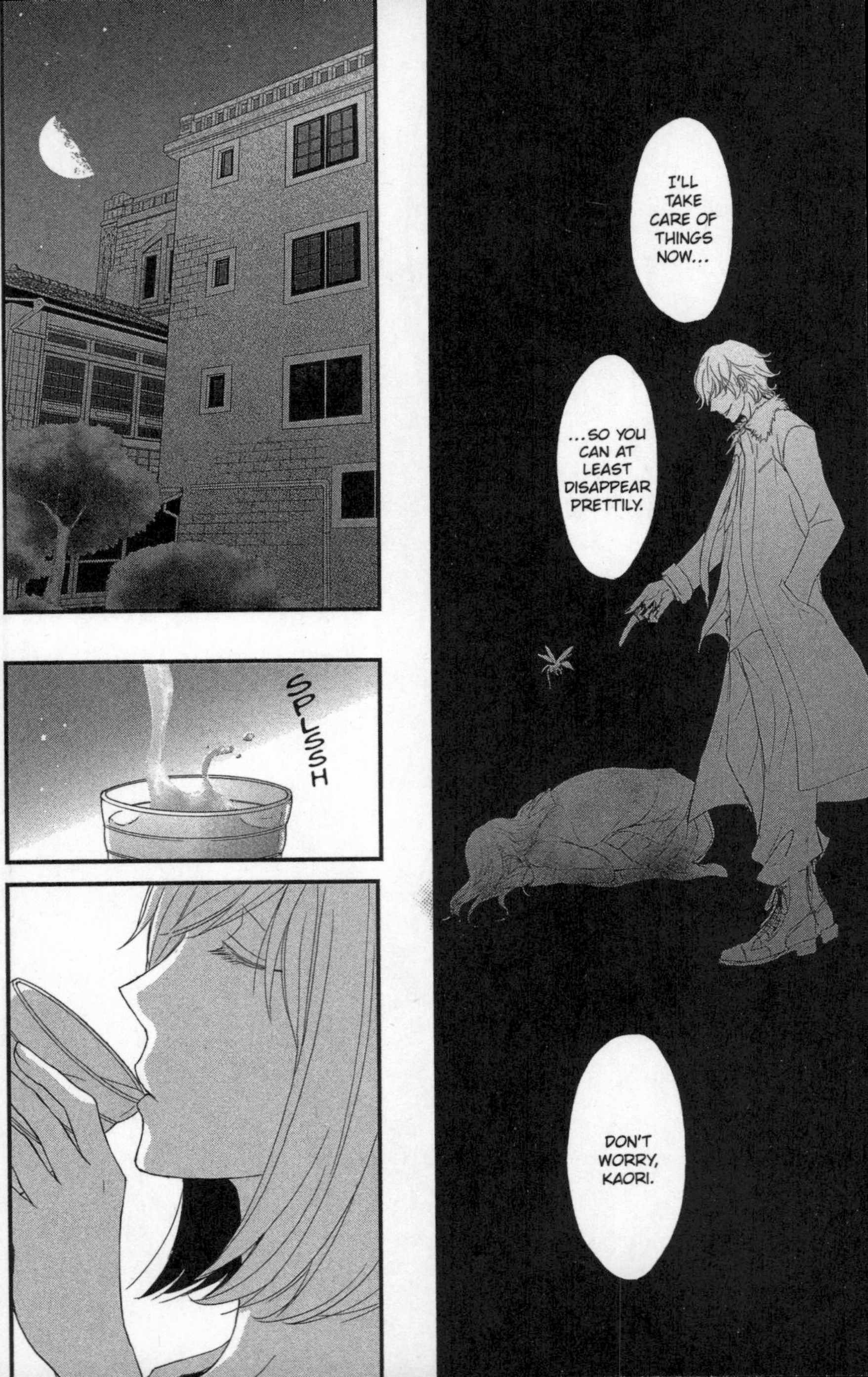
I'LL TAKE CARE OF THINGS NOW...
...SO YOU CAN AT LEAST DISAPPEAR PRETTILY.
DON'T WORRY, KAORI.
SPLSSH

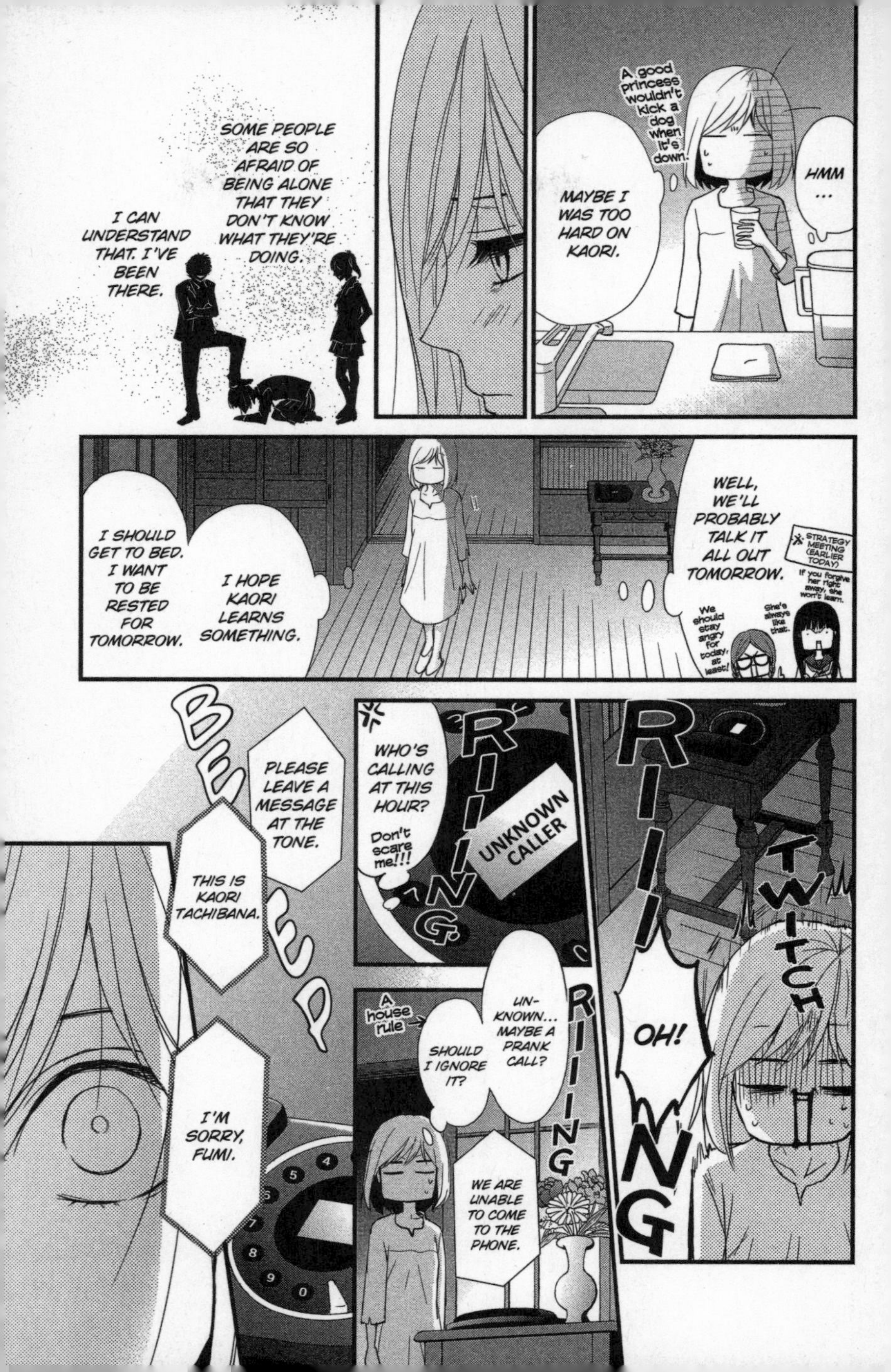
HMM ...
A good princess wouldn't kick a dog when it's down.
MAYBE I WAS TOO HARD ON KAORI.
SOME PEOPLE ARE SO AFRAID OF BEING ALONE THAT THEY DON'T KNOW WHAT THEY'RE DOING.
I CAN UNDERSTAND THAT. I'VE BEEN THERE.
WELL, WE'LL PROBABLY TALK IT ALL OUT TOMORROW.
※ STRATEGY MEETING (EARLIER TODAY)
If you forgive her right away, she won't learn.
She's always like that.
We should stay angry for today, at least!
I HOPE KAORI LEARNS SOMETHING.
I SHOULD GET TO BED. I WANT TO BE RESTED FOR TOMORROW.
RIIING
TWITCH
OH!
RIIING
WHO'S CALLING AT THIS HOUR?
Don't scare me!!!
RIIING
UNKNOWN CALLER
UN-KNOWN... MAYBE A PRANK CALL?
A house rule
SHOULD I IGNORE IT?
RIIING
WE ARE UNABLE TO COME TO THE PHONE.
PLEASE LEAVE A MESSAGE AT THE TONE.
BEEP
THIS IS KAORI TACHIBANA.
I'M SORRY, FUMI.

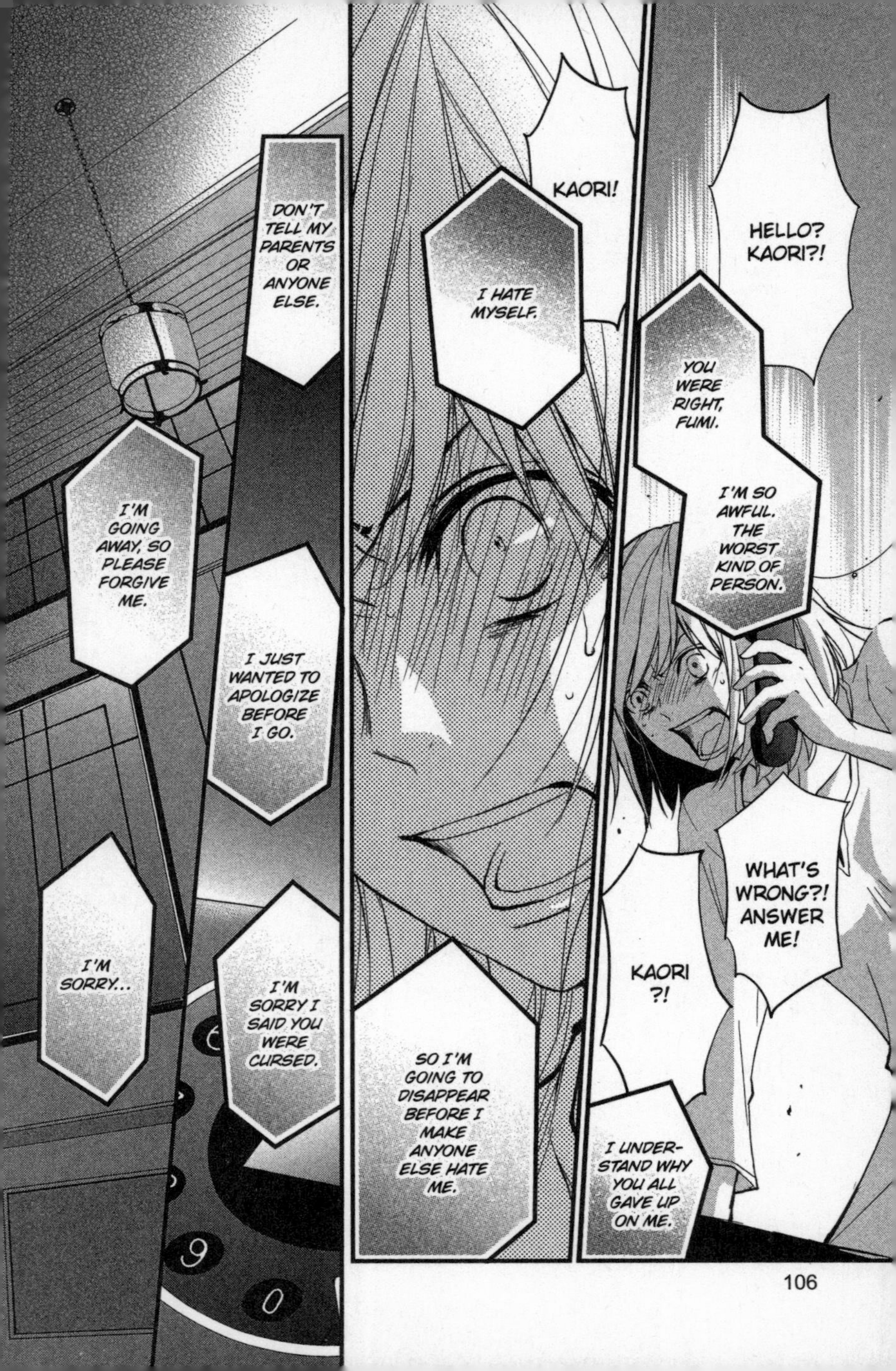
HELLO? KAORI?!
YOU WERE RIGHT, FUMI.
I'M SO AWFUL. THE WORST KIND OF PERSON.
WHAT'S WRONG?! ANSWER ME!
KAORI ?!
I UNDER-STAND WHY YOU ALL GAVE UP ON ME.
KAORI!
I HATE MYSELF.
SO I'M GOING TO DISAPPEAR BEFORE I MAKE ANYONE ELSE HATE ME.
DON'T TELL MY PARENTS OR ANYONE ELSE.
I'M GOING AWAY, SO PLEASE FORGIVE ME.
I JUST WANTED TO APOLOGIZE BEFORE I GO.
I'M SORRY I SAID YOU WERE CURSED.
I'M SORRY...

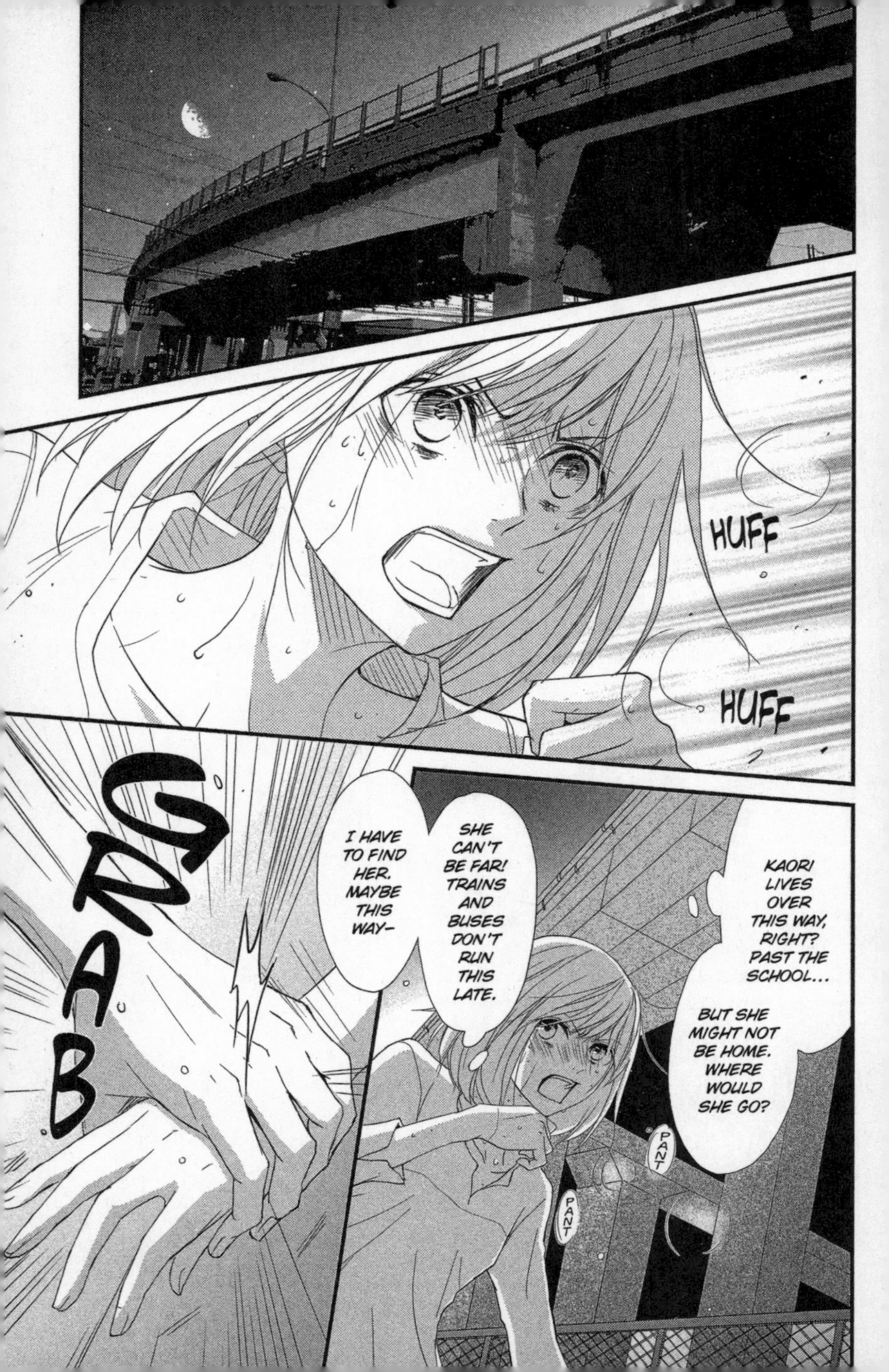
HUFF
HUFF
KAORI LIVES OVER THIS WAY, RIGHT? PAST THE SCHOOL...
BUT SHE MIGHT NOT BE HOME. WHERE WOULD SHE GO?
SHE CAN'T BE FAR! TRAINS AND BUSES DON'T RUN THIS LATE.
I HAVE TO FIND HER. MAYBE THIS WAY-
PANT
PANT
GRAB

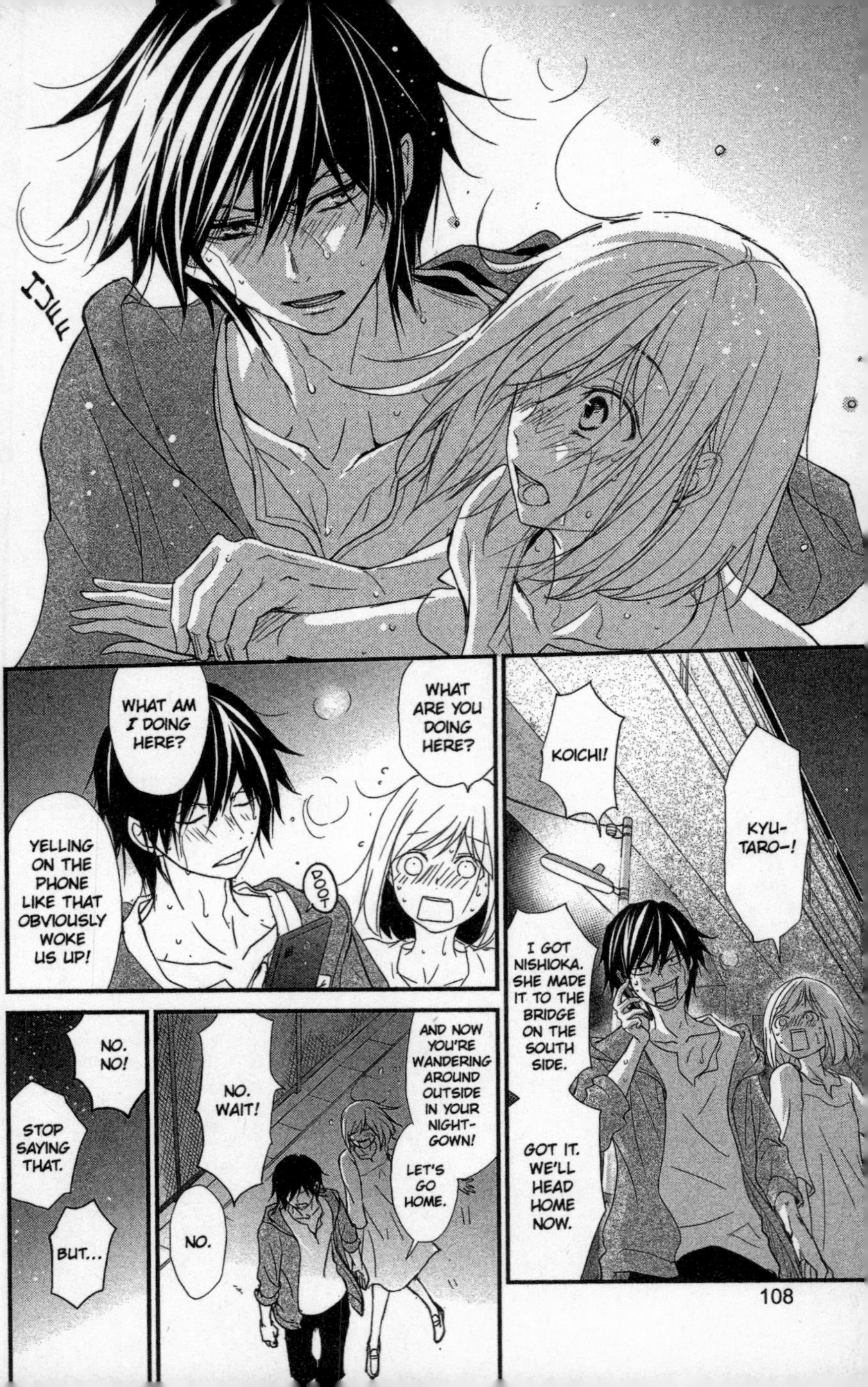
KYU-
TARO-!
KOICHI!
I GOT NISHIOKA. SHE MADE IT TO THE BRIDGE ON THE SOUTH SIDE.
GOT IT. WE'LL HEAD HOME NOW.
WHAT ARE YOU DOING HERE?
WHAT AM I DOING HERE?
DOOT
YELLING ON THE PHONE LIKE THAT OBVIOUSLY WOKE US UP!
AND NOW YOU'RE WANDERING AROUND OUTSIDE IN YOUR NIGHT-GOWN!
NO. WAIT!
LET'S GO HOME.
NO.
NO. NO!
STOP SAYING THAT.
BUT...

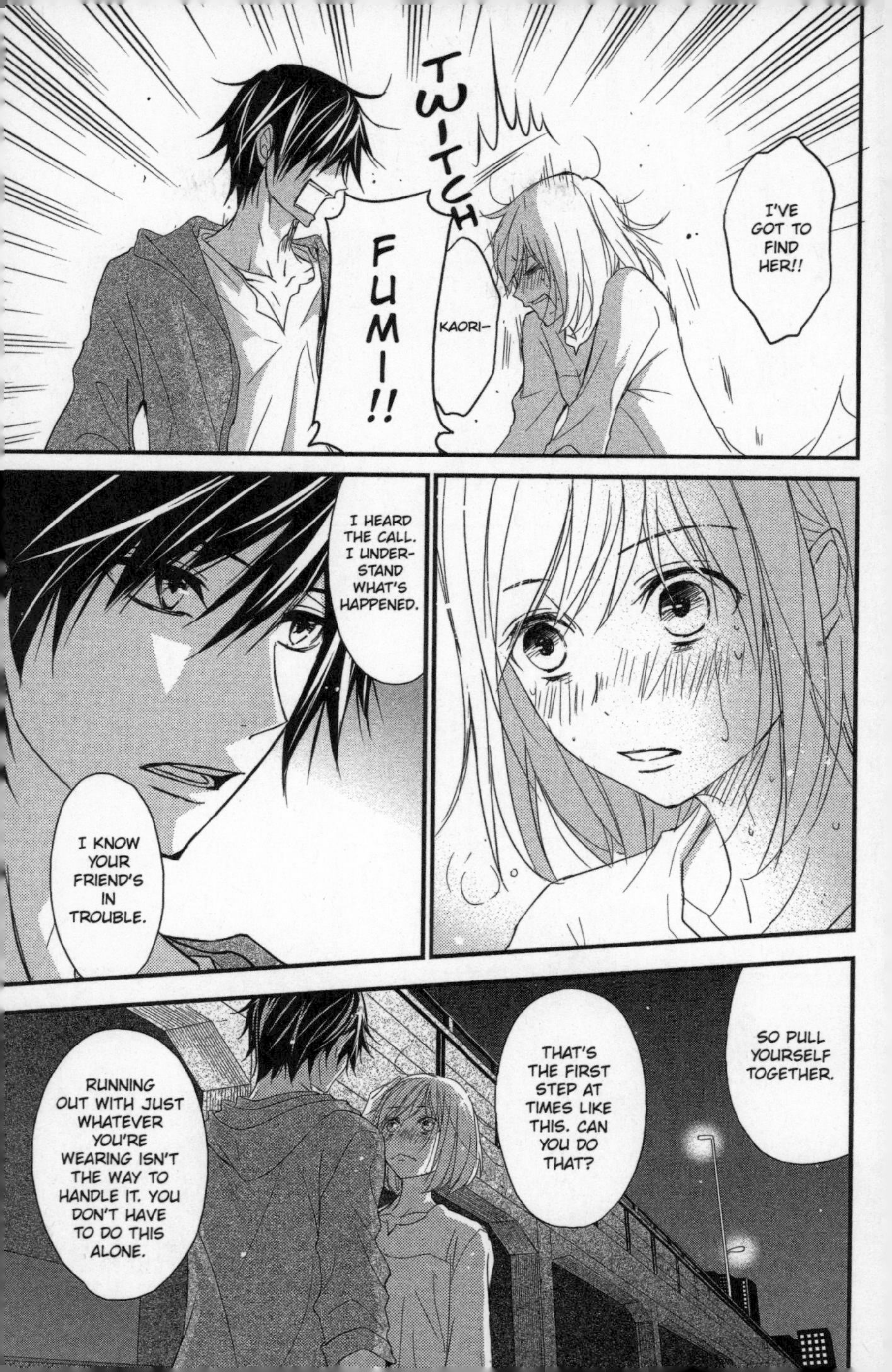
I'VE GOT TO FIND HER!!
KAORI- FUMI!!
TWITCH
I HEARD THE CALL. I UNDER-STAND WHAT'S HAPPENED.
I KNOW YOUR FRIEND'S IN TROUBLE.
SO PULL YOURSELF TOGETHER.
THAT'S THE FIRST STEP AT TIMES LIKE THIS. CAN YOU DO THAT?
RUNNING OUT WITH JUST WHATEVER YOU'RE WEARING ISN'T THE WAY TO HANDLE IT. YOU DON'T HAVE TO DO THIS ALONE.

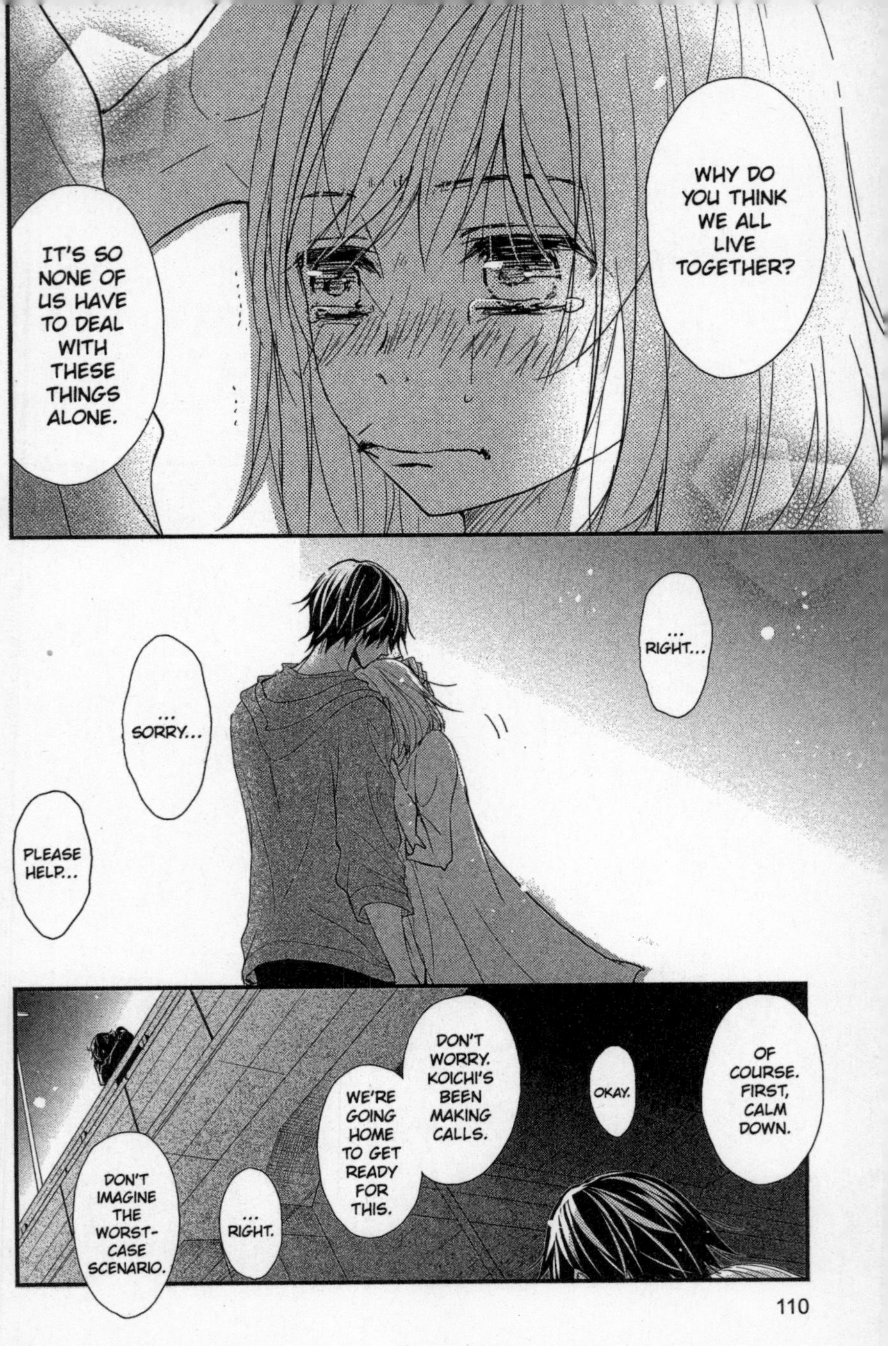
WHY DO YOU THINK WE ALL LIVE TOGETHER?
IT'S SO NONE OF US HAVE TO DEAL WITH THESE THINGS ALONE.
... RIGHT...
... SORRY...
PLEASE HELP...
OF COURSE. FIRST, CALM DOWN.
OKAY.
DON'T WORRY. KOICHI'S BEEN MAKING CALLS.
WE'RE GOING HOME TO GET READY FOR THIS.
... RIGHT.
DON'T IMAGINE THE WORST-CASE SCENARIO.

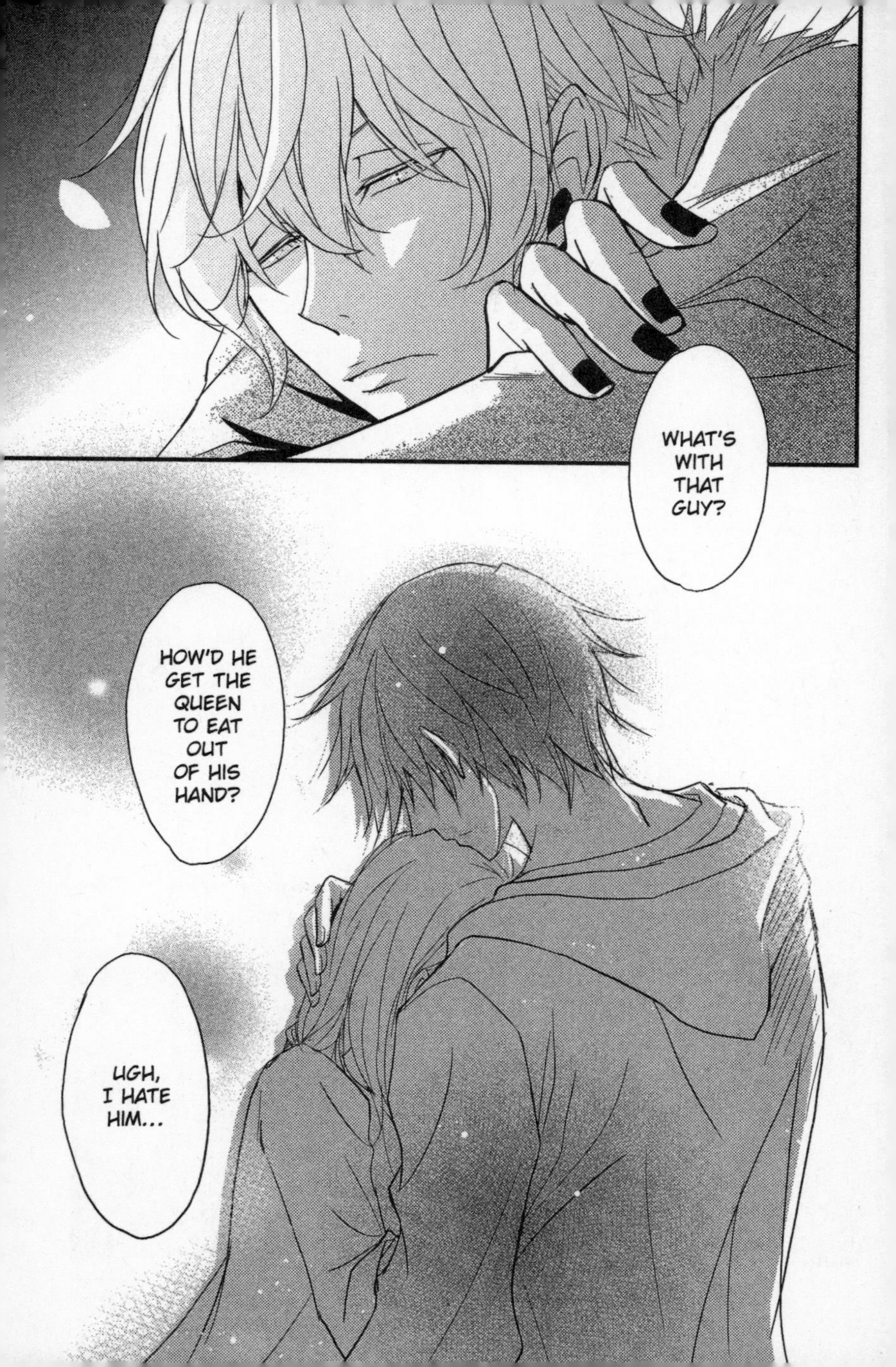
WHAT'S WITH THAT GUY?
HOW'D HE GET THE QUEEN TO EAT OUT OF HIS HAND?
UGH, I HATE HIM...

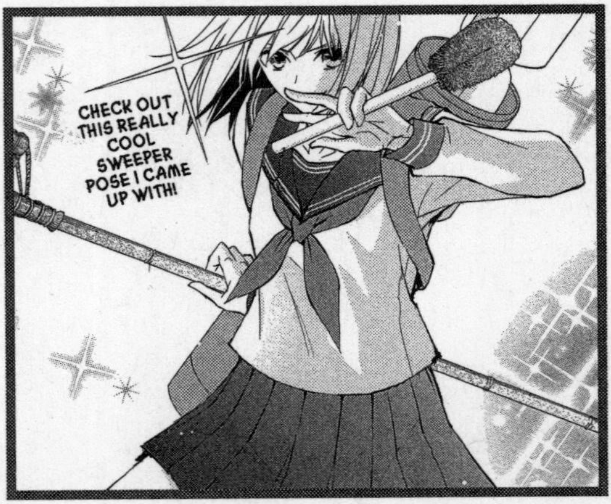
CHECK OUT THIS REALLY COOL SWEEPER POSE I CAME UP WITH!

SWEEP 14

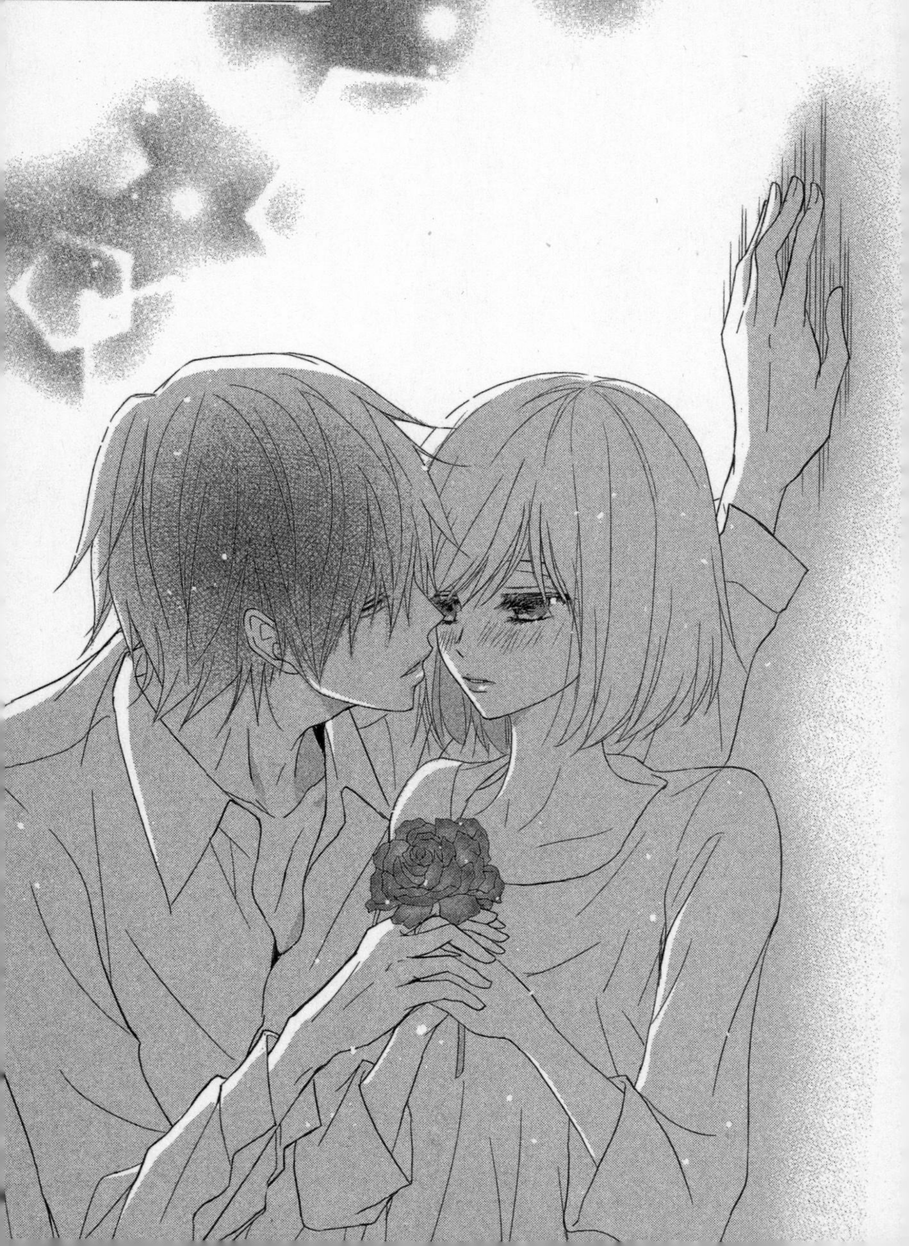

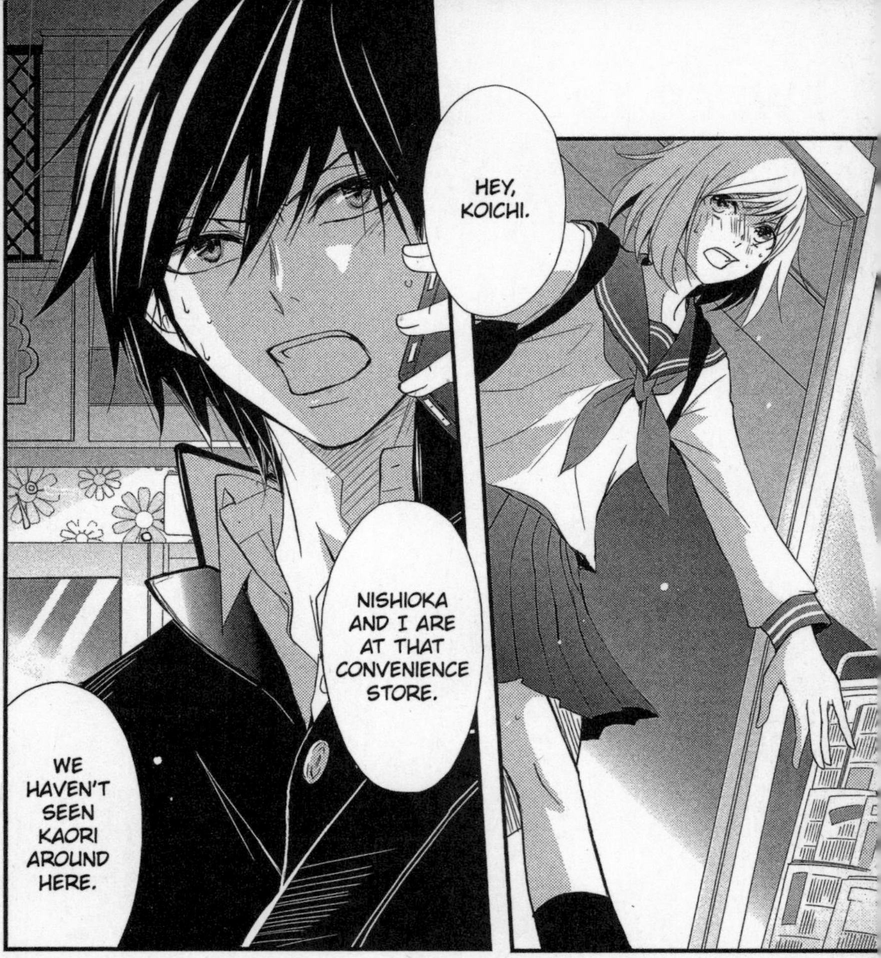
HEY, KOICHI.
NISHIOKA AND I ARE AT THAT CONVENIENCE STORE.
WE HAVEN'T SEEN KAORI AROUND HERE.

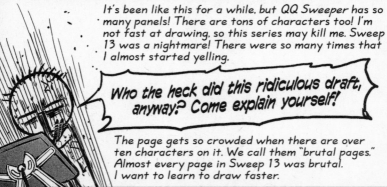

It's been like this for a while, but QQ *Sweeper* has so many panels! There are tons of characters too! I'm not fast at drawing, so this series may kill me. Sweep 13 was a nightmare! There were so many times that I almost started yelling.

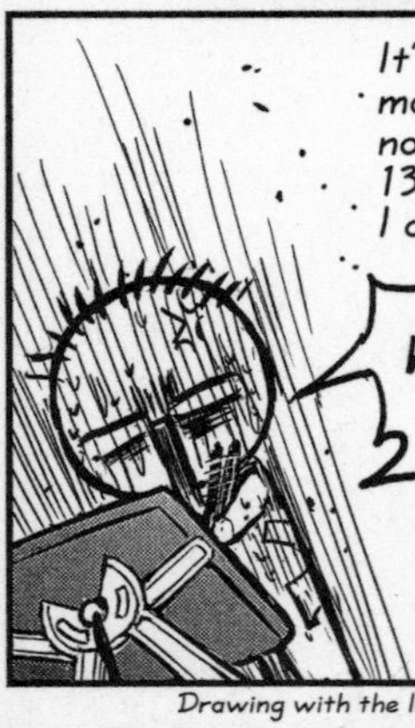
Who the heck did this ridiculous draft, anyway? Come explain yourself!

The page gets so crowded when there are over ten characters on it. We call them "brutal pages." Almost every page in Sweep 13 was brutal. I want to learn to draw faster.

Drawing with the left hand. Huh.

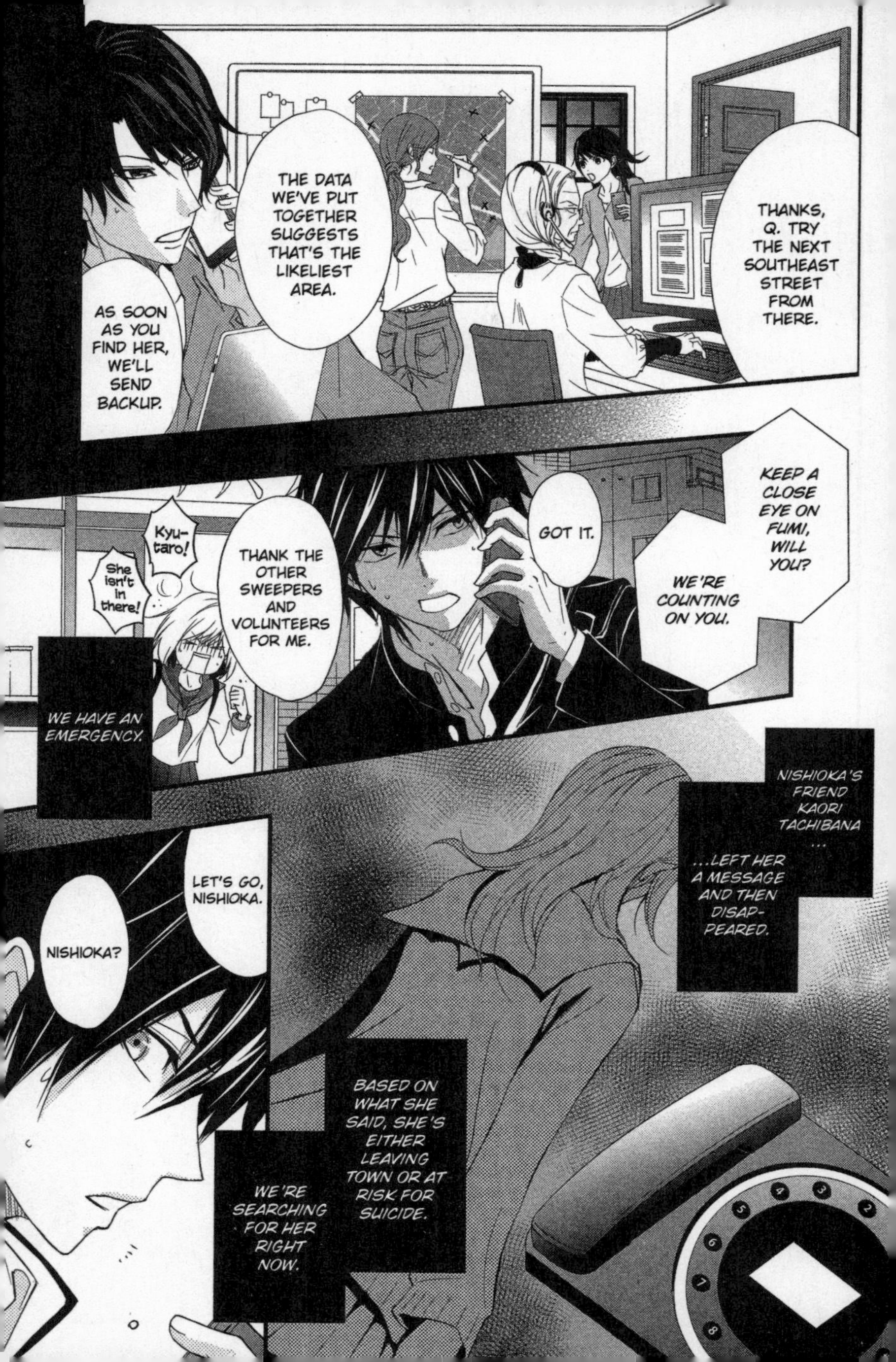
THANKS, Q. TRY THE NEXT SOUTHEAST STREET FROM THERE.
THE DATA WE'VE PUT TOGETHER SUGGESTS THAT'S THE LIKELIEST AREA.
AS SOON AS YOU FIND HER, WE'LL SEND BACKUP.
KEEP A CLOSE EYE ON FUMI, WILL YOU?
WE'RE COUNTING ON YOU.
GOT IT.
THANK THE OTHER SWEEPERS AND VOLUNTEERS FOR ME.
Kyu-taro!
She isn't in there!
WE HAVE AN EMERGENCY.
NISHIOKA'S FRIEND KAORI TACHIBANA...
...LEFT HER A MESSAGE AND THEN DISAP-PEARED.
LET'S GO, NISHIOKA.
NISHIOKA?
BASED ON WHAT SHE SAID, SHE'S EITHER LEAVING TOWN OR AT RISK FOR SUICIDE.
WE'RE SEARCHING FOR HER RIGHT NOW.

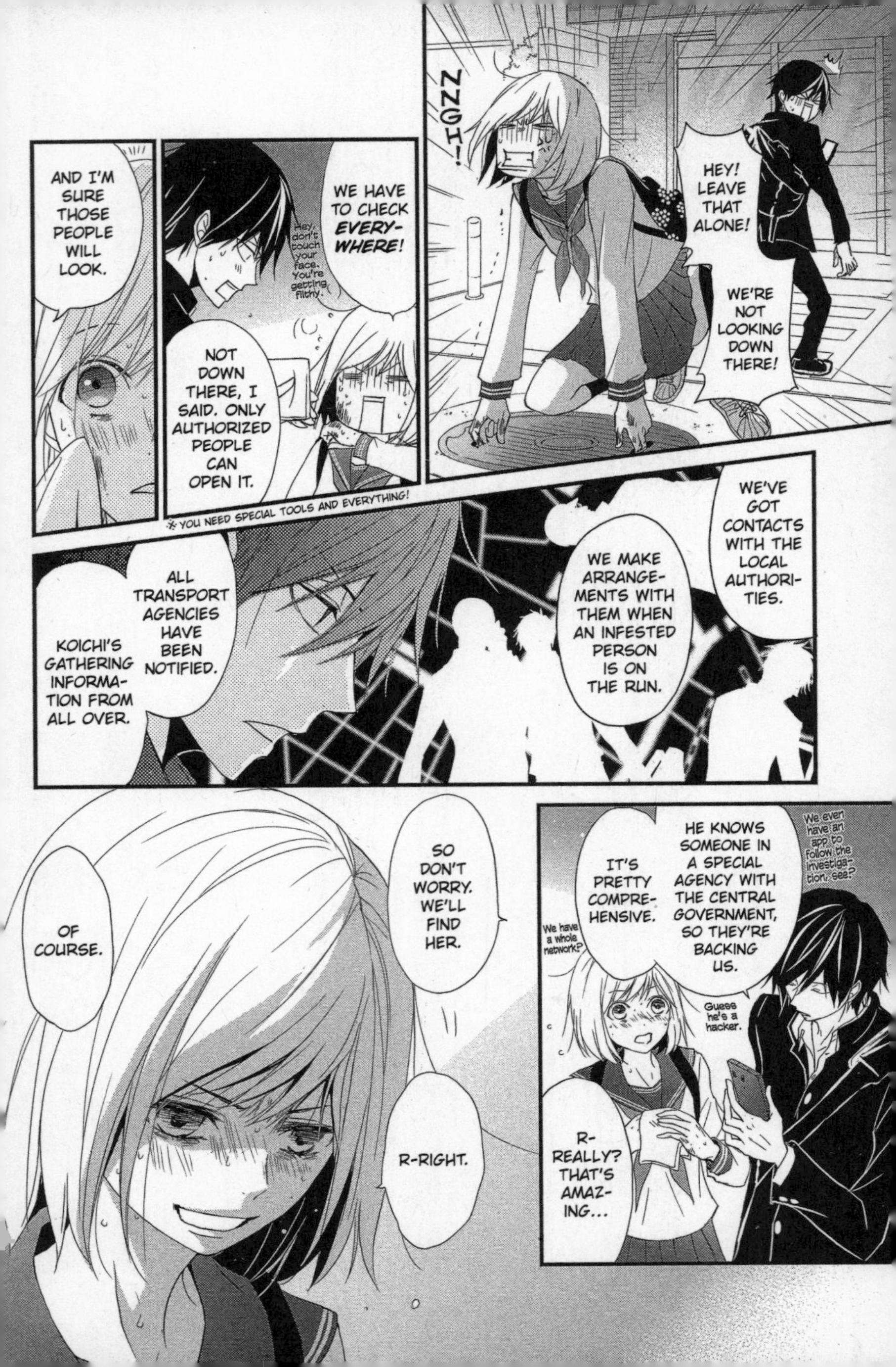
NNGH!
HEY! LEAVE THAT ALONE!
WE'RE NOT LOOKING DOWN THERE!
WE HAVE TO CHECK *EVERYWHERE!*
Hey, don't touch your face. You're getting filthy.
NOT DOWN THERE, I SAID. ONLY AUTHORIZED PEOPLE CAN OPEN IT.
※YOU NEED SPECIAL TOOLS AND EVERYTHING!
AND I'M SURE THOSE PEOPLE WILL LOOK.
WE'VE GOT CONTACTS WITH THE LOCAL AUTHORITIES.
WE MAKE ARRANGEMENTS WITH THEM WHEN AN INFESTED PERSON IS ON THE RUN.
ALL TRANSPORT AGENCIES HAVE BEEN NOTIFIED.
KOICHI'S GATHERING INFORMATION FROM ALL OVER.
We even have an app to follow the investigation, see?
HE KNOWS SOMEONE IN A SPECIAL AGENCY WITH THE CENTRAL GOVERNMENT, SO THEY'RE BACKING US.
IT'S PRETTY COMPREHENSIVE.
We have a whole network?
Guess he's a hacker.
R-REALLY? THAT'S AMAZING...
SO DON'T WORRY. WE'LL FIND HER.
OF COURSE.
R-RIGHT.

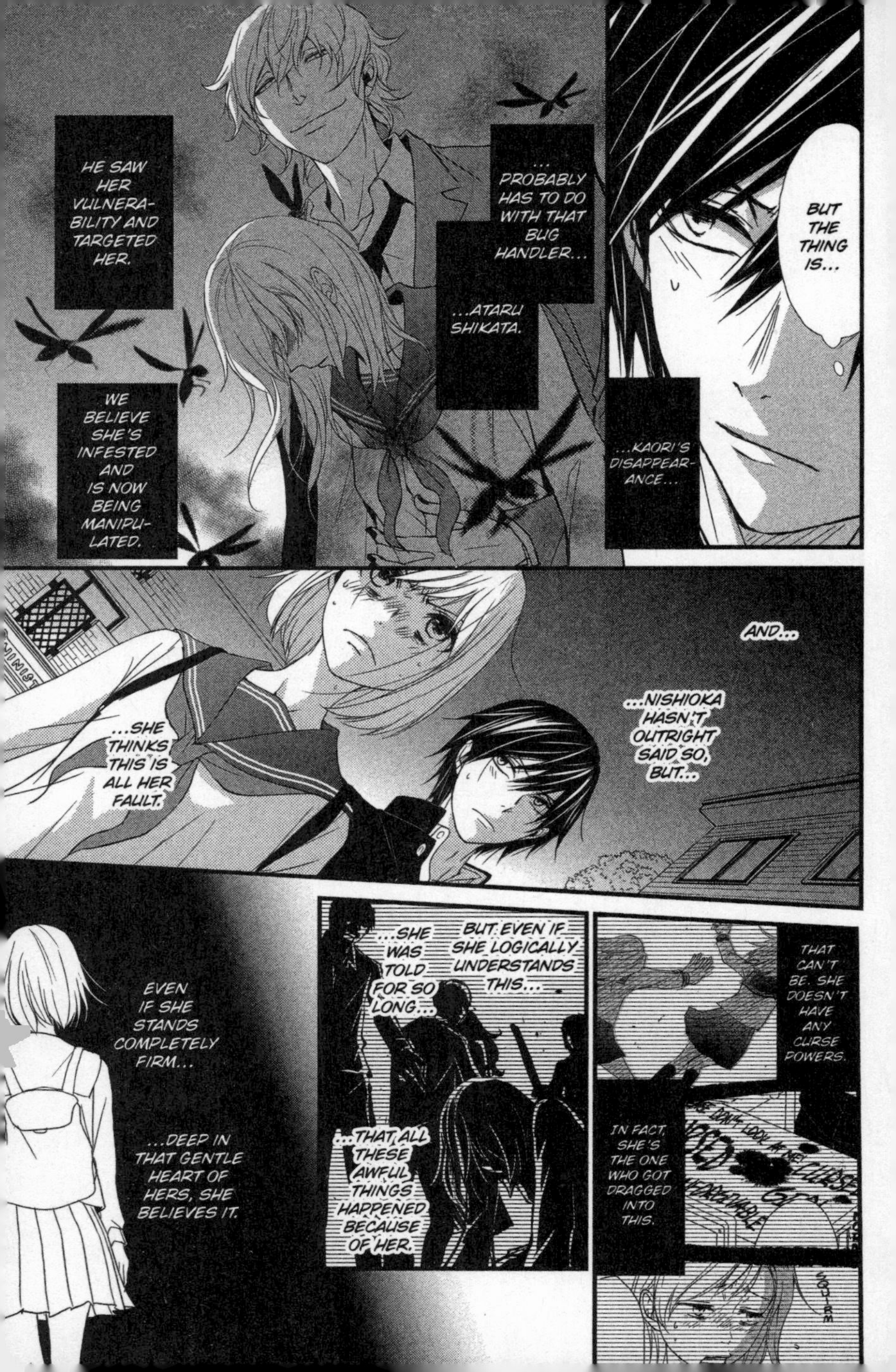
BUT THE THING IS...
...KAORI'S DISAPPEARANCE...
...PROBABLY HAS TO DO WITH THAT BUG HANDLER...
...ATARU SHIKATA.
HE SAW HER VULNERABILITY AND TARGETED HER.
WE BELIEVE SHE'S INFESTED AND IS NOW BEING MANIPULATED.
AND...
...NISHIOKA HASN'T OUTRIGHT SAID SO, BUT...
...SHE THINKS THIS IS ALL HER FAULT.
THAT CAN'T BE. SHE DOESN'T HAVE ANY CURSE POWERS.
IN FACT, SHE'S THE ONE WHO GOT DRAGGED INTO THIS.
SQUIRM
BUT EVEN IF SHE LOGICALLY UNDERSTANDS THIS...
...SHE WAS TOLD FOR SO LONG...
...THAT ALL THESE AWFUL THINGS HAPPENED BECAUSE OF HER.
EVEN IF SHE STANDS COMPLETELY FIRM...
...DEEP IN THAT GENTLE HEART OF HERS, SHE BELIEVES IT.

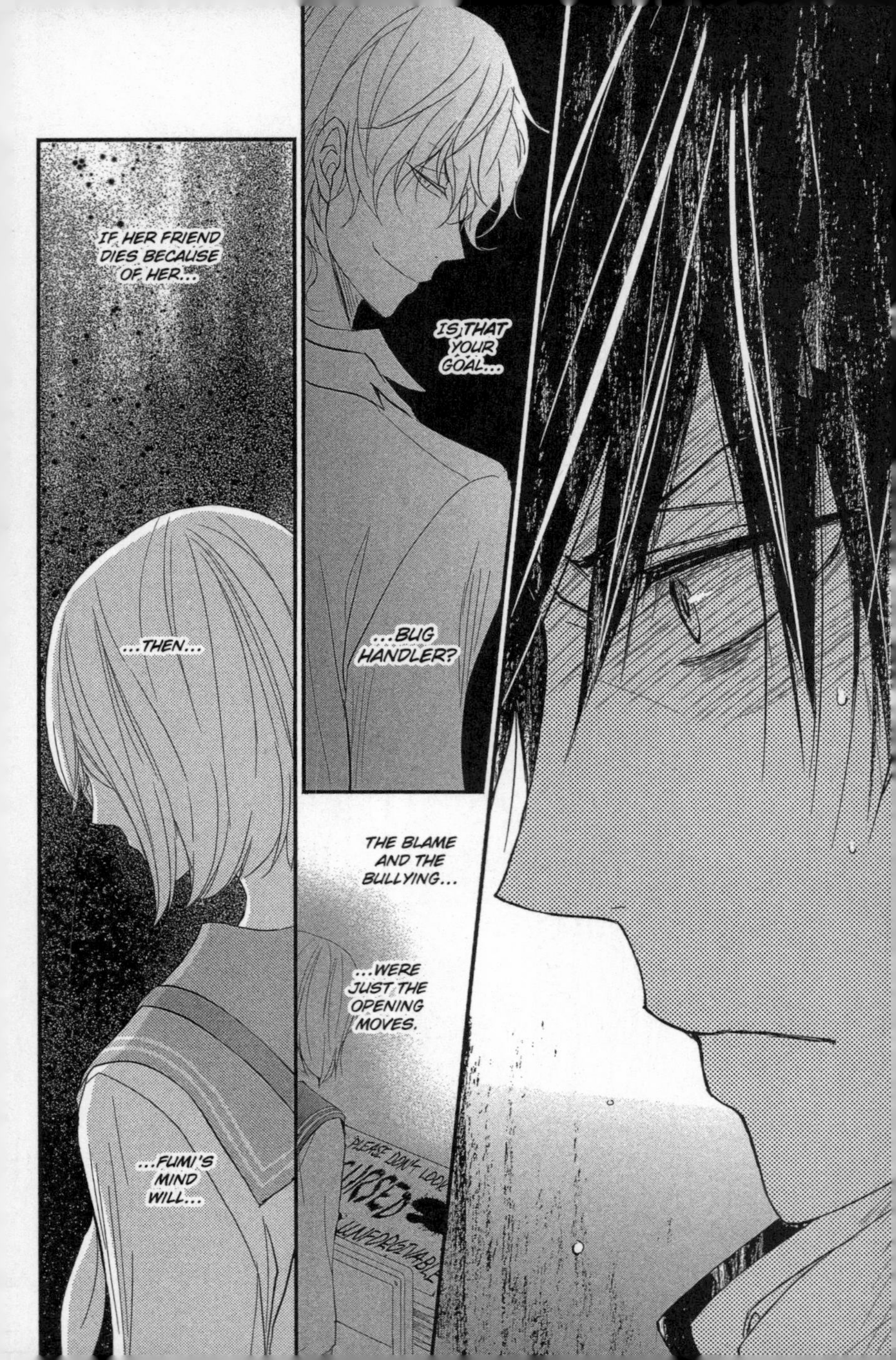
THE BLAME AND THE BULLYING...
...WERE JUST THE OPENING MOVES.
IS THAT YOUR GOAL...
...BUG HANDLER?
IF HER FRIEND DIES BECAUSE OF HER...
...THEN...
...FUMI'S MIND WILL...
PLEASE DON'T LOOK
CURSED
UNFORGETTABLE

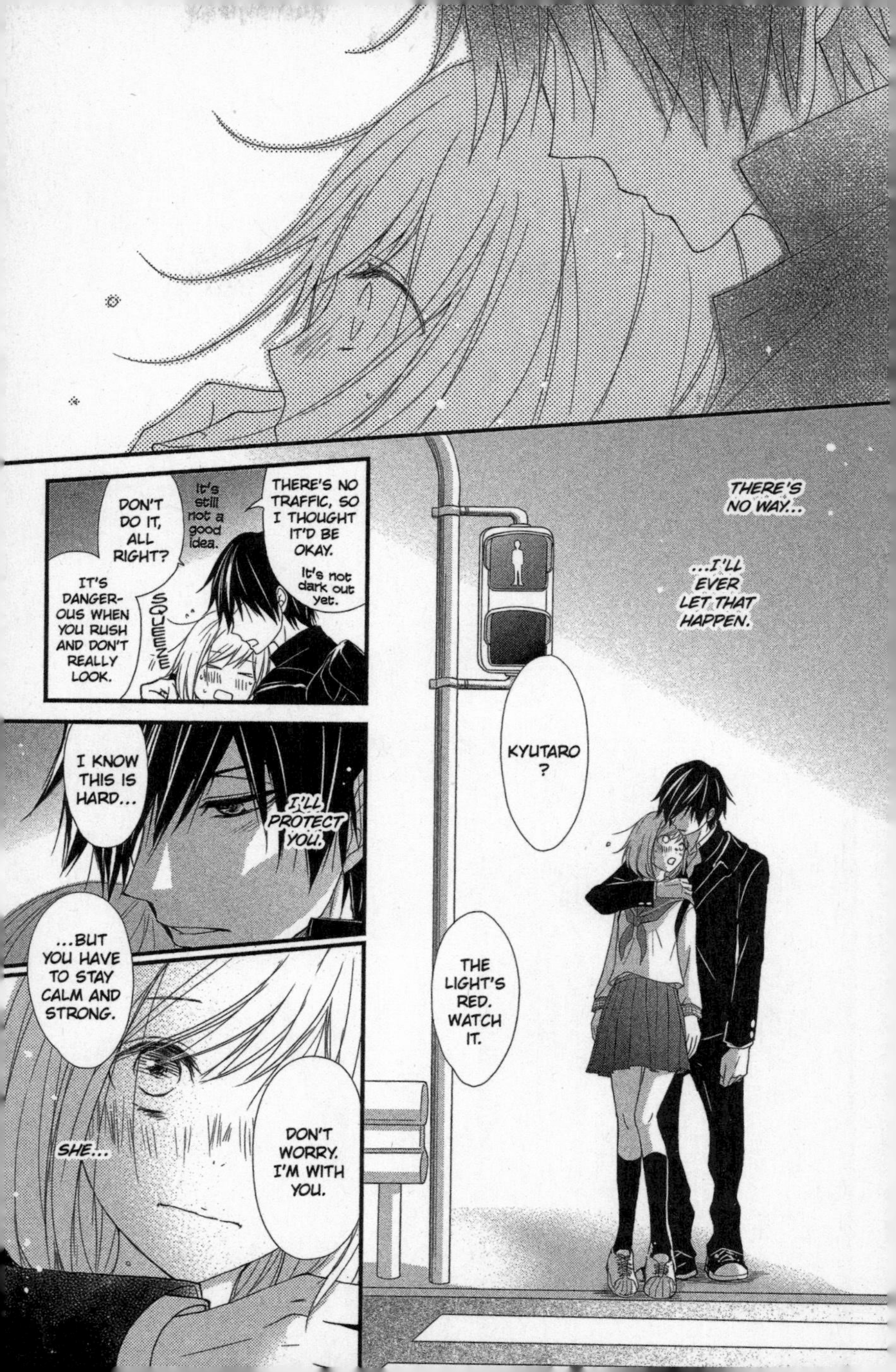
THERE'S NO WAY...
...I'LL EVER LET THAT HAPPEN.
KYUTARO?
THE LIGHT'S RED. WATCH IT.
THERE'S NO TRAFFIC, SO I THOUGHT IT'D BE OKAY.
It's not dark out yet.
It's still not a good idea.
DON'T DO IT, ALL RIGHT?
SQUEEZE
IT'S DANGER-OUS WHEN YOU RUSH AND DON'T REALLY LOOK.
I'LL PROTECT YOU.
I KNOW THIS IS HARD...
...BUT YOU HAVE TO STAY CALM AND STRONG.
DON'T WORRY. I'M WITH YOU.
SHE...

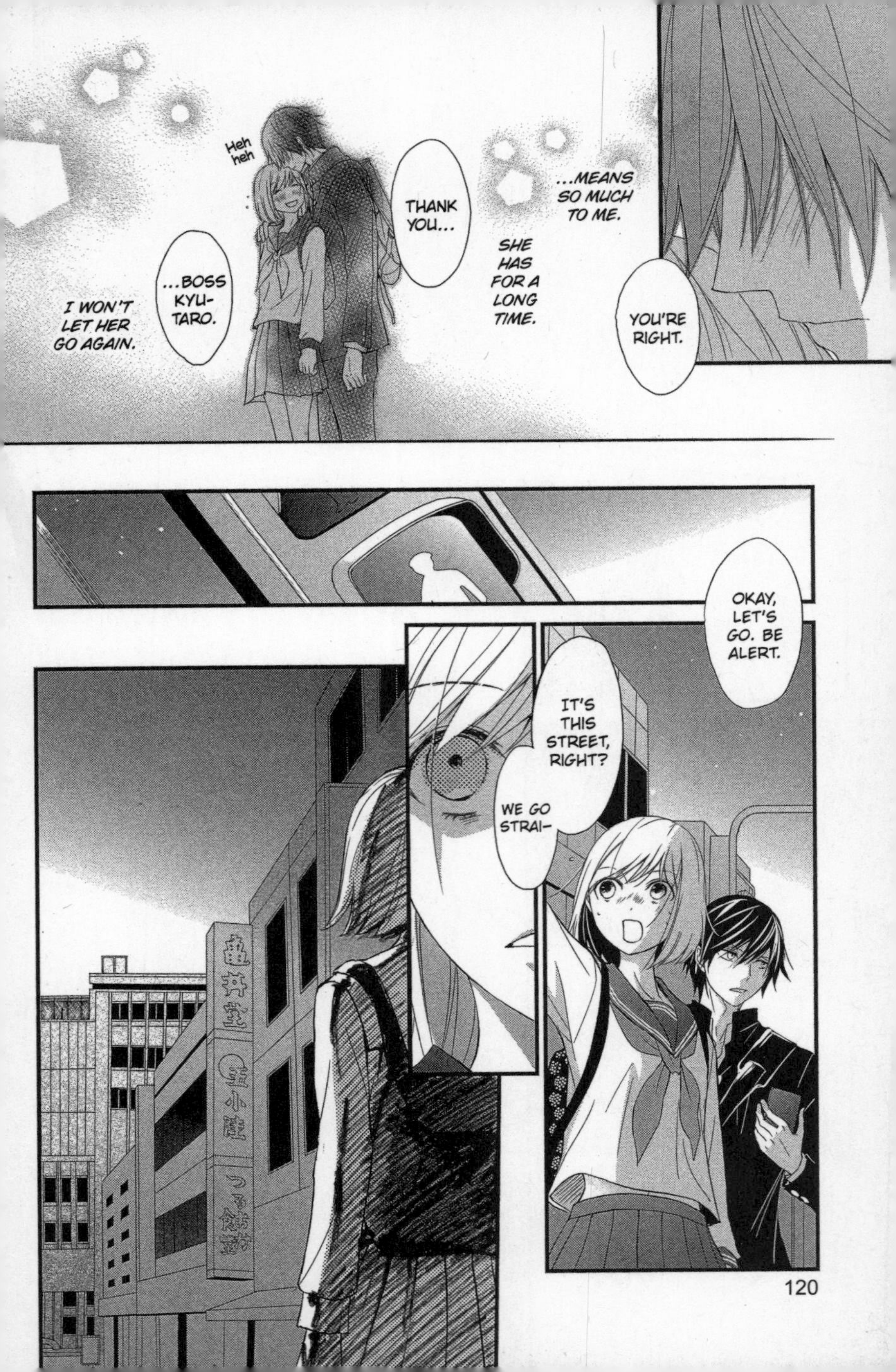
YOU'RE RIGHT.
...MEANS SO MUCH TO ME.
SHE HAS FOR A LONG TIME.
THANK YOU...
Heh heh
...BOSS KYU-TARO.
I WON'T LET HER GO AGAIN.
OKAY, LET'S GO. BE ALERT.
IT'S THIS STREET, RIGHT?
WE GO STRAI-

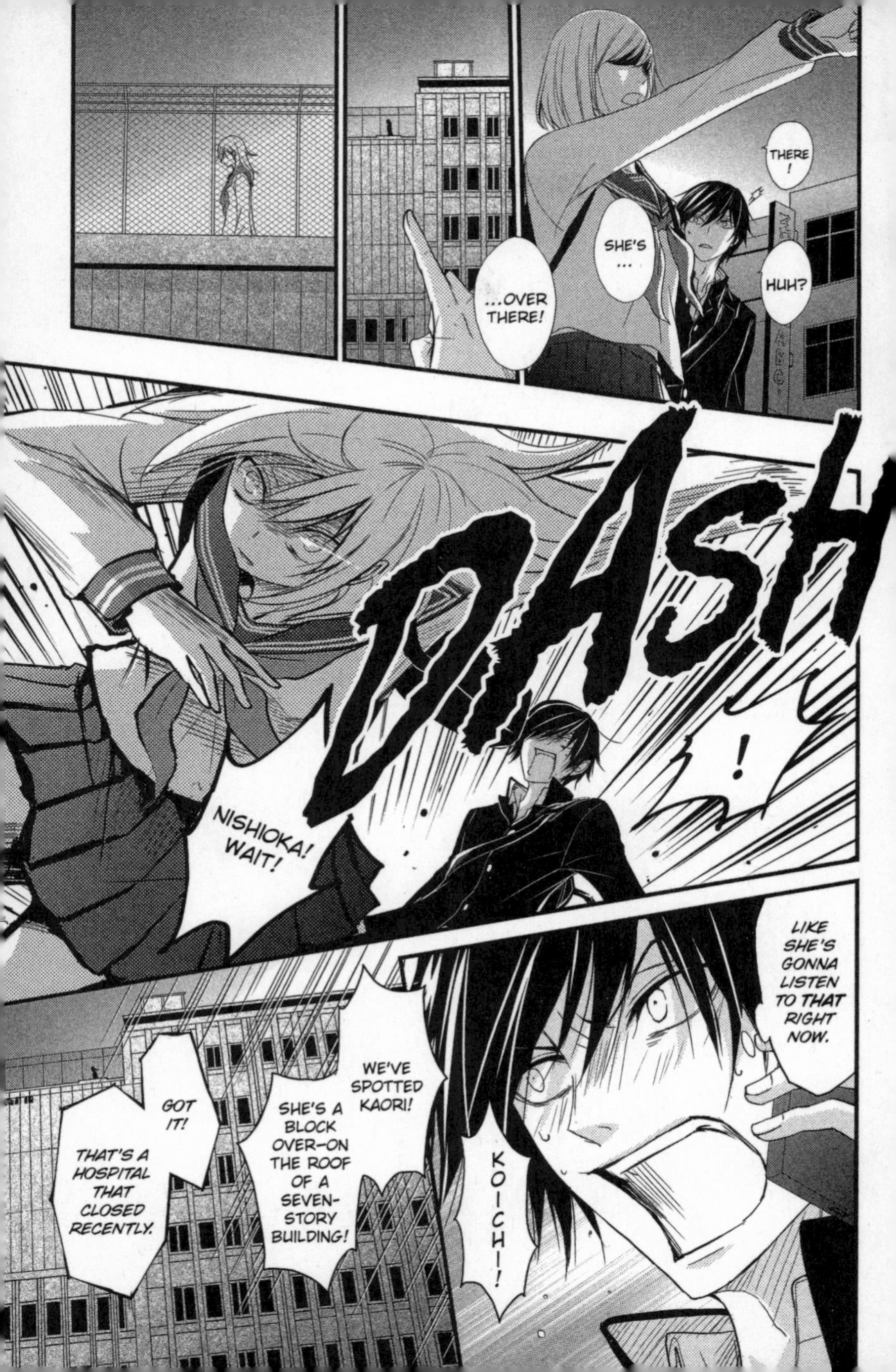
THERE!
HUH?
SHE'S...
...OVER THERE!
DASH
!
NISHIOKA! WAIT!
LIKE SHE'S GONNA LISTEN TO THAT RIGHT NOW.
KOICHI!
WE'VE SPOTTED KAORI!
SHE'S A BLOCK OVER—ON THE ROOF OF A SEVEN-STORY BUILDING!
GOT IT!
THAT'S A HOSPITAL THAT CLOSED RECENTLY.

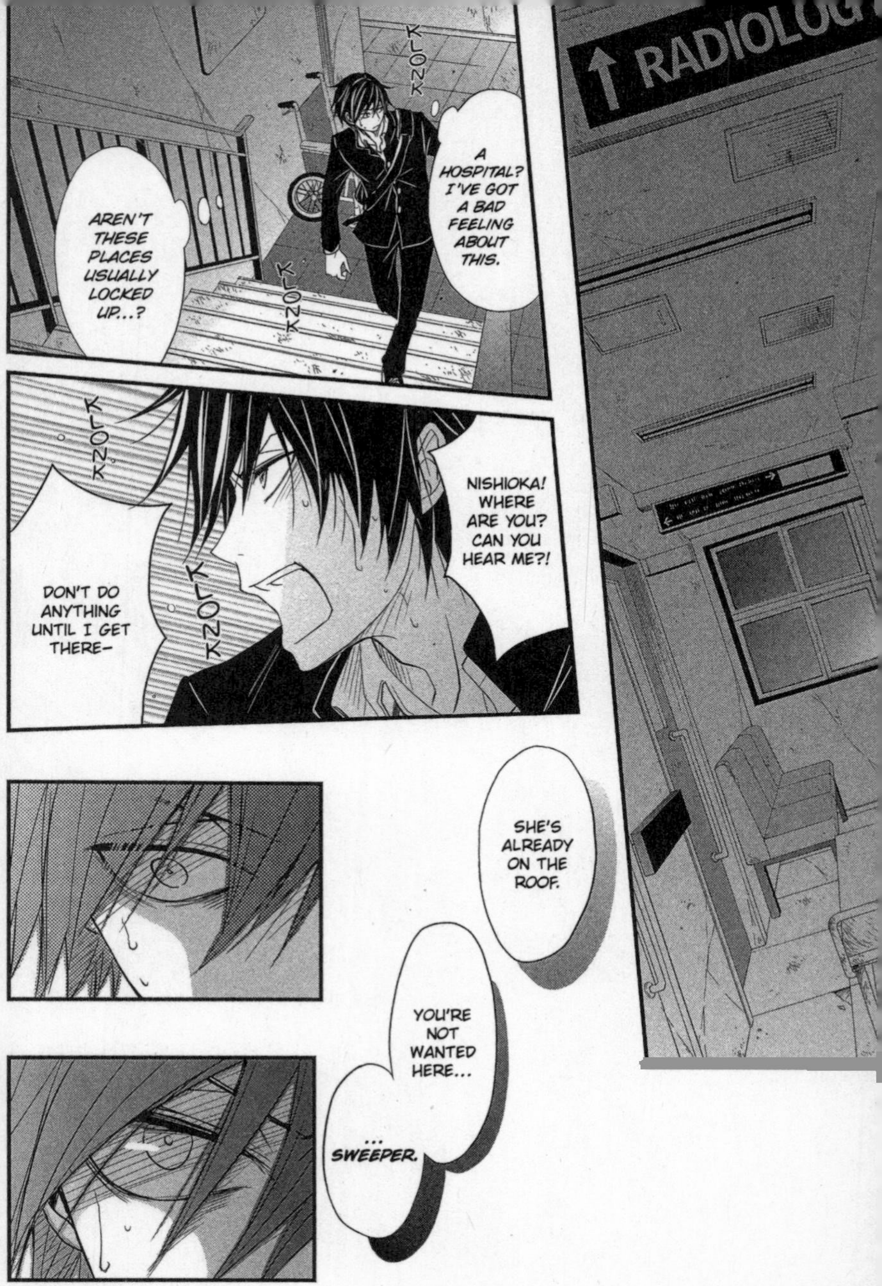
RADIOLOG
KLONK
A HOSPITAL? I'VE GOT A BAD FEELING ABOUT THIS.
KLONK
AREN'T THESE PLACES USUALLY LOCKED UP...?
NISHIOKA! WHERE ARE YOU? CAN YOU HEAR ME?!
KLONK
KLONK
DON'T DO ANYTHING UNTIL I GET THERE–
SHE'S ALREADY ON THE ROOF.
YOU'RE NOT WANTED HERE...
...SWEEPER.

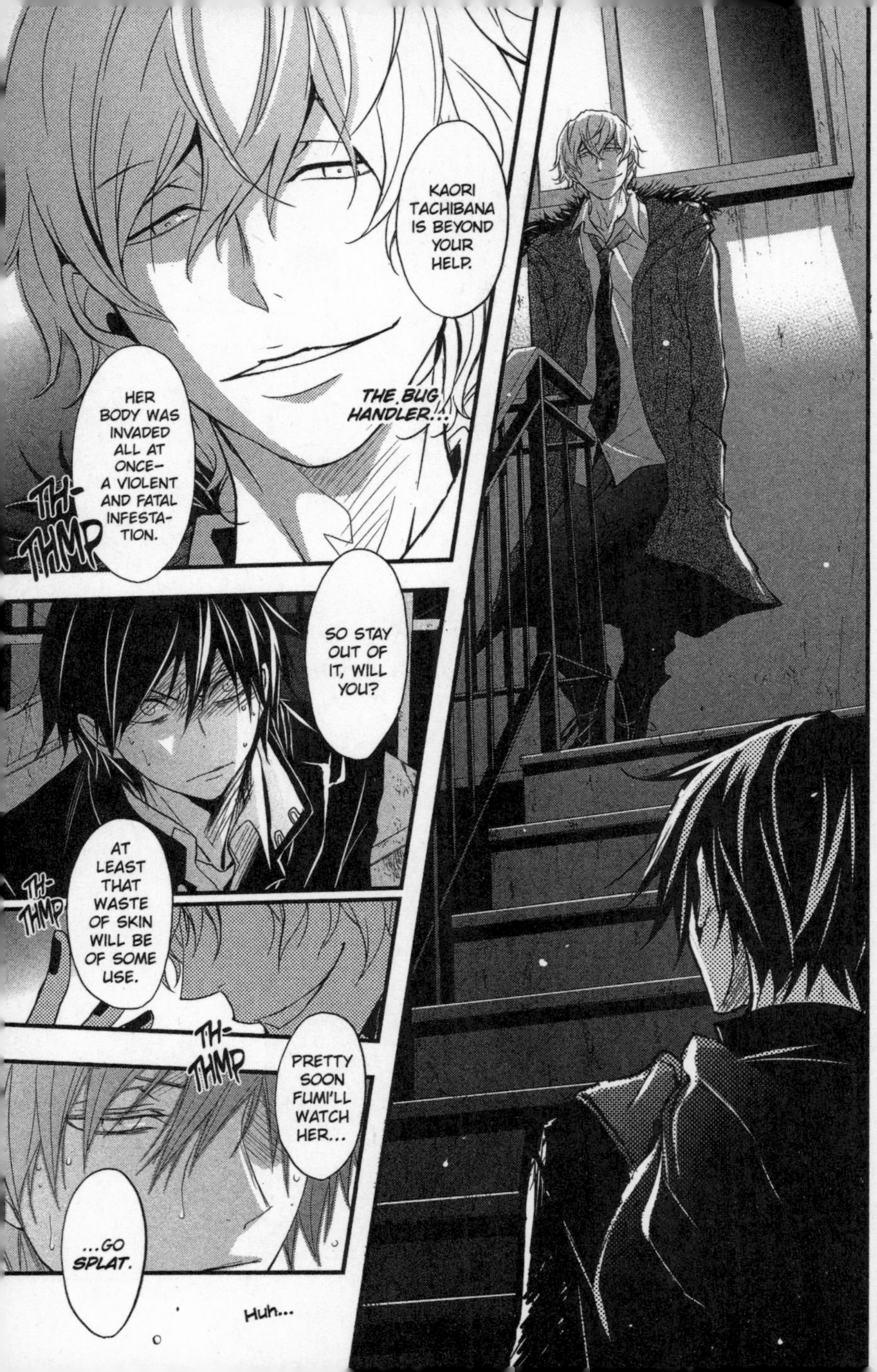
KAORI TACHIBANA IS BEYOND YOUR HELP.
THE BUG HANDLER...
HER BODY WAS INVADED ALL AT ONCE— A VIOLENT AND FATAL INFESTATION.
TH-THMP
SO STAY OUT OF IT, WILL YOU?
TH-THMP
AT LEAST THAT WASTE OF SKIN WILL BE OF SOME USE.
PRETTY SOON FUMI'LL WATCH HER...
TH-THMP
...GO SPLAT.
Huh...

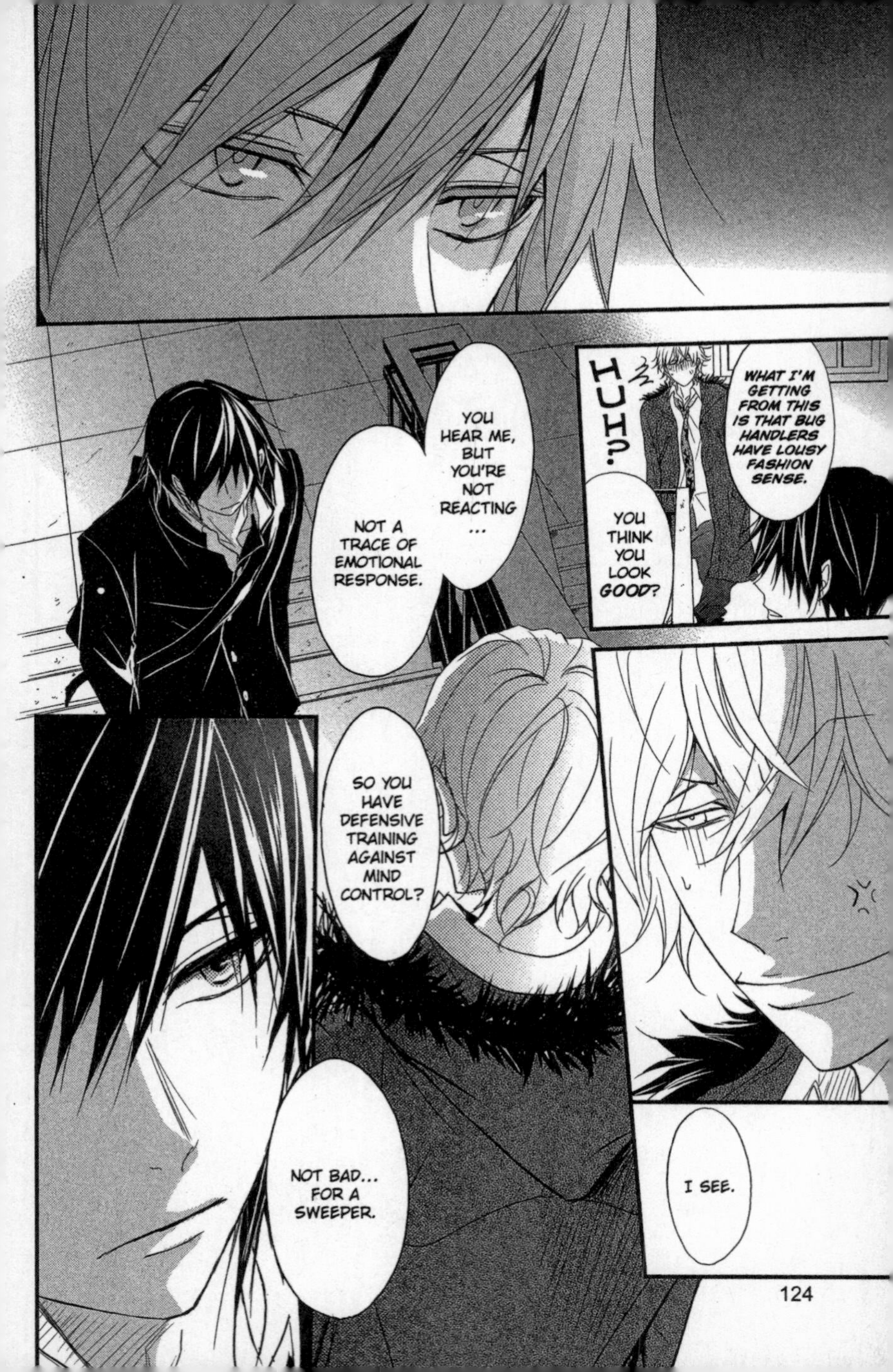
WHAT I'M GETTING FROM THIS IS THAT BUG HANDLERS HAVE LOUSY FASHION SENSE.
HUH?
YOU THINK YOU LOOK GOOD?
YOU HEAR ME, BUT YOU'RE NOT REACTING...
NOT A TRACE OF EMOTIONAL RESPONSE.
SO YOU HAVE DEFENSIVE TRAINING AGAINST MIND CONTROL?
I SEE.
NOT BAD... FOR A SWEEPER.

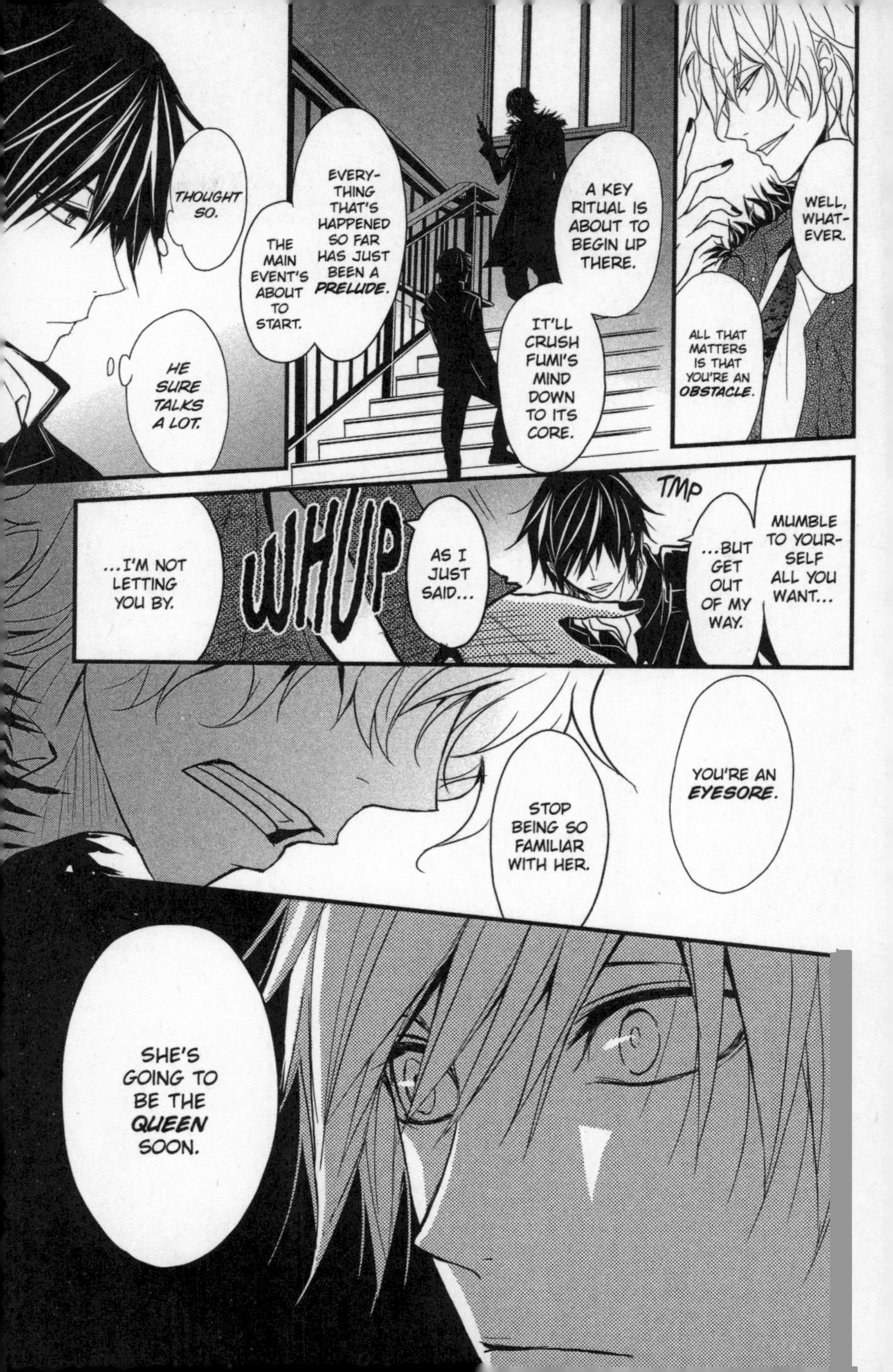
WELL, WHAT-EVER.
ALL THAT MATTERS IS THAT YOU'RE AN OBSTACLE.
A KEY RITUAL IS ABOUT TO BEGIN UP THERE.
IT'LL CRUSH FUMI'S MIND DOWN TO ITS CORE.
EVERY-THING THAT'S HAPPENED SO FAR HAS JUST BEEN A PRELUDE.
THE MAIN EVENT'S ABOUT TO START.
THOUGHT SO.
HE SURE TALKS A LOT.
TMP
MUMBLE TO YOUR-SELF ALL YOU WANT...
...BUT GET OUT OF MY WAY.
AS I JUST SAID...
WHUP
...I'M NOT LETTING YOU BY.
YOU'RE AN EYESORE.
STOP BEING SO FAMILIAR WITH HER.
SHE'S GOING TO BE THE QUEEN SOON.

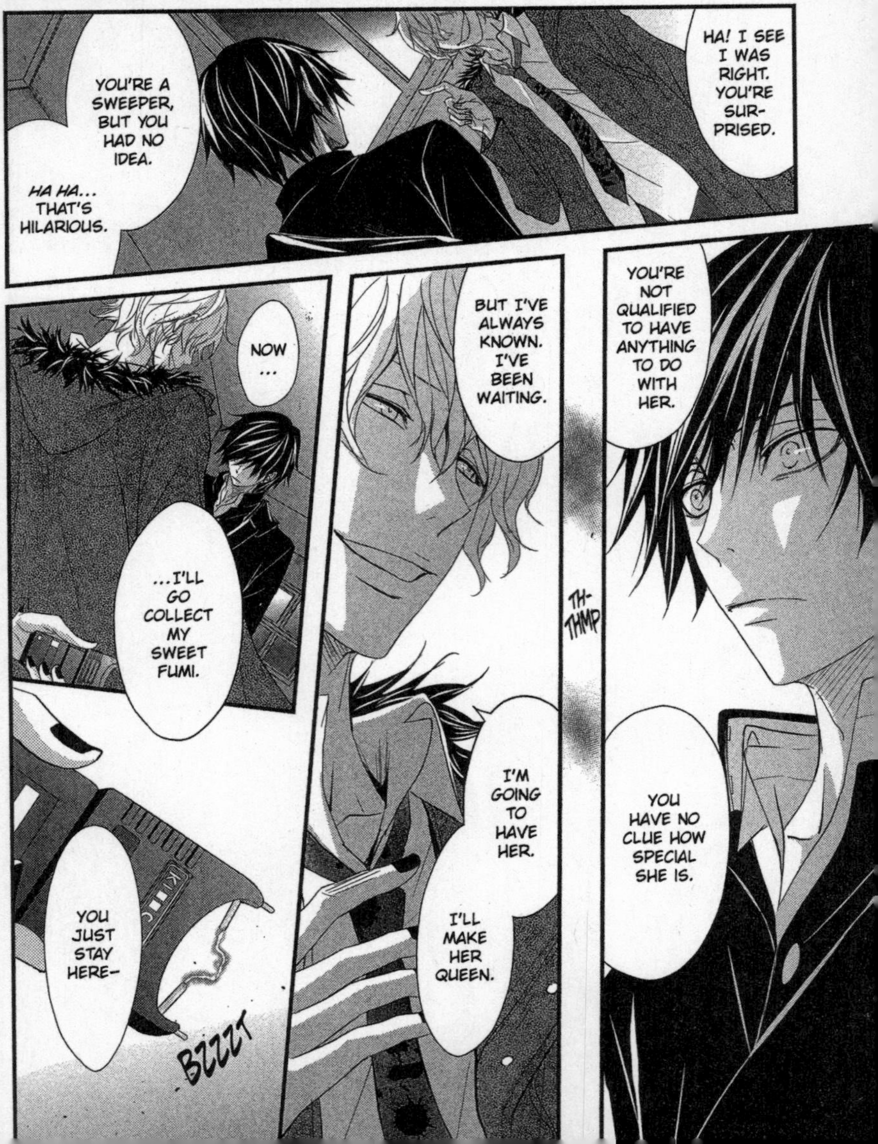
HA! I SEE I WAS RIGHT. YOU'RE SUR-PRISED.
YOU'RE A SWEEPER, BUT YOU HAD NO IDEA.
HA HA... THAT'S HILARIOUS.
YOU'RE NOT QUALIFIED TO HAVE ANYTHING TO DO WITH HER.
TH-THMP
YOU HAVE NO CLUE HOW SPECIAL SHE IS.
BUT I'VE ALWAYS KNOWN. I'VE BEEN WAITING.
I'M GOING TO HAVE HER.
I'LL MAKE HER QUEEN.
NOW...
...I'LL GO COLLECT MY SWEET FUMI.
YOU JUST STAY HERE-
BZZZT

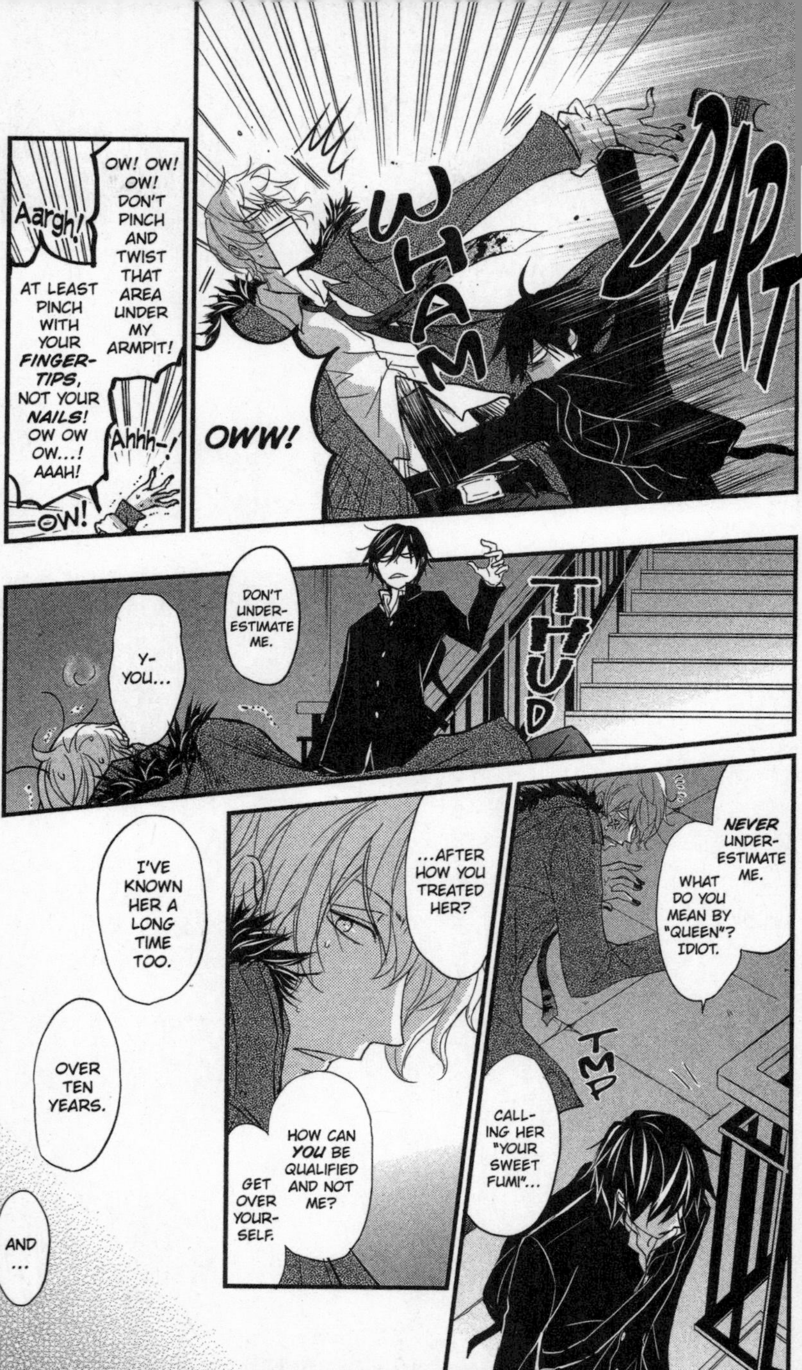
DART
WHAM
OWW!
OW! OW! OW! DON'T PINCH AND TWIST THAT AREA UNDER MY ARMPIT!
Aargh!
AT LEAST PINCH WITH YOUR *FINGER-TIPS*, NOT YOUR *NAILS*! OW OW OW...! AAAH!
Ahhh-!
OW!
THUD
DON'T UNDER-ESTIMATE ME.
Y-YOU...
NEVER UNDER-ESTIMATE ME.
WHAT DO YOU MEAN BY "QUEEN"? IDIOT.
TMP
CALL-ING HER "YOUR SWEET FUMI"...
...AFTER HOW YOU TREATED HER?
HOW CAN *YOU* BE QUALIFIED AND NOT ME?
GET OVER YOUR-SELF.
I'VE KNOWN HER A LONG TIME TOO.
OVER TEN YEARS.
AND ...

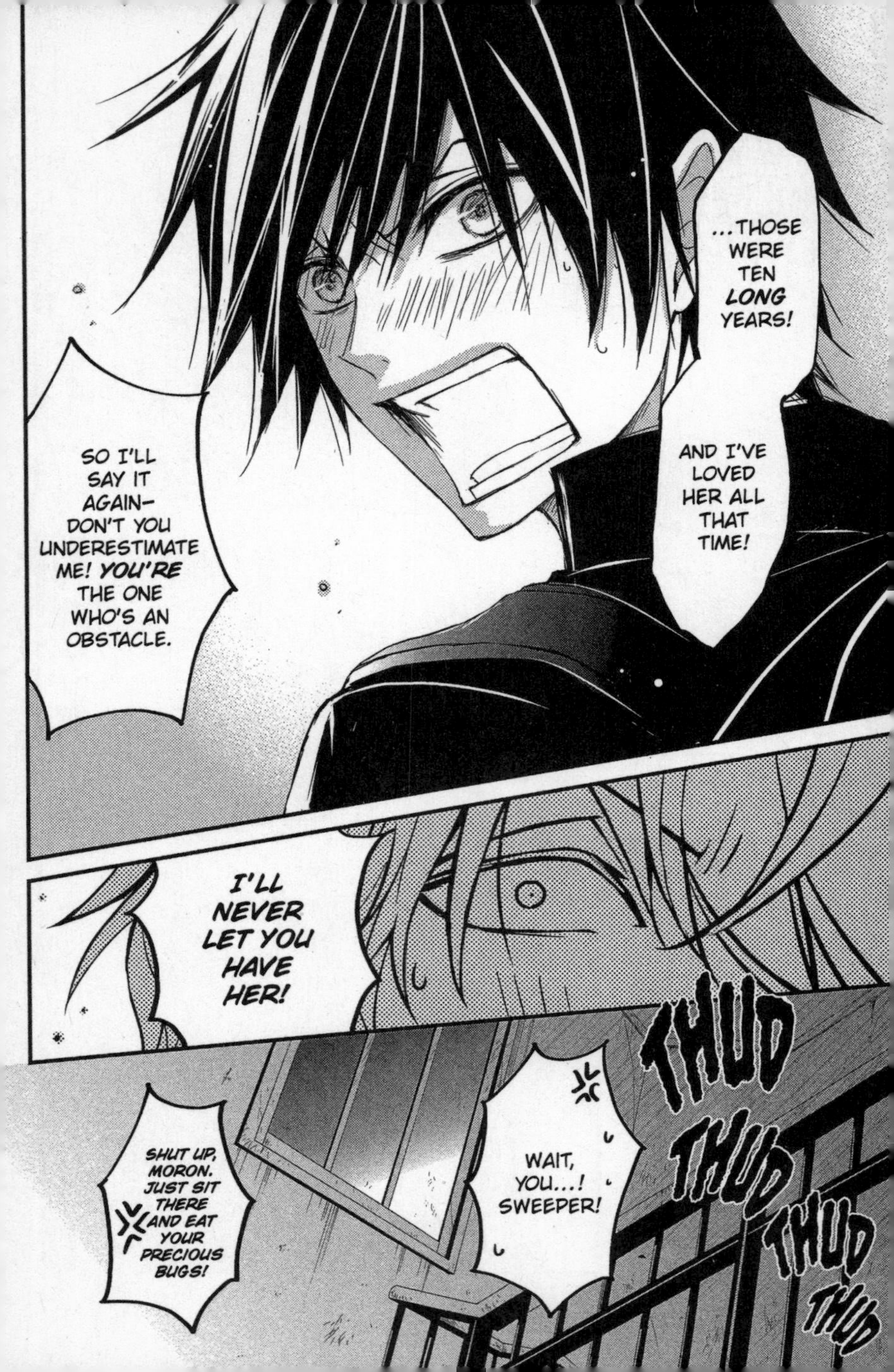
...THOSE WERE TEN LONG YEARS!
AND I'VE LOVED HER ALL THAT TIME!
SO I'LL SAY IT AGAIN—DON'T YOU UNDERESTIMATE ME! YOU'RE THE ONE WHO'S AN OBSTACLE.
I'LL NEVER LET YOU HAVE HER!
THUD THUD THUD THUD
WAIT, YOU...! SWEEPER!
SHUT UP, MORON. JUST SIT THERE AND EAT YOUR PRECIOUS BUGS!

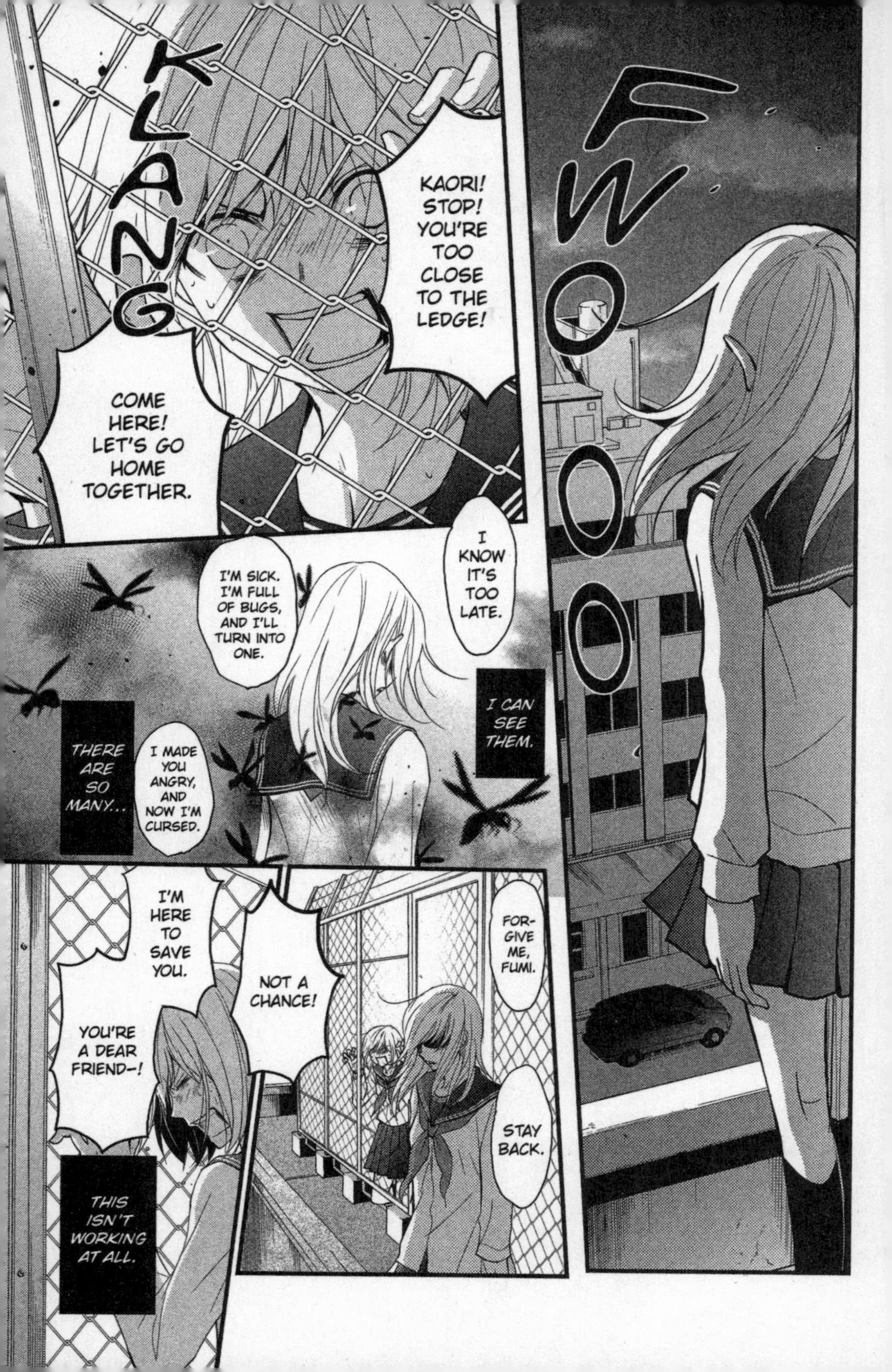
FWOOOOO
KLANG
KAORI! STOP! YOU'RE TOO CLOSE TO THE LEDGE!
COME HERE! LET'S GO HOME TOGETHER.
I KNOW IT'S TOO LATE.
I CAN SEE THEM.
I'M SICK. I'M FULL OF BUGS, AND I'LL TURN INTO ONE.
I MADE YOU ANGRY, AND NOW I'M CURSED.
THERE ARE SO MANY...
FOR-GIVE ME, FUMI.
NOT A CHANCE!
I'M HERE TO SAVE YOU.
YOU'RE A DEAR FRIEND—!
STAY BACK.
THIS ISN'T WORKING AT ALL.

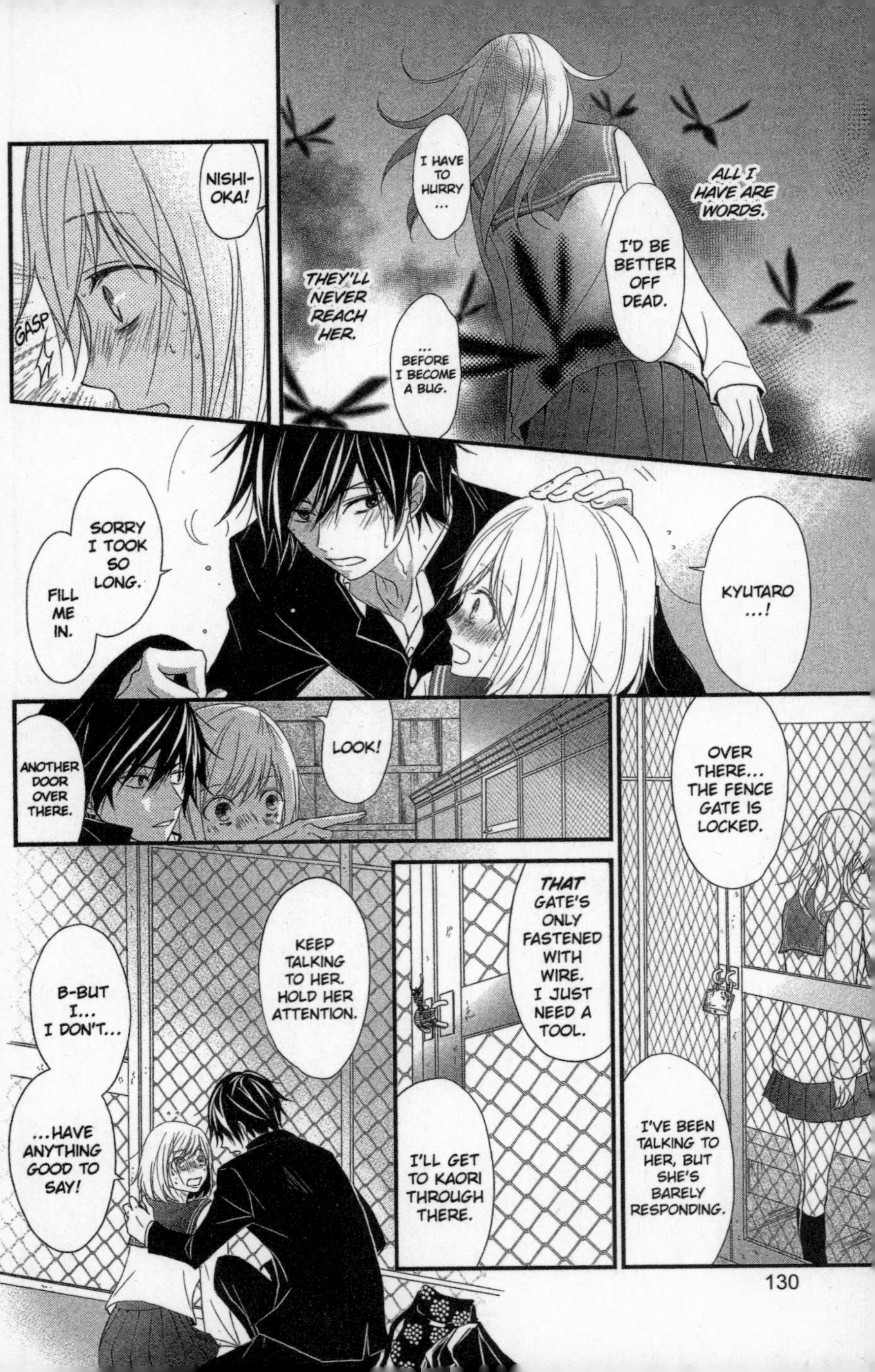
ALL I HAVE ARE WORDS.
I'D BE BETTER OFF DEAD.
I HAVE TO HURRY...
...BEFORE I BECOME A BUG.
THEY'LL NEVER REACH HER.
NISHI-OKA!
GASP
KYUTARO ...!
SORRY I TOOK SO LONG.
FILL ME IN.
OVER THERE... THE FENCE GATE IS LOCKED.
I'VE BEEN TALKING TO HER, BUT SHE'S BARELY RESPONDING.
LOOK!
ANOTHER DOOR OVER THERE.
THAT GATE'S ONLY FASTENED WITH WIRE. I JUST NEED A TOOL.
KEEP TALKING TO HER. HOLD HER ATTENTION.
I'LL GET TO KAORI THROUGH THERE.
B-BUT I... I DON'T...
...HAVE ANYTHING GOOD TO SAY!

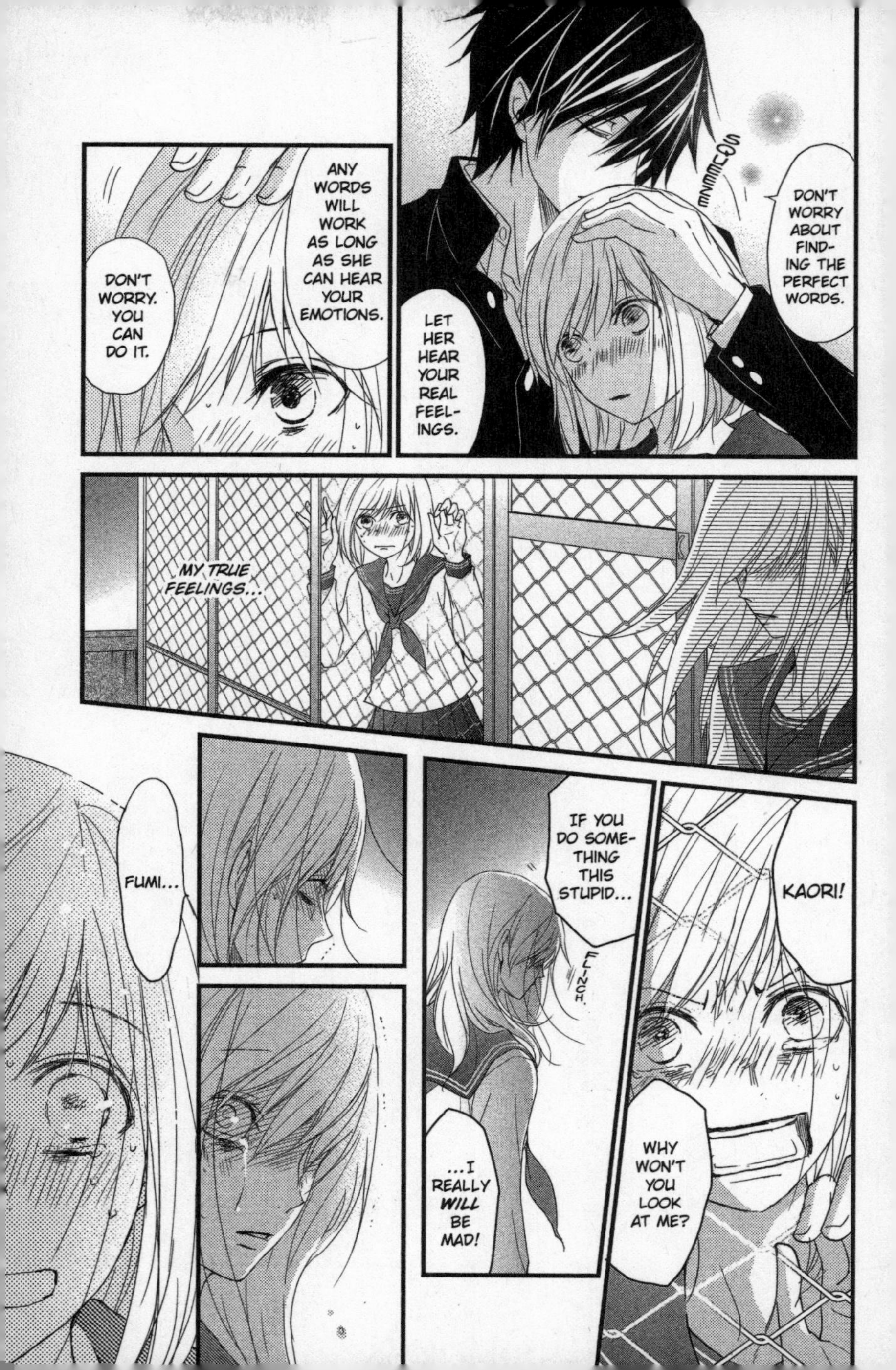
SQUEEEE
DON'T WORRY ABOUT FINDING THE PERFECT WORDS.
LET HER HEAR YOUR REAL FEELINGS.
ANY WORDS WILL WORK AS LONG AS SHE CAN HEAR YOUR EMOTIONS.
DON'T WORRY. YOU CAN DO IT.
MY TRUE FEELINGS...
KAORI!
WHY WON'T YOU LOOK AT ME?
IF YOU DO SOMETHING THIS STUPID...
FLINCH
...I REALLY **WILL** BE MAD!
FUMI...

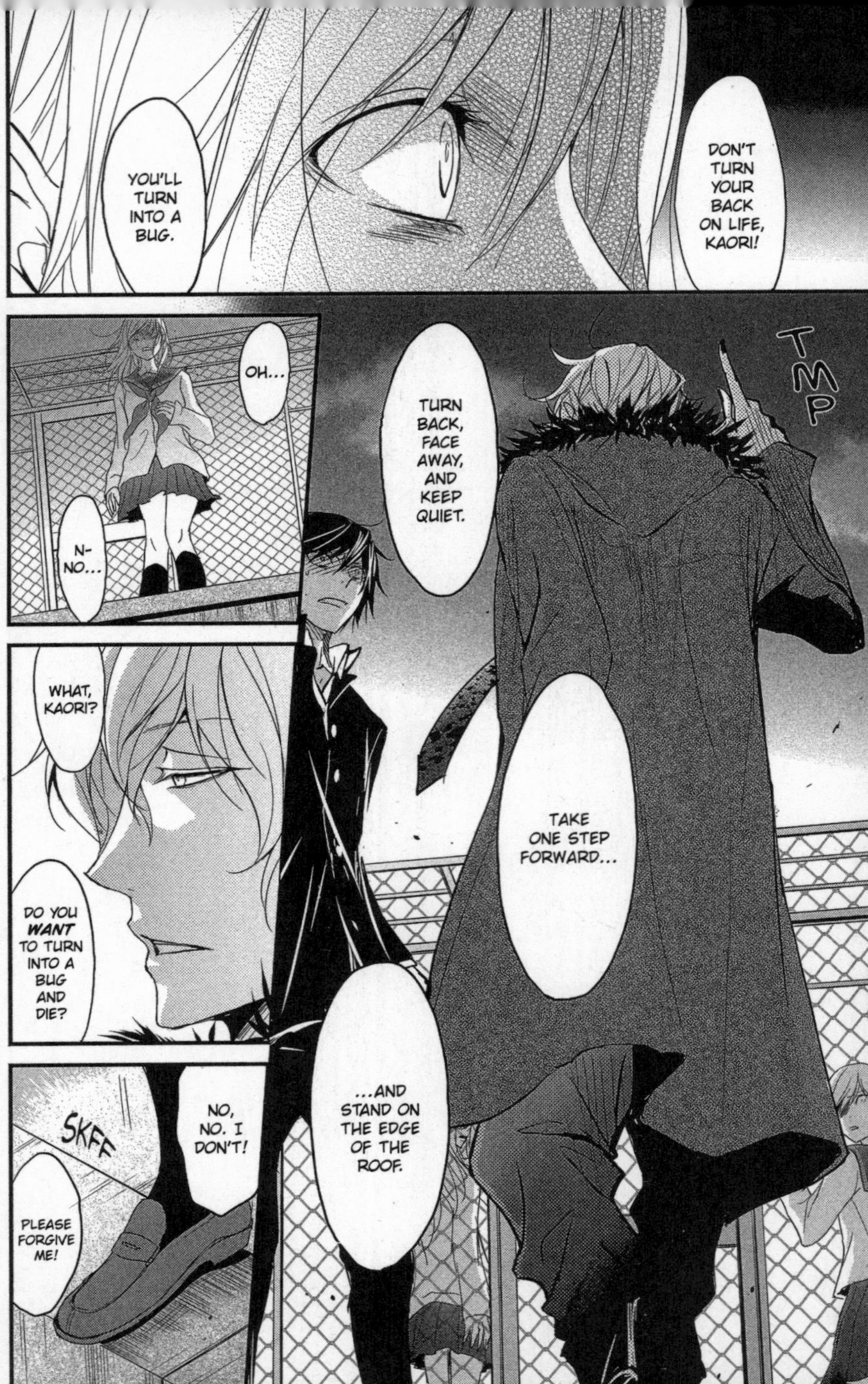
DON'T TURN YOUR BACK ON LIFE, KAORI!
YOU'LL TURN INTO A BUG.
TMP
TURN BACK, FACE AWAY, AND KEEP QUIET.
TAKE ONE STEP FORWARD...
...AND STAND ON THE EDGE OF THE ROOF.
OH...
N-NO...
WHAT, KAORI?
DO YOU **WANT** TO TURN INTO A BUG AND DIE?
NO, NO. I DON'T!
SKFF
PLEASE FORGIVE ME!

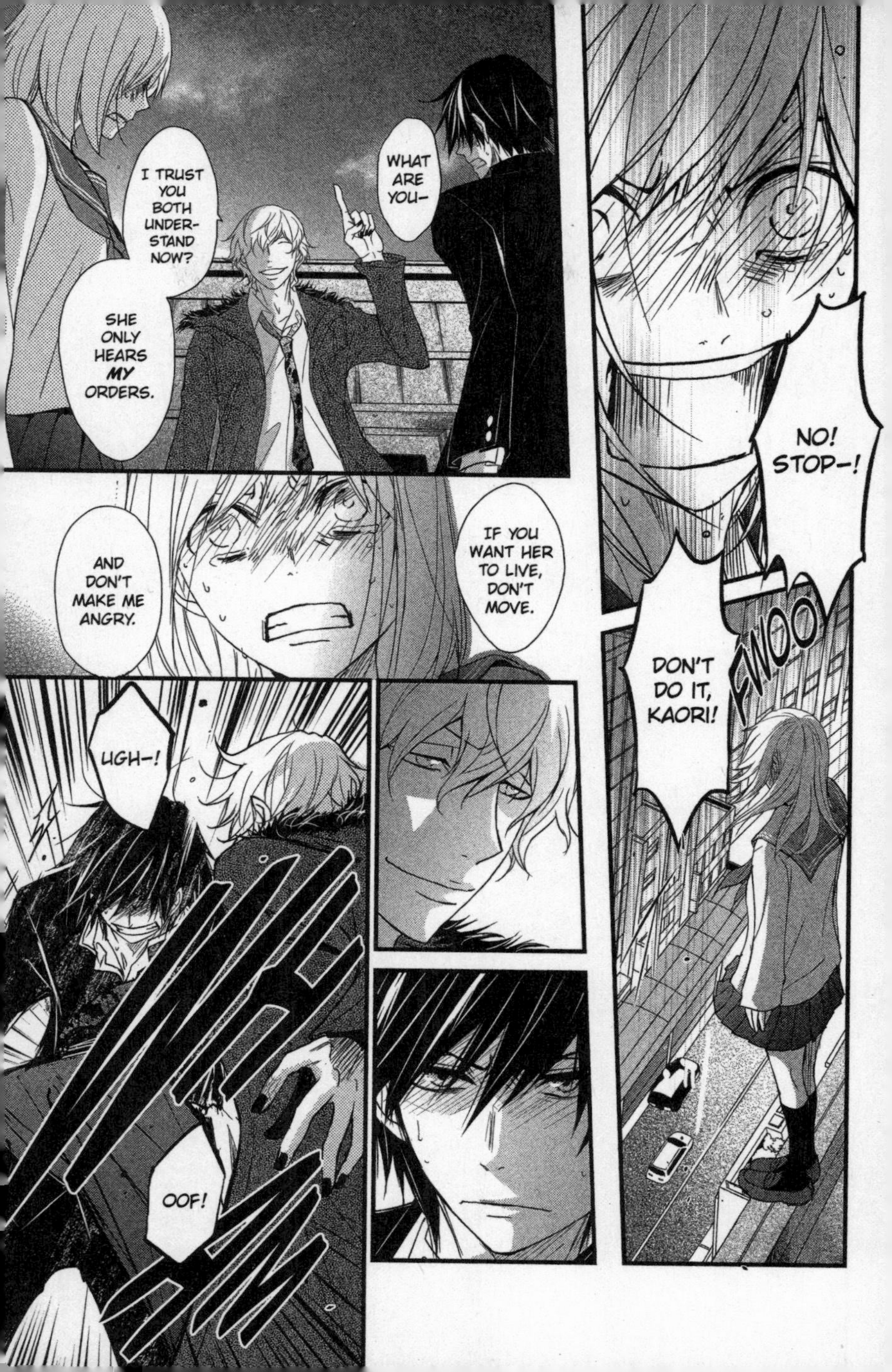
NO! STOP-!
FWOO
DON'T DO IT, KAORI!
WHAT ARE YOU-
I TRUST YOU BOTH UNDER-STAND NOW?
SHE ONLY HEARS *MY* ORDERS.
IF YOU WANT HER TO LIVE, DON'T MOVE.
AND DON'T MAKE ME ANGRY.
UGH-!
OOF!

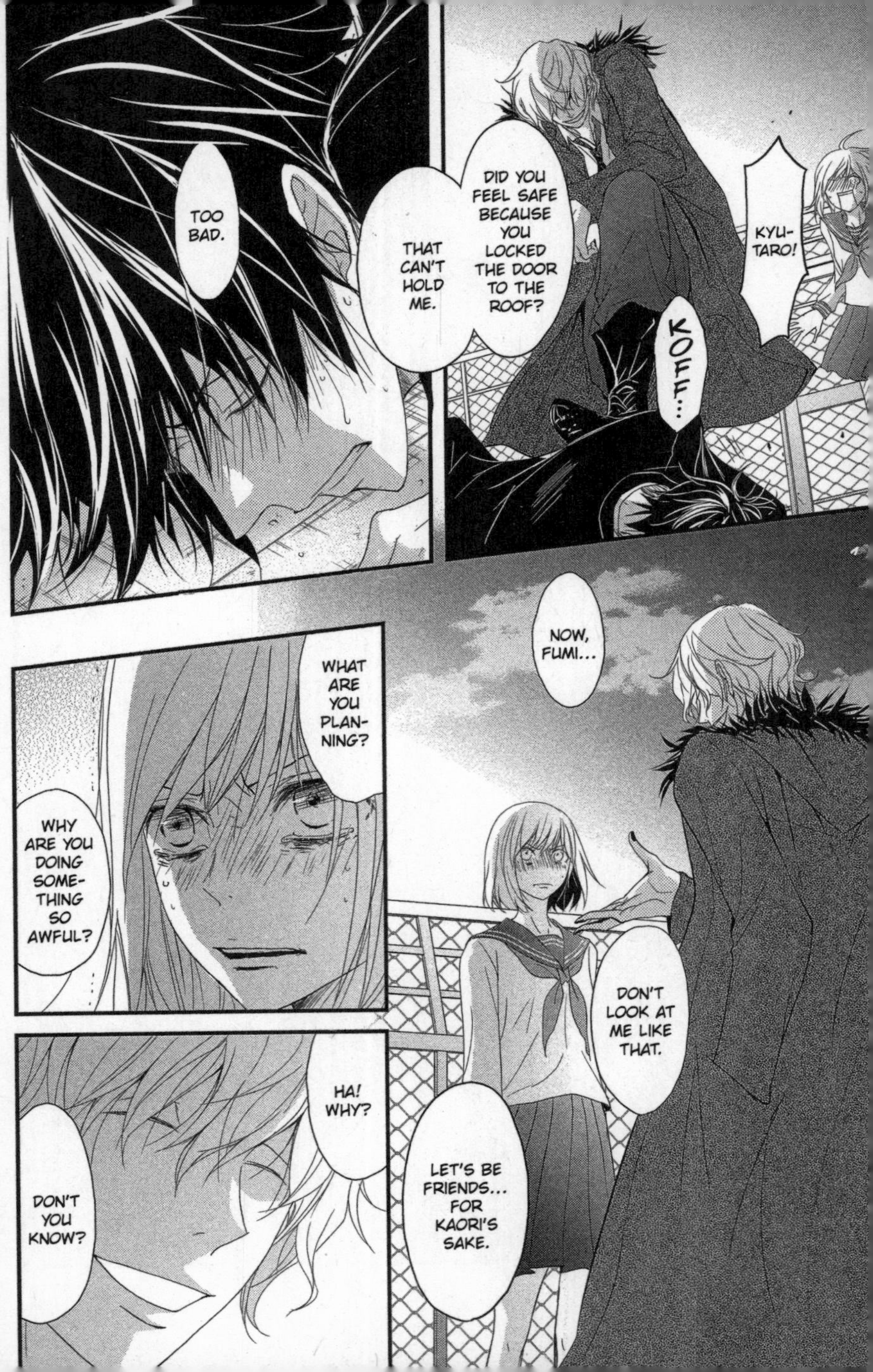
KYU-TARO!
DID YOU FEEL SAFE BECAUSE YOU LOCKED THE DOOR TO THE ROOF?
THAT CAN'T HOLD ME.
KOFF...
TOO BAD.
NOW, FUMI...
DON'T LOOK AT ME LIKE THAT.
LET'S BE FRIENDS... FOR KAORI'S SAKE.
WHAT ARE YOU PLANNING?
WHY ARE YOU DOING SOMETHING SO AWFUL?
HA! WHY?
DON'T YOU KNOW?

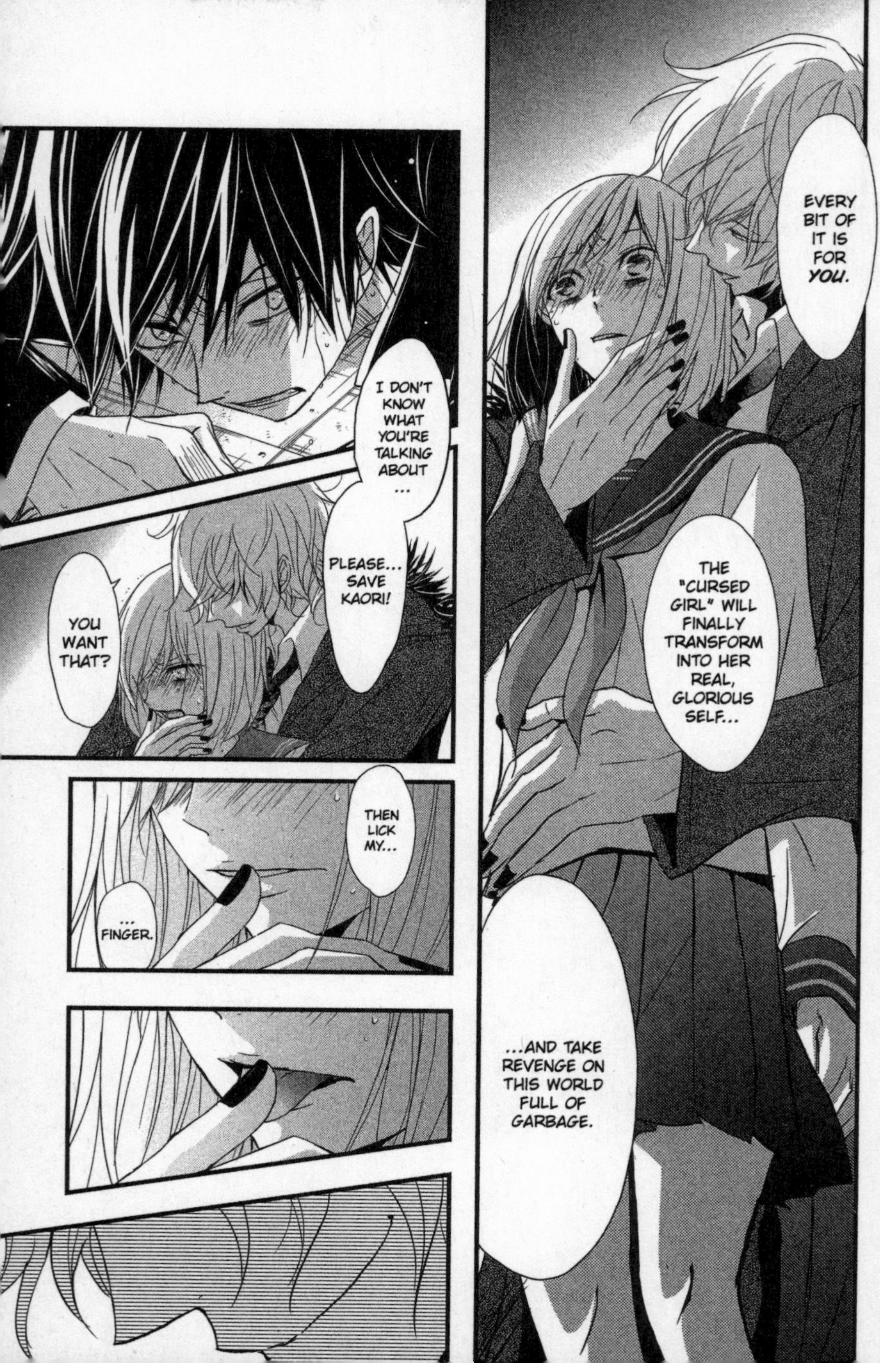
EVERY BIT OF IT IS FOR *YOU*.
THE "CURSED GIRL" WILL FINALLY TRANSFORM INTO HER REAL, GLORIOUS SELF...
...AND TAKE REVENGE ON THIS WORLD FULL OF GARBAGE.
I DON'T KNOW WHAT YOU'RE TALKING ABOUT...
PLEASE... SAVE KAORI!
YOU WANT THAT?
THEN LICK MY...
...FINGER.

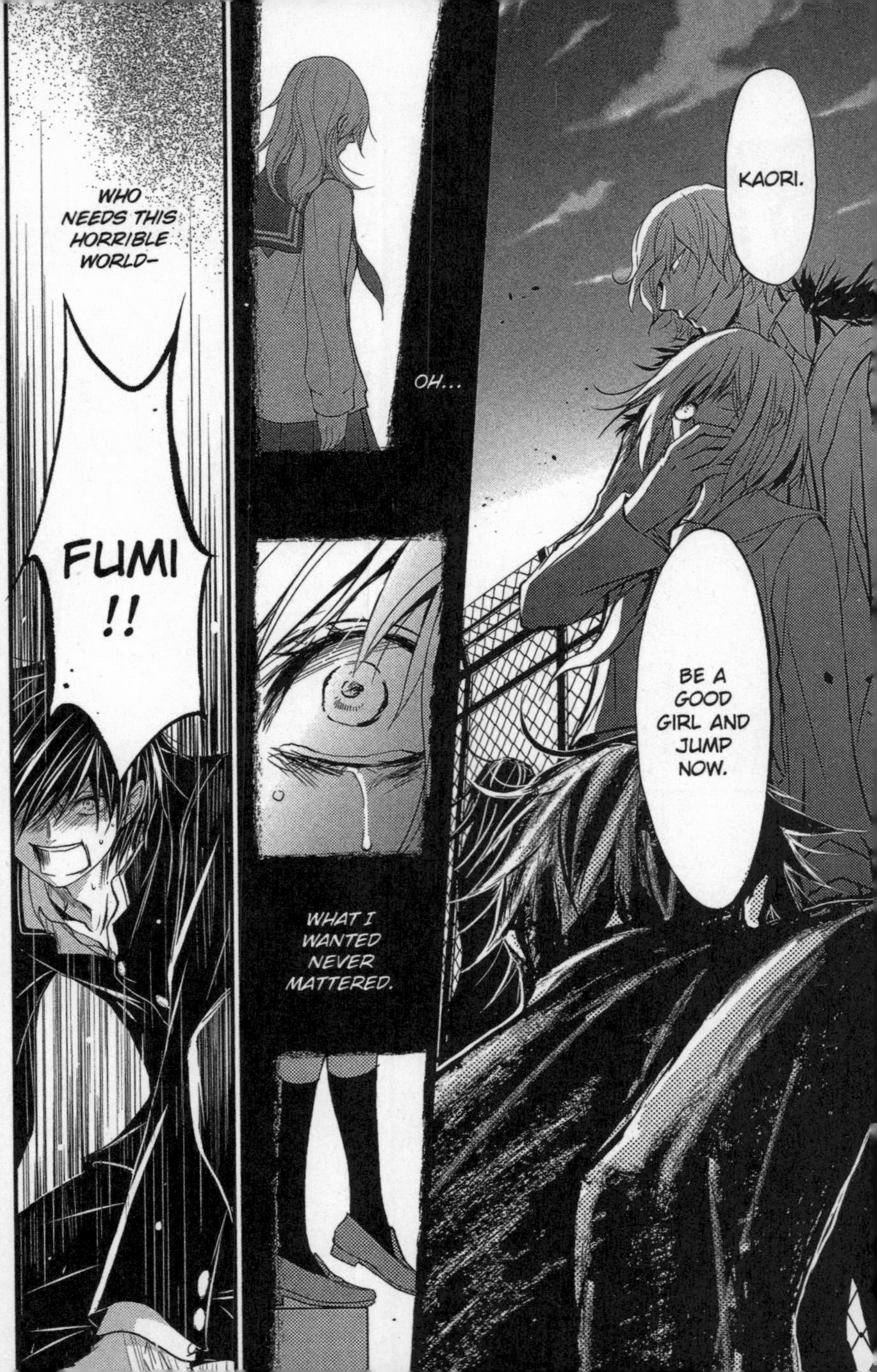

KAORI.
BE A GOOD GIRL AND JUMP NOW.
OH...
WHAT I WANTED NEVER MATTERED.
WHO NEEDS THIS HORRIBLE WORLD-
FUMI!!

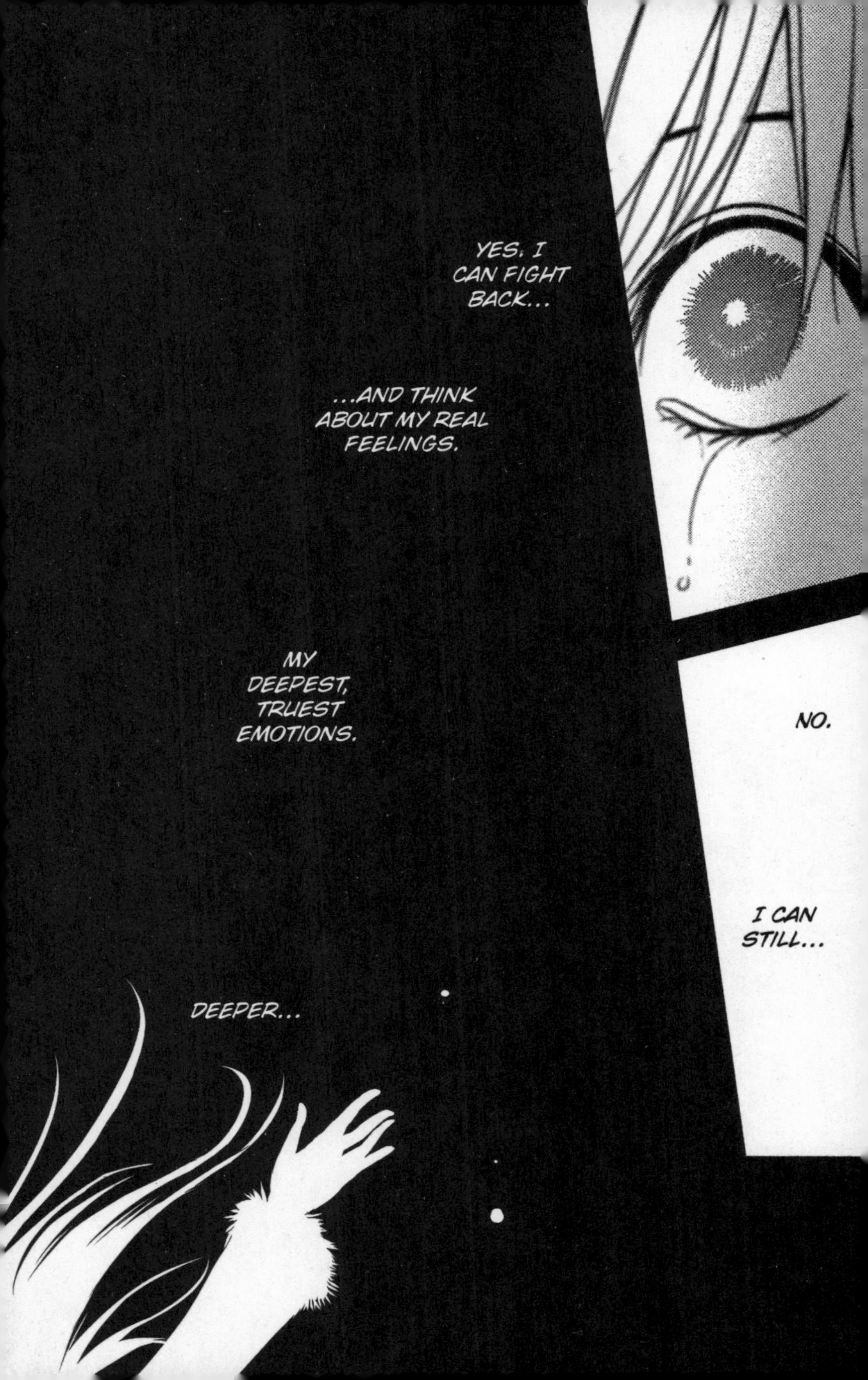
NO.
I CAN STILL...
YES, I CAN FIGHT BACK...
...AND THINK ABOUT MY REAL FEELINGS.
MY DEEPEST, TRUEST EMOTIONS.
DEEPER...

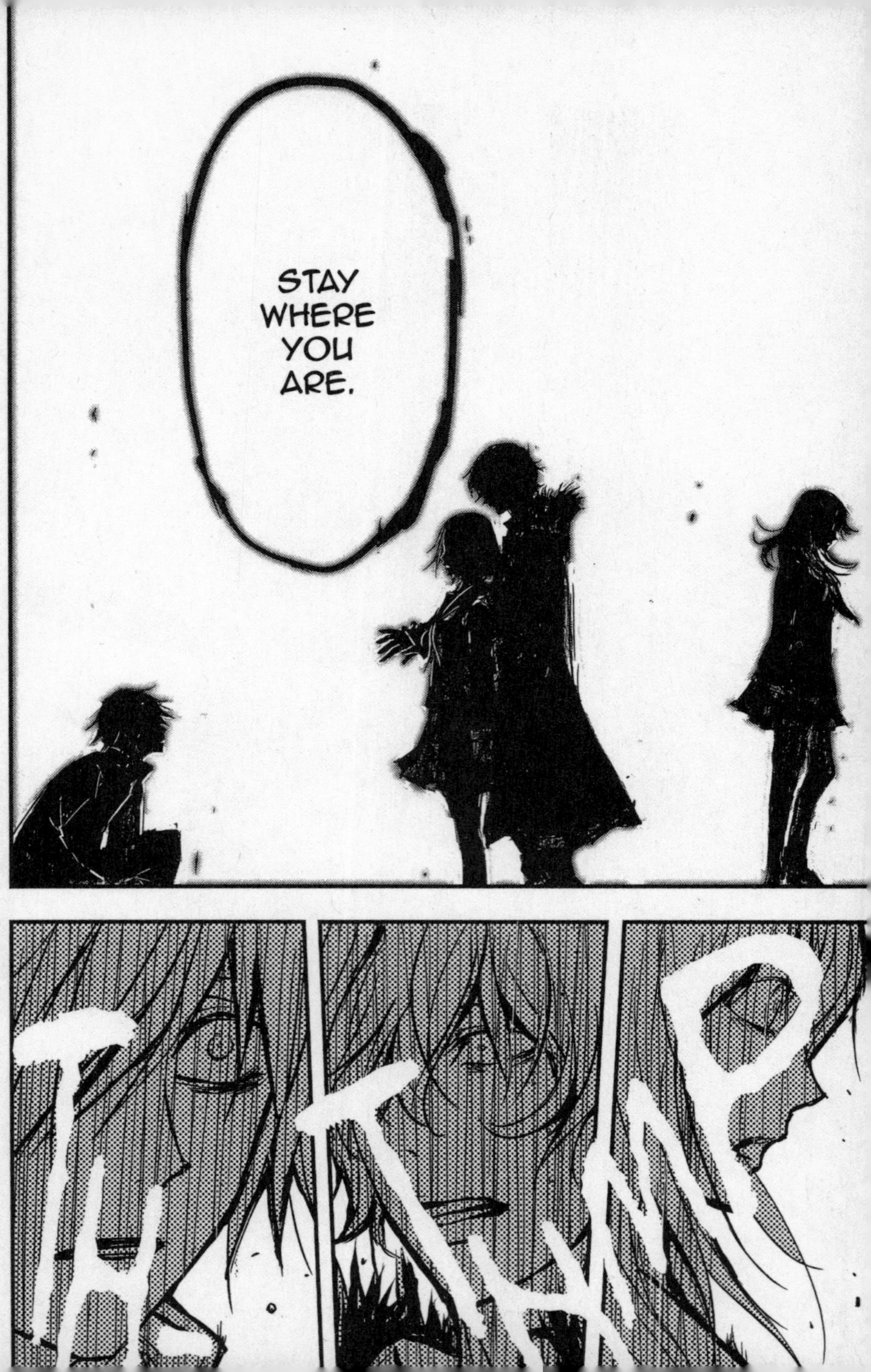
STAY WHERE YOU ARE.

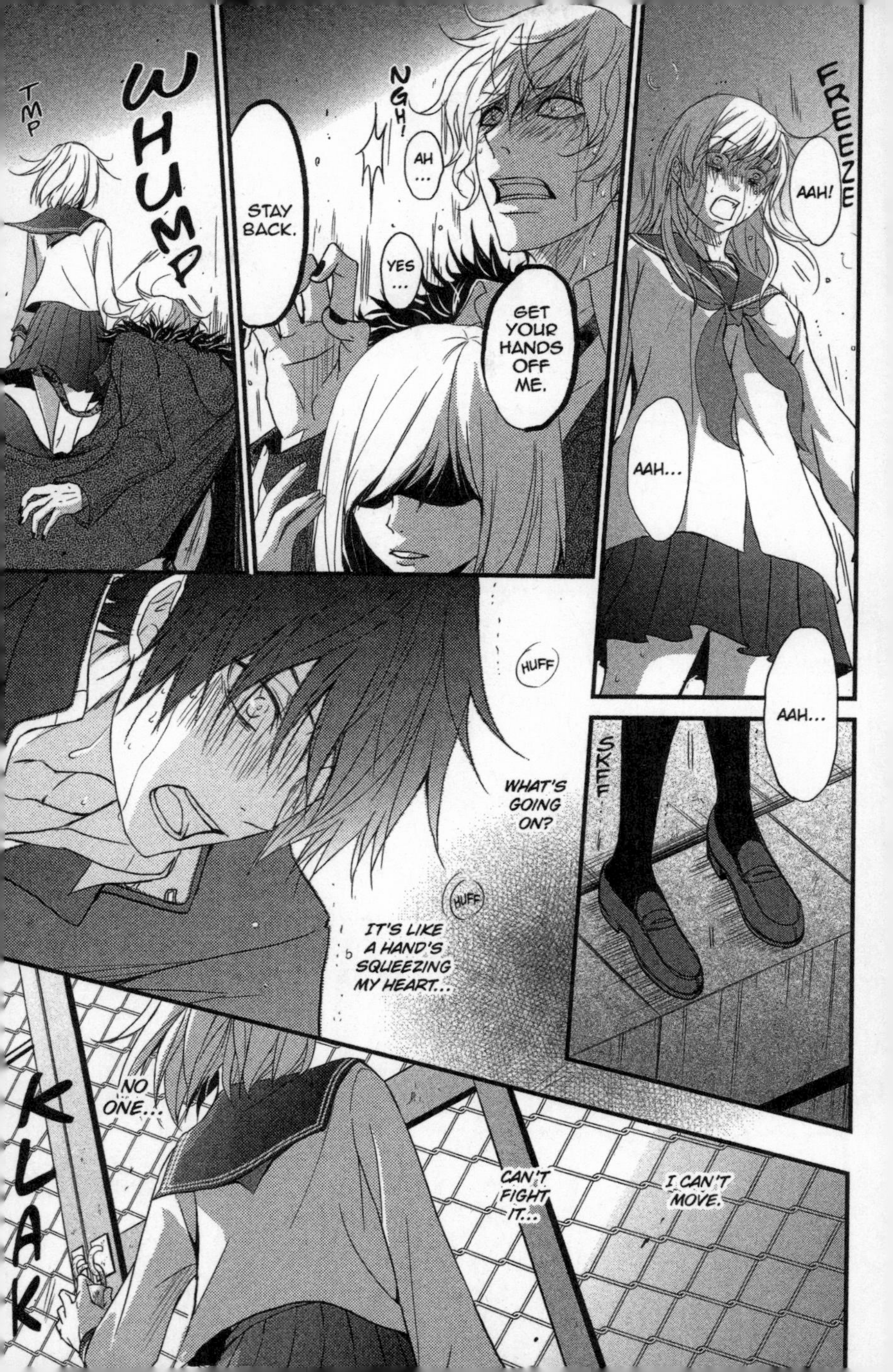
FREEZE
AAH!
AAH...
AH...
NGH!
GET YOUR HANDS OFF ME.
YES...
STAY BACK.
TMP
WHUMP
AAH...
SKFF
HUFF
WHAT'S GOING ON?
HUFF
IT'S LIKE A HAND'S SQUEEZING MY HEART...
I CAN'T MOVE.
CAN'T FIGHT IT...
NO ONE...
KLAK

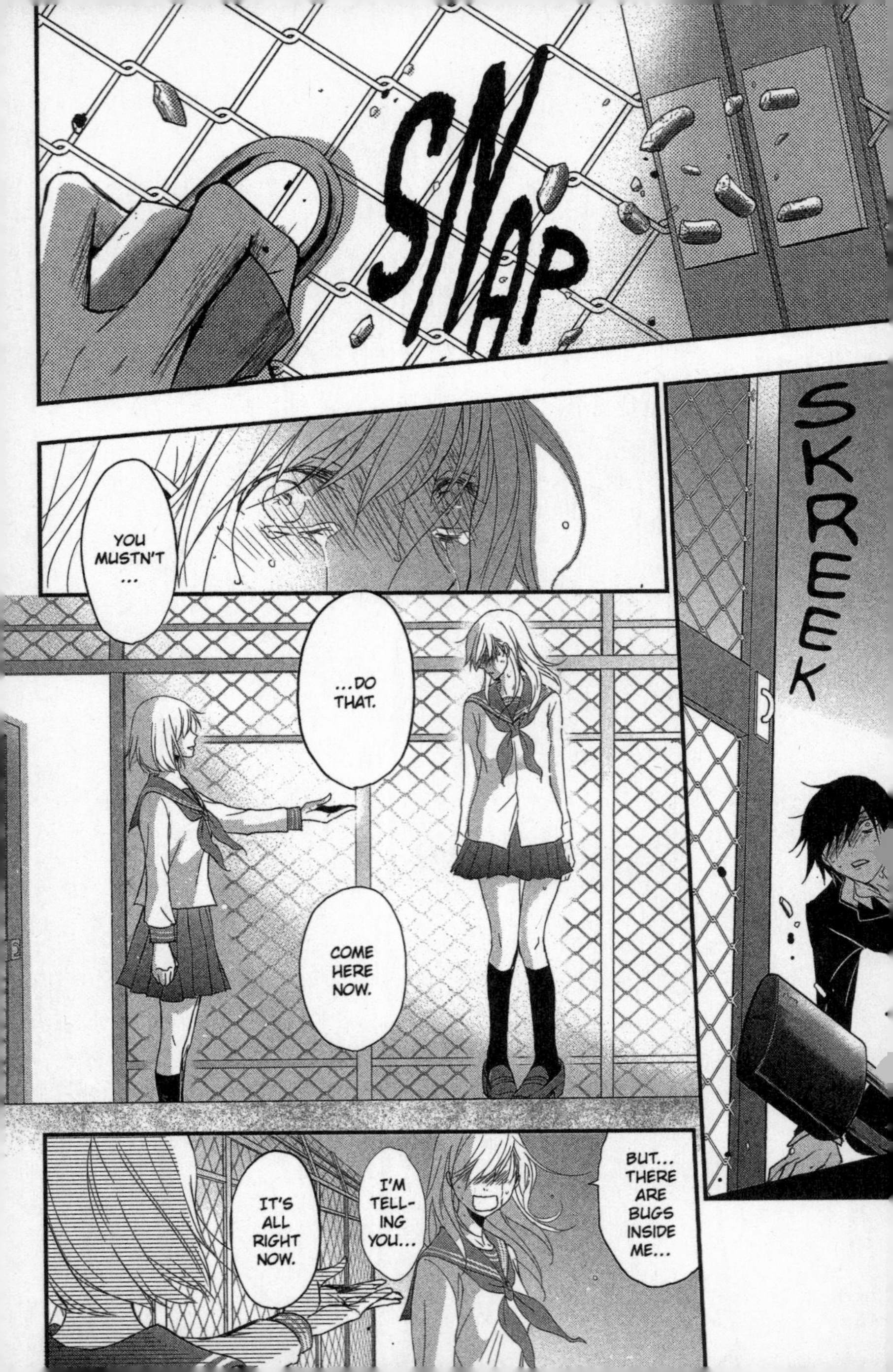
SNAP
SKREEK
YOU MUSTN'T ...
...DO THAT.
COME HERE NOW.
BUT... THERE ARE BUGS INSIDE ME...
I'M TELL-ING YOU...
IT'S ALL RIGHT NOW.

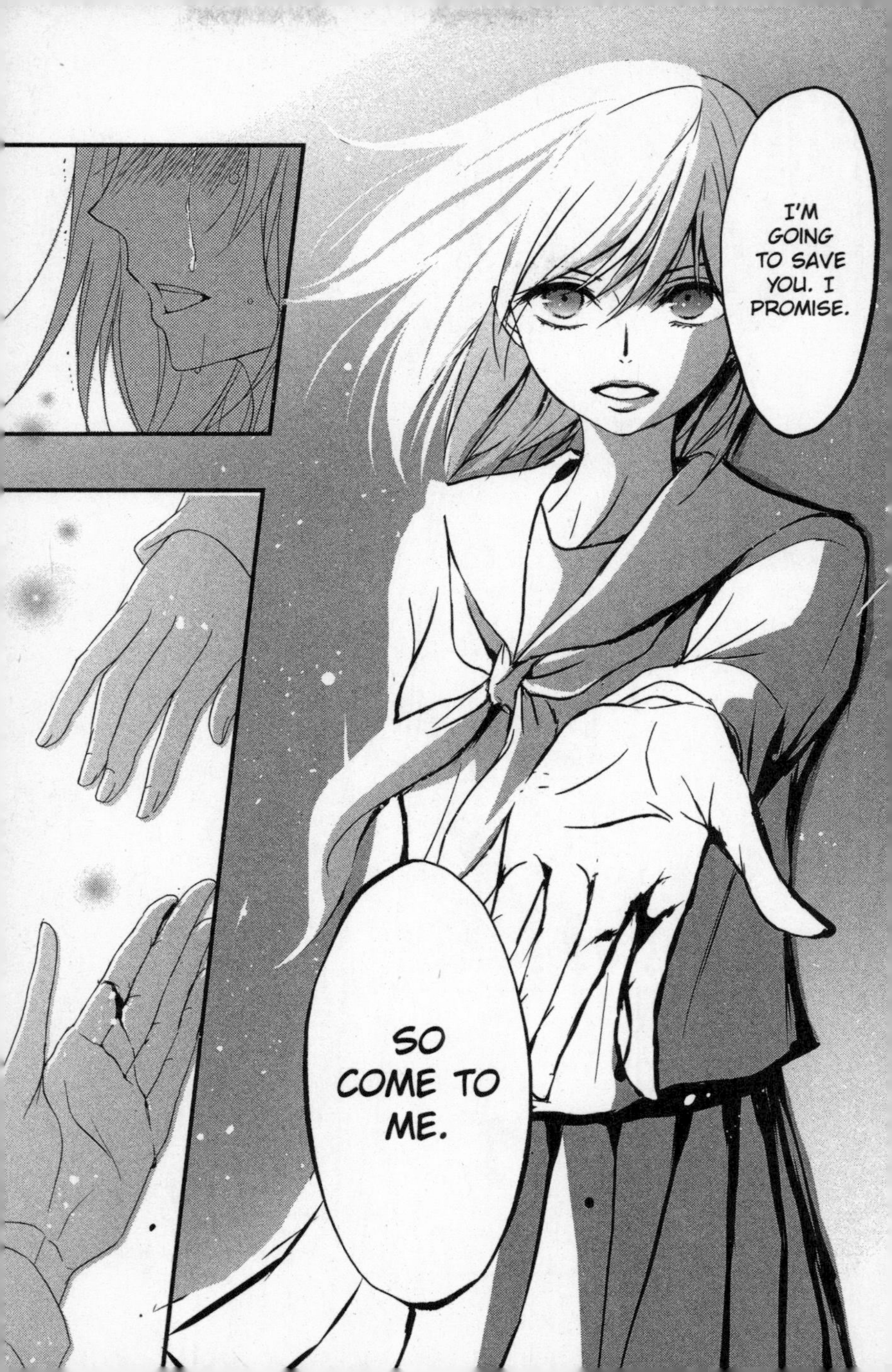
I'M GOING TO SAVE YOU. I PROMISE.
SO COME TO ME.

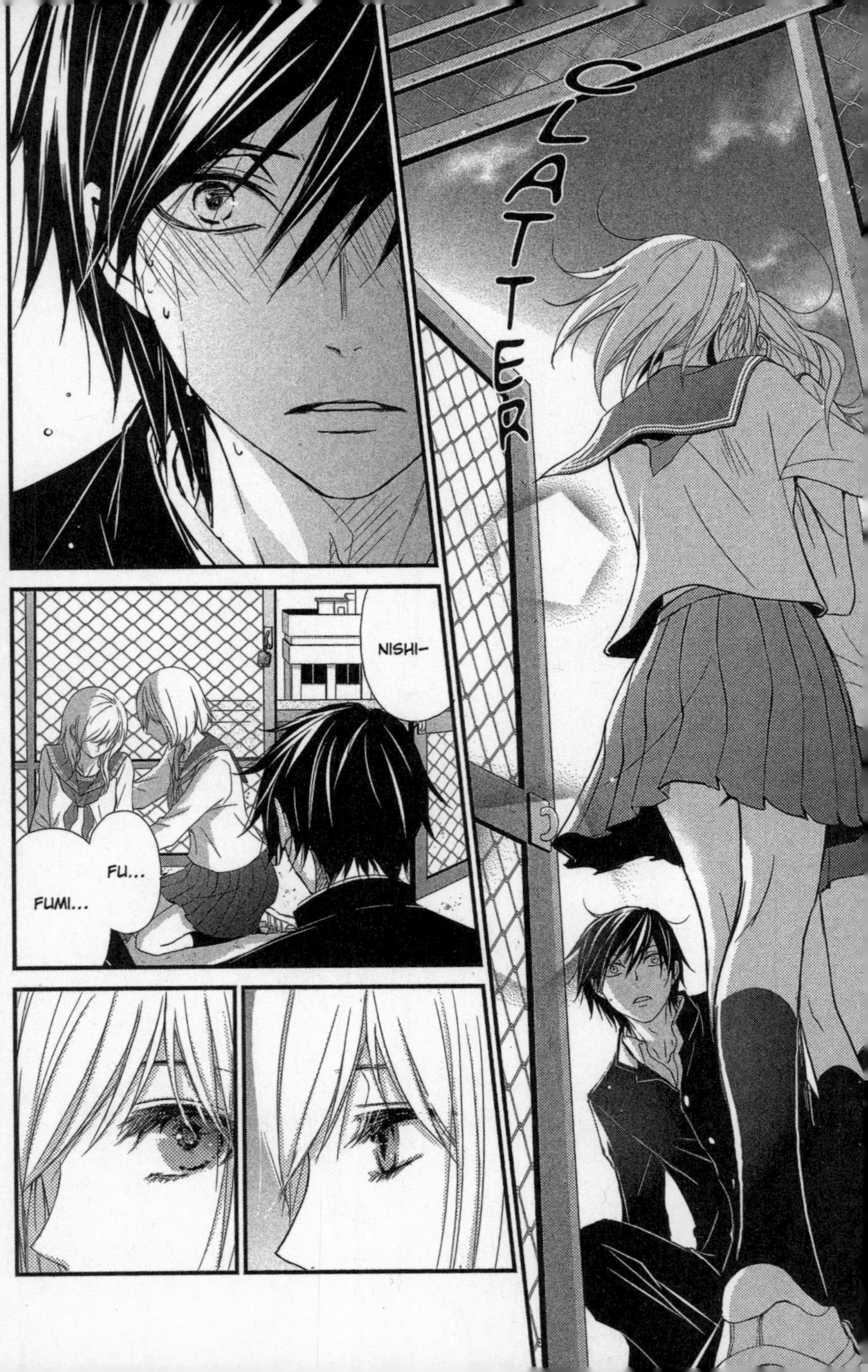
CLATTER
NISHI-
FU... FUMI...

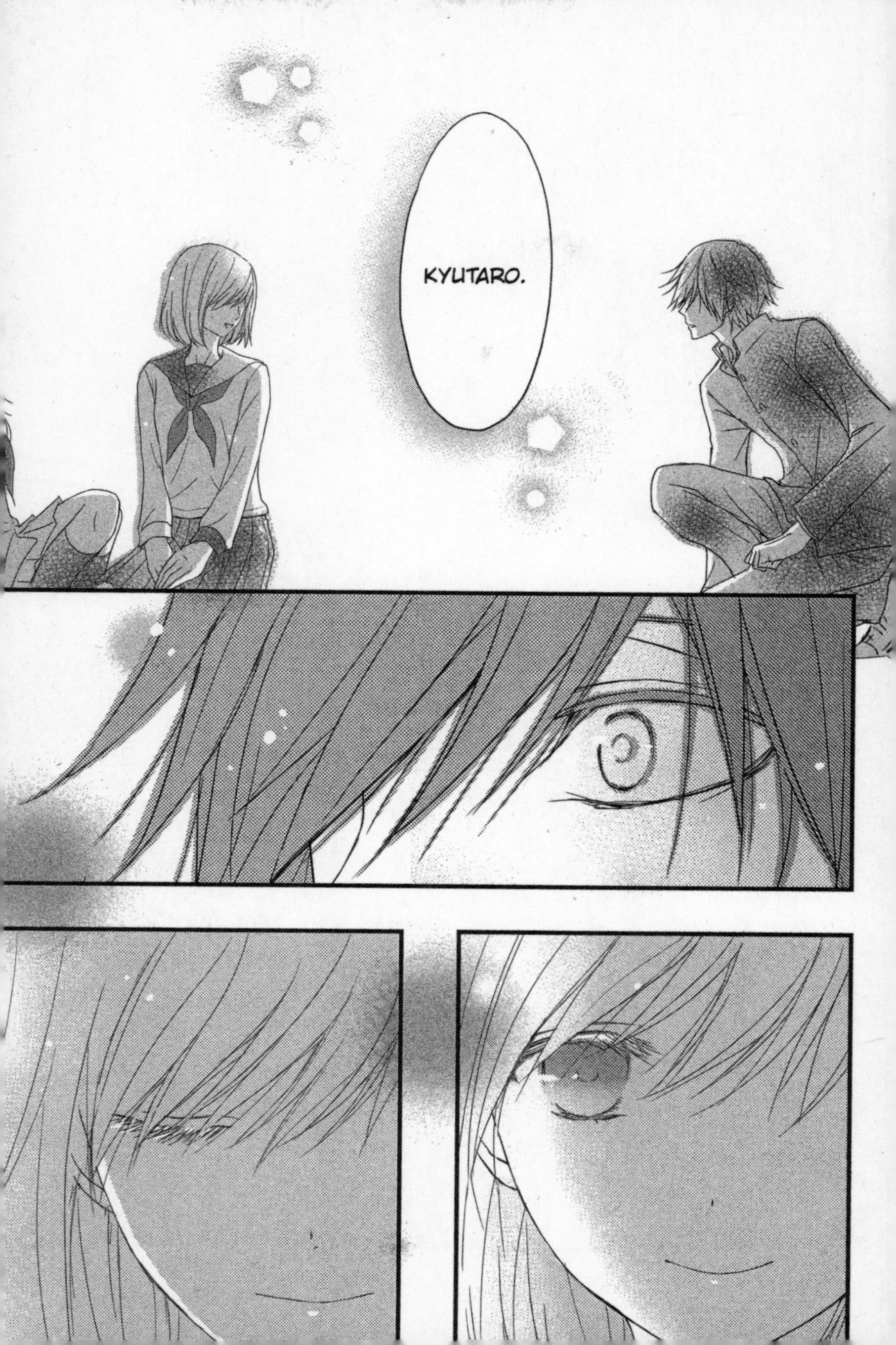
KYUTARO.

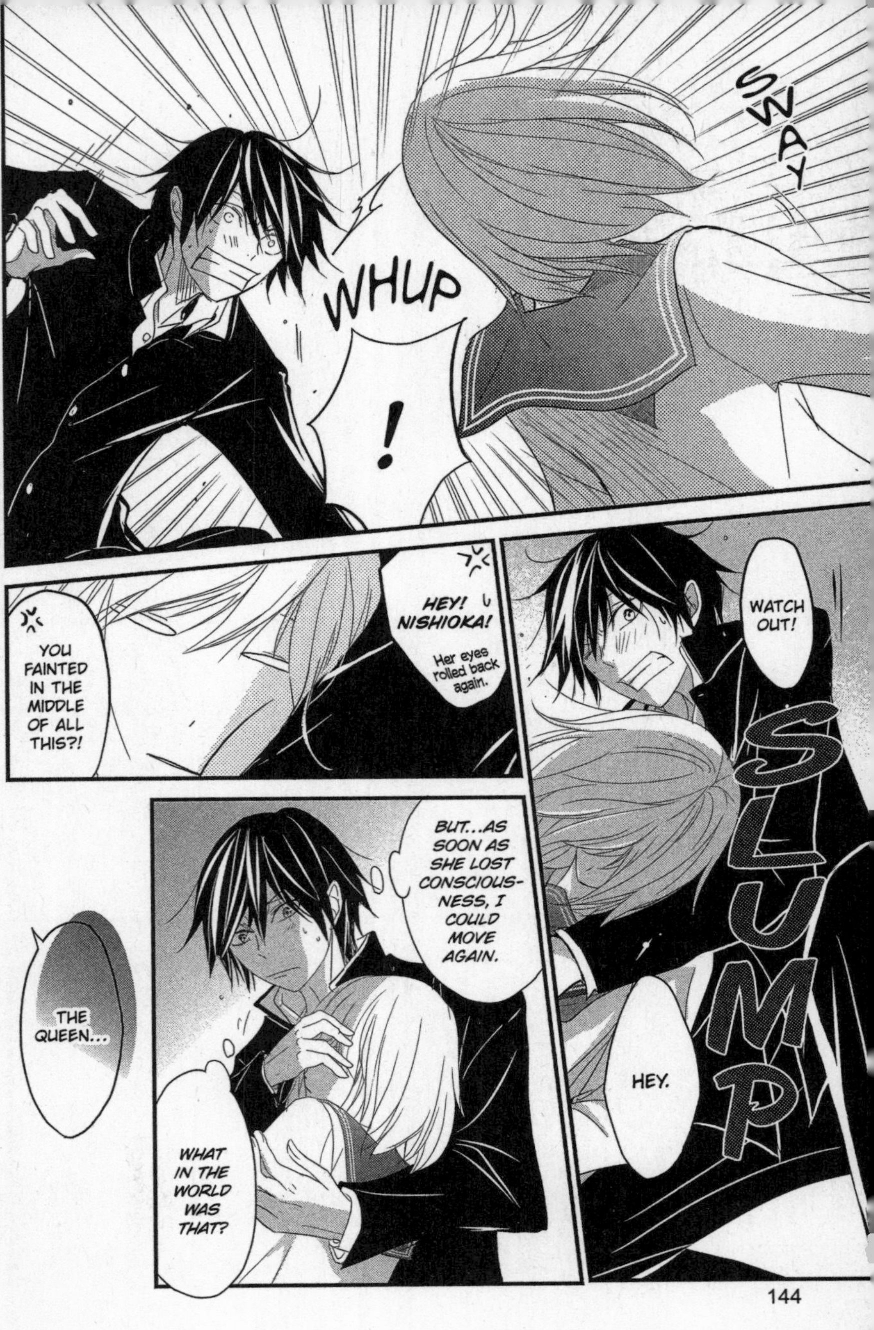
SWAY
WHUP
!
WATCH OUT!
SLUMP
HEY.
HEY! NISHIOKA!
Her eyes rolled back again.
YOU FAINTED IN THE MIDDLE OF ALL THIS?!
BUT...AS SOON AS SHE LOST CONSCIOUSNESS, I COULD MOVE AGAIN.
THE QUEEN...
WHAT IN THE WORLD WAS THAT?

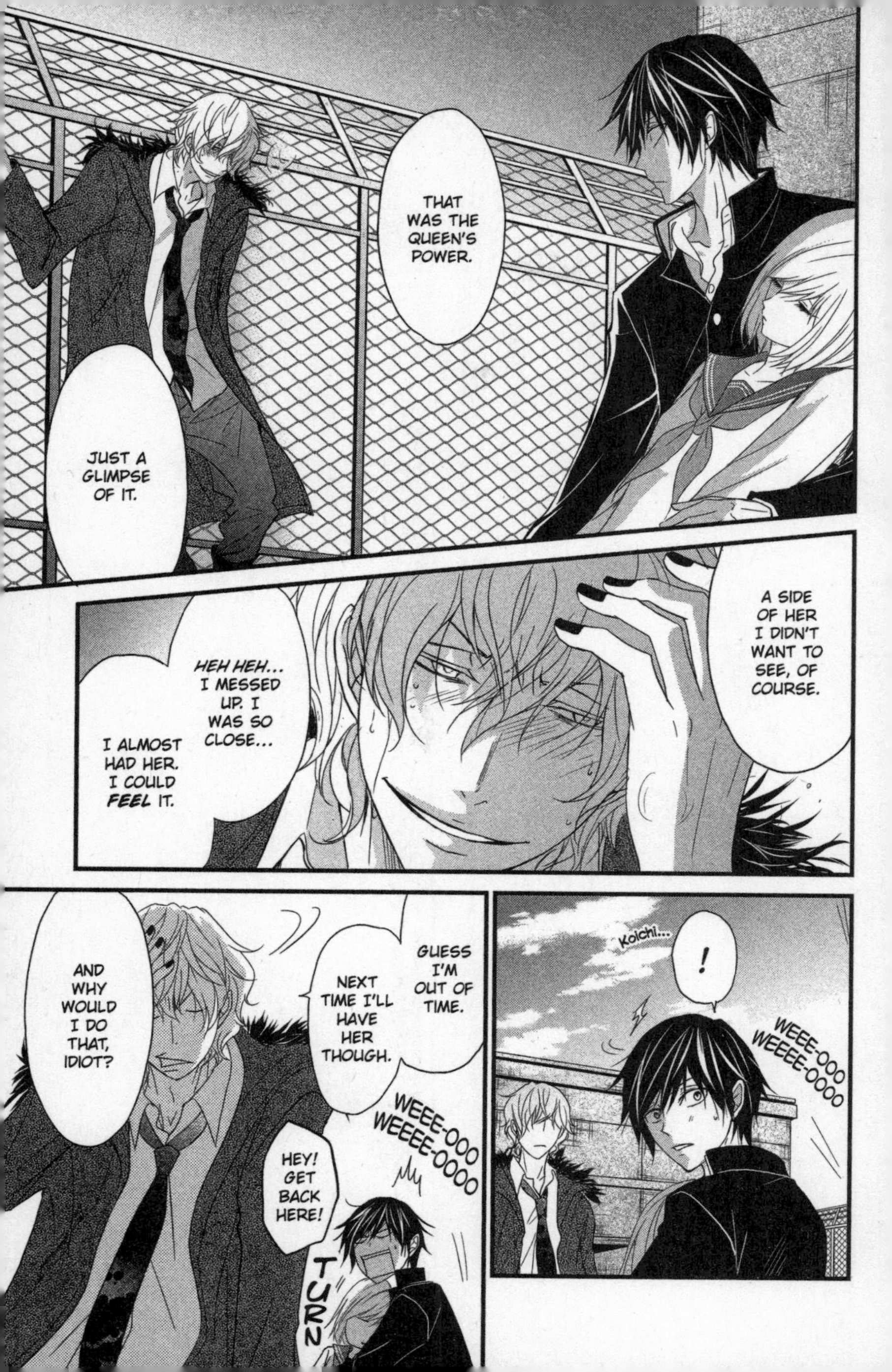
THAT WAS THE QUEEN'S POWER.
JUST A GLIMPSE OF IT.
A SIDE OF HER I DIDN'T WANT TO SEE, OF COURSE.
HEH HEH... I MESSED UP. I WAS SO CLOSE...
I ALMOST HAD HER. I COULD ***FEEL*** IT.
Koichi...
!
WEEE-OOO WEEEE-OOOO
GUESS I'M OUT OF TIME.
NEXT TIME I'LL HAVE HER THOUGH.
AND WHY WOULD I DO THAT, IDIOT?
WEEE-OOO WEEEE-OOOO
HEY! GET BACK HERE!
TURN

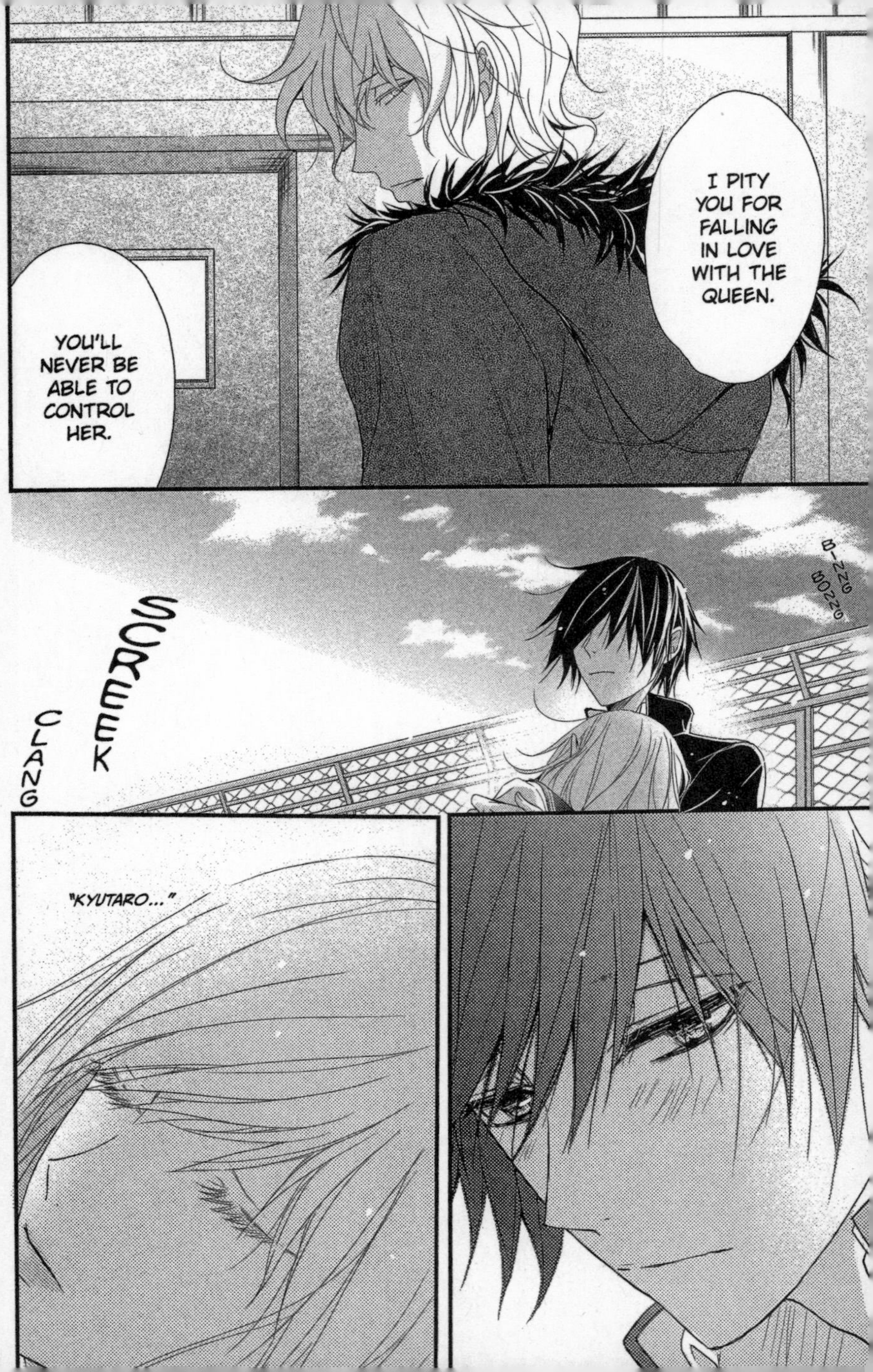
I PITY YOU FOR FALLING IN LOVE WITH THE QUEEN.
YOU'LL NEVER BE ABLE TO CONTROL HER.
BINNG BONNG
SCREEK
CLANG
"KYUTARO..."

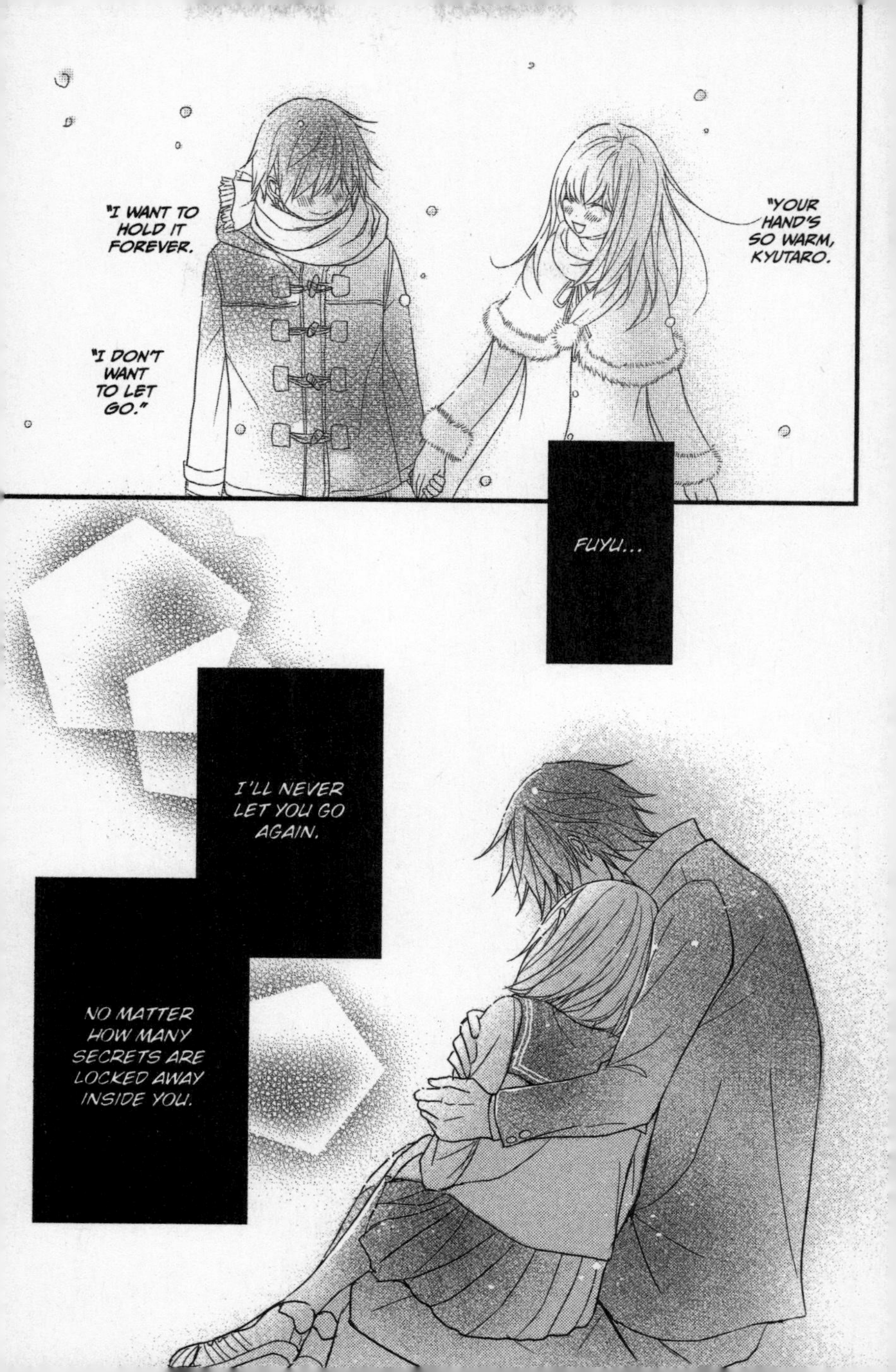
"YOUR HAND'S SO WARM, KYUTARO.
"I WANT TO HOLD IT FOREVER.
"I DON'T WANT TO LET GO."
FUYU...
I'LL NEVER LET YOU GO AGAIN.
NO MATTER HOW MANY SECRETS ARE LOCKED AWAY INSIDE YOU.

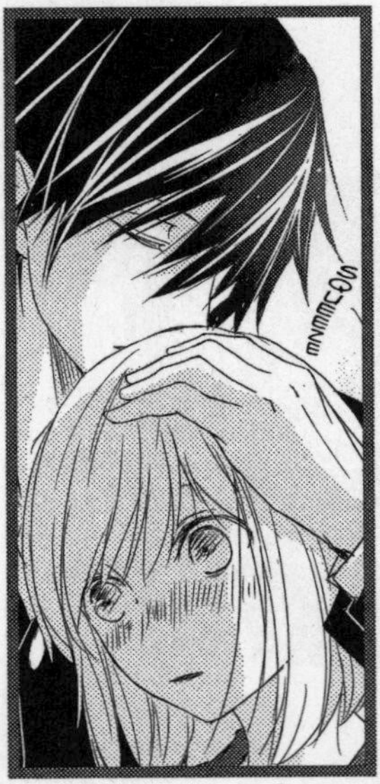
SQUEEZE

SWEEP 15

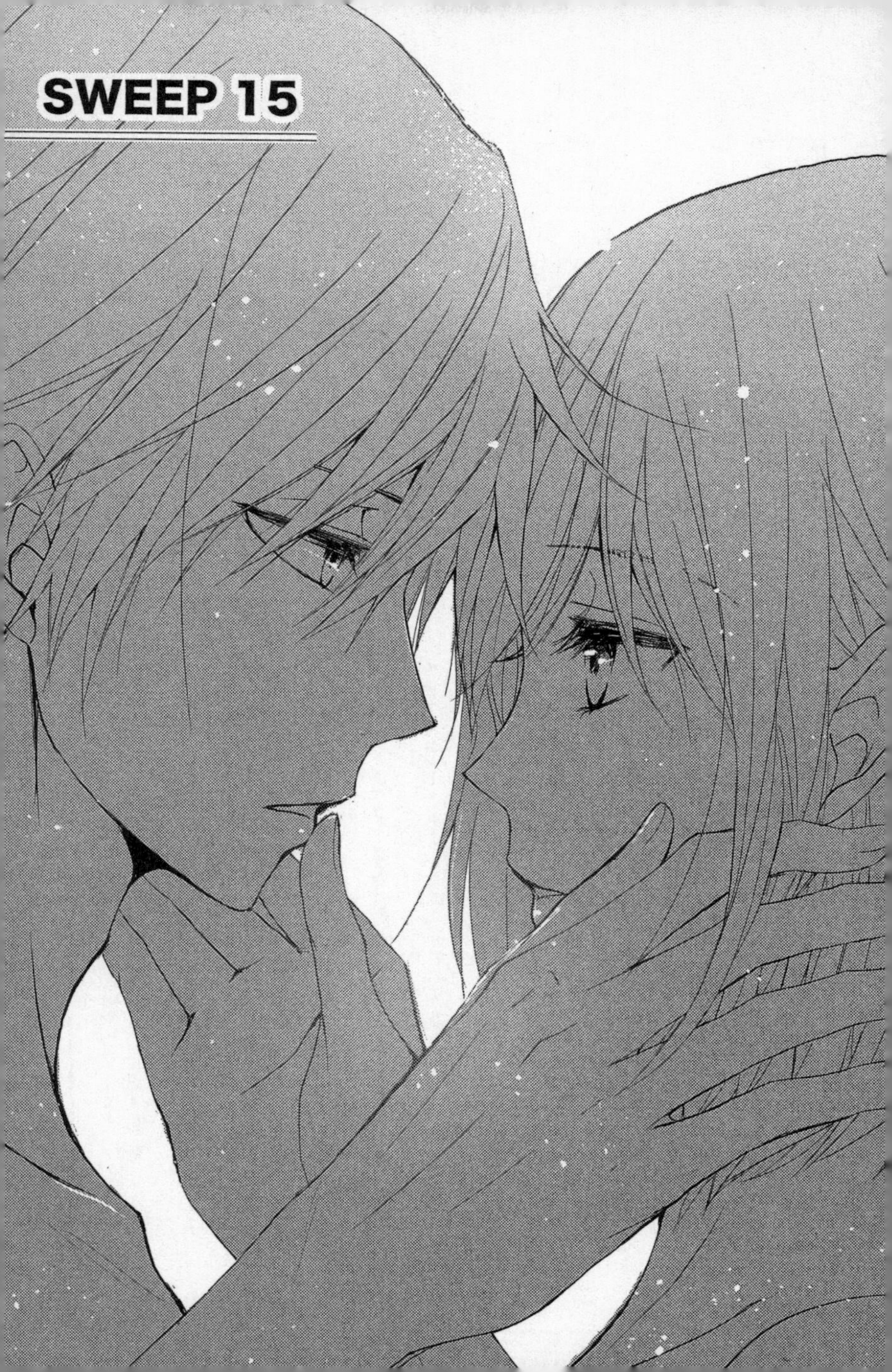

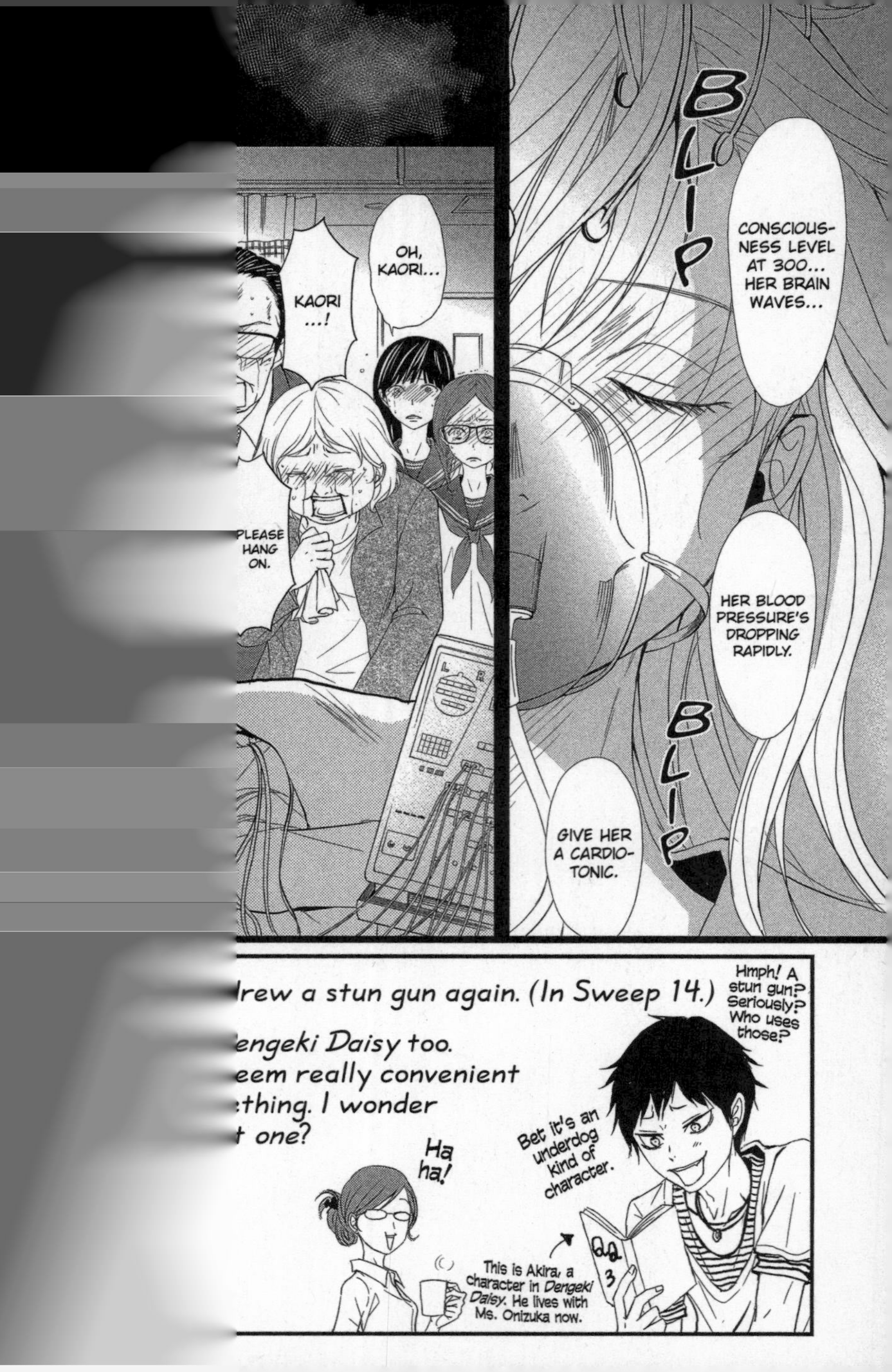
BLIP
CONSCIOUSNESS LEVEL AT 300... HER BRAIN WAVES...
HER BLOOD PRESSURE'S DROPPING RAPIDLY.
BLIP
GIVE HER A CARDIOTONIC.
OH, KAORI...
KAORI ...!
PLEASE HANG ON.
rew a stun gun again. (In Sweep 14.)
engeki Daisy too.
eem really convenient
ething. I wonder
t one?
Hmph! A stun gun? Seriously? Who uses those?
Bet it's an underdog kind of character.
Ha ha!
This is Akira, a character in Dengeki Daisy. He lives with Ms. Onizuka now.
QQ 3

IT'S SO
DARK AND
COLD...

WILL I
DISAPPEAR?

AM...AM
I DYING?

BUT...

"SO
COME
TO
ME."

"I'M
GOING
TO SAVE
YOU. I
PROMISE.

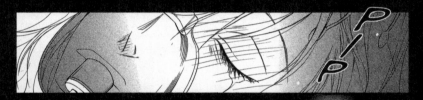

P/P

TH-
THMP

FUMI...

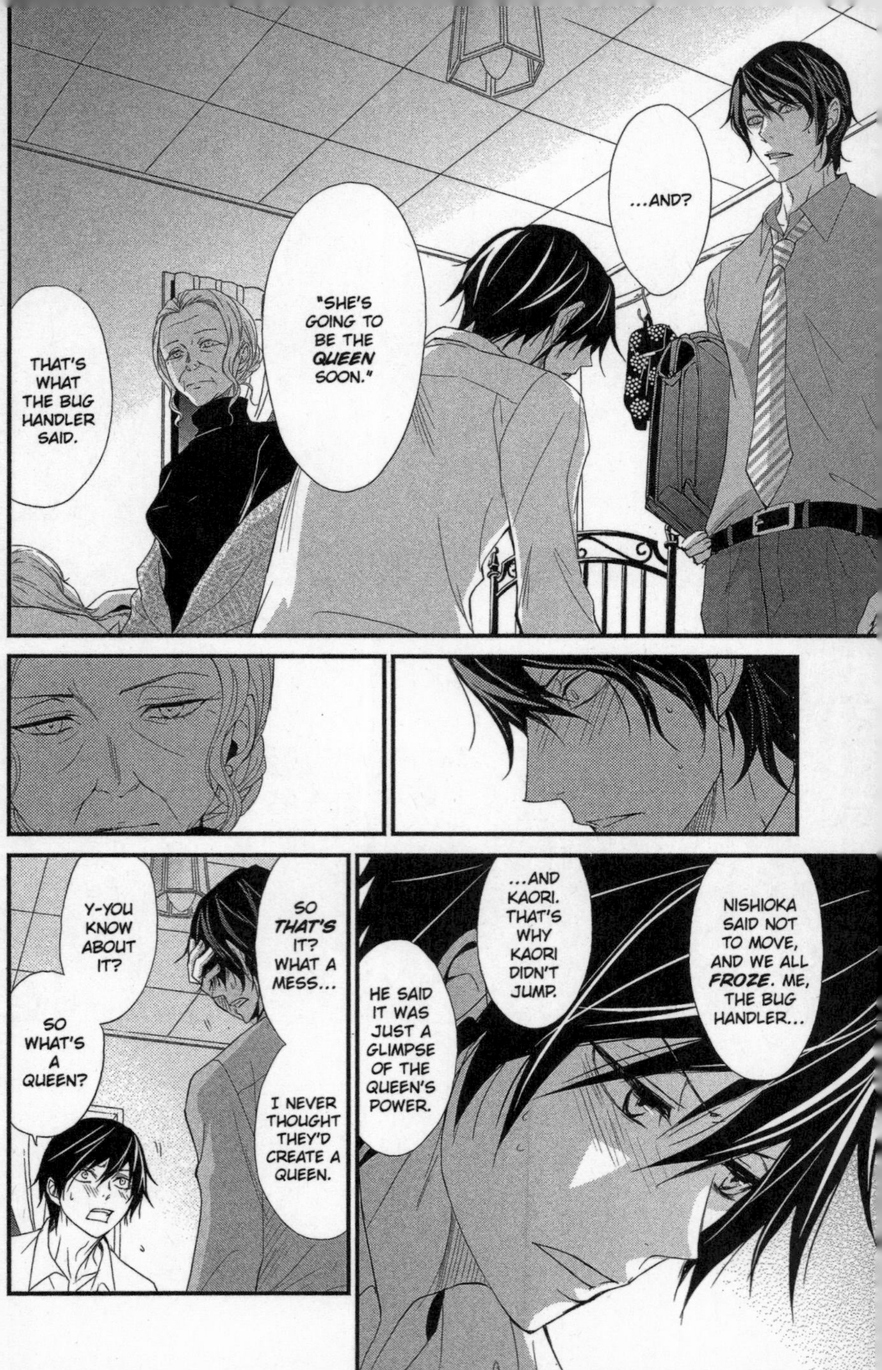
...AND?
"SHE'S GOING TO BE THE *QUEEN* SOON."
THAT'S WHAT THE BUG HANDLER SAID.
NISHIOKA SAID NOT TO MOVE, AND WE ALL *FROZE*. ME, THE BUG HANDLER...
...AND KAORI. THAT'S WHY KAORI DIDN'T JUMP.
HE SAID IT WAS JUST A GLIMPSE OF THE QUEEN'S POWER.
SO *THAT'S* IT? WHAT A MESS...
I NEVER THOUGHT THEY'D CREATE A QUEEN.
Y-YOU KNOW ABOUT IT?
SO WHAT'S A QUEEN?

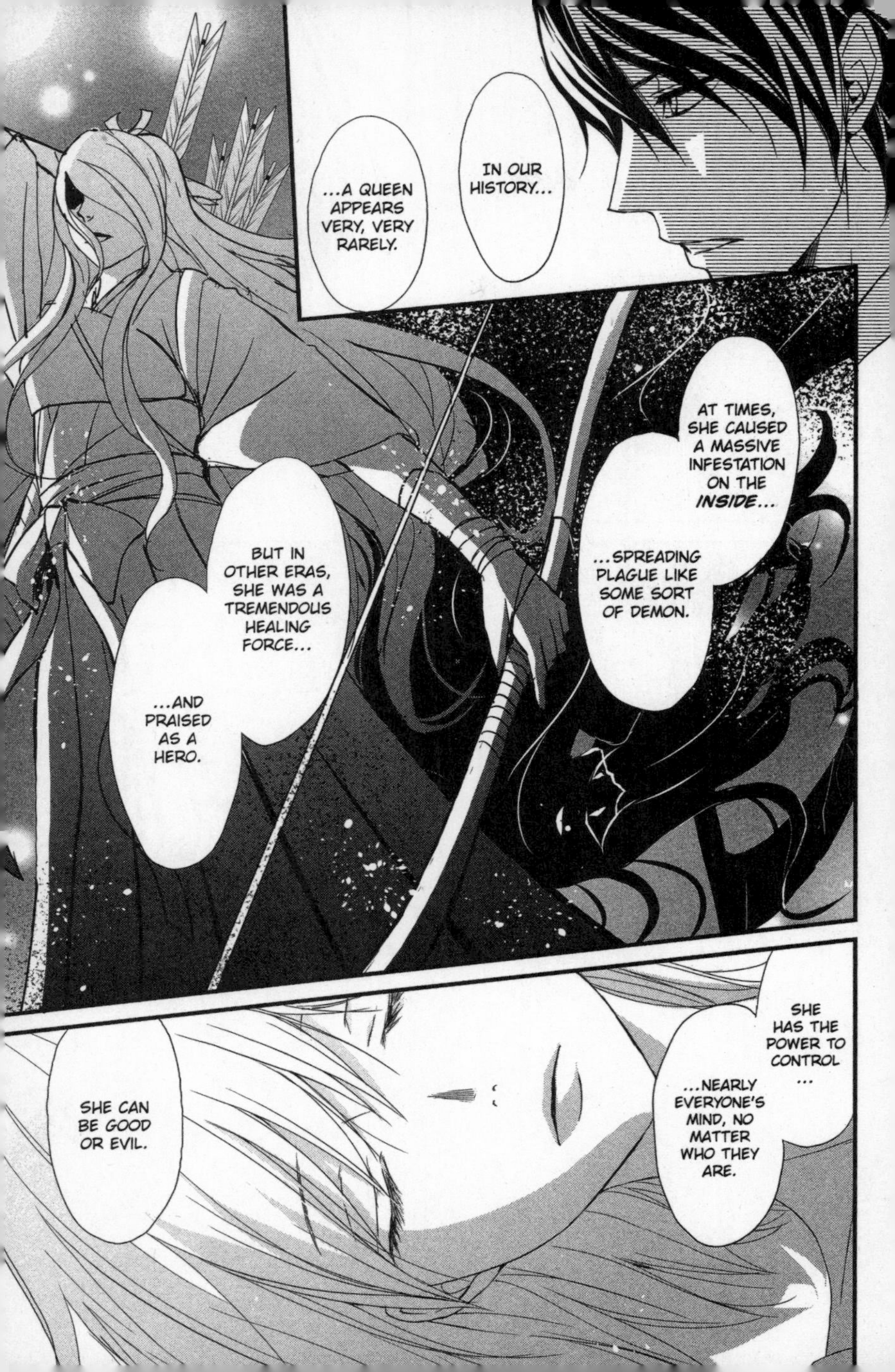
IN OUR HISTORY...
...A QUEEN APPEARS VERY, VERY RARELY.
AT TIMES, SHE CAUSED A MASSIVE INFESTATION ON THE *INSIDE*...
...SPREADING PLAGUE LIKE SOME SORT OF DEMON.
BUT IN OTHER ERAS, SHE WAS A TREMENDOUS HEALING FORCE...
...AND PRAISED AS A HERO.
SHE HAS THE POWER TO CONTROL ...
...NEARLY EVERYONE'S MIND, NO MATTER WHO THEY ARE.
SHE CAN BE GOOD OR EVIL.

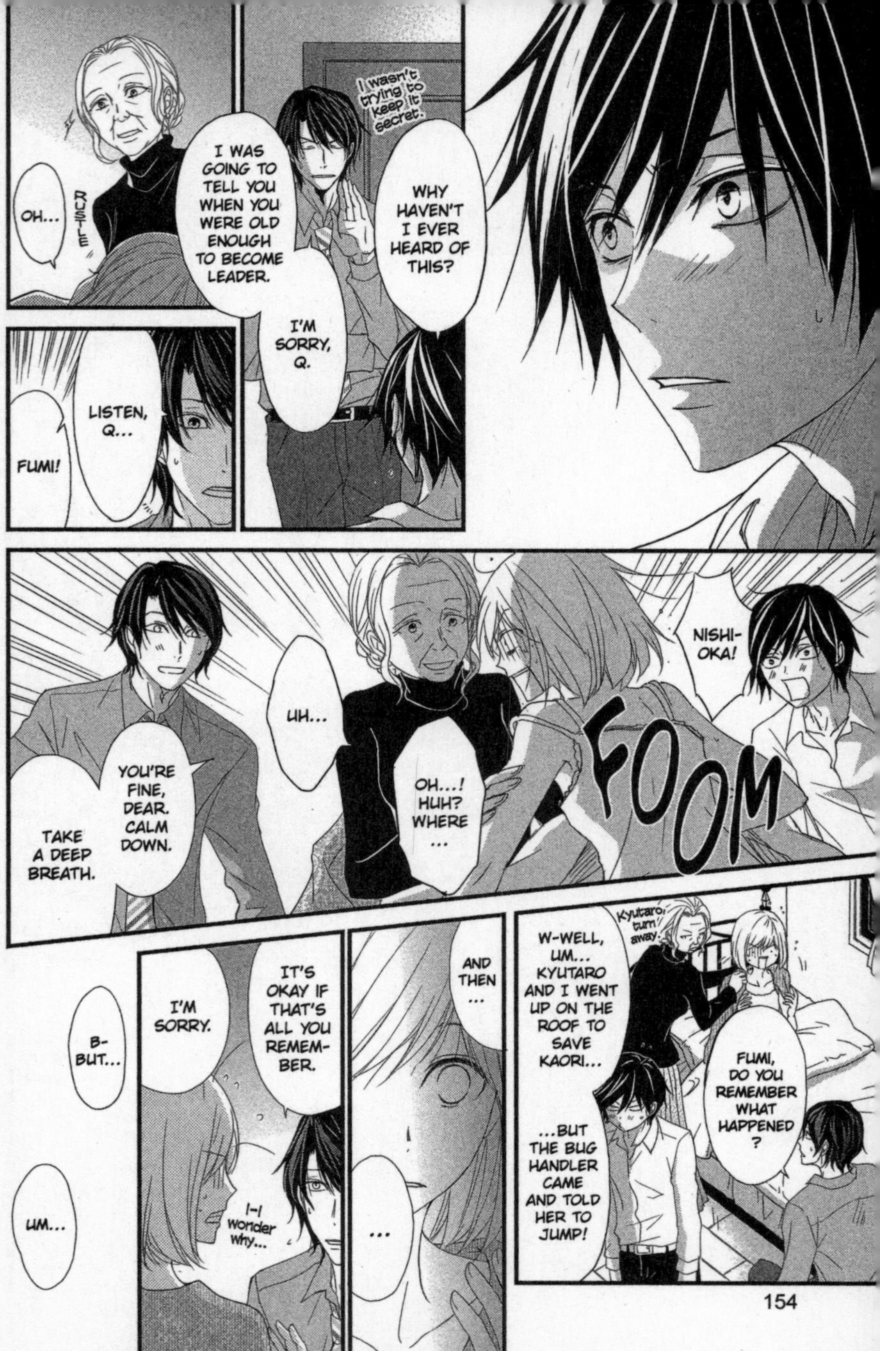
WHY HAVEN'T I EVER HEARD OF THIS?
I wasn't trying to keep it secret.
I WAS GOING TO TELL YOU WHEN YOU WERE OLD ENOUGH TO BECOME LEADER.
I'M SORRY, Q.
RUSTLE
OH...
LISTEN, Q...
FUMI!
NISHI-OKA!
FOOM
OH...! HUH? WHERE...
UH...
YOU'RE FINE, DEAR. CALM DOWN.
TAKE A DEEP BREATH.
Kyutaro, turn away.
FUMI, DO YOU REMEMBER WHAT HAPPENED?
W-WELL, UM... KYUTARO AND I WENT UP ON THE ROOF TO SAVE KAORI...
...BUT THE BUG HANDLER CAME AND TOLD HER TO JUMP!
AND THEN...
...
IT'S OKAY IF THAT'S ALL YOU REMEMBER.
I'M SORRY.
I-I wonder why...
B-BUT...
UM...

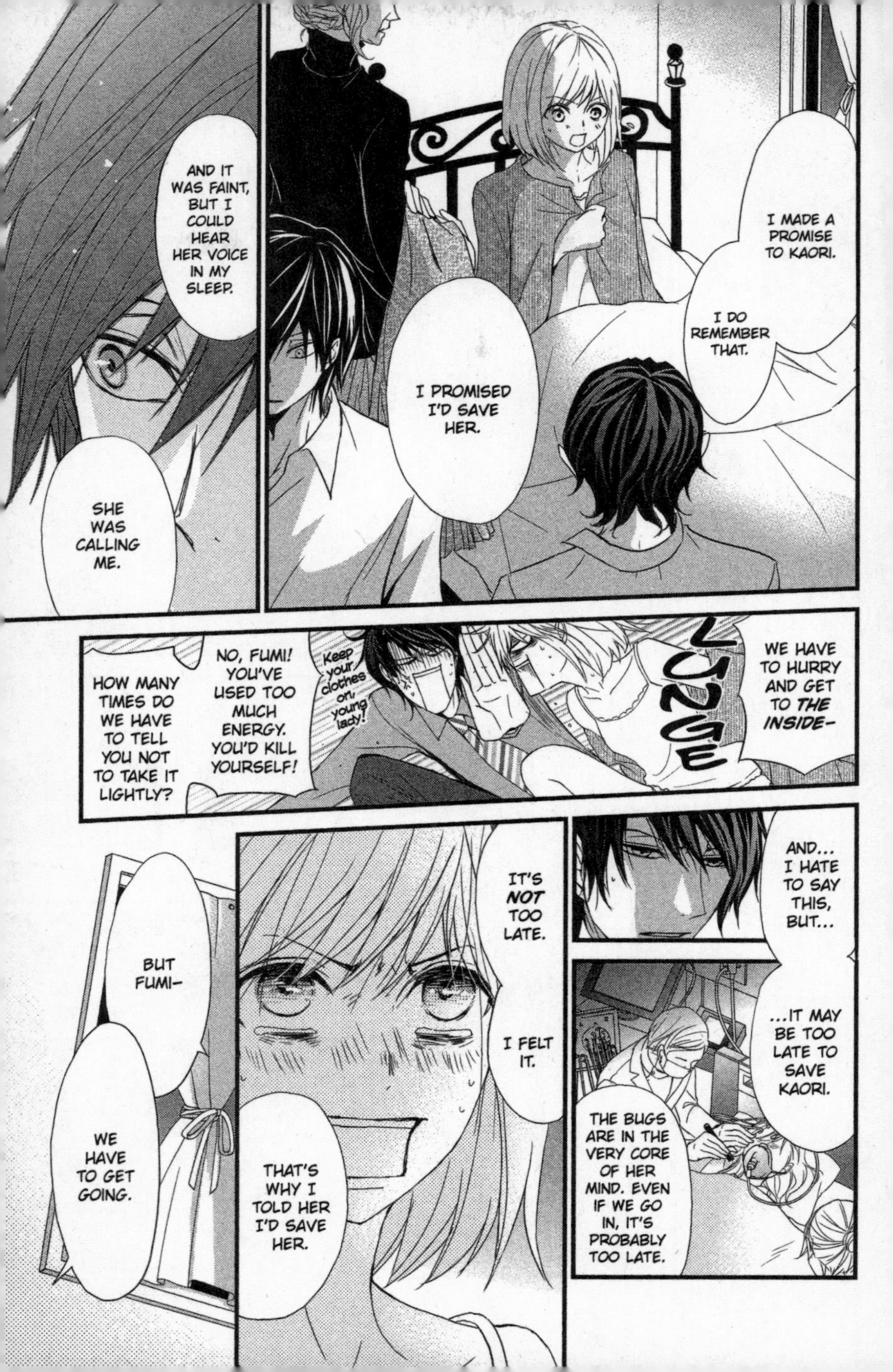
I MADE A PROMISE TO KAORI.
I DO REMEMBER THAT.
I PROMISED I'D SAVE HER.
AND IT WAS FAINT, BUT I COULD HEAR HER VOICE IN MY SLEEP.
SHE WAS CALLING ME.
WE HAVE TO HURRY AND GET TO *THE INSIDE*-
LUNGE
Keep your clothes on, young lady!
NO, FUMI! YOU'VE USED TOO MUCH ENERGY. YOU'D KILL YOURSELF!
HOW MANY TIMES DO WE HAVE TO TELL YOU NOT TO TAKE IT LIGHTLY?
AND... I HATE TO SAY THIS, BUT...
...IT MAY BE TOO LATE TO SAVE KAORI.
THE BUGS ARE IN THE VERY CORE OF HER MIND. EVEN IF WE GO IN, IT'S PROBABLY TOO LATE.
IT'S *NOT* TOO LATE.
I FELT IT.
THAT'S WHY I TOLD HER I'D SAVE HER.
BUT FUMI-
WE HAVE TO GET GOING.

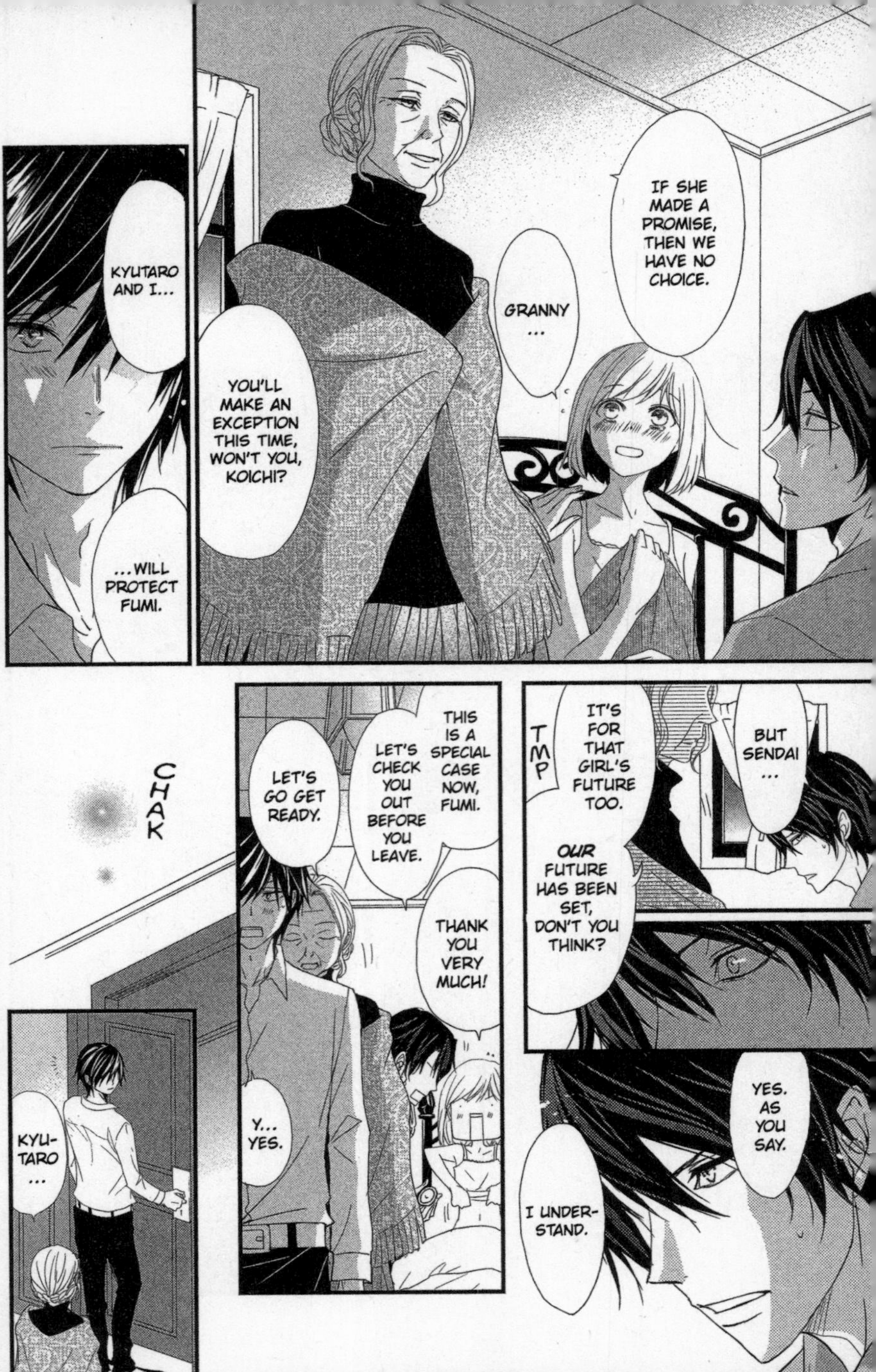
IF SHE MADE A PROMISE, THEN WE HAVE NO CHOICE.
GRANNY...
YOU'LL MAKE AN EXCEPTION THIS TIME, WON'T YOU, KOICHI?
KYUTARO AND I...
...WILL PROTECT FUMI.
BUT SENDAI...
IT'S FOR THAT GIRL'S FUTURE TOO.
TMP
OUR FUTURE HAS BEEN SET, DON'T YOU THINK?
YES. AS YOU SAY.
I UNDERSTAND.
THIS IS A SPECIAL CASE NOW, FUMI.
LET'S CHECK YOU OUT BEFORE YOU LEAVE.
LET'S GO GET READY.
THANK YOU VERY MUCH!
Y... YES.
CHAK
KYU-TARO...

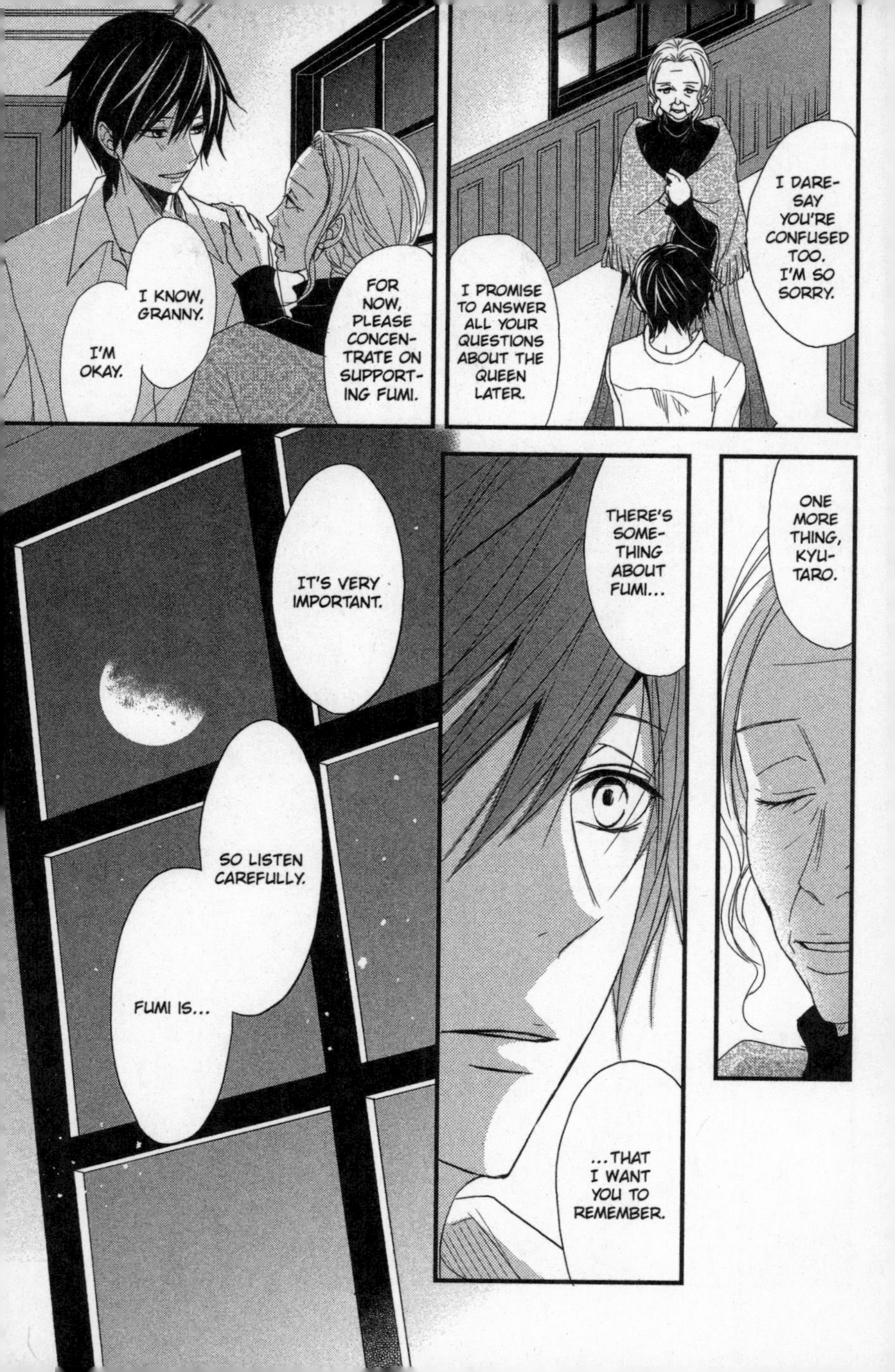
I DARE-SAY YOU'RE CONFUSED TOO. I'M SO SORRY.
I PROMISE TO ANSWER ALL YOUR QUESTIONS ABOUT THE QUEEN LATER.
FOR NOW, PLEASE CONCEN-TRATE ON SUPPORT-ING FUMI.
I KNOW, GRANNY.
I'M OKAY.
ONE MORE THING, KYU-TARO.
THERE'S SOME-THING ABOUT FUMI...
...THAT I WANT YOU TO REMEMBER.
IT'S VERY IMPORTANT.
SO LISTEN CAREFULLY.
FUMI IS...

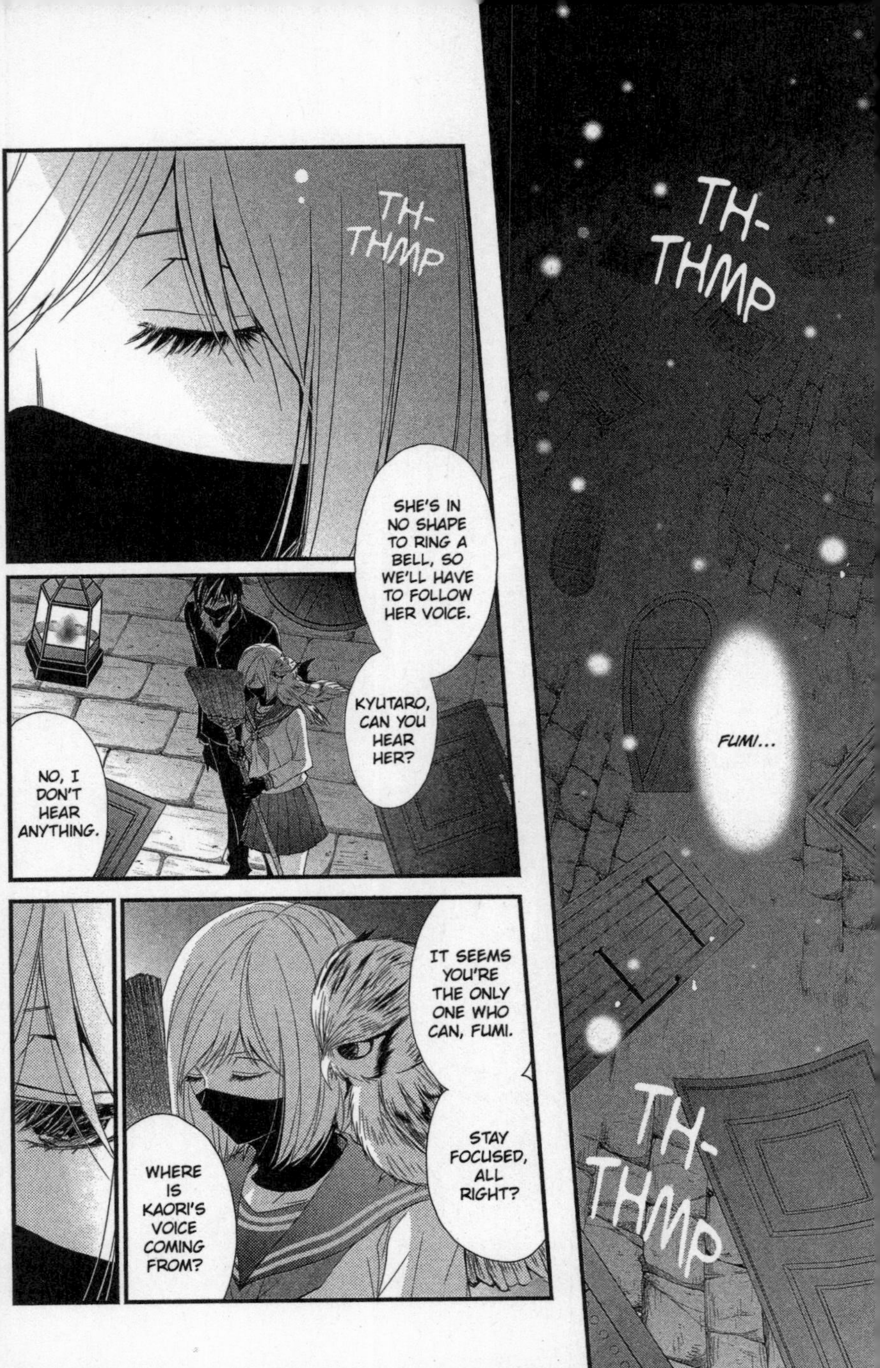
TH-THMP
FUMI...
TH-THMP
TH-THMP
SHE'S IN NO SHAPE TO RING A BELL, SO WE'LL HAVE TO FOLLOW HER VOICE.
KYUTARO, CAN YOU HEAR HER?
NO, I DON'T HEAR ANYTHING.
IT SEEMS YOU'RE THE ONLY ONE WHO CAN, FUMI.
STAY FOCUSED, ALL RIGHT?
WHERE IS KAORI'S VOICE COMING FROM?

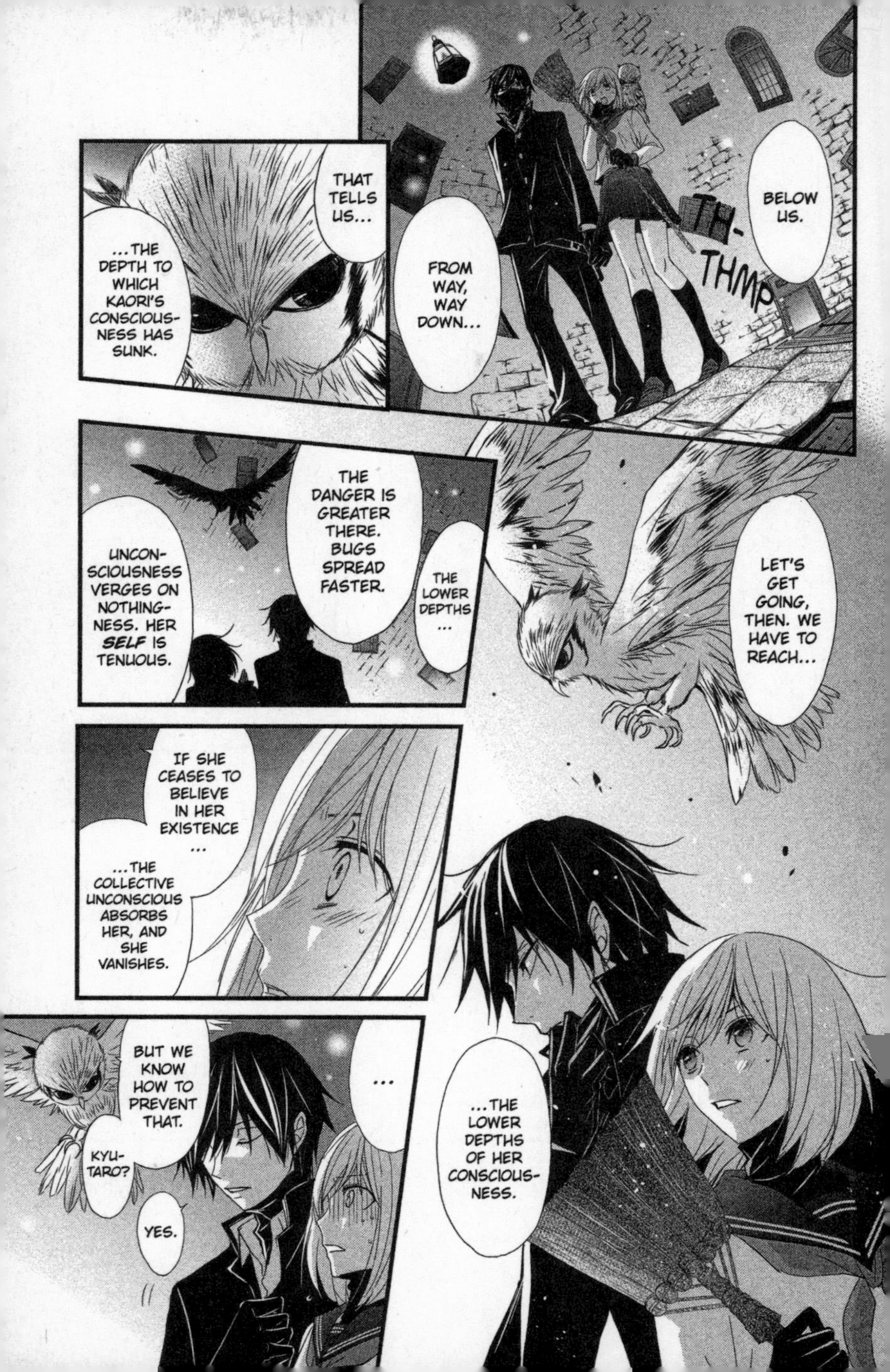
BELOW US.
TH-THMP
FROM WAY, WAY DOWN...
THAT TELLS US...
...THE DEPTH TO WHICH KAORI'S CONSCIOUSNESS HAS SUNK.
LET'S GET GOING, THEN. WE HAVE TO REACH...
...THE LOWER DEPTHS OF HER CONSCIOUS-NESS.
THE LOWER DEPTHS...
THE DANGER IS GREATER THERE. BUGS SPREAD FASTER.
UNCON-SCIOUSNESS VERGES ON NOTHING-NESS. HER *SELF* IS TENUOUS.
IF SHE CEASES TO BELIEVE IN HER EXISTENCE...
...THE COLLECTIVE UNCONSCIOUS ABSORBS HER, AND SHE VANISHES.
...
BUT WE KNOW HOW TO PREVENT THAT.
KYU-TARO?
YES.

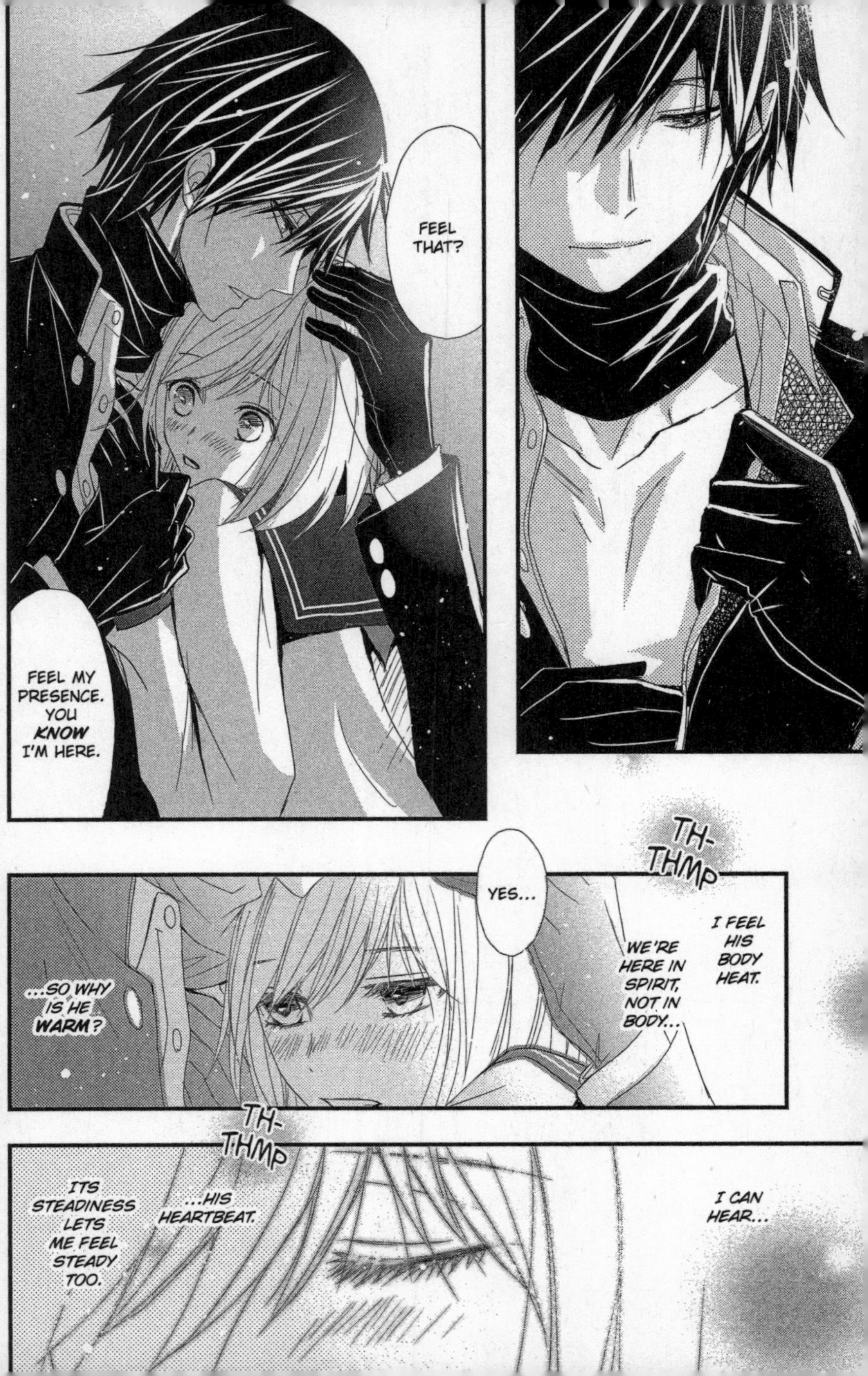
FEEL THAT?
FEEL MY PRESENCE. YOU KNOW I'M HERE.
TH-THMP
YES...
I FEEL HIS BODY HEAT.
WE'RE HERE IN SPIRIT, NOT IN BODY...
...SO WHY IS HE WARM?
TH-THMP
I CAN HEAR...
...HIS HEARTBEAT.
ITS STEADINESS LETS ME FEEL STEADY TOO.

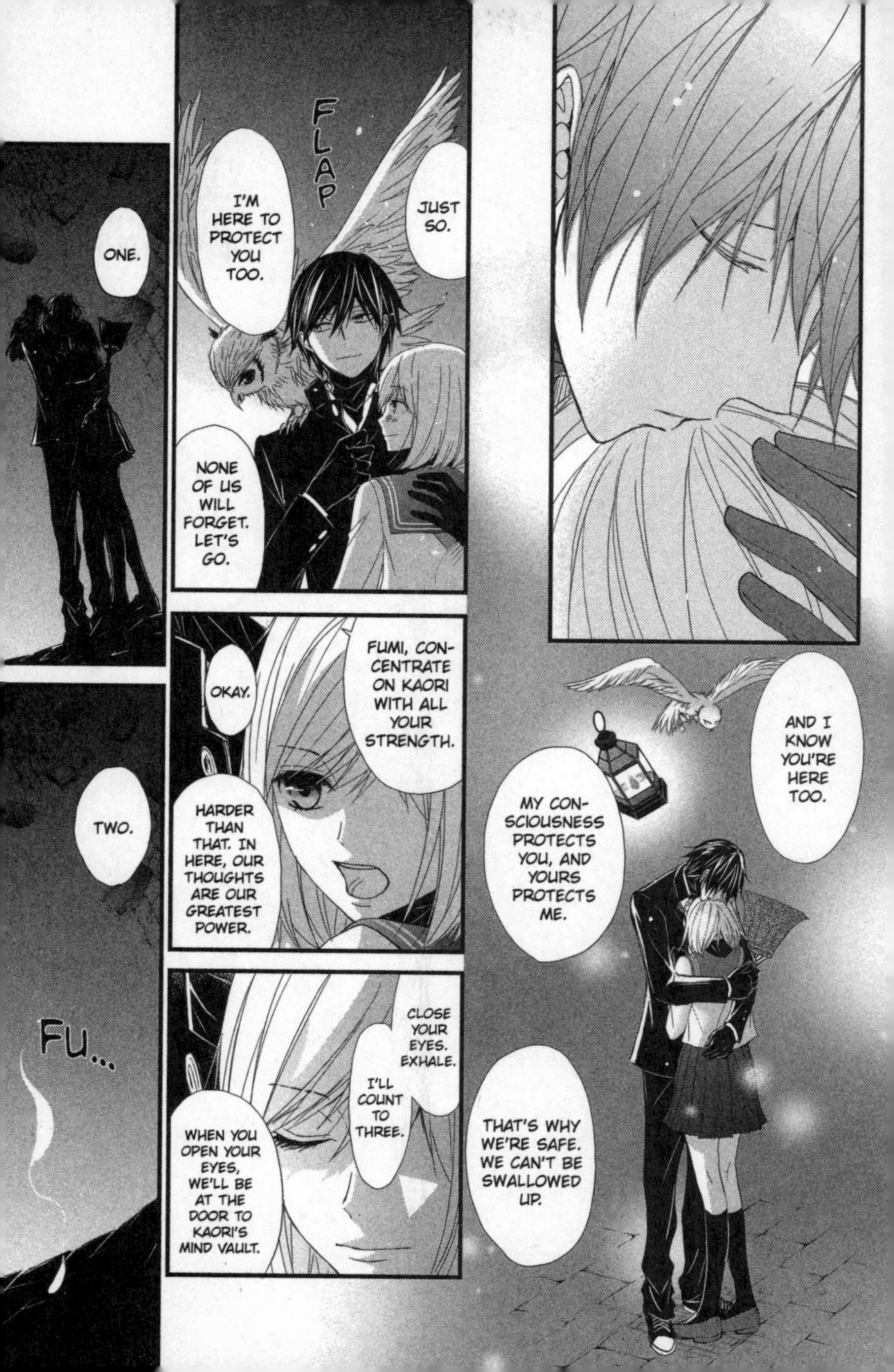
AND I KNOW YOU'RE HERE TOO.
MY CON-SCIOUSNESS PROTECTS YOU, AND YOURS PROTECTS ME.
THAT'S WHY WE'RE SAFE. WE CAN'T BE SWALLOWED UP.
JUST SO.
FLAP
I'M HERE TO PROTECT YOU TOO.
NONE OF US WILL FORGET. LET'S GO.
ONE.
FUMI, CON-CENTRATE ON KAORI WITH ALL YOUR STRENGTH.
OKAY.
HARDER THAN THAT. IN HERE, OUR THOUGHTS ARE OUR GREATEST POWER.
TWO.
CLOSE YOUR EYES. EXHALE.
I'LL COUNT TO THREE.
WHEN YOU OPEN YOUR EYES, WE'LL BE AT THE DOOR TO KAORI'S MIND VAULT.
FU...

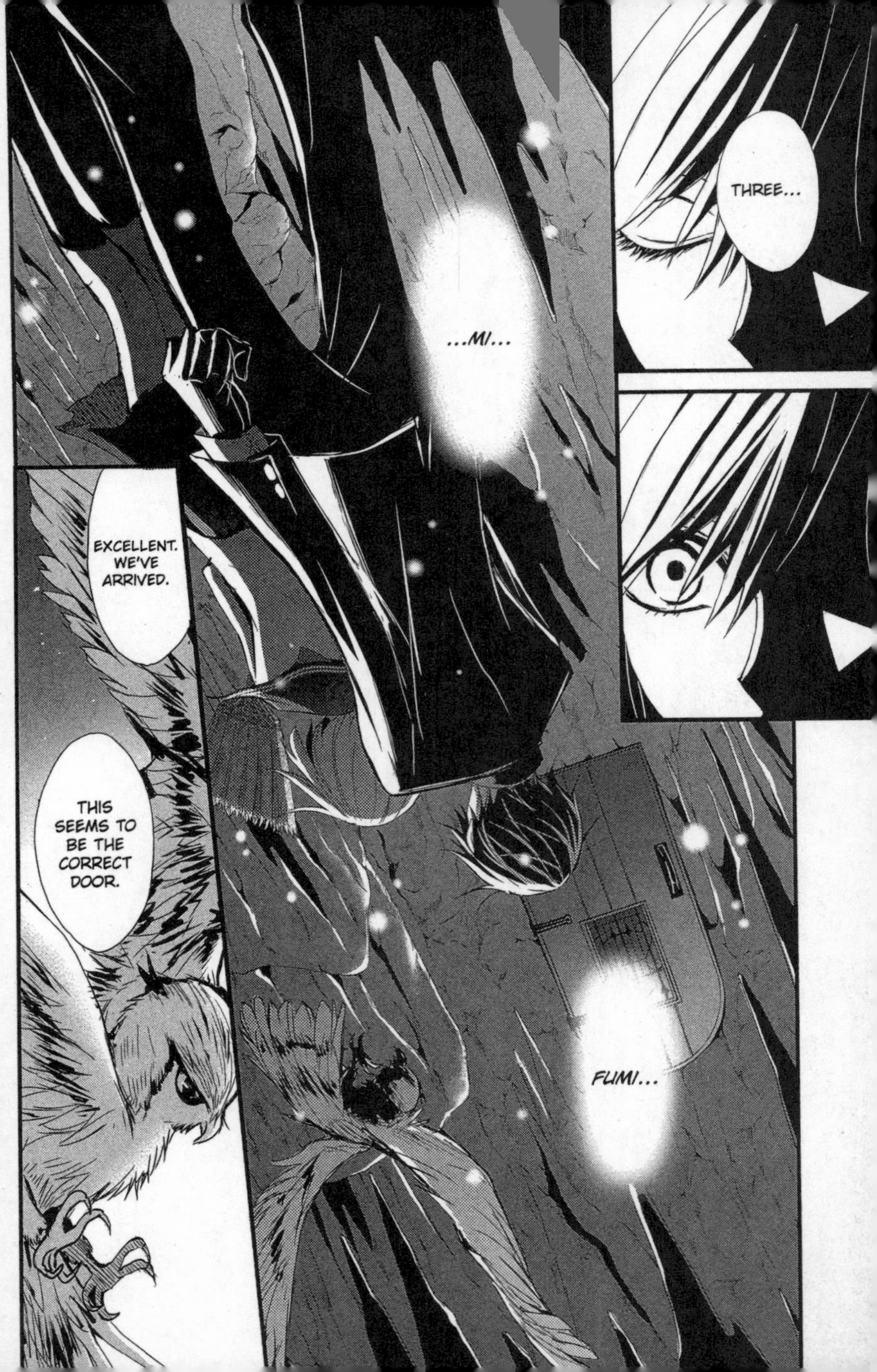
THREE...
...MI...
FUMI...
EXCELLENT. WE'VE ARRIVED.
THIS SEEMS TO BE THE CORRECT DOOR.

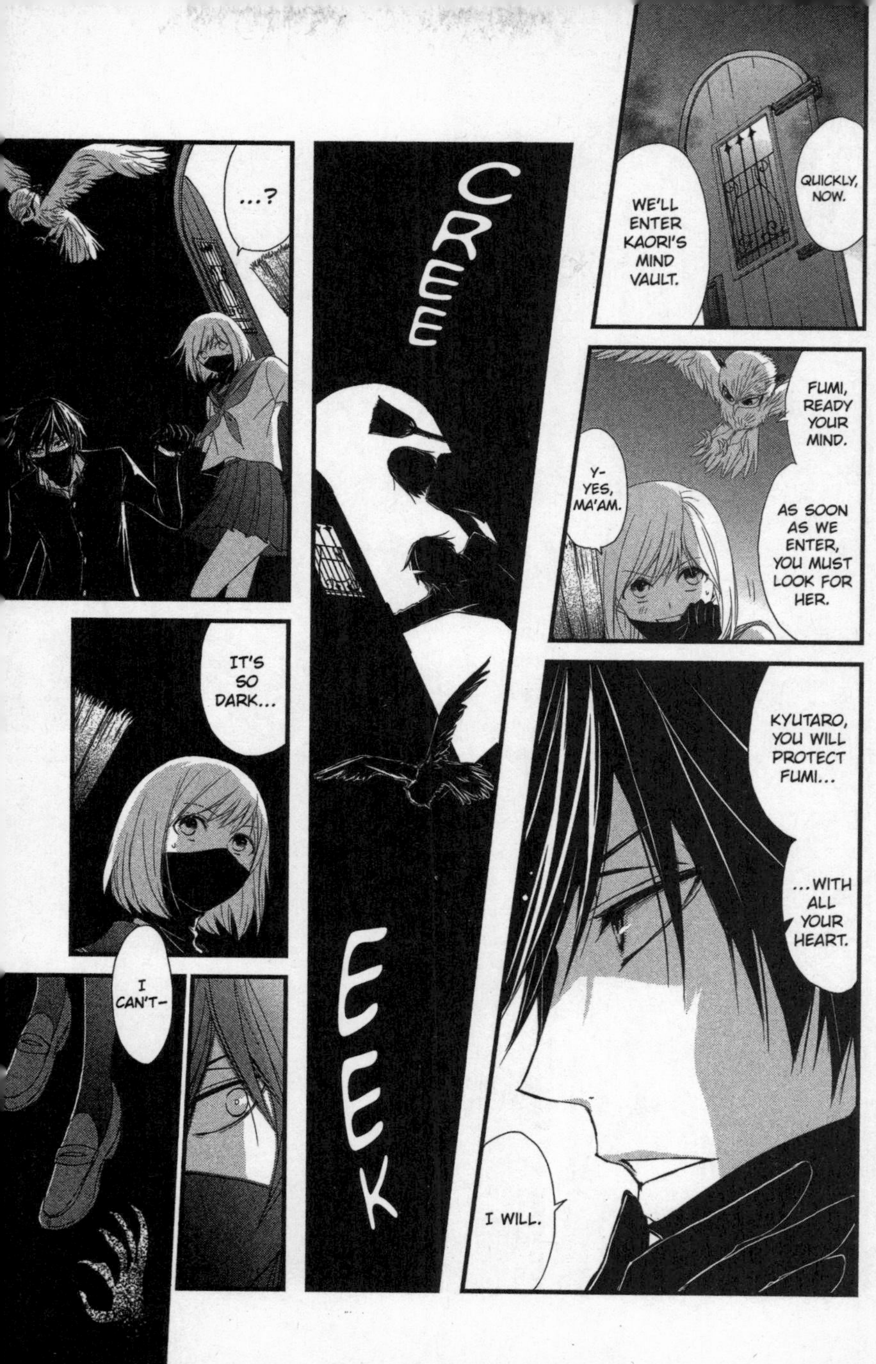
QUICKLY, NOW.
WE'LL ENTER KAORI'S MIND VAULT.
FUMI, READY YOUR MIND.
Y-YES, MA'AM.
AS SOON AS WE ENTER, YOU MUST LOOK FOR HER.
KYUTARO, YOU WILL PROTECT FUMI...
...WITH ALL YOUR HEART.
I WILL.
CREE
EEK
...?
IT'S SO DARK...
I CAN'T-

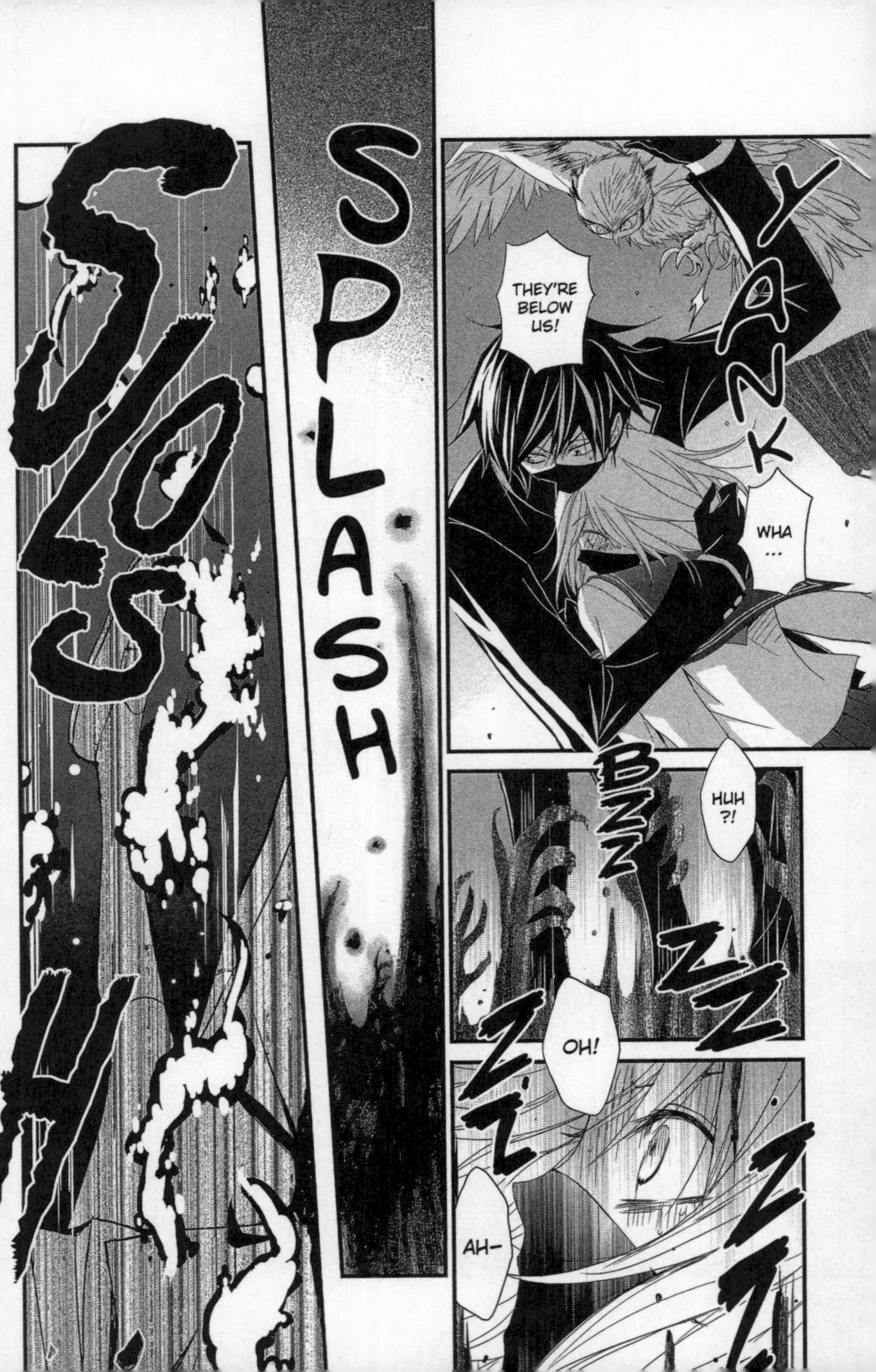
YANK
THEY'RE BELOW US!
WHA ...
BZZ
HUH ?!
ZZZ
OH!
ZZ
AH-
SPLASH

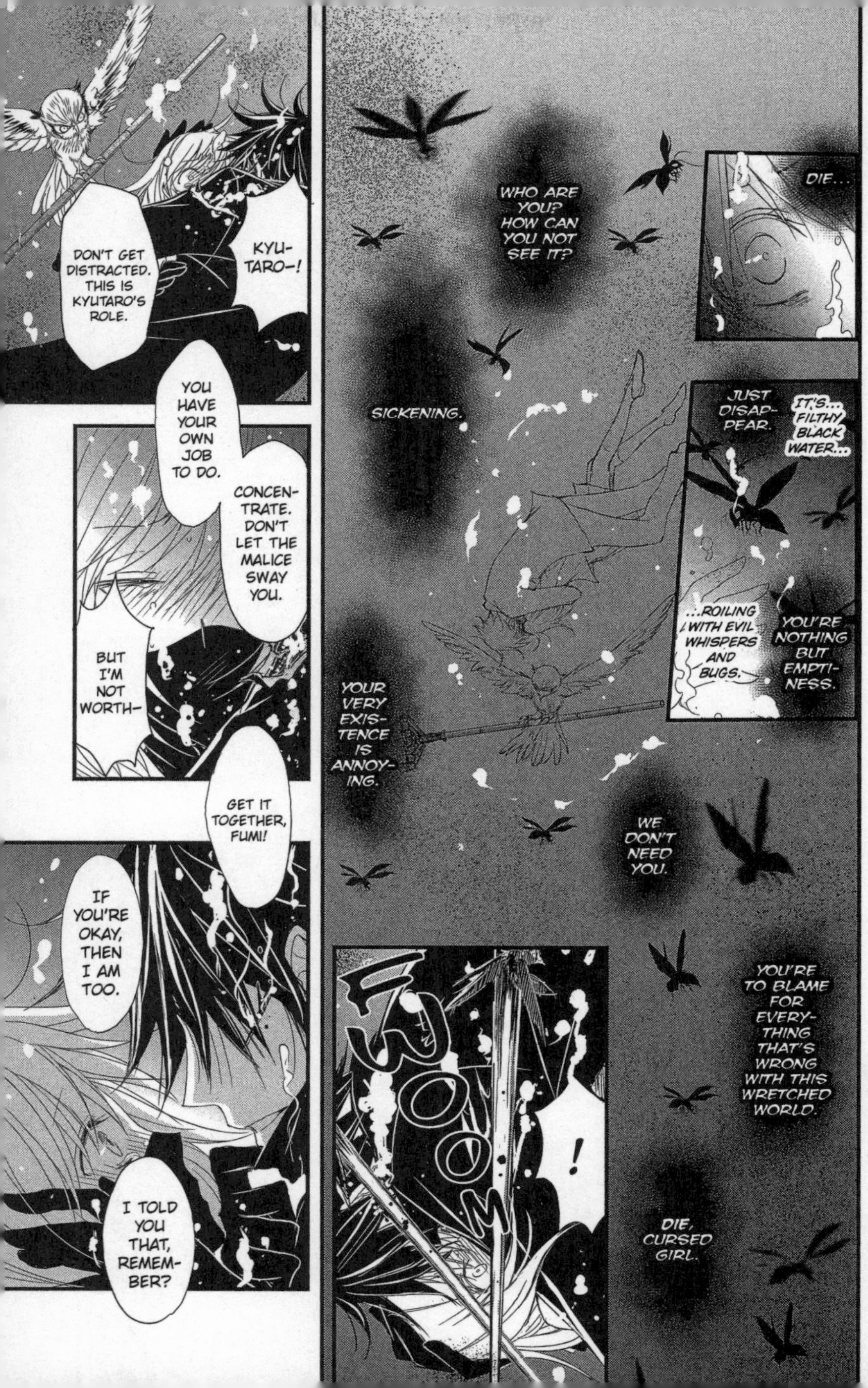
DIE...
WHO ARE YOU? HOW CAN YOU NOT SEE IT?
IT'S... FILTHY BLACK WATER...
JUST DISAPPEAR.
YOU'RE NOTHING BUT EMPTINESS.
...ROILING WITH EVIL WHISPERS AND BUGS.
SICKENING.
YOUR VERY EXISTENCE IS ANNOYING.
WE DON'T NEED YOU.
YOU'RE TO BLAME FOR EVERYTHING THAT'S WRONG WITH THIS WRETCHED WORLD.
DIE, CURSED GIRL.
!
BOOM
KYU-TARO-!
DON'T GET DISTRACTED. THIS IS KYUTARO'S ROLE.
YOU HAVE YOUR OWN JOB TO DO.
CONCENTRATE. DON'T LET THE MALICE SWAY YOU.
BUT I'M NOT WORTH-
GET IT TOGETHER, FUMI!
IF YOU'RE OKAY, THEN I AM TOO.
I TOLD YOU THAT, REMEMBER?

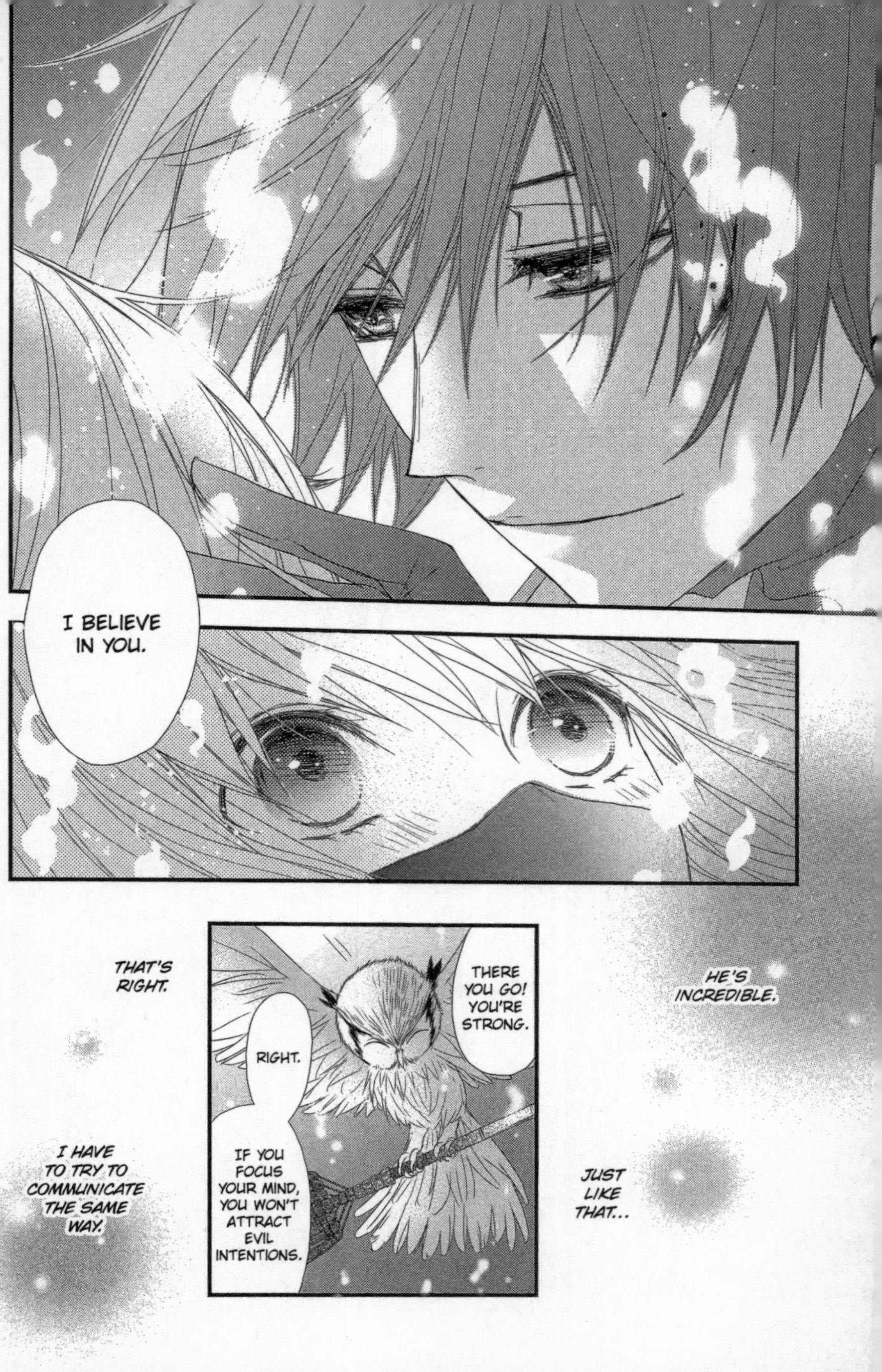
I BELIEVE IN YOU.
HE'S INCREDIBLE.
JUST LIKE THAT...
THERE YOU GO! YOU'RE STRONG.
RIGHT.
IF YOU FOCUS YOUR MIND, YOU WON'T ATTRACT EVIL INTENTIONS.
THAT'S RIGHT.
I HAVE TO TRY TO COMMUNICATE THE SAME WAY.

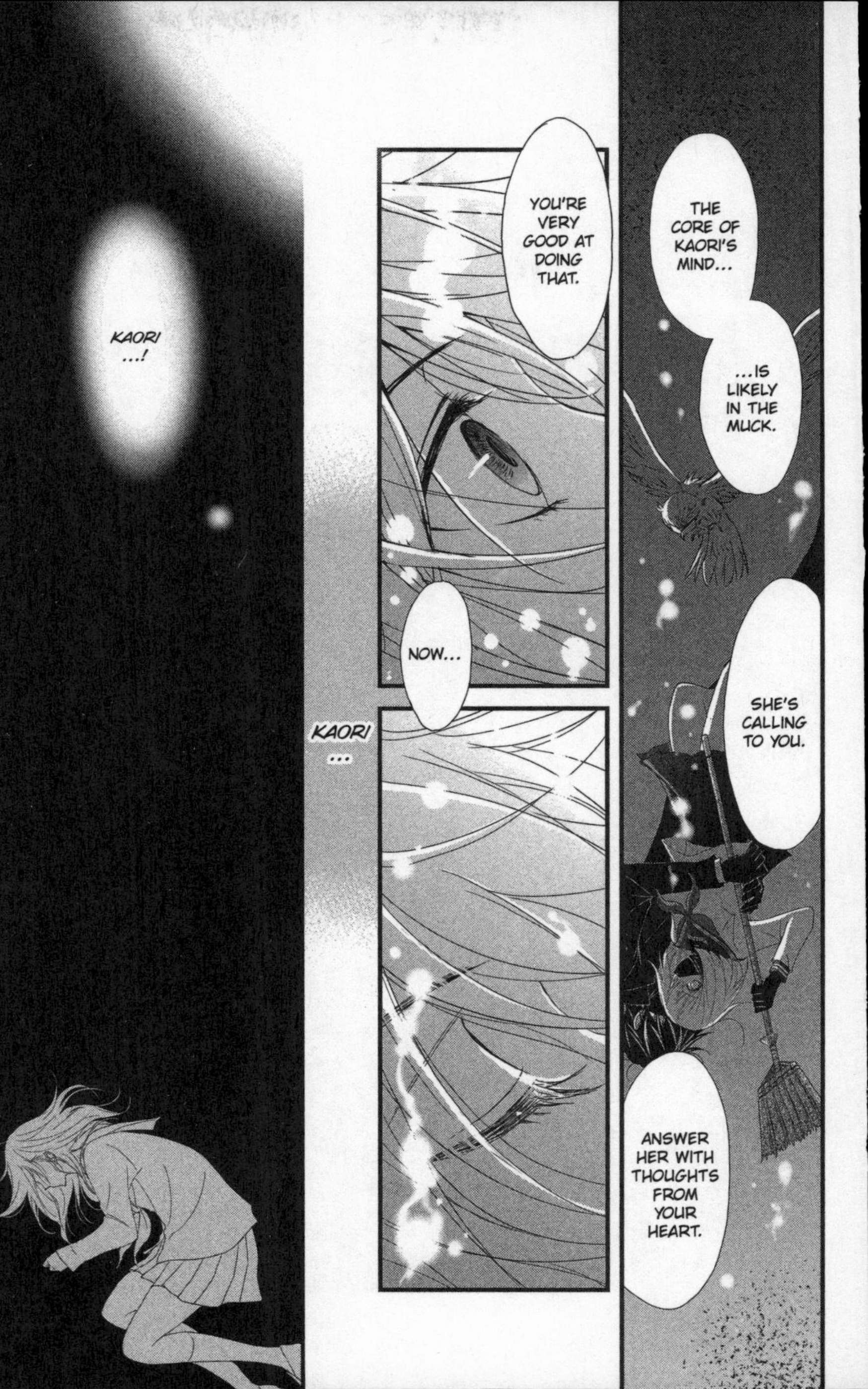
THE CORE OF KAORI'S MIND...
...IS LIKELY IN THE MUCK.
SHE'S CALLING TO YOU.
ANSWER HER WITH THOUGHTS FROM YOUR HEART.
YOU'RE VERY GOOD AT DOING THAT.
NOW...
KAORI...
KAORI...!

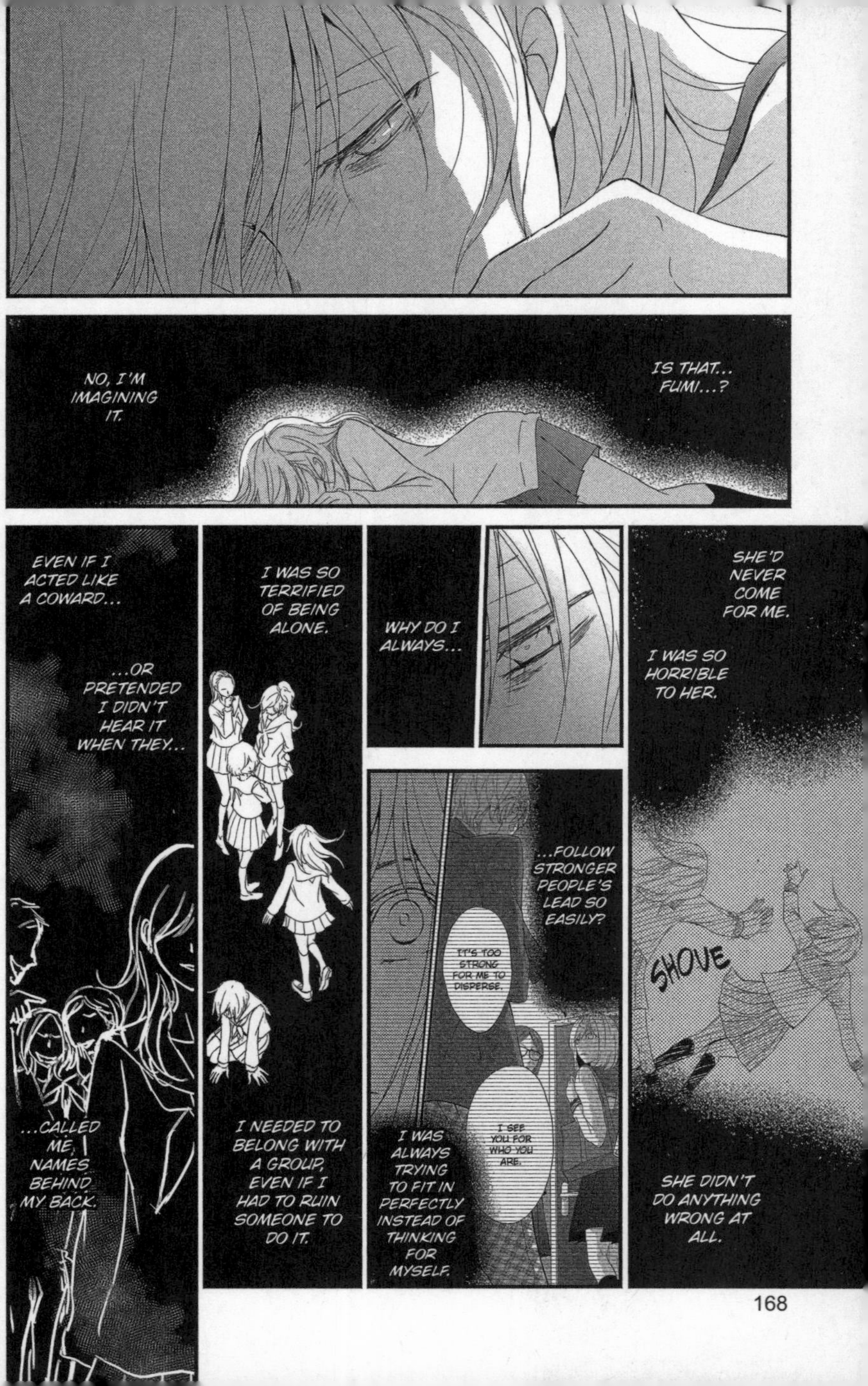
IS THAT... FUMI...?
NO, I'M IMAGINING IT.
SHE'D NEVER COME FOR ME.
I WAS SO HORRIBLE TO HER.
SHOVE
SHE DIDN'T DO ANYTHING WRONG AT ALL.
WHY DO I ALWAYS...
...FOLLOW STRONGER PEOPLE'S LEAD SO EASILY?
IT'S TOO STRONG FOR ME TO DISPERSE.
I SEE YOU FOR WHO YOU ARE.
I WAS ALWAYS TRYING TO FIT IN PERFECTLY INSTEAD OF THINKING FOR MYSELF.
I WAS SO TERRIFIED OF BEING ALONE.
I NEEDED TO BELONG WITH A GROUP, EVEN IF I HAD TO RUIN SOMEONE TO DO IT.
EVEN IF I ACTED LIKE A COWARD...
...OR PRETENDED I DIDN'T HEAR IT WHEN THEY...
...CALLED ME NAMES BEHIND MY BACK.

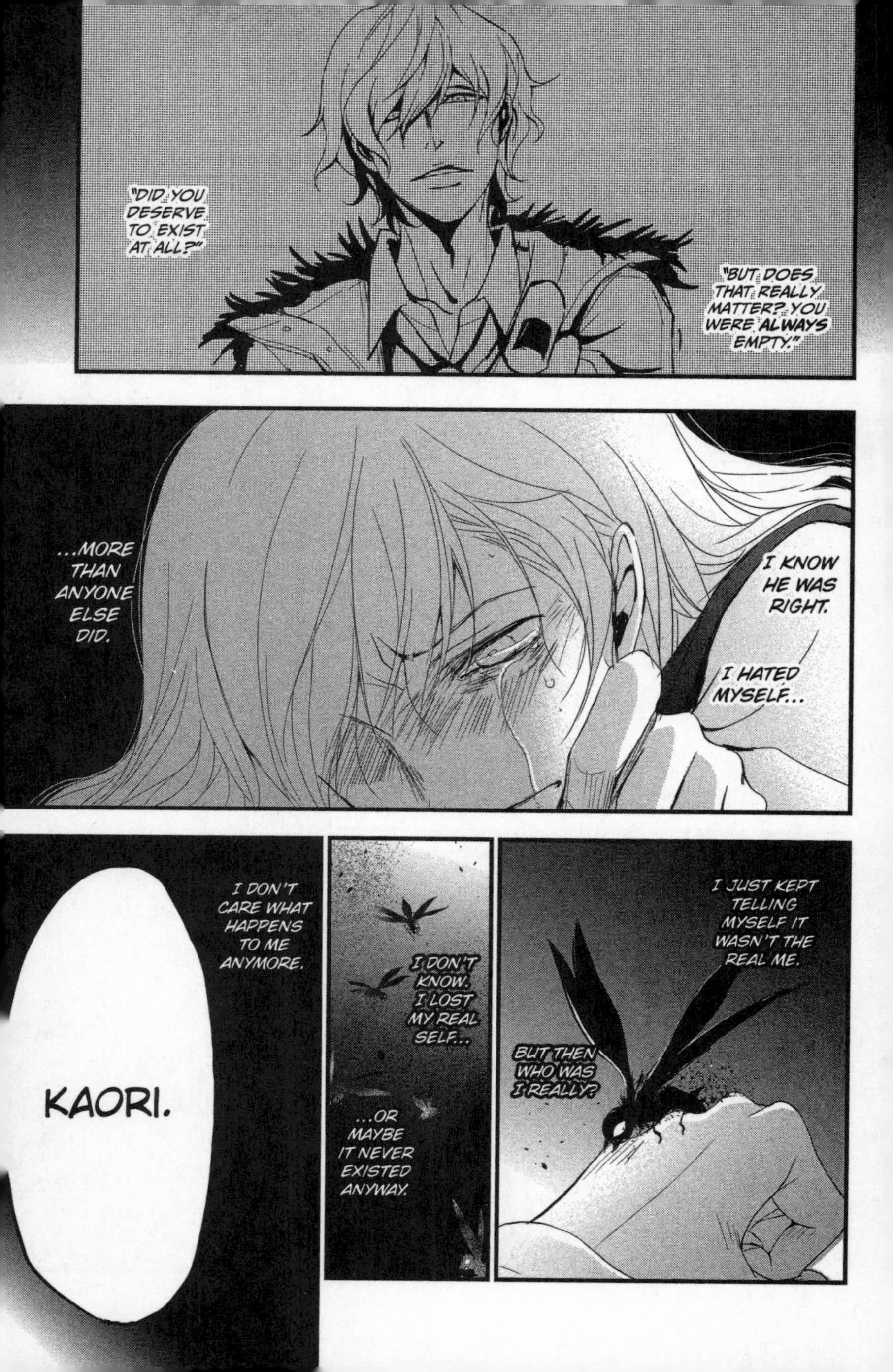
"DID YOU DESERVE TO EXIST AT ALL?"
"BUT DOES THAT REALLY MATTER? YOU WERE ALWAYS EMPTY."
I KNOW HE WAS RIGHT.
I HATED MYSELF...
...MORE THAN ANYONE ELSE DID.
I JUST KEPT TELLING MYSELF IT WASN'T THE REAL ME.
BUT THEN WHO WAS I REALLY?
I DON'T KNOW. I LOST MY REAL SELF...
...OR MAYBE IT NEVER EXISTED ANYWAY.
I DON'T CARE WHAT HAPPENS TO ME ANYMORE.
KAORI.

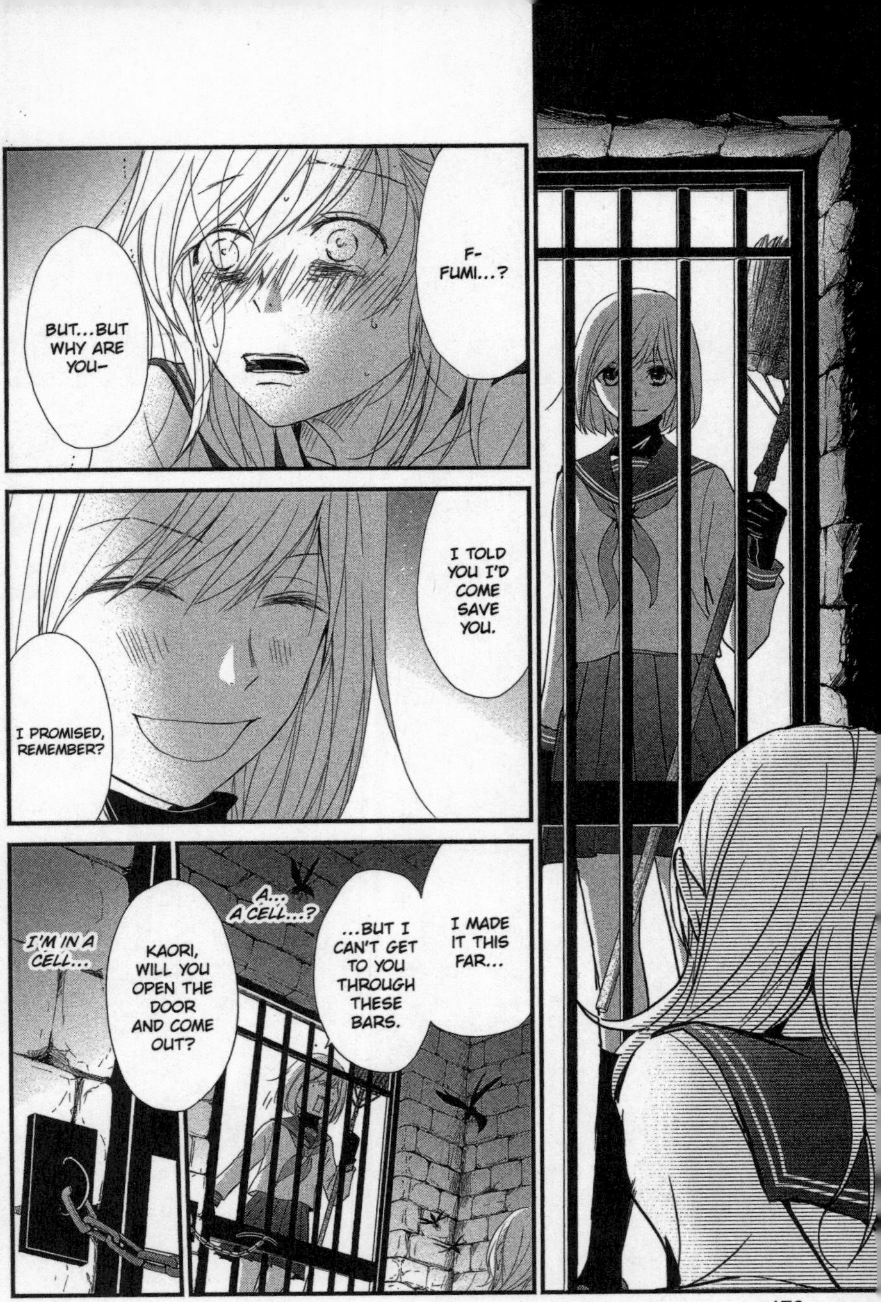
F-FUMI...?
BUT...BUT WHY ARE YOU-
I TOLD YOU I'D COME SAVE YOU.
I PROMISED, REMEMBER?
I MADE IT THIS FAR...
...BUT I CAN'T GET TO YOU THROUGH THESE BARS.
A... A CELL...?
KAORI, WILL YOU OPEN THE DOOR AND COME OUT?
I'M IN A CELL...

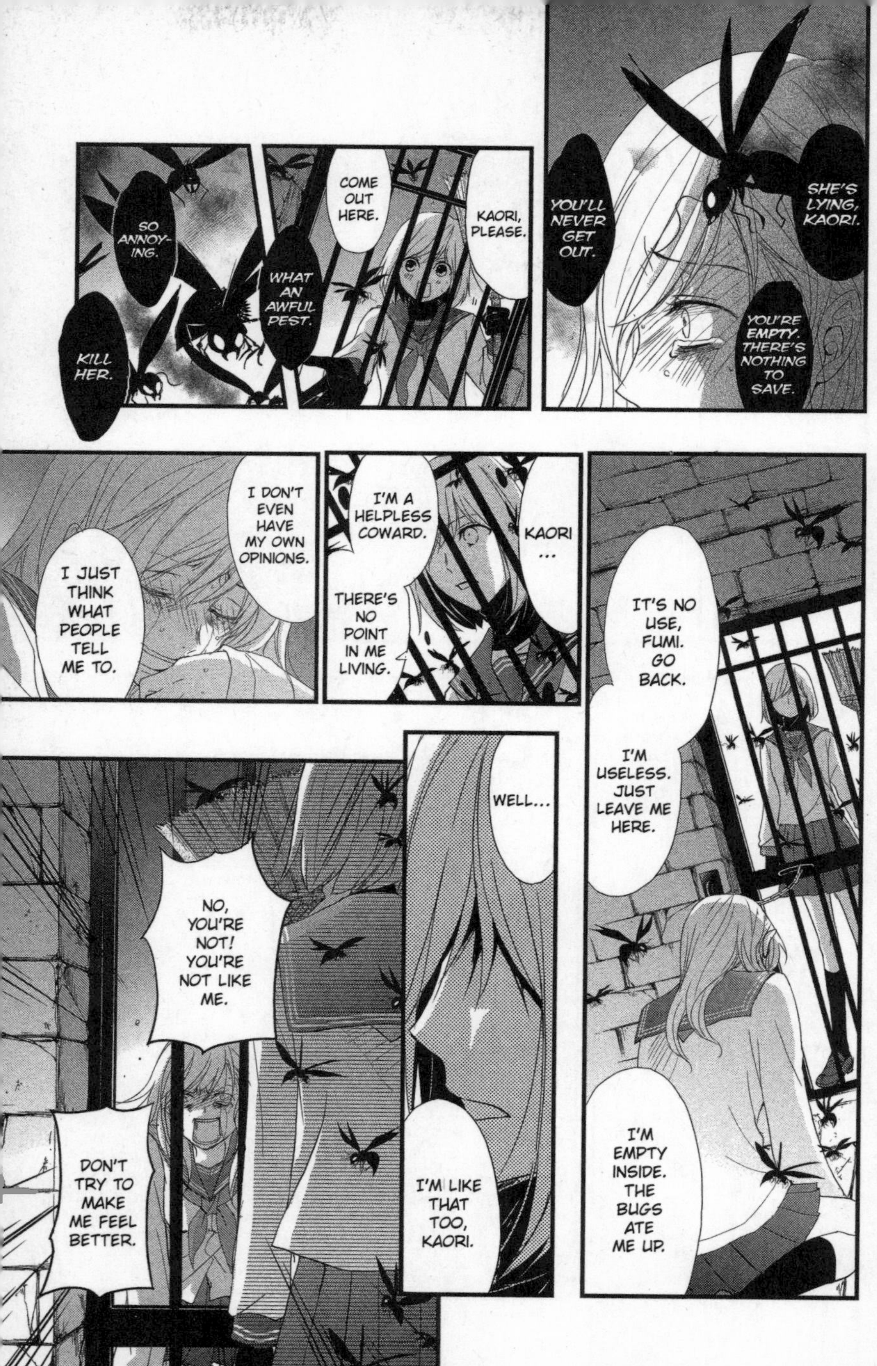
SHE'S LYING, KAORI.
YOU'LL NEVER GET OUT.
YOU'RE EMPTY. THERE'S NOTHING TO SAVE.
KAORI, PLEASE.
COME OUT HERE.
WHAT AN AWFUL PEST.
SO ANNOY-ING.
KILL HER.
IT'S NO USE, FUMI. GO BACK.
I'M USELESS. JUST LEAVE ME HERE.
I'M EMPTY INSIDE. THE BUGS ATE ME UP.
KAORI...
I'M A HELPLESS COWARD.
THERE'S NO POINT IN ME LIVING.
I DON'T EVEN HAVE MY OWN OPINIONS.
I JUST THINK WHAT PEOPLE TELL ME TO.
WELL...
I'M LIKE THAT TOO, KAORI.
NO, YOU'RE NOT! YOU'RE NOT LIKE ME.
DON'T TRY TO MAKE ME FEEL BETTER.

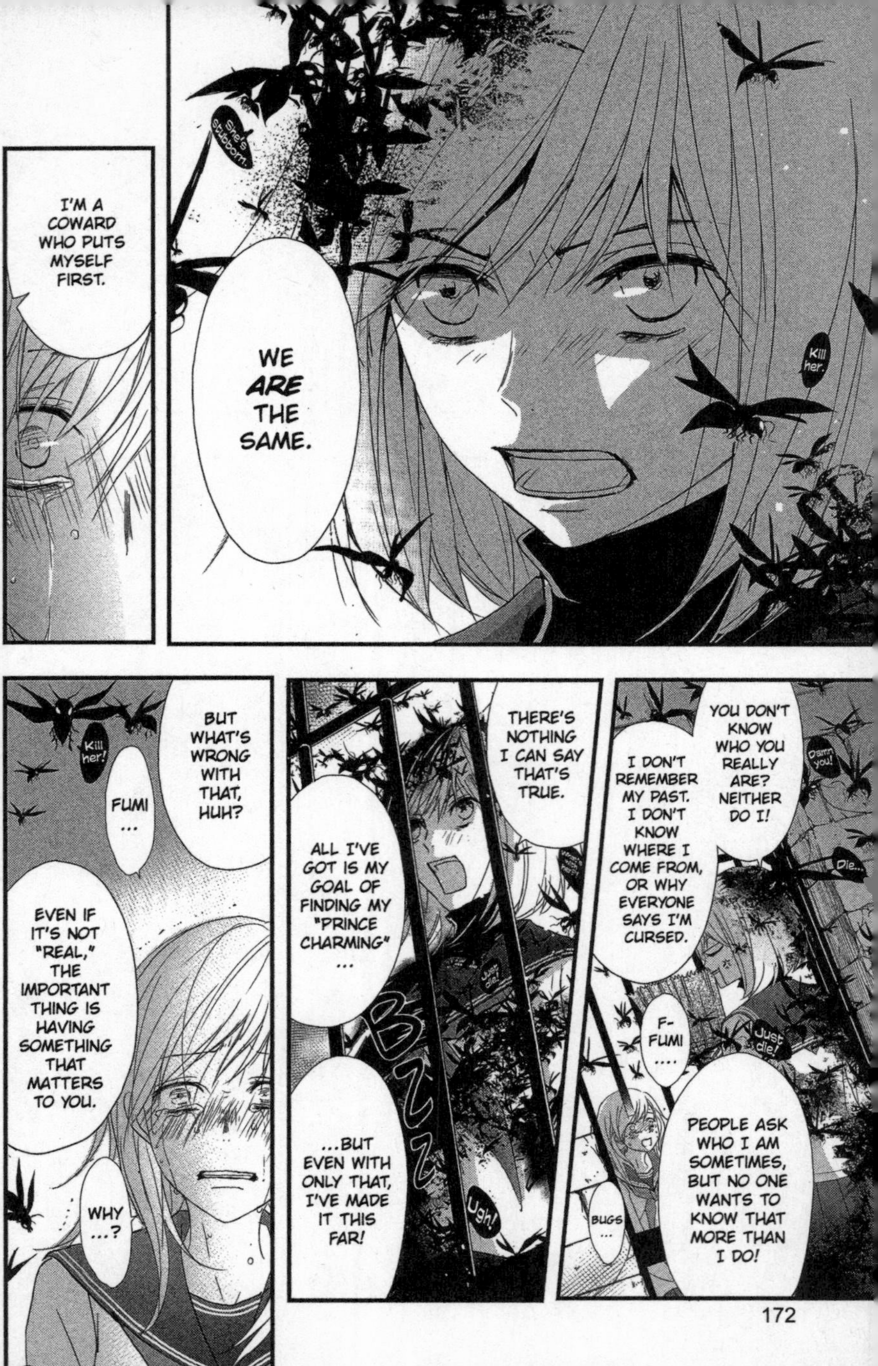

She's stubborn.
WE ARE THE SAME.
Kill her.
I'M A COWARD WHO PUTS MYSELF FIRST.
YOU DON'T KNOW WHO YOU REALLY ARE? NEITHER DO I!
I DON'T REMEMBER MY PAST. I DON'T KNOW WHERE I COME FROM, OR WHY EVERYONE SAYS I'M CURSED.
Damn you!
Die...
F-FUMI ....
Just die!
PEOPLE ASK WHO I AM SOMETIMES, BUT NO ONE WANTS TO KNOW THAT MORE THAN I DO!
BUGS ...
THERE'S NOTHING I CAN SAY THAT'S TRUE.
ALL I'VE GOT IS MY GOAL OF FINDING MY "PRINCE CHARMING" ...
Just die!
BZZ
...BUT EVEN WITH ONLY THAT, I'VE MADE IT THIS FAR!
Ugh!
BUT WHAT'S WRONG WITH THAT, HUH?
Kill her!
FUMI ...
EVEN IF IT'S NOT "REAL," THE IMPORTANT THING IS HAVING SOMETHING THAT MATTERS TO YOU.
WHY ...?

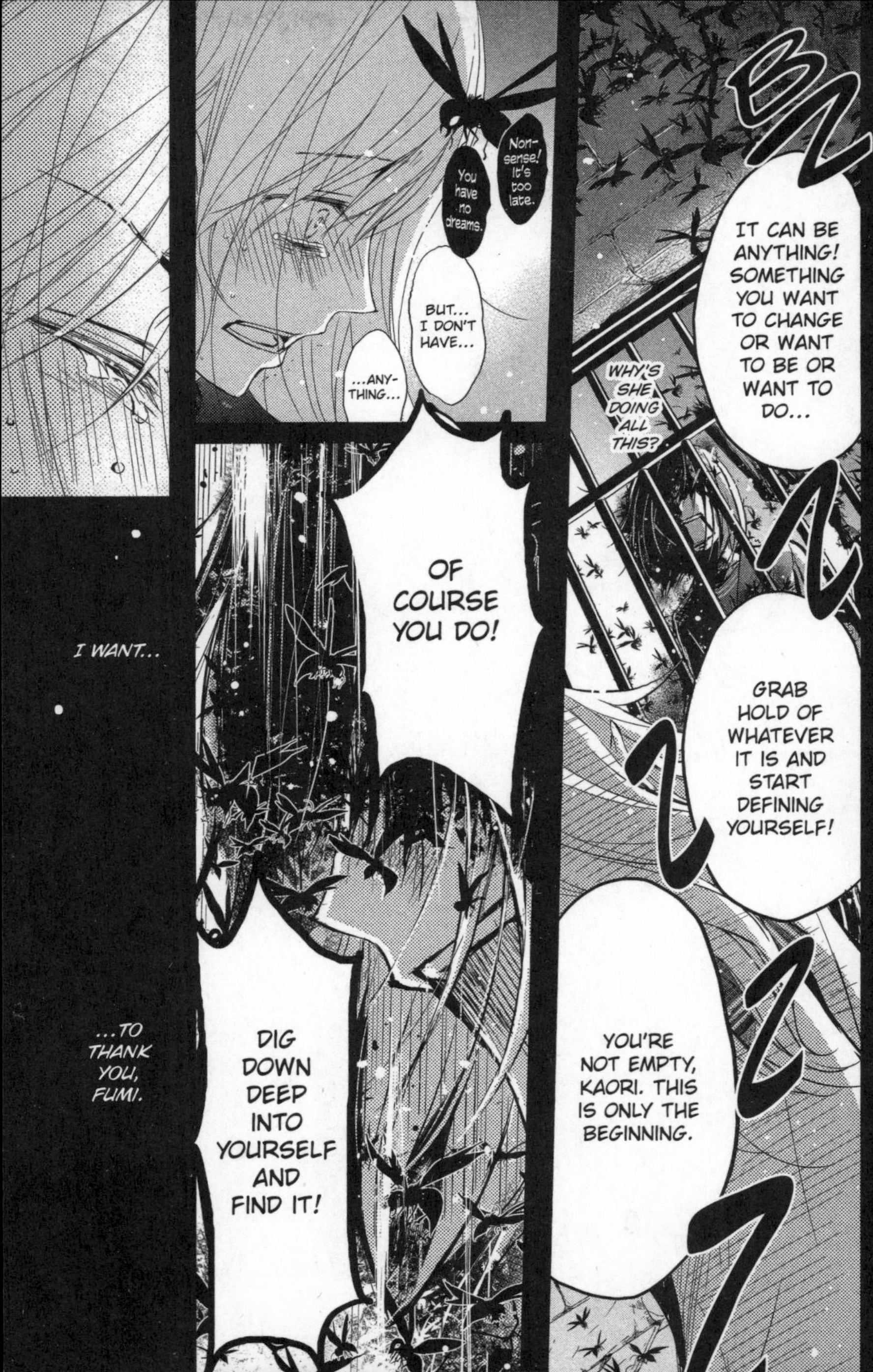
BZZZZZ
IT CAN BE ANYTHING! SOMETHING YOU WANT TO CHANGE OR WANT TO BE OR WANT TO DO...
WHY'S SHE DOING ALL THIS?
Non-sense! It's too late.
You have no dreams.
BUT... I DON'T HAVE...
...ANY-THING...
GRAB HOLD OF WHATEVER IT IS AND START DEFINING YOURSELF!
YOU'RE NOT EMPTY, KAORI. THIS IS ONLY THE BEGINNING.
OF COURSE YOU DO!
DIG DOWN DEEP INTO YOURSELF AND FIND IT!
I WANT...
...TO THANK YOU, FUMI.

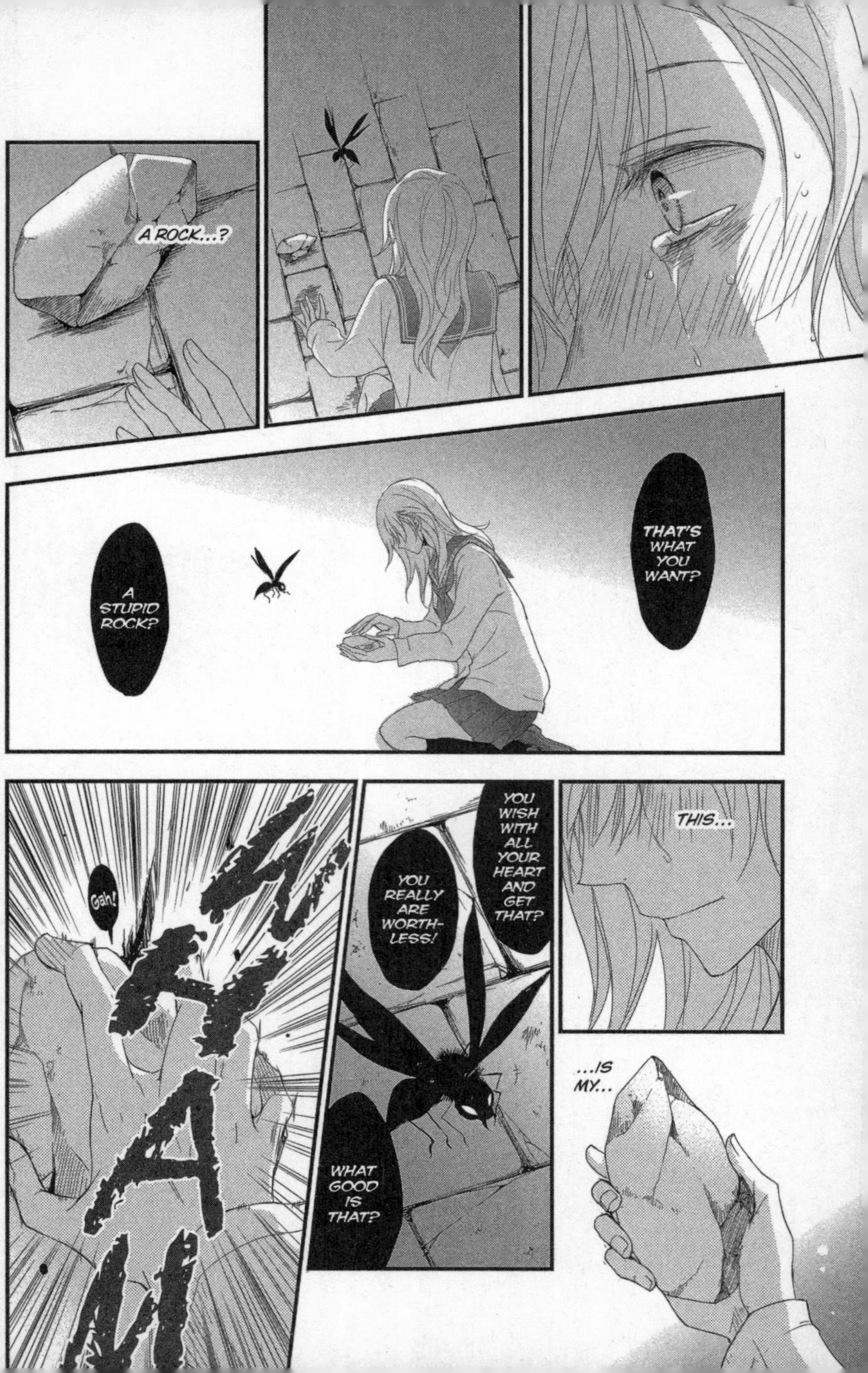
A ROCK...?
THAT'S WHAT YOU WANT?
A STUPID ROCK?
THIS...
...IS MY...
YOU WISH WITH ALL YOUR HEART AND GET THAT?
YOU REALLY ARE WORTHLESS!
WHAT GOOD IS THAT?
Gah!

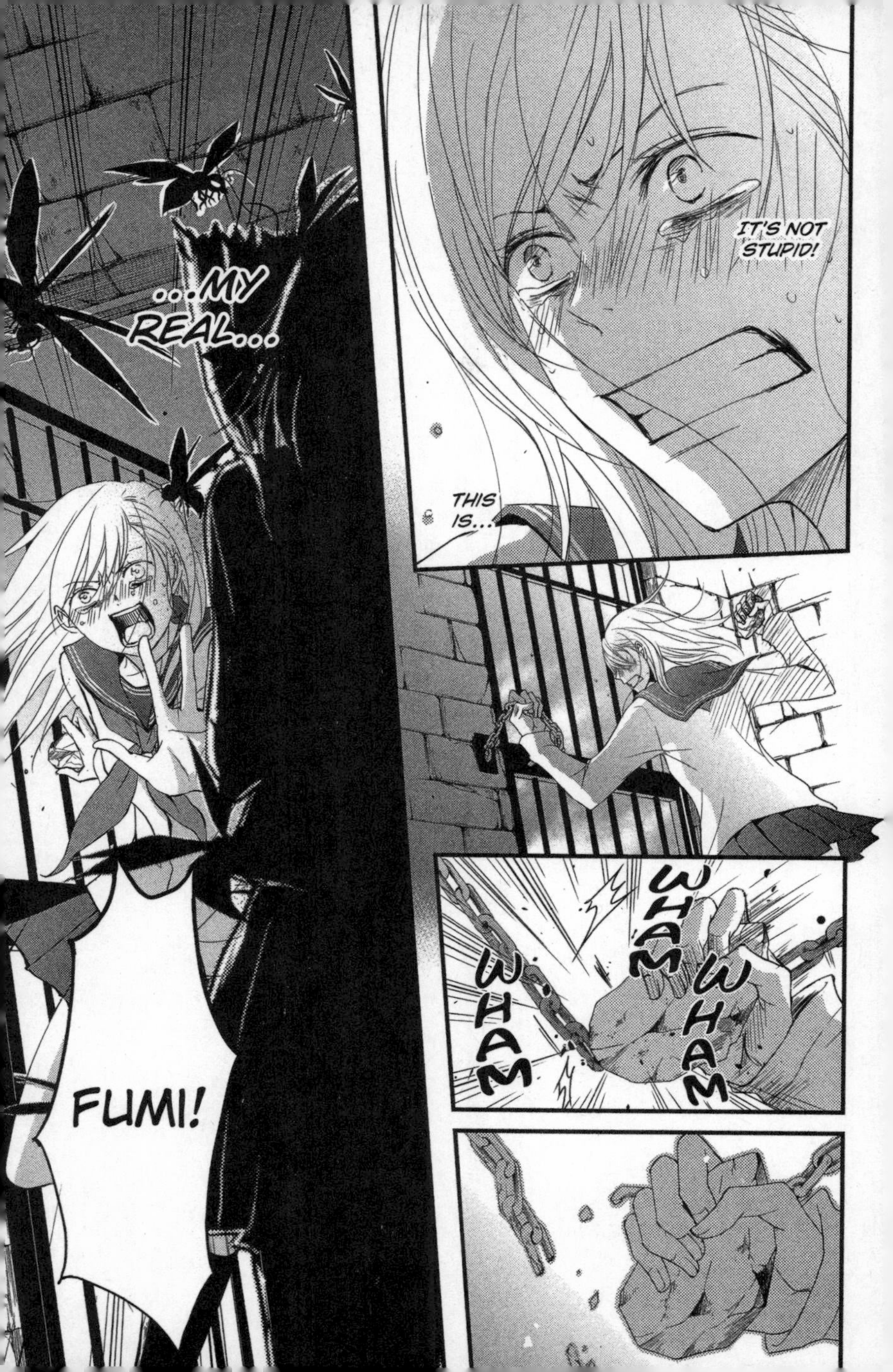
IT'S NOT STUPID!
THIS IS...
WHAM
WHAM
WHAM
WHAM
...MY REAL...
FUMI!

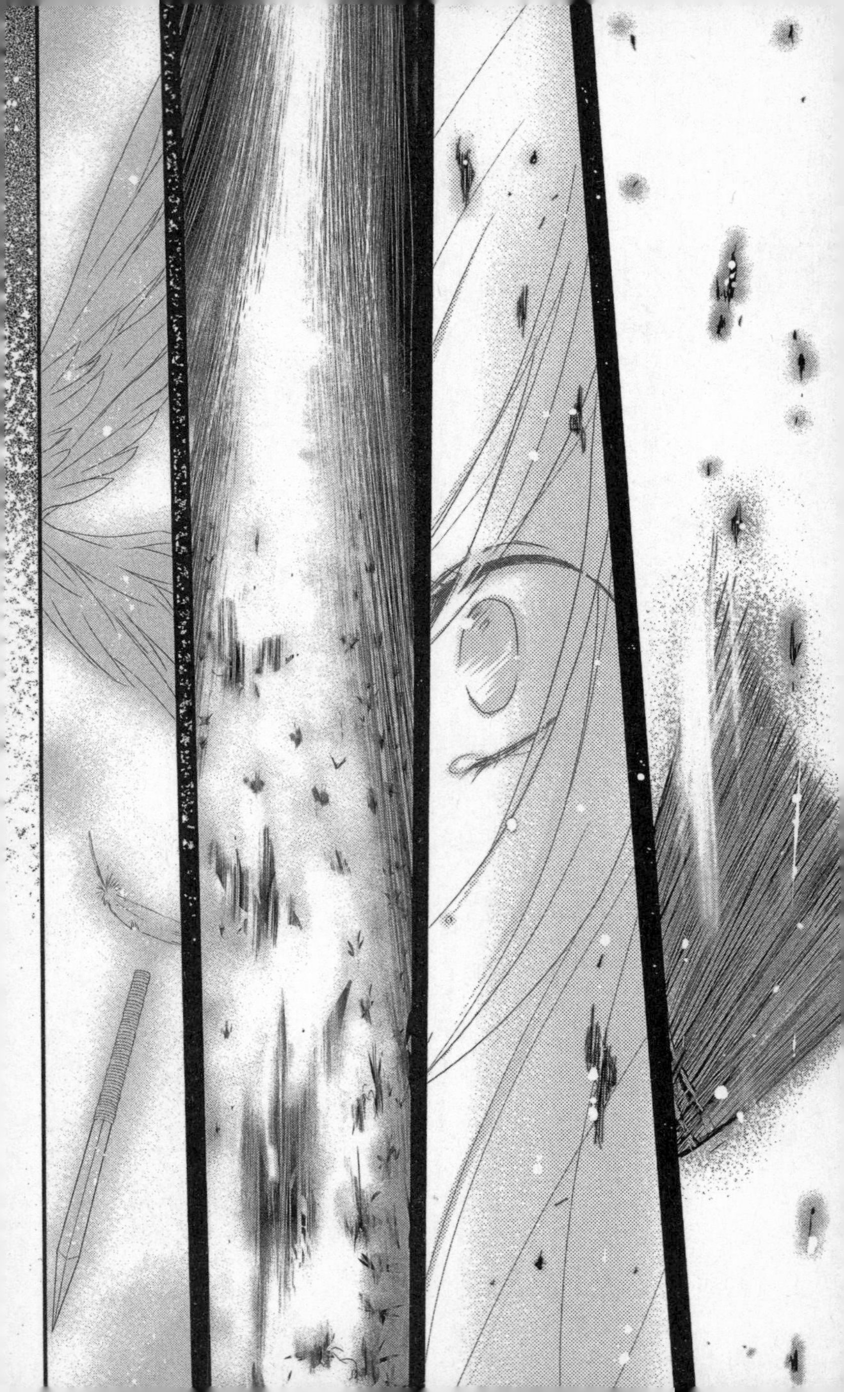

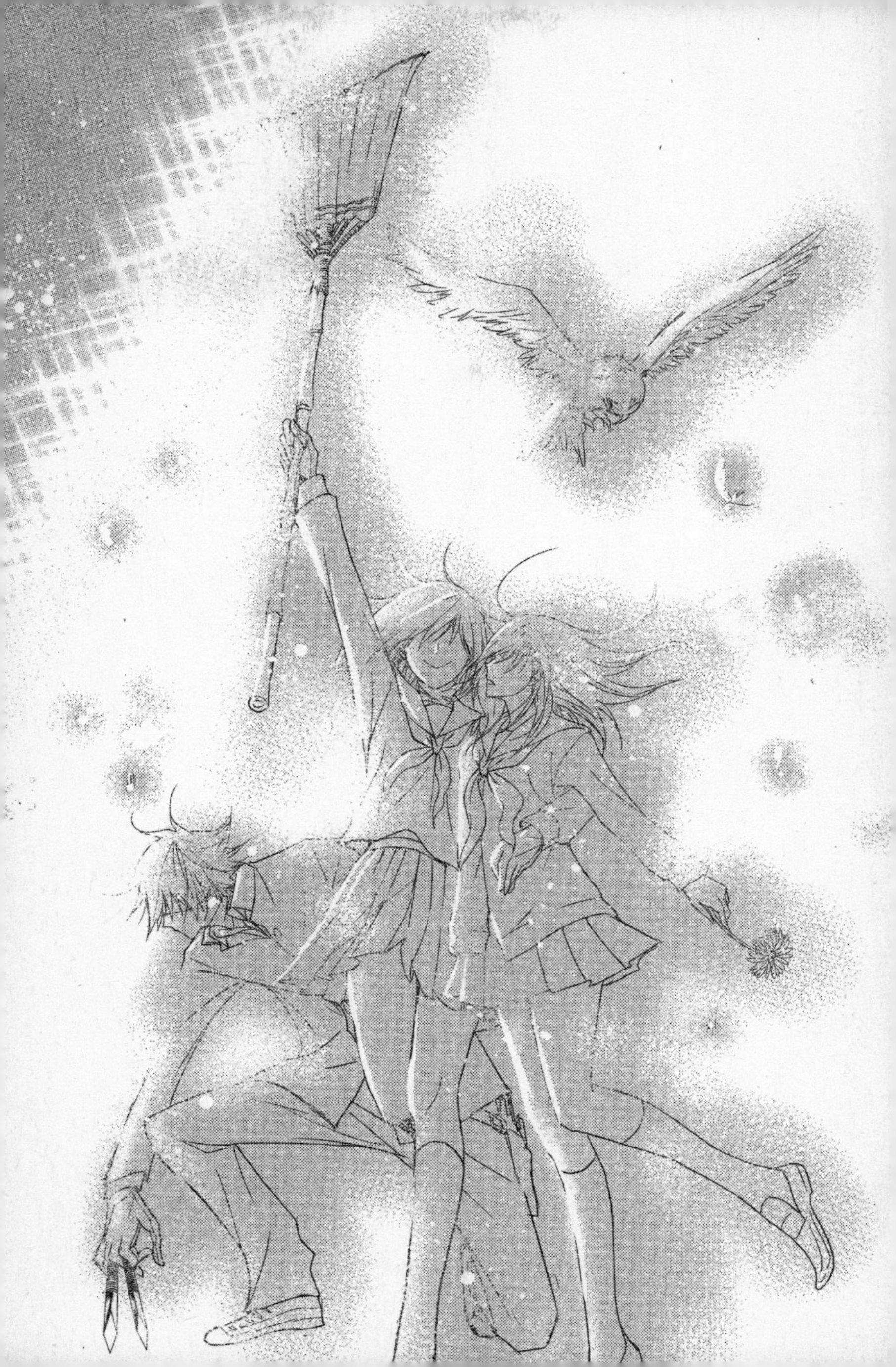

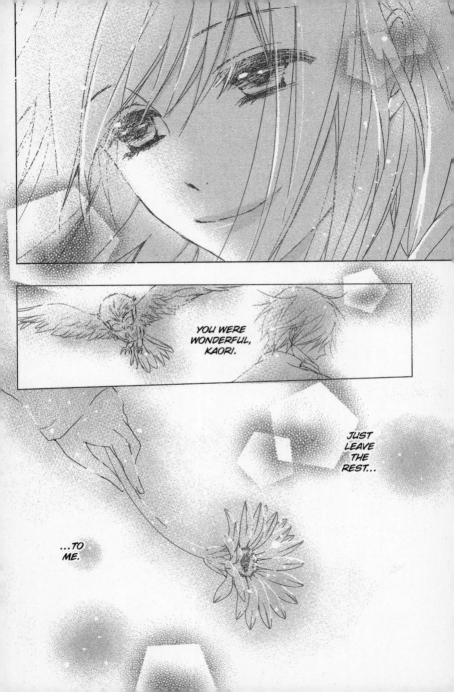

YOU WERE WONDERFUL, KAORI.

JUST LEAVE THE REST...

...TO ME.

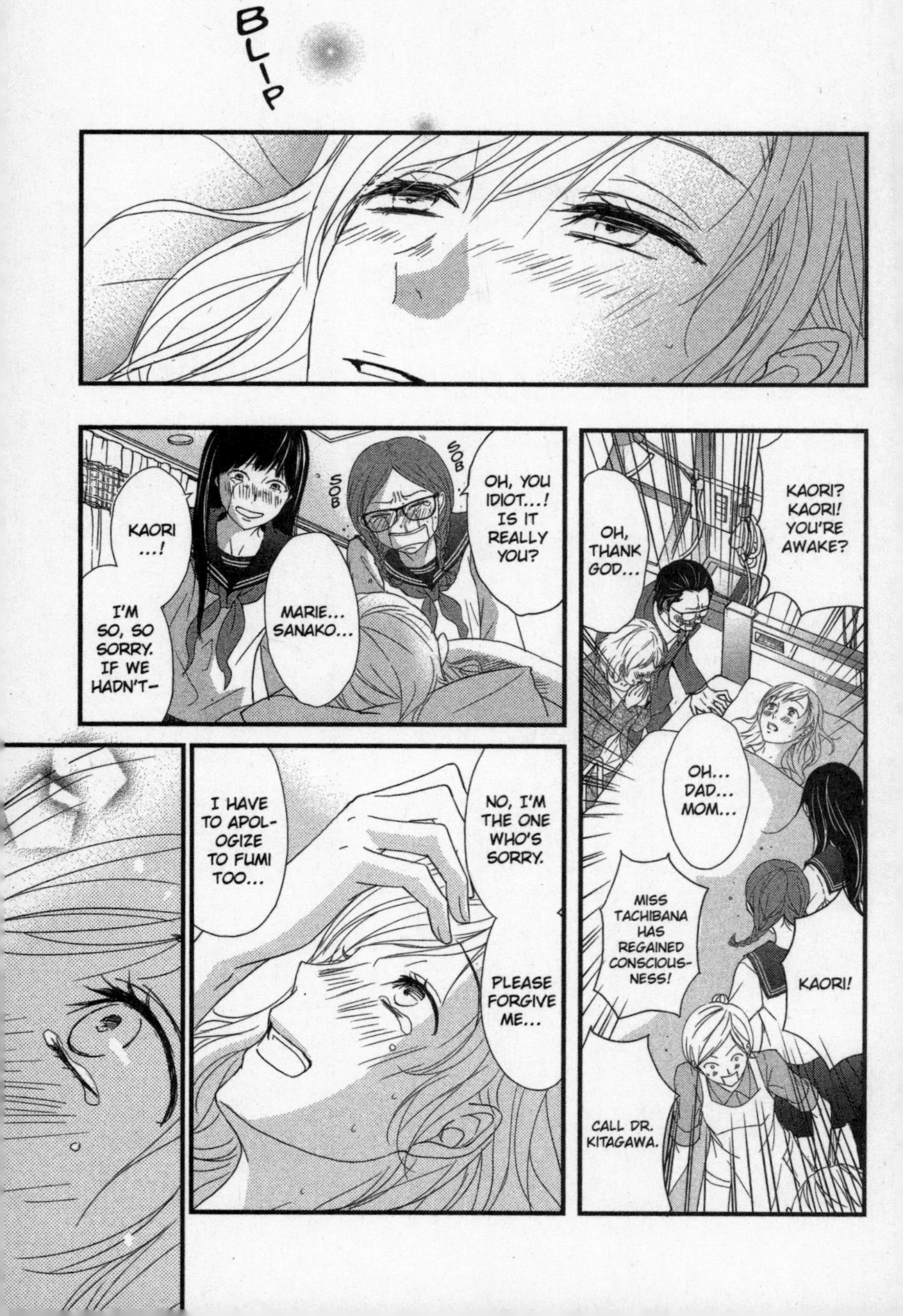
BLIP
KAORI? KAORI! YOU'RE AWAKE?
OH, THANK GOD...
OH... DAD... MOM...
MISS TACHIBANA HAS REGAINED CONSCIOUS-NESS!
KAORI!
CALL DR. KITAGAWA.
SOB
SOB
OH, YOU IDIOT...! IS IT REALLY YOU?
KAORI ...!
MARIE... SANAKO...
I'M SO, SO SORRY. IF WE HADN'T-
NO, I'M THE ONE WHO'S SORRY.
PLEASE FORGIVE ME...
I HAVE TO APOLOGIZE TO FUMI TOO...

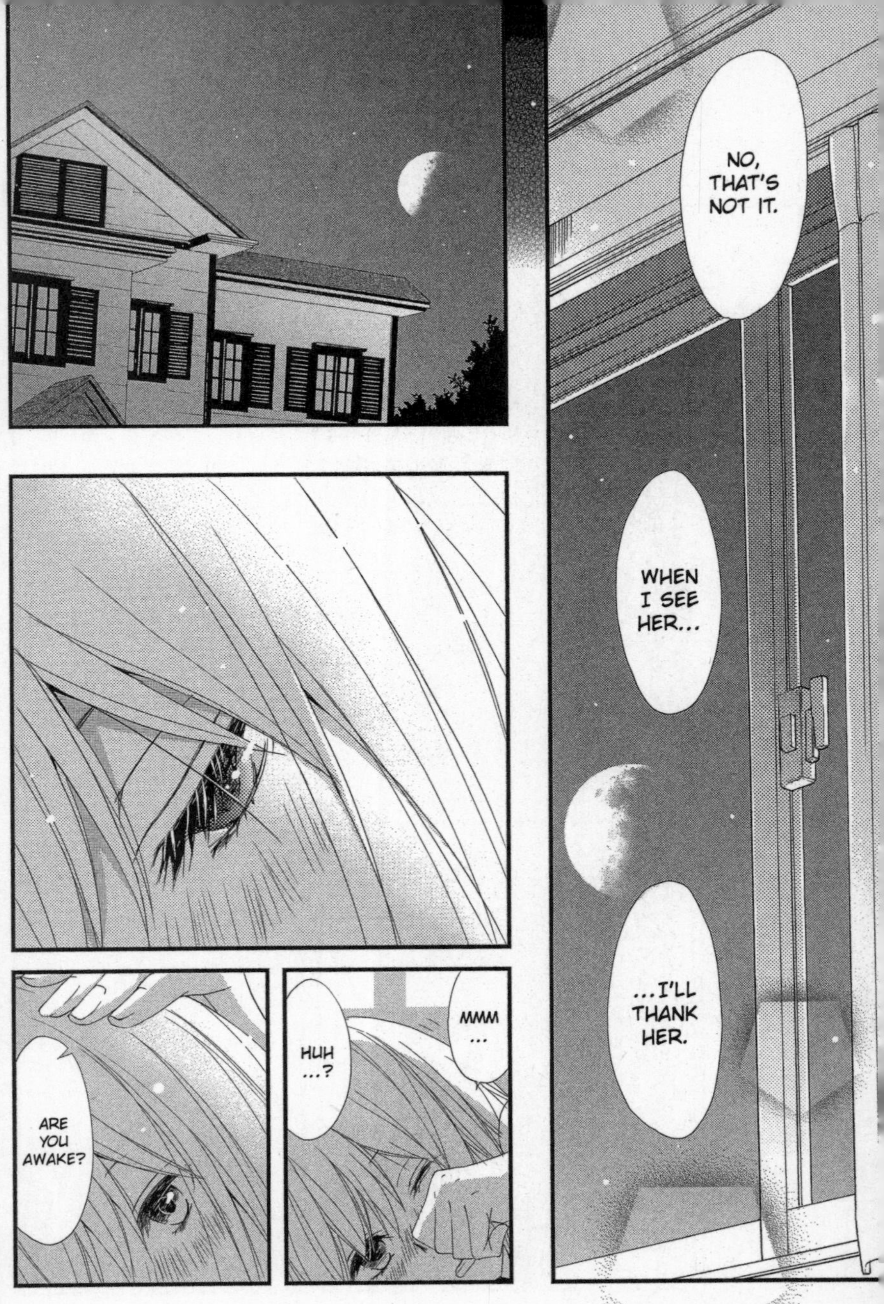
NO, THAT'S NOT IT.
WHEN I SEE HER...
...I'LL THANK HER.
MMM ...
HUH ...?
ARE YOU AWAKE?

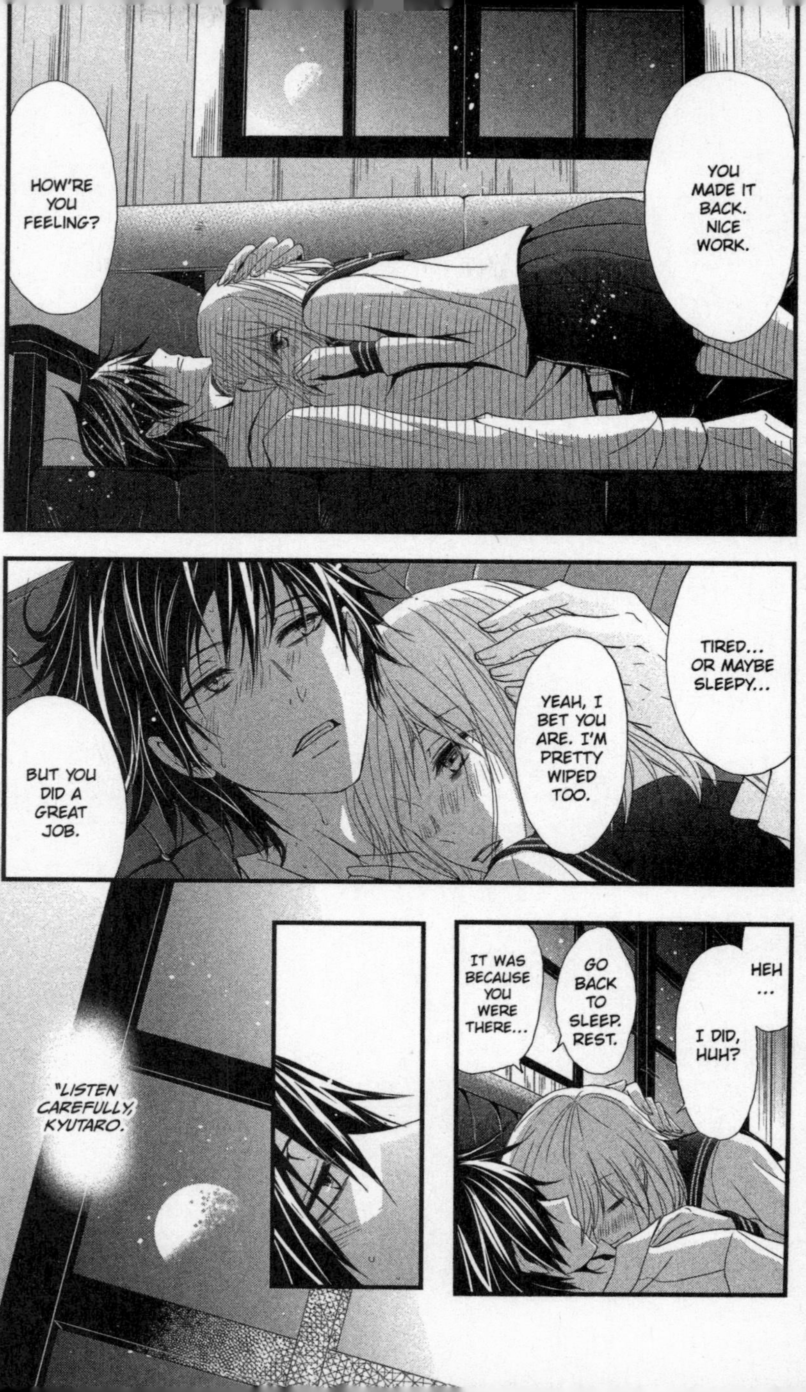
YOU MADE IT BACK. NICE WORK.
HOW'RE YOU FEELING?
TIRED... OR MAYBE SLEEPY...
YEAH, I BET YOU ARE. I'M PRETTY WIPED TOO.
BUT YOU DID A GREAT JOB.
HEH ... I DID, HUH?
GO BACK TO SLEEP. REST.
IT WAS BECAUSE YOU WERE THERE...
"LISTEN CAREFULLY, KYUTARO.

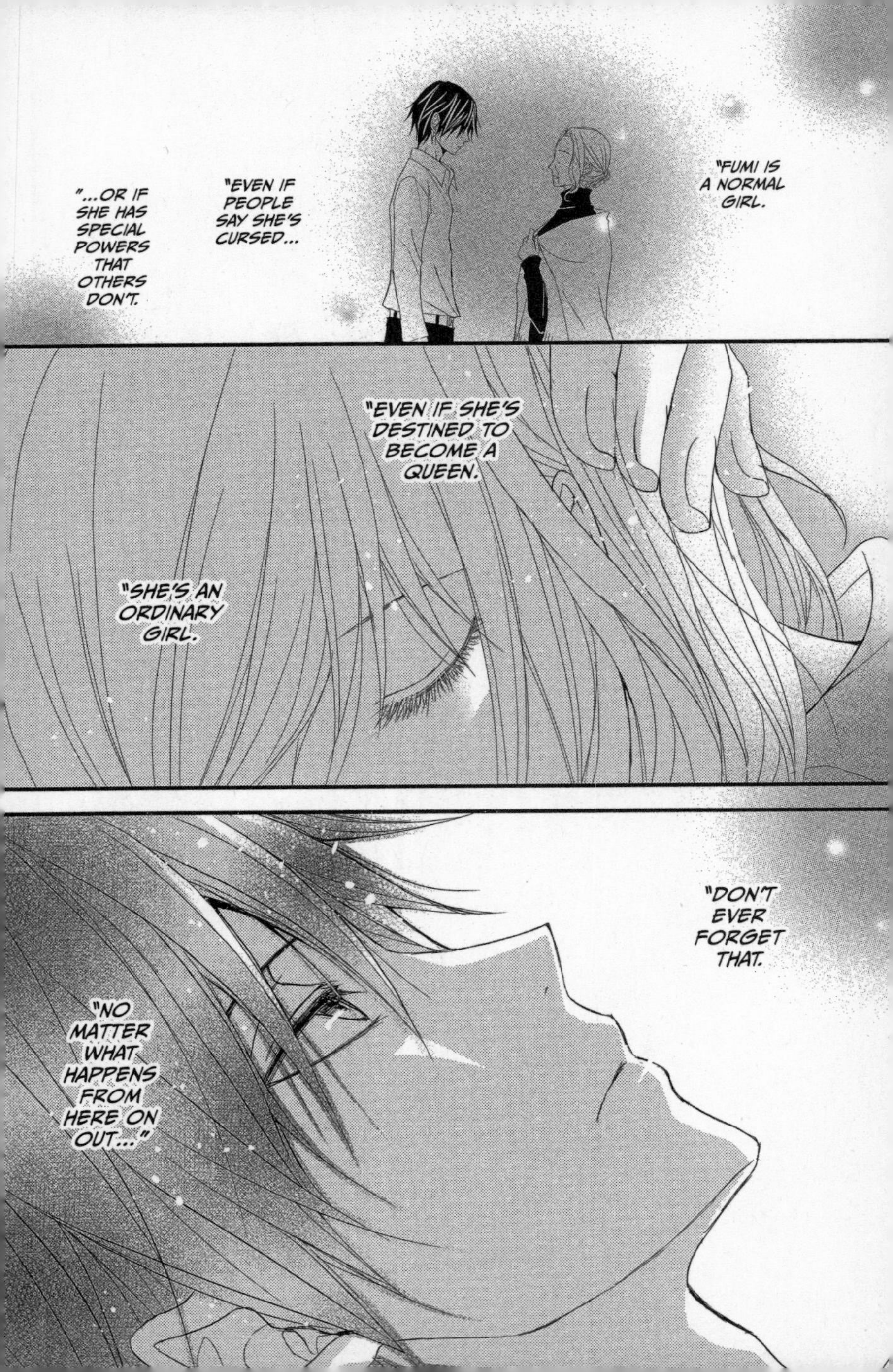
"FUMI IS A NORMAL GIRL.
"EVEN IF PEOPLE SAY SHE'S CURSED...
"...OR IF SHE HAS SPECIAL POWERS THAT OTHERS DON'T.
"EVEN IF SHE'S DESTINED TO BECOME A QUEEN.
"SHE'S AN ORDINARY GIRL.
"DON'T EVER FORGET THAT.
"NO MATTER WHAT HAPPENS FROM HERE ON OUT..."

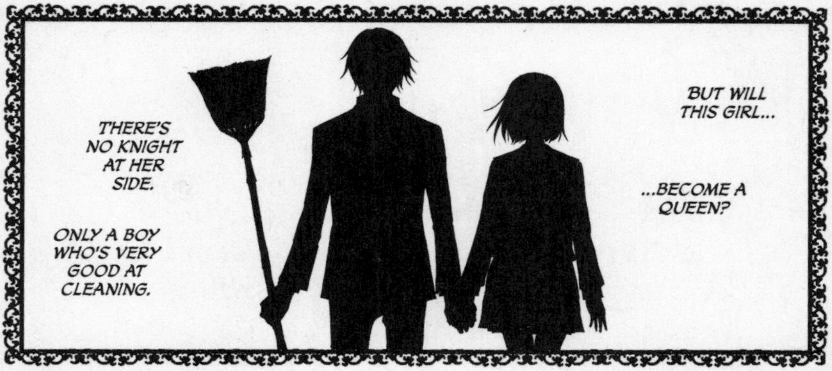
BUT WILL THIS GIRL...
...BECOME A QUEEN?
THERE'S NO KNIGHT AT HER SIDE.
ONLY A BOY WHO'S VERY GOOD AT CLEANING.

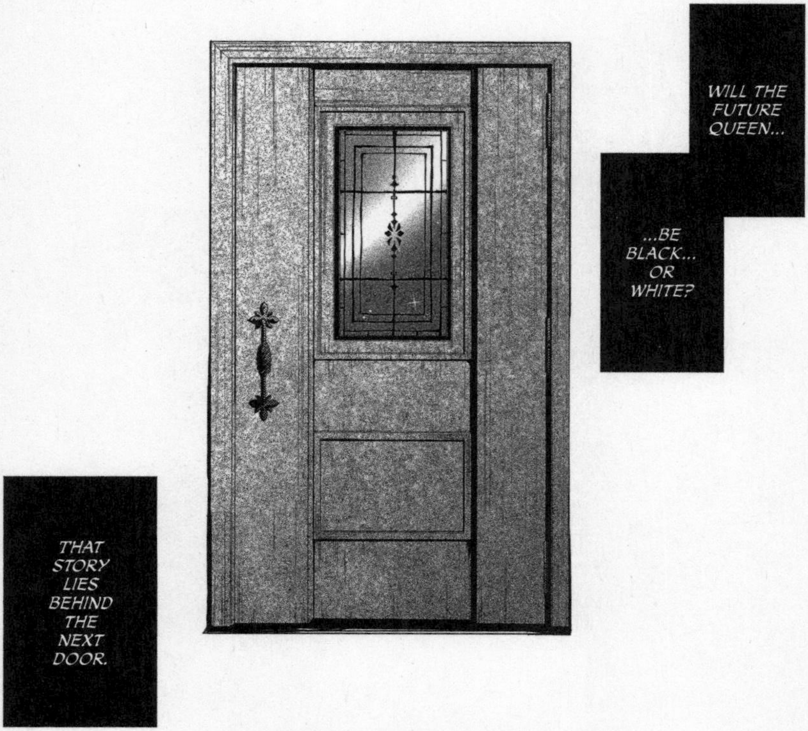
WILL THE FUTURE QUEEN...
...BE BLACK... OR WHITE?
THAT STORY LIES BEHIND THE NEXT DOOR.

QQ SWEEPER ③ *THE END*

Note ①

In Sweep 14 or so of *QQ Sweeper*, you can see brief appearances by characters like the glasses-wearing Onizuka, the girl with the scallion-shaped head and the hacker who created an app. See more of them in *Dengeki Daisy!* (16 volumes)

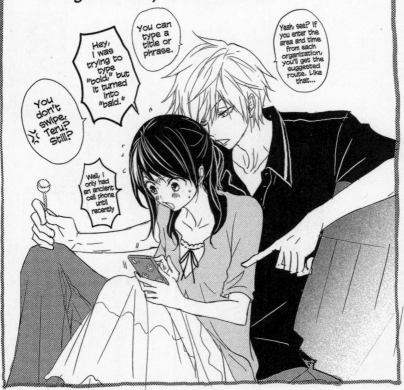

Yeah, see? If you enter the area and time from each organization, you'll get the suggested route. Like that...
You can type a title or phrase.
Hey, I was trying to type "bold," but it turned into "bald."
You don't swipe, Teru? Still?
Well, I only had an ancient cell phone until recently...

Note ②

Just wanted to let you all know that I now have a Twitter account! (@motomikyosuke).

I'll tweet news about my manga and some stuff from my everyday life. I might also share some unpublished art, so please stop by sometimes!

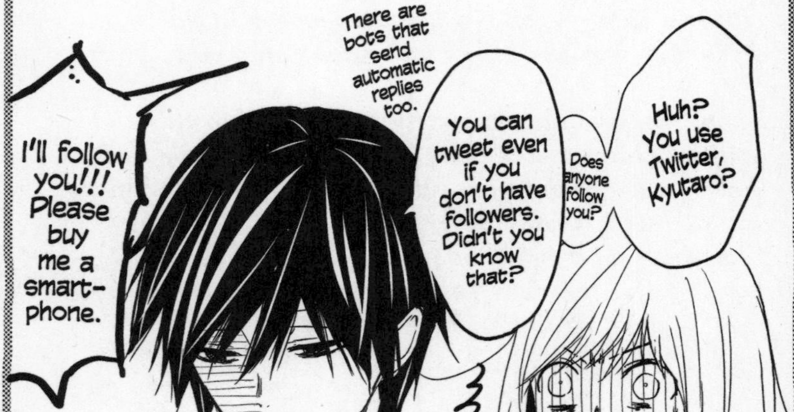
Huh? You use Twitter, Kyutaro?
Does anyone follow you?
You can tweet even if you don't have followers. Didn't you know that?
There are bots that send automatic replies too.
I'll follow you!!! Please buy me a smart-phone.
TAP TAP

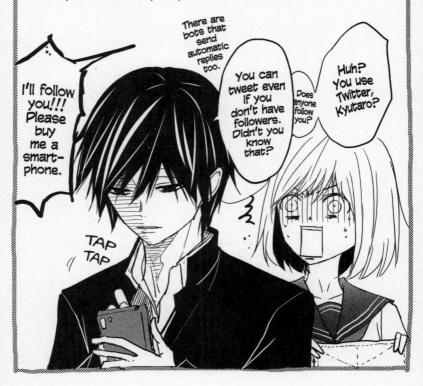

AFTERWORD

Oh—hi! I know it's a little sudden, but we've reached the end of QQ Sweeper. Thank you for reading it!

Hmm... I can hear people going, "What? But that wasn't a real ending!" I'm sorry! I understand why you're annoyed!

Actually, the story's continuing under a new title, Queen's Quality. So it's going to look a little different, but the story just keeps on going.

I don't really understand the reasons for this unusual change, so I can't explain it, but I can tell you it was an unusual and big opportunity for me, so I couldn't turn it down. I'll work even harder from now on! And I hope you'll keep reading about what happens to Fumi and Kyutaro next!

最圀キョウスケ

Kyousuke Motomi

Send your letters to: ♡

KYOUSUKE MOTOMI
C/O QQ SWEEPER EDITOR
VIZ MEDIA
P.O. BOX 77010
SAN FRANCISCO, CA 94107

Let's go to the next door.

"QUEEN'S QUALITY"

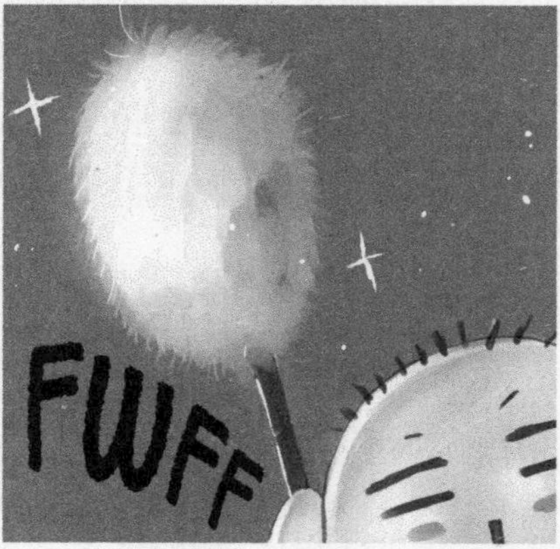
FWFF

I bought myself a wool duster recently. It's great for dusting the furniture, and it's nice and fluffy. Touching it when I'm stressed gives me a sense of calm. It's becoming like a pet to me (since I'm not allowed to have an actual animal).

—Kyousuke Motomi

Author Bio

Born on August 1, Kyousuke Motomi debuted in *Deluxe Betsucomi* with *Hetakuso Kyupiddo* (No Good Cupid) in 2002. She is the creator of *Dengeki Daisy* and *Beast Master*, both available in North America from Viz Media. Motomi enjoys sleeping, tea ceremonies and reading Haruki Murakami.

QQ SWEEPER

VOL. 3
Shojo Beat Edition

STORY AND ART BY
KYOUSUKE MOTOMI

QQ SWEEPER Vol. 3
by Kyousuke MOTOMI
© 2014 Kyousuke MOTOMI
All rights reserved.
Original Japanese edition published by SHOGAKUKAN.
English translation rights in the United States of America, Canada, United Kingdom and Ireland, arranged with SHOGAKUKAN.

English Adaptation/Ysabet Reinhardt MacFarlane
Translation/JN Productions
Touch-Up Art & Lettering/Eric Erbes
Design/Izumi Evers
Editor/Amy Yu

Printed in the U.S.A.

Published by VIZ Media, LLC
P.O. Box 77010
San Francisco, CA 94107

10 9 8 7 6 5 4 3 2 1
First printing, June 2016

 www.viz.com   www.shojobeat.com

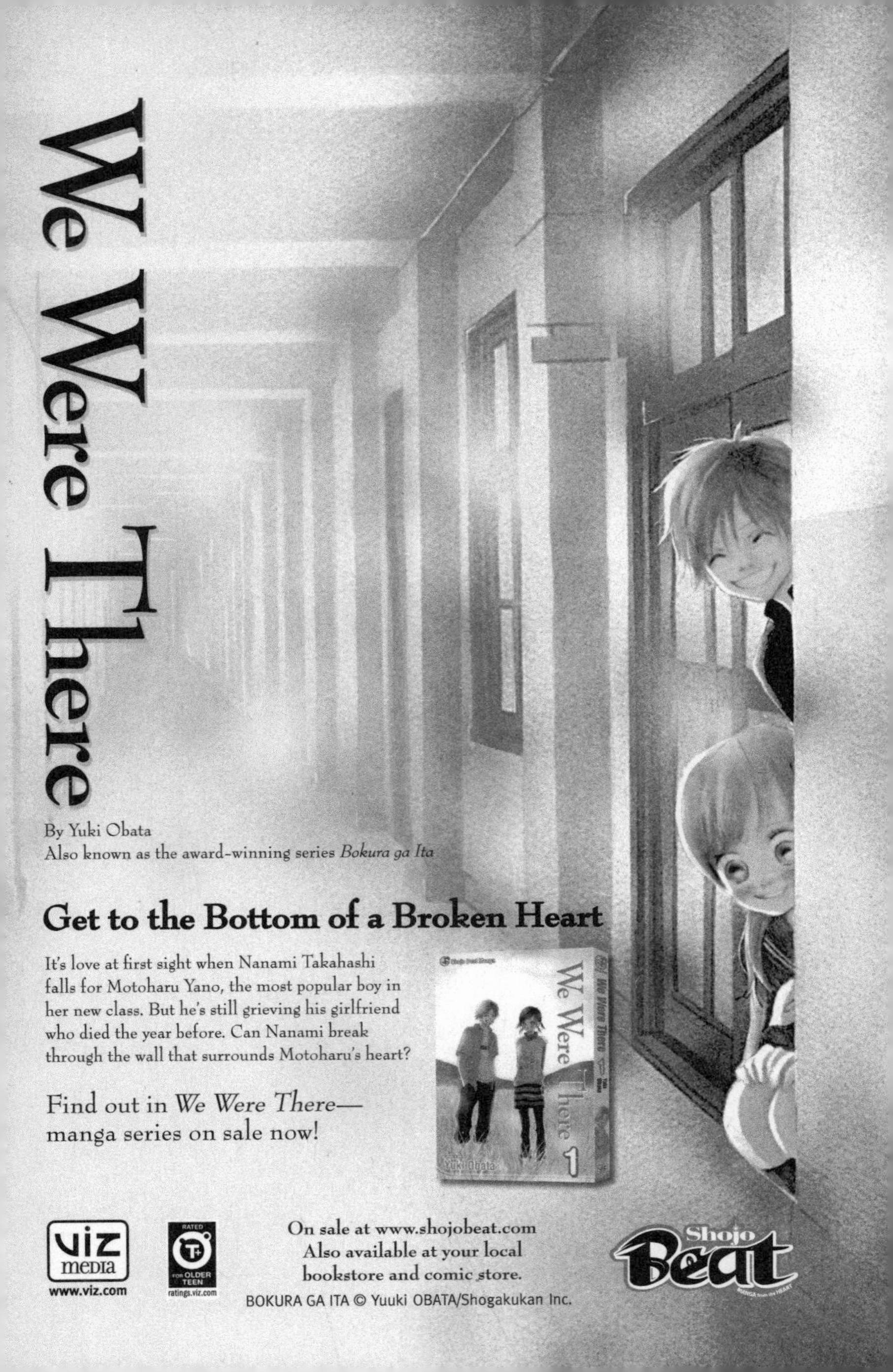
We Were There
By Yuki Obata
Also known as the award-winning series Bokura ga Ita
Get to the Bottom of a Broken Heart
It's love at first sight when Nanami Takahashi falls for Motoharu Yano, the most popular boy in her new class. But he's still grieving his girlfriend who died the year before. Can Nanami break through the wall that surrounds Motoharu's heart?
Find out in We Were There—manga series on sale now!
We Were There
Yuki Obata
1
VIZ media
www.viz.com
RATED T+ FOR OLDER TEEN
ratings.viz.com
On sale at www.shojobeat.com
Also available at your local bookstore and comic store.
BOKURA GA ITA © Yuuki OBATA/Shogakukan Inc.
Shojo Beat

Honey Blood

Story & Art by Miko Mitsuki

Hinata can't help but be drawn to Junya, but could it be that he's actually a vampire?

When a girl at her school is attacked by what seems to be a vampire, high school student Hinata Sorazono refuses to believe that vampires even exist. But then she meets her new neighbor, Junya Tokinaga, the author of an incredibly popular vampire romance novel… Could it be that Junya's actually a vampire—and worse yet, the culprit?!

This is the last page.

In keeping with the original Japanese comic format, this book reads from right to left—so action, sound effects and word balloons are completely reversed. This preserves the orientation of the original artwork—plus, it's fun! Check out the diagram shown here to get the hang of things, and then turn to the other side of the book to get started!

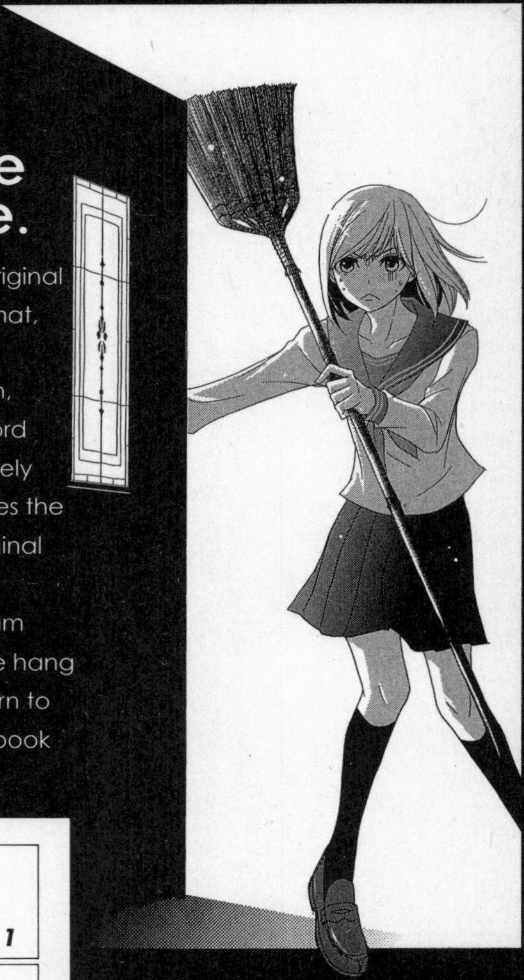

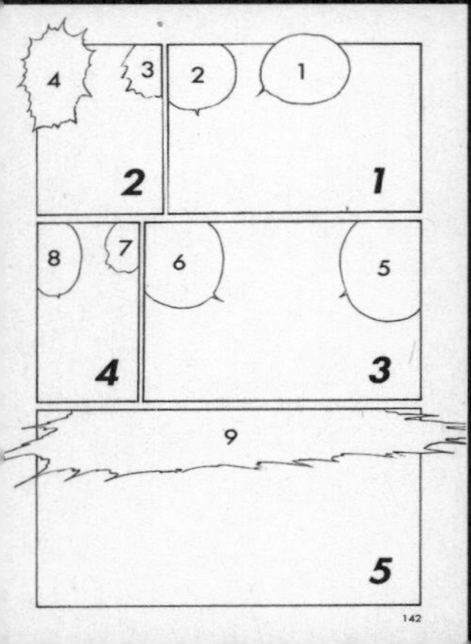

1
2
1
3
4
2
5
6
3
7
8
4
9
5
142